the PALEO
SLOW COOKER

the PALEO SLOW COOKER

HEALTHY, GLUTEN-FREE MEALS THE *easy* WAY

Arsy Vartanian

Founder & Chef of rubiesandradishes.com
with Amy Kubal, Registered Dietitian

Foreword by Chris Kresser, L.Ac

Race Point
PUBLISHING

Race Point
PUBLISHING

A division of Book Sales, Inc.
276 Fifth Avenue Suite 206
New York, New York 10001

RACE POINT PUBLISHING and the distinctive Race Point Publishing logo are trademarks
of Book Sales, Inc.

ISBN-13: 978-1-937994-07-5

Photography by Tamara Lee Sang

Printed in China

2 4 6 8 10 9 7 5 3 1

www.racepointpub.com

To my husband, Brooke

my daughter, Indyanna

my parents, Eda & Hayrik

my brothers, Arbi and Aren

and

in memory of my aunt, Valentine

Thank you for the overwhelming love and support.

CONTENTS

FOREWORD BY
CHRIS KRESSER

I'm different than some of the other contributors in the burgeoning Paleo community because I work with patients on a one-on-one basis. I see clients with a variety of different health concerns, ranging from difficulty losing weight to more serious health problems. This is how I met Arsy a couple of years ago.

Achieving optimal health can be complex, often requiring a variety of lifestyle changes, ranging from sleep to stress management. However, eating real food that will nourish your body is a great starting point. When I took Arsy on as a patient, she had already removed many of the toxins from her diet and her health was beginning to improve significantly as a result. But she was still experiencing some symptoms, such as headaches and lethargy. I worked with her to change her diet even further, emphasizing nutrient-dense foods like bone broth on a regular basis. Arsy was one of my star patients and her story underscores the power of eating a diet void of toxins and rich in nutrients, such as the Paleo diet. And as she mentions in this book, this worked wonders for her. She no longer has headaches and is feeling better than ever. This book reflects the knowledge Arsy has gained by experimenting with her diet to achieve optimal health. Slow-cooking became a tool that she utilized often to help her stay committed to these changes, while balancing her busy schedule.

When people are confronted with the concept of following this whole foods approach, they may be hesitant to make the necessary changes thinking that it will require gourmet cooking daily. In reality, many of us do not have the time or money to cook three elaborate meals a day. That is why this book is so necessary. The key to Arsy's success with the Paleo diet has been her interest and skills as a cook and in this book she offers us a way to prepare delicious and healthy meals in a simple and affordable way. Furthermore, this book demonstrates that the Paleo diet does not have to be boring. Arsy brings her Middle-Eastern background with several Armenian and Persian recipes, as well as other ethnic recipes that she has learned about from friends, proving that with the elimination of grains, legumes and dairy, boundless amounts of options still exist.

I have mentioned elsewhere that I prefer the term Paleo Template to Paleo diet, as no single diet is optimal for all individuals. This book does an excellent job of offering recipes that help those with a more individualized approach, from low-carbers to endurance athletes. There are also recipes that are safe for those following an autoimmune protocol. It also includes many recipes using nutritious foods. Animal products, particularly organ meats, are some of the real super foods, but can also be some of the most time-consuming and intimidating to prepare. There are several recipes such as oxtail soup and liver and onions that are valuable for Paleo newbies and seasoned vets alike looking to add more vitamins and minerals into their diet.

I often use a slow cooker myself, and one of my favorite slow-cooked meals is pot roast. It's easy, tastes great and makes enough so that during the week we can open the fridge, heat it up and have a delicious gourmet Paleo meal ready in a few minutes. The slow cooker does a great job of preserving the moisture, tenderness and flavor of a great meal. I will be using this book often to prepare some new healthy dishes.

Most people who switch to a Paleo diet, like Arsy, see significant benefits immediately. They have more energy. They lose weight effortlessly. Many people report increased virility and fertility. Athletes often break their own records. It improves and stabilizes your mood. Many people who were taking anti-depressant medications have been able to lower their doses or get off the drugs completely. It also helps people reconnect with their food and food sources, simultaneously strengthening relationships with local farmers and helping people understand just how important food is to our everyday life.

So if you're wondering why I believe in the Paleo diet, it is because I have seen it work in my practice time and time again to reduce inflammation, regulate the immune system and super-charge metabolism by nourishing our bodies with healthy food we crave and need. This book will be a great resource to help you change your eating habits for the better and to stay committed.

—**CHRIS KRESSER**, chriskresser.com, Medicine for the 21st Century

INTRODUCTION

MY TAKE ON THE PALEO DIET

"Ten thousand years ago the Agricultural Revolution was the beginning of a drastic change in the human diet that continues to this day. Today more than 70% of our dietary calories come from foods that our Paleolithic ancestors rarely, if ever, ate. The result is epidemic levels of cardiovascular disease, cancer, diabetes, osteoporosis, arthritis, gastrointestinal disease, and more."

- Dr. Loren Cordain

When I first read *The Paleo Diet* by Dr. Loren Cordain back in 2008, the above quote immediately resonated with me. A light bulb went off in my head, and I began to understand my own health problems, as well the issues that those around me were experiencing. From that moment on, I could not read enough books, blogs and articles. This is my take on the Paleo diet as a result of everything I have read and experimented with over the past four years.

WHAT IS THE PALEO DIET AND HOW DO YOU FOLLOW IT?

It's a lifestyle that aspires to achieve optimal health by following a diet based on what and how our Paleolithic ancestors ate. The current Paleo movement uses our ancestors as a starting point, but leverages modern science to expand from there. Essentially, it is a diet focused on consuming whole, natural foods, such as meats, eggs, vegetables, fruits, nuts and healthy fats.

How to get started: Eat plenty of meats, seafood, vegetables, eggs, healthy fats and some fruit and nuts. Eliminate the top three food toxins – gluten, industrial/vegetable oils and sugar!

Always purchase the highest-quality ingredients that you can afford. Foods that are organic and grass-fed are not only void of pesticides and antibiotics but are also highly nutritious.

Avoid grains and legumes: It's especially important to avoid wheat and other gluten-containing grains, such as rye and barley. But also avoid soy, corn, beans, and peanuts (they are actually a legume, not a nut).

Avoid added sugars: This includes artificial sweeteners. Only occasionally consume natural sweeteners, such as honey and maple syrup.

Avoid vegetable oils and other processed oils: This includes canola, corn, soybean, cottonseed oil, among others. If you are confused about which fats and oils to consume, check out my "Guide to Using Fats & Oils" on page 14.

Don't be afraid to include healthy fats in your diet: This includes animal fats, avocado, olive oil, coconut oil, palm oil, ghee, grass-fed butter, lard and tallow, among others.

Eat foods with minimal ingredients: If you don't recognize something in the ingredients list or if it is something your grandma didn't eat, chances are neither should you.

Typically a Paleo diet does not include dairy, only consume dairy if you digest it well. If you are not sure how well you tolerate dairy, I suggest cutting it out for a month and then reintroducing it. If you are going to include dairy, it is best to use high-quality dairy from grass-fed sources. Grass-fed dairy is richer in nutrients and has a better fat composition, plus it tastes amazing! The only dairy foods I personally include regularly in my diet are raw milk, heavy cream, grass-fed butter and ghee. However, I will indulge in some high-quality cheese on occasion.

Is the paleo diet a low-carb diet? No, because you can eat certain carbs like yams. There are people who choose to take a low-carb approach, particularly if weight loss is the goal. Depending on your needs, you can adjust accordingly. Athletes may choose to include more starchy options such as sweet potatoes, potatoes, tubers, plantains and bananas.

WHAT ARE SOME OF THE BENEFITS OF THE PALEO DIET?

🔥 Weight loss

🔥 Omega-3/Omega-6 balance in the diet

🔥 Reduced inflammation

🔥 Reduced risk of modern day diseases such as diabetes, osteoporosis, cancer, heart disease

🔥 Increased energy and focus

🔥 Better athletic performance

SOME TIPS FOR FOLLOWING A PALEO DIET

Clean out your fridge and pantry: Throw out all the foods that you will not be consuming on the Paleo diet.

Eat enough food. Eat until you are full. This may seem counter-intuitive because we have been told so often to eat smaller portions. However, when we are eating the foods our bodies were designed to eat, our bodies also know when they have had enough. Trust your body. The Paleo diet typically has a much lighter caloric load than grain-based diets, so you may need to eat more in volume to stay full. If you eat larger meals, you will also need fewer snacks. Snack foods even on a Paleo diet are the ones that are easy to overeat, such as nuts and fruits.

Be very strict the first 2 weeks: Do not "cheat" at all in the first phase. I have found from my own experience and from talking to friends that the first two weeks are the most difficult. You may not feel great at this time because your body is adjusting to the changes in your diet. You may still be craving the foods you used to eat. Stick with it. It will become much easier after this point. I promise!

Be prepared: Preparation is key, especially when you are first starting out. Plan what you are going to eat in advance and prepare whatever you can ahead of time.

I tend to focus on preparing meat in advance, as I find this to be the most time consuming, hence my obsession with the slow cooker. I make a large roast every Sunday and this lasts us for a few meals. This way at dinner time, we can throw together a well-balanced meal quickly.

As the typical American diet is heavily made up of grains, at first glance it seems overwhelming to exclude these foods. As we look at what we can eat, we see that the options are endless on the Paleo Diet. You can have meats, seafood, fruits, vegetables, nuts/seeds, herbs/spices, and healthy sources of fat. Any combination of these foods makes for a fantastic meal!

WHY THE SLOW COOKER?

The slow cooker has many benefits. What initially drew me to it was its convenience. The slow cooker has been my biggest ally in keeping my Paleo diet. I work a day job that requires much commitment and I have a 2-3 hour-a-day commute. Between the hours spent at work, and time with friends and family, I knew that as much as I loved cooking, I could not cook a meal from scratch every night. I also knew that I could not go back to making a quick sandwich for dinner either. I loved how I felt when I ate Paleo-friendly food and wanted a way to continue it. I found the key to my success with the Paleo diet was cooking meat in bulk. When we got home from work, we could just heat it up along with some veggies and have a quick and healthy meal. Then we could spend our evenings enjoying a healthy dinner and catching up about our day!

Besides convenience, the slow cooker is also economical. I know that grass-fed beef can get pricey, especially premium cuts. The slow cooker is a great way to cook inexpensive cuts of meat that tend to be tough but flavorful. The slow-cooking process allows these tough cuts of meat to become tender, juicy and flavorful.

Also it's healthy. Since the food is being cooked at a very low temperature, we never have an opportunity to scorch it and sacrifice the integrity of the ingredients.

SOME SLOW COOKER TIPS

Liquid does not evaporate in the slow cooker, raising the risks of ending up with a bland, watery dish. It requires using flavorful bases, and using more herbs and spices than in conventional cooking. Adding herbs and spices again towards the end of cooking time also helps with flavor.

Browning, although you don't have to do this step if you are busy, really helps to add flavor to your dish!

Also salt tends to dissipate, especially as the vegetables give up liquid. We recommend salting your dishes well at the end to make sure they taste their best.

Sometimes you can end up with quite a bit of liquid when slow-cooking. The best thing to do is remove the meat and vegetables when they are done and place the liquid in a sauce pan. Heat over medium heat until you see the sauce thicken, about 5 to 10 minutes. This will also help to concentrate the flavors. Salt after this process so you don't get too much when the liquid evaporates.

FAT IS "WHERE IT'S AT'!

Fat: Artery clogging, heart disease causing, and obesity stimulating—all around BAD stuff. Whoa, wait a minute, that's not right. However it is unfortunately what the health, medical and food industry have led us to believe. The message that 'fat is bad' has been pushed on society for decades. There are 'fat free' and 'low fat' versions of nearly every food and sadly, people are buying them. The truth of the matter is that fat is essential to life and good for us! Now, we're not talking about Crisco, vegetable oils and margarine, rather natural fats found in grass-fed meats, butter, coconut products, and olive oil.

WHY FAT IS GOOD AND WHAT IT DOES:

Fat provides linoleic and linolenic acid to the body. These are essential fatty acids that the body can't make and must be obtained from what we eat. Linoleic and linolenic play important roles in blood clotting, brain development and inflammation control. Additionally, these essential fatty acids can be converted to other fatty acids that the body needs to function and be healthy.

Fat is our energy bank! It's where we store extra calories that can be used when we do not have access to food. It is also used during exercise when glycogen stores have been depleted.

Fat is also an insulator! It helps us to maintain our body temperature and protects our organs from injury and shock.

Without dietary fat we would not absorb the fat-soluble vitamins A, D, E and K; which all play important roles in health maintenance.

Fat plays a vital role in the brain and nervous system.

It is an important component of cell membranes and plays an important role in skin structure.

And without fat, hormone production would be next to impossible!

Fat also stimulates the flow of bile, emptying of the gall bladder, is a vital component of human milk and is extremely important in infant brain development.

GUIDE TO USING FATS AND OILS

FATS/OILS SAFE FOR FRYING, SAUTÉING AND BROWNING (OPT FOR ORGANIC AND UNREFINED OPTIONS)

Saturated fats are the best options for cooking; since they are chemically stable, they are resistant to damage from heat. Contrary to popular belief, they also play an important role in our health. They provide us with energy, they satiate us and they help us absorb important fat-soluble vitamins such as Vitamins A, D, E and K.

ANIMAL FATS

- Butter
- Ghee
- Lard

- Goose fat
- Duck fat
- Chicken fat (consume in moderation, due to high omega-6 content)
- Tallow (rendered beef or lamb fat)

NON-ANIMAL SATURATED FATS

🔥 Coconut oil

🔥 Palm oil

FATS/OILS SAFE FOR COLD USE

Use in moderation or as a condiment due to high omega-6 content

🔥 Olive oil

🔥 Avocado oil

🔥 Nut oils (macadamia, walnut, etc.)

🔥 Seed oils (sesame, flax, hemp, pumpkin, etc.)

UNHEALTHY FAT/OILS TO AVOID

These fats are either man-made or highly processed. These oils oxidize easily and become rancid, causing inflammation in the body. Avoid anything that is hydrogenated or partially hydrogenated.

🔥 Margarine or other fake butters

🔥 Vegetable oil

🔥 Canola oil

🔥 Corn oil

🔥 Cottonseed oil

🔥 Safflower oil

🔥 Sunflower oil

🔥 Rice bran oil

🔥 Grapeseed oil

🔥 Soybean oil

🔥 Shortening

REFERENCES

The Skinny on Fats by Mary G. Enig, PhD and Sally Fallon // January 1 2000

Canola Oil May Be "Paleo Diet" Approved, But I Won't Eat It by Diane Sanfilippo // JUNE 14, 2010

FAQs: What Are Safe Cooking Fats and Oils? by Diane Sanfilippo // September 19, 2011

The Definitive Guide to Oils by Mark Sisson

A Primal Primer: Animal Fats by Mark Sisson

TIPS FOR DINING OUT AND TRAVELING

I travel about once a month for work, and here are a few tips that help me keep Paleo on the road.

On the flight: If taking a longer flight, I pack snacks such as nuts, dried fruit, fresh fruit, coconut flakes and beef jerky. Some of these items I might not indulge in often at home, however, they are still much healthier options than snacks served on the plane. I also bring extra snacks for the trip or stop at a store and load up when I arrive, just in case I am in a situation where there isn't something suitable to eat.

You may have to compromise on quality: At home we always use organic and grass-fed ingredients. However while traveling for work, this is not always an option so I sometimes settle for conventional food as long as it is dairy, grain and legume-free.

Vegetable Oils/Industrial Seed Oils: The major issue with dining out is most foods in restaurants are cooked using vegetable oil (corn oil, soybean oil, cottonseed oil, etc.). I believe this is very unhealthy food, and I try my best to avoid it. I choose dishes that are cooked without oil whenever possible, such as grilled meats and steamed veggies. I have also found it difficult to completely avoid vegetable oil when dining out regularly. In those cases, I focus on staying dairy-grain-and legume free and understand that I may be consuming some vegetable oil. I still try my best to avoid it, but I also try not to worry about it so I can enjoy the meal.

Communication is key: When I first started my current job, I did not mention my Paleo lifestyle to my co-workers, but I always managed to find something to eat regardless of where we went. However, now that they know how I eat, they are accommodating about selecting restaurants and nice about it all. If you explain a little bit about your diet to colleagues, choosing Paleo-friendly restaurants becomes much easier. Maybe you will influence others to make healthier choices, too.

Review restaurant menus in advance: If I know in advance the restaurant where we will be dining, I research the menu and find some options that will work for me before we arrive so it doesn't take me extra time to find that right dish.

Ask the server: If I am unsure about anything, I ask the server questions. They are usually happy to confirm with the chef. I always ask if the fish is farmed or wild-caught. I always confirm that the item does not have gluten, because not all ingredients are always listed on the menu. More and more servers are becoming familiar with the term gluten-free. In fact, when I've mentioned that I can't eat gluten, the server has been great about making suggestions.

DINING OUT OPTIONS THAT WORK BEST FOR ME:

American/Continental: These seem to be the easiest places to stay Paleo. I choose foods that are gently cooked or grilled to limit the use of vegetable oils. If I am unsure about any sauces (sometimes flour is added as a thickening agent, or soy-sauce, sugar, vegetable oil are used), I skip the sauce and let the meat and veggies stand on their own.

Salads: The good old go-to! When in doubt, you can always order a salad with meat and ask for olive oil and vinegar for dressing.

Grocery stores with prepared food area (like Whole Foods): You can often get some organic meat and veggies from the prepared meal area. Read the ingredients closely because they sometimes use canola oil.

Mexican food: You can usually get some sort of plate with beef, pork or chicken and ask to substitute the rice and beans for a side of veggies, plus salsa and guacamole.

Thai food: This is always a good option because you can get some sort of vegetable/meat dish or curry and skip the rice. However with most options, you are going to get some vegetable oil. Make sure to choose dishes made without soy sauce. Thai-beef salads are a good option.

Burgers Protein-style: It seems like many places are popping up lately that specialize in grass-fed burgers.

Sushi: I either order sashimi or a hand-roll with no rice, plus some sides. Also, ask if the restaurant has wheat-free soy sauce; most places do now. I personally tolerate white rice pretty well, so every once in a while I might just have rice with my sushi.

WHEN YOUR PARTNER IS NOT PALEO...

In the best case scenario, the entire family will adopt a Paleo lifestyle. This will definitely help to make it easier to stay committed. However, just because your partner is not committed doesn't mean you can't be. I have been living this way for several years and although my husband mostly eats a Paleo diet, he is not strict. The hardest thing to exclude is the only thing I truly miss—a delicious microbrew! It's difficult to watch my husband enjoy one in the yard on a sunny day. With my intolerance to gluten, cheating here is not an option.

Our deal is all the groceries we buy and meals we cook at home are Paleo-friendly. He cooks paleo meals and agrees that our kids will eat this way. Then he eats what he wants when he or we go out. I will admit when I first started, I wanted badly to "convert" him, I would lecture him over dinner and try to pressure him. I was definitely the "pushy Paleo" wife/sister/daughter/friend. When I eventually got tired and realized my nagging and pleading were not working, I gave up and just tried to lead by example. As he observed my health problems diminish, my energy to become consistent even through my pregnancy, he took it upon himself to decide on a strict 30-day trial.

—ARSY VARTANIAN

FALLING OFF THE PALEO WAGON

It happens to the best of us! To be completely honest, I fell off the Paleo wagon several times prior to making the complete lifestyle change.

In the long run, what has worked for me is the idea that all "cheats" are not created equal. I've found that I react most to gluten. This seems to be true of most people I've talked to. If I momentarily fall of the wagon, I stay focused on avoiding gluten-containing items such as wheat, rye, and barley. These foods are the harshest on our bodies. One function of the Paleo diet is to reduce inflammation in the body and improve health and performance by removing food toxins. If you do indulge in a treat such as rice, beans or corn tortilla chips, don't beat yourself up about it, just enjoy it and make sure to get back on track during your next meal.

After a month of eating this way, chances are you won't want to cheat very often. I don't know if there is any scientific evidence on this, but from my own experience and from talking to friends, it seems that after consuming only real foods for a while your tastes change. Sugary foods taste much sweeter than before and artificial foods that you used to love to indulge in (like, in my case, Sour Patch Kids), taste—well, artificial. These foods become less satisfying.

HOW DOES THE PALEO LIFESTYLE REDUCE INFLAMMATION?

Inflammation is caused by an activation of the immune system in response to a stressor. The sources of the stress in our lives are numerous and can be biological (sleep, autoimmune disease, infection), physical (injury, exercise), mental/emotional (work/family/life factors), environmental (chemicals, pollution), and/or dietary (processed foods, unhealthy fats, etc.). While some inflammation is natural, normal and healthy; a prolonged inflammatory state is a catalyst in the development of many diseases. Diabetes, Alzheimer's, cancer, arthritis, heart disease, IBS, Parkinson's and many other conditions are the products of chronic inflammation. Controlling inflammation is crucial in disease prevention and there are generally two ways in which we can accomplish this.

1. Avoid or minimize all agents/conditions that result in an inflammatory response (this is next to impossible).

2. Modify diet and lifestyle to favor an anti-inflammatory state.

HOW DOES A PALEO LIFESTYLE REDUCE INFLAMMATION?

Paleo foods are non-inflammatory foods (for the most part - watch out for high doses of nuts, traditionally raised meats, etc.)

Vegetables are packed with antioxidants and are naturally anti-inflammatory. It is important to eat a variety of vegetables in order to get the most benefit and nutrition.

Many herbs and spices used in paleo cooking have inflammation-reducing properties. Some of the heavy hitters include cumin, basil, capsaicin, garlic, turmeric, and oregano.

There are no processed foods which contain unnatural trans fats, refined grains, high doses of sugar, omega-6 fatty acids, and overabundance of chemicals and artificial ingredients.

The paleo eating style emphasizes the importance of limiting the omega-6 fatty acids (inflammatory) and focusing more on the omega-3's (anti-inflammatory). Wild caught fish and grassfed meats, minimal amounts of nuts and no processed food are key to achieving an optimal omega-6 to omega-3 ratio.

Paleo promotes a healthy gut! Fermented foods have a place on your plate. Kimchi, sauerkraut, and other fermented vegetables help bolster healthy gut bacteria.

Sensible - not too much, not too little - exercise is promoted. Excessive, high intensity hammerings drive inflammation. Periodization and a smart training program helps to limit the inflammatory response exercise creates (remember, small amounts of inflammation are healthy and natural!)

Good night! Sleep is a key component to a paleo way of life. During sleep is when the body heals and repairs. Lack of sleep results in a natural stress response and therefore results in an inflammatory response.

That's how it works! Paleo is the way to go to reduce and avoid further inflammation. In a world full of stressors it's a great tool!

chapter one

IN–THE–BEGINNING
APPETIZERS

I AM A HUGE FAN OF FINGER FOODS. I love having guests over and serving a variety of appetizers, so guests actually have a chance to mingle. The slow cooker is great for this, as you can prepare the meal in advance and have it warm and ready when guests arrive!

Also guests barely notice they are eating Paleo-friendly foods. So if you serve heavy appetizers as I normally do for a game or party, your guests will have enjoyed a truly Paleo experience. If they weren't drinking beer, you might ask them how they felt the next day. I'll bet they had more energy and felt great.

PALEO **SPICY RIB** APPETIZER

This simple and easy appetizer is great as a finger food and will delight both Paleo and non-Paleo dieting guests.

INGREDIENTS

3 lbs pork spare ribs

2 tbsp paprika

1 tsp chili powder

1 tsp cayenne

1 tsp sweet basil, dried

1 tsp cumin

Salt and pepper to taste after dish is cooked

SAUCE

1 cup tomatoes, peeled and chopped

2 serrano peppers, chopped and peeled

2 tbsp apple cider vinegar

3 cloves garlic, crushed

½ small onion, minced

1 tbsp fresh lime juice

Two pinches of salt

COOKING INSTRUCTIONS

> Cut ribs into single pieces.

> Rub pieces with the spices and place in the slow cooker.

> Put tomatoes in a bowl, smash them with a fork and mix in the rest of the sauce ingredients.

> Pour mixture over the ribs, cover and cook on low for 4-6 hours until ribs are tender.

> Be sure to add salt and pepper after cooking.

CAPONATA SICILIANA

This dish is usually served chunky, but I often put it through the food processor and make it more of a dip. It makes it much easier when serving with sliced cucumbers. I am a spicy food lover, so I also tend to roast the peppers first and add a couple of jalapenos for some extra kick.

INGREDIENTS

4 tomatoes, peeled and chopped, cut into ½-inch pieces

2 large eggplant, peeled and cut into ½-inch pieces

2 tbsp ghee

2 medium zucchini, cut into ½-inch pieces

2 bell peppers, chopped

1 onion, chopped

3-4 cloves garlic, crushed

2 celery stalks, sliced

¼ cup chopped fresh parsley

1 cup chopped fresh basil

2 tbsp apple cider vinegar

¼ cup tomato paste

1 tsp sea salt

¼ tsp ground black pepper

½ cup green or black olives

2 tbsp capers

¼ cup pine nuts

1-2 cucumbers, sliced

Salt and pepper to taste

COOKING INSTRUCTIONS

❯ Roast the peppers in the broiler to add some extra flavor, 2-3 minutes a side (an optional step that adds a nice smoky flavor) and transfer to the slow cooker.

❯ Sauté the eggplant in 1 tablespoon ghee in a heavy-bottomed pan over medium heat until browned on all sides, about 5 minutes, then transfer to the slow cooker.

❯ Use remaining ghee to sauté the onions, garlic, and celery for 5 minutes until the onions are translucent, then transfer the mixture to the slow cooker.

❯ Add the remaining ingredients to the slow cooker except the olives, capers, basil, parsley, pine nuts and cucumbers.

❯ Cook on low for 4 hours until the vegetables are tender.

❯ Stir in the olives, capers, basil and pine nuts.

❯ Serve on cucumber rounds. This dish can be served warm or cold.

HONEY MUSTARD
CAVEMAN DRUMSTICKS

Here's a more traditional and favorite appetizer with a Paleo twist. Honey is Paleo-friendly but not encouraged in large amounts. Here it is a bit of a treat. The longer you stay on the Paleo diet, the more sensitive you will become to sweet flavors and the less you will desire to sweeten things.

INGREDIENTS

3 lbs chicken drumsticks

⅓ cup honey 2 tbsp, stone ground mustard

3 cloves garlic, crushed

¼ cup coconut oil

Salt and pepper for browning and just before serving

COOKING INSTRUCTIONS

❯ Salt and pepper drumsticks and brown them in a broiler for 5 minutes, turning once.

❯ Each broiler is different so watch closely to make sure drumsticks don't burn.

❯ Meanwhile, melt the coconut oil and mix it with the rest of the ingredients in a large bowl.

❯ Place browned chicken in bowl and mix until coated with the sauce.

❯ Pour everything into the slow cooker and cook on low heat for five hours.

❯ Salt and pepper the drumsticks before serving.

LAMB **MEATBALLS**

Grass-fed lamb is a great way to get more nutritents into your diet. This dish has a Middle Eastern flair with the cumin and is a favoite among my friends, even those who don't usually eat lamb.

INGREDIENTS

2 lbs ground lamb
2 tsps cumin
2 tsps fennel
1 tsp cayenne
½ tsp turmeric
Pinch of saffron
2 large eggs, lightly beaten
¼ white onion, finely minced
3 cloves garlic, crushed
Salt and pepper just before serving
Toothpicks for serving
1 tbsp ghee

COOKING INSTRUCTIONS

> Heat ghee in a frying pan over medium heat.

> Mix all the ingredients in a bowl to combine well.

> Shape into meatballs and drop into the pan.

> Brown for 5 minutes, turning the meatballs once.

> Add meatballs to the slow cooker.

> Add ¼ cup beef or chicken stock, cover and cook on low for 3-4 hours.

CILANTRO MINT PESTO SAUCE (OPTIONAL)

INGREDIENTS

3 tbsp olive oil
1 tbsp lemon juice
1 tsp fresh ginger
2 cups cilantro
1 cup mint
½ cup chopped onion
2 cloves garlic, crushed
salt and pepper
½ jalapeno pepper, chopped

COOKING INSTRUCTIONS

To make the sauce, place all ingredients in a food processor and mix until smooth.

CURRIED CHICKEN WINGS

Here's a different take on chicken wings that I love. They are really easy to make so I whip them up when we have last-minute guests over to watch a game, and the wings are often gone before game time.

INGREDIENTS

4 lbs chicken wings

1 cup coconut milk

2 tbsp fish sauce

3 tbsp red curry paste

¼ cup onion, minced

2 cloves garlic, crushed

2 tsps fresh ginger, grated

Salt and pepper before serving

COOKING INSTRUCTIONS

❯ Broil the chicken wings for 5 minutes, turning once, watching carefully so they don't burn.

❯ Mix all the ingredients and chicken in the slow cooker and cook on low for 4-5 hours.

❯ Remove the wings and thicken the sauce by cooking it on the stovetop over medium-high heat, stirring constantly for 1-2 minutes.

❯ Pour the sauce over the wings, salt and pepper to taste and serve.

CONDIMENTS & SUBSTITUTIONS

Condiments tend to be a matter of personal preference in the Paleo lifestyle. Depending on your goals or health concerns you may be stricter or less strict than me.

Here is my approach: I'm comfortable using non-paleo condiments in my cooking, as long as they are in small amounts, and I don't have an adverse reaction to them. What I mean by non-paleo is that they may have sugar or soy in them. However, I never use condiments that have wheat in them.

THE MAIN CONDIMENTS THAT YOU MAY NOTICE ME USING ARE:

Tamari (gluten-free soy sauce): Which is actually just fermented soybeans, but I say gluten-free because the first ingredient in conventional soy sauce is wheat and not soy so make sure to read the label. If you choose not to use any soy in your diet, you can always substitute coconut aminos. Coconut aminos have a similar salty flavor with a slight sweetness.

Another ingredient I will occasionally use with Asian dishes is **mirin**, which is rice wine vinegar. If you choose to not include any rice products in your diet, you can always substitute coconut vinegar for mirin.

From time to time, I will use **Worcestershire sauce**. Again, make sure to read the label to ensure that there is no wheat in it. If you choose not to include non-paleo condiments, you can always skip this ingredient.

Cooking with alcohol: You will notice that several recipes use fruit based alcohol like wine, brandy, cognac or hard cider. Most of the alcohol used in these recipes evaporates as it cooks. However if you're sensitive to alcohol or don't want to use it, here are a few alternatives for ensuring that the meat stays tender: broth, apple juice, tomato juice or blanched tomatoes, and filtered water.

Ghee and grass-fed butter: Although, not strictly paleo, these are still a healthy fat choice. Butter is a good source of vitamin K-2, which has been found to help protect us from heart disease. It promotes brain function and even helps prevent cancer. Once the milk is removed, butter is left with very minimal traces of lactose and casein (the main problems with dairy) and ghee is left with even less. I also prefer these fats for browning, as they don't compromise the flavor of the dish with other strong flavors like bacon when using bacon grease. If you are sensitive to butter and ghee, or you choose not to use them, refer to my guide for using fats and oils on page 14. I almost always brown my meats and veggies using ghee, but if ghee is hard to find in your area, butter will always do!

Cooking liquids: We prefer to make our own cooking liquids as it is easy and much healthier. When testing my recipes, I always used homemade coconut milk, broth and blanched tomatoes. However, if there are time constraints, canned varieties can also be substituted.

Tomato paste: Tomato paste is a great ingredient for adding flavor to slow-cooker meals. I highly urge you to find a variety sold in a glass jar, opposed to in a can.

AUTOIMMUNE DISORDERS

The prevalence of autoimmune disease in today's society seems to be skyrocketing. The diseases are many: celiac, diabetes, rheumatoid arthritis, lupus, thyroid maladies, MS, ALS, fibromyalgia, Crohn's, ulcerative colitis, etc. Autoimmune disorders refer to any and all conditions in which the body cannot distinguish between foreign materials/ proteins and itself. Then the body begins attacking its own tissues and organs. It is believed that 70% of autoimmune disease can be blamed on environmental or lifestyle elements. Some believe that "leaky gut" or increased intestinal permeability is a key factor in the development of autoimmune conditions. Many dietary components contribute to the development of leaky gut. Some of the most common offenders are wheat, grains, legumes, dairy and nightshade vegetables; NSAIDS, oral contraceptives and antacids can also play roles in leaky-gut development. Avoiding the foods and agents that contribute to the development and progression of autoimmune conditions can remarkably improve health which is one of the reasons the Paleo lifestyle has become so popular.

Those with pre-existing autoimmune conditions are advised to follow an 'Autoimmune Paleo' protocol. In this plan nightshade vegetables (peppers, potatoes, eggplant, green tomatoes, capsacin), eggs, and nuts are also excluded due to possible reactions. These guidelines may be loosened in time based on individual response and progression.

chapter two

SAVORY, SUCCULENT AND SLOW COOKED
BEEF DISHES

BEEF AND RED MEAT IN GENERAL HAVE RECEIVED MUCH MISGUIDED NEGATIVE ATTENTION IN THE MAINSTREAM. We now believe that choosing healthy beef from grass-fed cattle has proven health benefits. Beef is not only an excellent source of protein, but also of B vitamins, iron and zinc! Studies have found that grass-fed beef is higher in Omega-3 fatty acids, conjugated linoleic acid (CLA) and vitamin E! Omega-3s are present in the grass eaten by cattle; when cows eat grain they don't store this essentially fatty acid to pass on to us. By choosing grass-fed beef we are also avoiding digesting hormones, antibiotics and other drugs. Grass feeding is also better for the animals and the environment. It promotes humane treatment of animals and reduces the use of chemical fertilizers and pesticides to grow unsustainable amounts of corn and soy.

When making a health-conscious choice about eating animal proteins, we shouldn't ask ourselves, is this red or white meat? We should ask, did this animal eat what it was naturally meant to eat?

Grass-fed beef can be pricey. Purchasing through a CSA is a great way to save money. Also, purchasing tough, inexpensive cuts such as roasts and cooking them gently and slowly in a slow cooker is another great way to incorporate grass-fed meat into our diets.

TRADITIONAL
BEEF BOURGUIGNON

This French twist on a regular beef stew conatins less sauce, is more elegant and delivers a delicious tangy red-wine flavor that is to die for. Shallots can be time consuming to peel so feel free to save shallots for guests and swap in a large yellow onion cut into eighths for regular meals, though I'm not sure who would call this a "regular meal." It's easy gourmet, French country cooking at its best and will fill your house with tantalizing aromas all day, presaging the great meal ahead.

INGREDIENTS

½ lb bacon, diced

2 lbs beef chuck, big cubed

8 shallots, peeled and left whole

2 cloves garlic, crushed

1 tbsp Herbes de Provence

1 lb mushrooms, stems removed and sliced

1 lb carrots, sliced

1½ cups red wine

1 cup beef stock

½ cup cognac

Salt and pepper just before serving

COOKING INSTRUCTIONS

> Sauté the bacon over medium high until just crisp, about 3-5 minutes.

> Remove the bacon and brown the meat in the bacon grease in batches for about 5 minutes each, turning the meat only a few times and allowing it to brown well.

> If the bacon grease is smoking, turn the heat down to medium.

> Place the beef, bacon and all other ingredients into the slow cooker and cook on low for 6-8 hours.

> You may have extra liquid, so use a slotted spoon to serve the meat and vegetables in a bowl and then ladle just enough sauce over the dish to cover the bottom of the bowl.

> Be sure to put a good amount of salt and pepper on the dish before serving.

SERVINGS: 6

COOK'S NOTE: SLOW COOKING DRAWS THE SALT OUT OF MEATS AND VEGETABLES SO IT'S BEST TO PUT A GOOD AMOUNT OF SALT ON JUST BEFORE SERVING TO BRING OUT THE FLAVORS.

BEEF AND FENNEL STEW

The fennel gives this dish Mediterranean flair and a lighter flavor. I'd recommend you brown the beef for this one to give the dish more body. As with almost all beef stews, the homemade bone broth offers big health benefits and is packed with minerals that are great for your body.

INGREDIENTS

2 lbs beef stew meat

1 onion, chopped

1 tbsp ghee

2 fennel bulbs, cored and thinly sliced

2 carrots, cored and sliced

1 bell pepper, chopped

2 cloves garlic, smashed

3 cups beef broth

2 tbsp tomato paste

1 tsp fennel seeds

1 tsp paprika

1 tsp thyme

2 bay leaves

Salt and pepper just before serving

COOKING INSTRUCTIONS

❯ Brown the meat in batches in a heavy-bottomed pan over medium-high heat for 5 minutes.

❯ Be careful to not crowd the pan and make sure it is well heated before you put in the meat.

❯ Sauté onion in the ghee until translucent.

❯ Put all the other ingredients in the slow cooker with the meat and cook on low for 8 hours. Salt and pepper to taste before serving.

SERVINGS: 6

OXTAIL SOUP

This is a very nutrient-dense meal, rich in gelatin which builds strong bones and is good for your skin, heart and muscles. This rich dish is also very tasty, sort of a supercharged beef stew. When following the Paleo diet, fatty and nutrient-rich meals stop you from overeating while keeping you satisfied naturally by providing what your body needs. You don't need to starve yourself to stay fit.

INGREDIENTS

3 lbs oxtails, cut into sections

1 onion, chopped

2 large carrots, sliced

1 large leek, cleaned well and sliced

2 bay leaves

1 red spicy pepper (optional)

3 cups beef stock

1 cup red wine

2 tomatoes, peeled and chopped

1 tsp thyme

¼ cup chopped parsley, to be added at the end

Salt and pepper just before serving

COOKING INSTRUCTIONS

❯ Brown the oxtail in a heavy-bottomed pan over medium-high heat in batches about 5 minutes each, then transfer to the slow cooker.

❯ Put all ingredients into the slow cooker except the parsley.

❯ Cook for 8 hours on low heat.

❯ Stir in parsley, and add salt and pepper before serving.

SERVINGS: 6-8

BEEF BRISKET IN
ESPRESSO BEAN BBQ SAUCE

This is a great recipe for hosting an outdoor party in the summer. You can prepare it in advance and keep it warm in the pot on your counter or plugged in outside. This dish is nicely balanced, not too sweet or sugary like some barbecue sauces but full of flavor. Brisket is a lean cut of meat so is a good option for people restricting calories and works well for the crockpot, a tough cut that comes out nice and fork-tender. This dish takes a little extra prep time but is worth it.

INGREDIENTS

2 ½ lbs beef brisket
Salt and pepper just before serving

ESPRESSO BBQ SAUCE

1 medium onion, diced
4 cloves garlic, crushed
2 tbsp ghee for sautéing
5 whole tomatoes, peeled and seeds removed
½ cup apple cider vinegar
Juice of 1 lemon
½ cup honey
2 dried chipotle peppers
1 tsp smoked paprika
¼ tsp of fresh ginger
¼ cup brewed espresso or a ½ cup of strong regular coffee
2 tbsp Dijon mustard
2 tbsp Worcestershire sauce (make sure it is a gluten-free brand)
2 tsps chili powder
½ tbsp salt
½ tbsp pepper

COOKING INSTRUCTIONS

❭ To make the sauce, sauté the onions in a large saucepan over medium heat, until translucent, about 8 minutes.

❭ Add garlic and chipotle peppers, and sauté until the garlic is fragrant, about 3 minutes. Add tomatoes and simmer for a few minutes.

❭ Using either an immersion blender or food processor, puree the mixture.

❭ Return the pan to medium heat, put the pureed barbecue sauce in the pan and add the rest of the ingredients.

❭ Stir everything together until completely combined and continue to cook at a low simmer for about 30 minutes, stirring occasionally until the sauce is thickened and a dark burgundy color.

❭ Brown the brisket in a clean pan over medium-high heat for 5 minutes.

❭ Place in the slow cooker with 1 cup of the barbecue sauce.

❭ Save second cup to serve directly on the meat.

❭ Cook on low for 6-8 hours, then shred in the slow cooker with 2 forks, being careful to not burn your hands on the sides.

❭ Add salt and pepper before serving.

SERVINGS: 6

ROPA VIEJA

The slow cooker is a great way to cook this traditional Latin American dish. While it is traditionally served with rice, I like it over steamed vegetables.

INGREDIENTS

2½ lbs chuck roast

2 onions, sliced

2 tbsp ghee

4 cloves garlic, minced

2 bell peppers, sliced, 1 red and 1 green to add some color

8 tomatoes, peeled, seeded and chopped

2 tbsp tomato paste

1 tsp salt

½ tsp pepper

1 tbsp cumin

1 tsp oregano

1 tsp smoked paprika

½ cup beef broth

Fresh cilantro for garnish

Salt and pepper just before serving

COOKING INSTRUCTIONS

❯ Melt 2 tablespoons of ghee in a heavy-bottomed pan over medium heat and sauté the onions until translucent.

❯ Add the peppers and garlic, sauté another 3 minutes until garlic is fragrant, then transfer to the slow-cooker.

❯ Brown the roast on all sides about 5 minutes, then transfer it to the slow-cooker.

❯ Stir together tomatoes, tomato paste, broth, spices, salt and pepper, pour over the beef and cook on low for 6-7 hours.

❯ Shred the beef with 2 forks and cook for an additional hour.

SERVINGS: 4-6

COOK'S NOTE: WHEN THE BEEF IS READY, IT SHOULD SHRED EASILY. IF YOU END UP WITH TOO MUCH LIQUID, TASTE THE MEAT, AND IF YOU ARE HAPPY WITH THE FLAVORS JUST REMOVE THE MEAT AND VEGETABLES WITH A SLOTTED SPOON. IF IT NEEDS MORE FLAVOR, YOU CAN MOVE THE DISH TO A SAUTÉ PAN AND SIMMER ON LOW FOR 30 MINUTES TO CONCENTRATE THE FLAVORS AND REDUCE THE LIQUID.

CHILI COLORADO

This dish is easy to make and a good alternative to a typical comfort food meal at the end of a long day. It features bold Southwestern flavors that are classic favorites.

INGREDIENTS

1 onion, chopped

1 tbsp butter

3 lbs stew beef, cut into 1-inch chunks

8 dried chiles, stems and seeds removed

2 tbsp tomato paste

3 cloves garlic, chopped

2 cups beef stock

1 tbsp chili powder

2 tsp cumin

1 tbsp dried oregano

1 tsp dried parsley

4 tomatoes, peeled and chopped

Garnish with chopped cilantro

Salt and pepper just before serving

COOKING INSTRUCTIONS

> Lightly sauté onions in the butter in a heavy-bottomed pan set over medium heat, about 8 minutes until the onions are translucent.

> Add to the slow cooker.

> Return the pan to the heat, increased to medium high.

> Brown the beef on all sides in batches for 5 minutes a batch.

> Add the browned beef and all other ingredients to the slow cooker and cook on low for 8 hours.

> Salt and pepper to taste before serving.

SERVINGS: 6

SHORT RIBS
IN TOMATO FENNEL SAUCE

This is one of the easiest recipes I know. The light flavor of fennel pairs nicely with the rich tomato sauce to create a terrific, fork-tender dish for a summer evening while barely lifting a finger.

INGREDIENTS

8 short ribs

4 garlic cloves, crushed

1 onion, diced

2 carrots, sliced

1 fennel bulb, chopped

6 tomatoes, peeled and chopped or 1 14-ounce can of whole tomatoes

1 tsp paprika

1 cups beef broth

½ cup red wine

1 red chile pepper

½ tsp thyme

½ tsp oregano

2 bay leaves

Salt and pepper just before serving

COOKING INSTRUCTIONS

> Put all the ingredients into the slow cooker and cook on low for 4 to 6 hours.

> Be careful not to overcook or the meat will slide off the bones before you get them out of the slow cooker.

> Salt and pepper and then serve.

SERVINGS: 2-3

PALEO **BEEF CASSEROLE**

This is a great inexpensive one-dish meal. It's very satisfying and the perfect meal right after a workout. It has carbs, fat and protein! Protein is extremely important to muscle recovery, growth and regeneration.

INGREDIENTS

1 onion, diced
1 tbsp ghee
3-4 cloves garlic
2 lbs ground beef
1 tsp oregano
1 tsp basil
3 yams, peeled and thinly sliced
1 cup sliced mushrooms
1 green pepper, seeded and chopped
1 red bell pepper, seeded and chopped
1 cup tomato sauce
Salt and pepper just before serving

COOKING INSTRUCTIONS

> In a large frying pan set over medium heat, sauté the onions in ghee for 5 minutes. Add the garlic and cook until fragrant, about 3 minutes.

> Turn the heat to medium high and add the ground beef, breaking up the meat with a spatula.

> Add the oregano and basil to the meat as it is browning.

> Cook for another 5 minutes.

> Lay the yams on the bottom of the slow cooker, then add the green and red peppers and mushrooms.

> Place the beef on top and pour tomato sauce over it.

> Cook on low for 6 hours.

SERVINGS: 6

PRIME RIB CHILI

This is an upscale chili with a more sophisticated and gourmet taste. There's no chili powder; the fresh peppers do the work here and deliver a nice, more subtle flavor. Beans are not Paleo-friendly so are not included but you won't miss them.

INGREDIENTS

3 lbs beef prime rib, cubed

2 tbsp ghee

1 white onion, diced

3 cloves garlic, crushed

2 anaheim peppers, seeded and diced

1 pablano pepper, seeded and diced

1 serrano pepper, seeded and diced

1 red bell pepper, chopped

6 tomatoes, peeled and chopped

2 tbsp tomato paste

2 cups beef stock

2 tsp smoked paprika

¼ tsp cayenne pepper

1 tsp cumin

1 tsp oregano

Salt and pepper just before serving

¼ cup cilantro, chopped for garnish

COOKING INSTRUCTIONS

❯ Brown the beef in 1 tablespoon of ghee in a heavy-bottomed pan over medium-high heat for 5 minutes and place in the slow cooker.

❯ Lower the temperature to medium and sauté the onions, garlic and peppers in the remaining ghee for 5 minutes, until the onions are translucent.

❯ Place vegetables in the slow cooker with the remaining ingredients and spices.

❯ Be sure to stir in the tomato paste so it doesn't clump up.

❯ Cook on low for 6 to 8 hours.

SERVINGS: 6-8

COOK'S NOTE: YOU CAN ADD A NICE SMOKY FLAVOR BY BROILING THE PEPPERS FOR FIVE MINUTES BEFORE CHOPPING THEM.

BEEF ROAST WITH CHILES

This is a nice twist on a traditional pot roast, giving it a Tex-Mex flavor.

INGREDIENTS

3-4 lbs beef brisket
1 tsp cumin
1 tsp caraway seeds
1 tsp ground fennel seeds
2 tbsp ghee
1 large onion, chopped
2 cloves garlic, crushed
6 dried chiles
1 cup beef broth
Salt and pepper just before serving

COOKING INSTRUCTIONS

› Rub beef with spices, except the chiles.

› Sauté onions in 1 tablespoon of ghee in a heavy-bottomed pan over medium heat, about 5 minutes.

› Place in the slow cooker.

› Turn heat to medium high and brown the beef on all sides in the other tablespoon of ghee, about 6 minutes.

› Add the rest of the ingredients to the slow cooker and cook on low for 8 hours.

› Salt to taste and serve.

SERVINGS: 6-8

BEEF **BRISKET**

A classic dish that's naturally Paleo-friendly, brisket offers easy flavors for the whole family. It freezes well and makes perfect leftovers for great Paleo lunches and fast dinners. I highly recommend you make your own broth for these and other dishes. You'll taste a big difference in the flavor, and the homemade broth has a greater nutritional value than bouillon cubes or canned stock.

INGREDIENTS

3-4 lb beef brisket

3-4 shallots, peeled

2 parsnips, chopped
(you can substitute 2 carrots)

2 tomatoes, chopped and peeled

2 bay leaves

1 cup beef broth

2 tbsp apple-cider vinegar

2 tbsp chili powder

1 tsp dry mustard

Salt and pepper just before serving

COOKING INSTRUCTIONS

❯ Preheat a heavy-bottomed pan to medium high for a couple minutes and brown the brisket all sides for about 6-8 minutes.

❯ Transfer the meat to the slow cooker.

❯ Add the rest of the ingredients to the slow cooker, making sure the dried spices are mixed into the liquid and not clumped or sitting dry on top of the meat.

❯ Cook on low for 6-8 hours.

❯ Add a good amount of salt and pepper, slice against the grain and serve in slices, spooning the sauce over the meat.

SERVINGS: 8-10

THAI **RED BEEF CURRY**

I love Thai food. I usually eat it with a side of steamed vegetables instead of rice. The lemongrass in this dish makes the flavor nice and light.

INGREDIENTS

2 lbs beef cut into slices ⅛- to ¼-inch thick

2 cups coconut milk

3 tbsp Thai red curry paste

3 kaffir lime leaves

2 small Asian eggplants, cut into slices

2 tbsp fresh ginger

3 cloves garlic, crushed

1 stalk lemongrass, finely sliced

1 tsp coriander

1 tsp cumin

2 tsp chili powder

Salt and pepper just before serving

COOKING INSTRUCTIONS

❯ Brown the beef in coconut oil in a heavy-bottomed pan over medium-high heat for 6 minutes.

❯ Place meat in slow cooker.

❯ Add the rest of ingredients.

❯ Cook on low for 6-8 hours.

❯ Add salt and pepper to taste, then serve.

SERVINGS: 4-6

LEMONGRASS AND CASHEW **BEEF**

Lemongrass in this dish is strong and underscored by the lime leaves. The cashews add a nice surprising crunch for a full-flavored Asian meal.

INGREDIENTS

2 tbsp fish sauce

1 tbsp honey

2 tbsp shallots, minced

3 cloves garlic, crushed

1 tsp cayenne

½ tbsp powdered coriander

2 stalks lemongrass, thinly sliced

3-4 kaffir lime leaves

1 tbsp fresh ginger, ground or grated

½ cup coconut aminos

2 lb flank steak, thickly sliced

1 onion, cut into wedges

2 red bell peppers, sliced

¼ cup coarsely crushed cashews

4 scallions, cut into ½-inch lengths for garnish

Salt and pepper just before serving

COOKING INSTRUCTIONS

> Put the fish sauce, honey, shallots, garlic, cayenne pepper, coriander, lemongrass, lime leaves, ginger and coconut aminos into the slow cooker.

> Stir until combined.

> Place the beef, onions and bell peppers into slow cooker with the sauce.

> Cook on low for 4-6 hours.

> Add cashews and half the scallions 30 minutes before serving.

> Garnish with the remaining scallions, salt and pepper to taste, then serve.

SERVINGS: 4-6

PERSIAN STEW WITH OKRA (BAAMIEH)

Okra is a seasonal vegetable that is not always easy to find. Every time I spot it, I snatch some up to make this traditional Persian stew. This dish is usually served over basmati rice so try it over cauliflower rice.

INGREDIENTS

2 lbs beef chuck, cut into 1-inch pieces

3 tbsp ghee

1 large onion, diced

4 cloves garlic, crushed

1 lb okra, stems cut off

2 tbsp fresh lime juice

½ tsps turmeric

2 tbsp tomato paste

4 fresh tomatoes peeled and chopped

½ cup beef broth

Juice of ½ a lime

Salt and pepper just before serving

COOKING INSTRUCTIONS

> Trim the stems of the okra, but make sure not to remove any of the base.

> Add 2 tablespoons ghee to a heavy-bottomed pan and sauté onions until soft, about 5 minutes.

> Add the meat, garlic and ¼ teaspoon of the turmeric.

> Sauté until meat is browned about another 6 minutes, being careful not to burn the garlic.

> Add tomatoes and tomato paste and sauté for 3 minutes longer.

> Add all the ingredients from the pan to the slow cooker.

> Add the broth and cook on low for 6 hours.

> Add okra and cook for an additional 1 hour, making sure to not over-cook the okra or they become slimy.

> Add an additional ¼ teaspoon turmeric, the lime juice, then salt and pepper to taste before serving.

SERVINGS: 6

SPICY THAI **BEEF SOUP**

I just love Thai food. It offers interesting flavors, and is sweet and savory.
A childhood friend was Thai, so I grew up eating Thai food with her family.
This is a tangy and satisfying soup with nice flavors of kaffir and lemongrass.
Be warned that Thai restaurants use a lot of soy sauce, so it's better
to make it at home so you can keep it Paleo-friendly.

INGREDIENTS

4 cups beef stock

2 stalks lemongrass, cut into pieces

4-5 kaffir lime leaves

4 red chilies

4 cloves garlic, crushed

1 lb thinly sliced beef

2-3 tbsp lime juice

2 tbsp fish sauce

2 tbsp red curry paste

¼ tsp cayenne pepper

2 scallions, chopped for garnish
Salt and pepper just before serving.

COOKING INSTRUCTIONS

> Put all the ingredients into the slow cooker.

> Cook on low for 4-6 hours until meat is tender.

> Salt and pepper to taste, and garnish with chopped scallions just before serving.

SERVINGS: 6

BEEF AND BOK CHOY

These ingredients are a popular combination in Asian cooking. The subtle flavors balance nicely in this light sauce with ginger adding a fresh zest. P.S. Don't use sesame oil to brown the meat. Use butter, ghee or coconut oil.

INGREDIENTS

2 lb flank steak, cut into inch-thick pieces and kept long

1 tbsp ghee

4 cloves garlic, crushed

1 onion, sliced

2 tbsp fresh ginger

½ cup beef broth

2 tbsp sesame oil

¼ cup coconut aminos or Tamari

5 cups bok choy, trimmed and cut into 1-inch pieces

1 red chili pepper, seeded and sliced

Garnish with green onions

COOKING INSTRUCTIONS

❯ In a heavy-bottomed pan over medium heat, sear the beef on all sides for about 5 minutes and place in the slow cooker.

❯ Add the ghee to the pan and sauté onions for 5 minutes until translucent.

❯ Add the garlic and cook another 3 minutes until fragrant.

❯ Place this and the rest of the ingredients in the slow cooker.

❯ Cook on low for 6-8 hours.

❯ Salt and pepper to taste and garnish with green onions.

SERVINGS: 4-6

PICADILLO

The slow cooker does really well with ground meats, which are also a great affordable way to eat grass-fed meat. This dish transforms regular old ground beef into a Cuban delight, with the surprising taste of olives adding an exotic and well-balanced flavor. It is also as a nice complement to eggs for breakfast.

INGREDIENTS

3 lbs ground beef

2 small onions, chopped

4 cloves, garlic crushed

½ cup beef stock

4 chopped tomatoes

2 tbsp tomato paste

1 jalapeño pepper, finely chopped

1 bell pepper, chopped

½ lb pitted green olives

1 tsp dried oregano

1 tsp dried basil

1 tsp cumin

Salt and pepper just before serving

COOKING INSTRUCTIONS

❯ Sauté onion in a 2 lb lean ground beef ½ cup sliced pimento stuffed green olives heavy pan over medium high for 5 minutes until transculent.

❯ Turn heat to medium high, add the garlic and brown the meat for 5 minutes, stirring occasionally to make sure the onions and garlic don't burn.

❯ Place meat, garlic and onions in the slow cooker with all the other ingredients, except the olives.

❯ Cook on low 6-8 hours.

❯ Add olives in the last hour of cooking.

❯ Salt and pepper to taste, then serve.

SERVINGS: 6-8

INDIAN **BEEF CURRY**

This very flavorful dish has a lot of health benefits. Turmeric is a spice with anti-inflamatory properties. It is thought that cinnamon helps lower blood-sugar levels and increases insulin production in the body, but I eat it because I love the exotic flavors.

INGREDIENTS

2 lb beef roast, cubed

3 tbsp ghee

1 onion, sliced

2 cloves garlic, crushed

1 tbsp fresh ginger, ground

1 tbsp ground coriander

2 tsp cumin

4 dried red chiles

1 tsp turmeric

1 tsp cinnamon

1 cup coconut milk

½ cup beef broth

Juice of one lemon

Salt and pepper just before serving

COOKING INSTRUCTIONS

❯ Heat a heavy-bottomed pan over medium high.

❯ Melt 1 tablespoon of ghee and then brown the beef in 2 or 3 batches, about 5 minutes each batch.

❯ Lower the heat to medium and sauté the onions and garlic in the remaining ghee for 5 minutes until translucent.

❯ Transfer to the slow cooker.

❯ Add the rest of the ingredients to the slow cooker.

❯ Cook for 6-8 hours.

❯ Salt and pepper to taste, then serve.

SERVINGS: 4-6

BEEF KALDERETA

Liver is a Paleo superfood as I might have mentioned before. Many people are not huge fans of liver, or not familiar with the taste. So this may be the perfect dish to help you include liver in your diet, as it hides the strong flavor a bit.

INGREDIENTS

2 lbs beef, cut into chunks

2 tbsp butter

3 onions, chopped

6 garlic cloves, crushed

½ lb chicken liver

3 bell peppers, diced

6 tomatoes, finely chopped

1 cup tomato sauce

2 cups beef stock

3 hot chili peppers

3 yams

2 bay leaves

Salt and pepper just before serving

COOKING INSTRUCTIONS

> In a heavy-bottomed pan, brown the beef in the butter in batches over medium heat, about 5 minutes a batch.

> Transfer to the slow cooker.

> Sauté the onions and bell peppers in the remaining butter until translucent, about 5 minutes. Add the garlic and sauté until fragrant, about 3 minutes.

> Meanwhile, chop the liver by pulsing it in a food processor.

> Add all the ingredients into the slow cooker.

> Cook on low for 6-8 hours.

> Salt and pepper to taste, then serve.

SERVINGS: 4-6

CROCKPOT KOREAN BEEF
(BULGOGI)

This recipe has a nice tangy twist. It goes really well with kimchi.
Don't forget to allow time to marinate the meat.

INGREDIENTS

4 cloves garlic, crushed

2 tbsp coconut vinegar or mirin

4 tbsp coconut aminos or Tamari

2 tbsp sesame oil

1 tbsp honey

½ onion, chopped

1 tbsp ghee

2 lb flank steak, thinly sliced

Salt and pepper just before serving

COOKING INSTRUCTIONS

❯ Mix all the ingredients except onions and meat.

❯ Pour marinade over meat and marinate for anywhere from a few hours to overnight in the refrigerator.

❯ Remove meat from marinade and let stand to dry a bit.

❯ Reserve the marinade.

❯ Sauté the onions in the ghee in a heavy-bottomed pan over medium heat for 5 minutes until translucent.

❯ Transfer to the slow cooker.

❯ Turn the heat up to medium-high and brown the beef in batches for about 5 minutes each batch.

❯ Place in slow cooker.

❯ Add the marinade to the slow cooker.

❯ Cook on low for 6-8 hours.

SERVINGS: 4-6

CABBAGE **DOLMAS**

This is a more involved recipe, but worth it. It's my mom's recipe and was a child-hood favorite of mine. She cooked it on the stove-top with rice, but I adapted it for the slow cooker and made it Paleo friendly. It has a lot of flavor and is very filling and satisfying. I usually make a large amount and freeze some for later use.

INGREDIENTS

20 white cabbage leaves

2 lbs ground beef

1 large onion, finely chopped

3 ripe tomatoes, 1 finely chopped for the stuffing and the other 2 peeled and coarsely chopped

3 cloves garlic, crushed

2 tbsp tomato paste

2 tsp salt

1 tsp pepper

1 tbsp cumin

½ cup mint, finely minced

1 cup parsley, finely minced

¼ tsp cayenne pepper

½ cup olive oil

More salt and pepper just before serving

COOKING INSTRUCTIONS

> To make the stuffing, combine the onion, finely chopped tomato, tomato paste, garlic, herbs, salt, pepper, cumin, olive oil and beef.

> You might cut down the cabbage leaves so they aren't too big for a tablespoon of the stuffing.

> Blanch the cabbage leaves by dunking them in boiling water for a minute.

> Place 1 heaping tablespoon of stuffing in the middle of each cabbage roll.

> Make into dolmas by folding the top and bottom over the filling, and then folding in the sides and rolling like a small burrito.

> Arrange dolmas in the slow cooker.

> Add the remaining tomatoes and the water.

> Drizzle with olive oil.

> Put a heatproof plate that fits in the slow cooker on top of dolmas, to weigh them down and keep leaves from opening.

> Cook for 4-6 hours on low.

> Salt and pepper to taste, then serve.

> To reheat a frozen dolma, put it in a pan or place it in a toaster oven on 350 degrees for 15 minutes.

SERVINGS: 4-6

STUFFED **EGGPLANT**

This is a fun dish to serve and comes with its own vegetable bowls. Here the mint lightens up the rich flavor of the ground beef. Armenians put a lot of mint in their food, but we aren't sure if this is a traditional dish or not. It's just tasty.

INGREDIENTS

6 eggplants
1 lb ground beef
1 tbsp fresh basil, chopped
2 tbsp fresh mint, chopped
1 tsp cumin
⅛ tsp cayenne
2 garlic cloves, minced
2 tbsp ghee
½ red onion, minced
2 Anaheim peppers, diced
3 tomatoes, chopped and peeled
Salt and pepper to taste
More salt and pepper just before serving

COOKING INSTRUCTIONS

❯ Cut eggplants lengthwise and scoop out the inside and reserve, leaving the shell about a half an inch thick.

❯ Cube the inside of the eggplant meat.

❯ Add to the ground beef the basil, mint, cumin, cayenne, salt, pepper and garlic.

❯ Heat the ghee in a heavy-bottomed pan over medium high and sauté the onions, peppers, and approximately one-third of the tomato and all the scooped-out eggplant for 5 minutes until the onions are translucent.

❯ Add the ground beef and brown for 6 minutes, breaking up the meat with a wooden spoon or spatula.

❯ Scoop the mixture into the eggplant shells and place them in the slow cooker.

❯ Arrange the rest of the tomatoes around the eggplant.

❯ Cook on low for 3-4 hours.

❯ Salt and pepper to taste, then serve.

SERVINGS: 6

STUFFED **PEPPERS**

This traditional dish is great in the slow cooker if you are careful when removing the perfectly done peppers. Each one is a hearty and delicious meal nicely presented.

INGREDIENTS

6 large peppers

2 lbs ground beef

1 onion, minced

3 cloves garlic, crushed

3 tomatoes, peeled and chopped

½ cup broth

1 tsp salt

½ tsp pepper

½ cup finely chopped flat-leaf parsley

¼ cup finely chopped fresh basil

1 tbsp cumin

1 tbsp dried oregano

More salt and pepper to taste just before serving

COOKING INSTRUCTIONS

❯ Wash peppers, cut the stem and clean inside.

❯ Mix ground beef with herbs, cumin, salt, pepper, onions, and garlic.

❯ Lightly brown the mixture in a heavy bottomed pan over medium heat for 5 minutes, breaking up the beef.

❯ Stuff the peppers with the mixture and arrange in slow cooker.

❯ Place tomatoes around peppers and pour in broth.

❯ Cook on low 4-6 hours.

❯ Salt and pepper to taste, then serve.

SERVINGS: 6

VENISON THYME STEW
WITH YAMS

This hearty stew is the perfect meal for a cold winter's night.

INGREDIENTS

2 lbs venison stew meat (leg or shoulder)

3 stalks celery, chopped

3 carrot sticks, peeled and sliced into ¼-inch rounds

4 cloves garlic, crushed

1 onion, chopped

2 tbsp ghee

1 bay leaf

2 yams, chopped

½ tsp oregano

1 tsp thyme

4 tomatoes, peeled and chopped

3 cups beef broth

Salt and pepper just before serving

COOKING INSTRUCTIONS

❭ Heat 1 tablespoon of ghee in a heavy-bottomed pan over medium heat.

❭ Brown the venison on all sides for 5 minutes and place in the slow cooker.

❭ Lightly sauté the vegetables in the remaining ghee for 5 minutes until the onions are translucent, and place them in the slow cooker.

❭ Add the rest of the ingredients and cook on low for 8 hours.

❭ Salt and pepper to taste, then serve.

SERVINGS: 6

POWERFUL PALEO **LIVER AND ONIONS WITH BACON**

Liver is really, really good for you. It's packed with vitamins. It has a rich flavor that turns some people off, but if you slow-cook it and drench in caramelized onions and fragrant bacon, people's complaints turn into compliments.

INGREDIENTS

4 strips bacon, diced

2 medium onions, halved and sliced

2 lb beef liver, cubed

3 tomatoes, chopped and peeled

1 cup beef broth

3 cloves garlic, smashed

1 tbsp dried parsley

Salt and pepper just before serving

COOKING INSTRUCTIONS

❯ In a heavy-bottomed pan, cook the bacon until crisp and transfer to the slow cooker.

❯ Lightly sauté the onions in the remaining bacon grease over medium-low heat for 12 minutes, stirring frequently until onions are nicely caramelized, then transfer to the slow cooker.

❯ Turn the heat to medium high, lightly sauté the liver for 5 minutes and transfer to the slow cooker.

❯ Add tomatoes, broth and parsley to the slow cooker

❯ Cook on low for 6-8 hours.

❯ Add salt and pepper to taste before serving.

SERVINGS: 6

BEEF ROAST WITH BEETS AND TARRAGON

This is a different take on a traditional roast that can last for many meals. The tarragon livens the flavor, while the beets are a nice alternative to potatoes and do well in the slow cooker.

INGREDIENTS

1 onion, chopped

3 tbsp butter

3-4 lb chuck roast

8-10 beets, roots trimmed and peeled

4 tbsp fresh tarragon

1 bay leaf

1 cup beef stock

Salt and pepper to taste just before serving

COOKING INSTRUCTIONS

❯ Sauté the onions in a tablespoon of butter in a heavy-bottomed pan over medium heat for 5 minutes until translucent.

❯ Transfer to the slow cooker.

❯ Turn the heat to medium high and brown the meat on all sides, about 8 minutes.

❯ Place the meat in the slow cooker with the remaining ingredients.

❯ Cook on low for 6-8 hours.

❯ Add salt and pepper to taste before serving.

SERVINGS: 6-8

PEPPERY VENISON ROAST

Pepper is a great complement to the rich and gamey flavors of venison.
This traditional roast is the perfect special treat for a holiday.

INGREDIENTS

2-3 lb venison roast

3 tbsp butter

2 onions, chopped

2 carrots, chopped

2 stalks celery, diced

3 cloves garlic, crushed

1½ tbsp black peppercorns

1 cup beef broth

1 tbsp parsley

½ tsp oregano

½ tsp basil

Salt just before serving

COOKING INSTRUCTIONS

❯ Heat a heavy-bottomed pan over medium high heat. Add 1 tablespoon of the butter and brown the roast on all sides, about 8 minutes total.

❯ Add meat to the slow cooker.

❯ Lower heat on the stove to medium and melt the remaining butter.

❯ Crack the peppercorns with a mortar and pestle or by rolling over the corns with a wine bottle.

❯ Sauté the onions, carrots, celery and about one-third of the pepper until the onions are translucent, about 5 minutes.

❯ Add the garlic and sauté another 3 minutes until fragrant.

❯ Place mixture in slow cooker around the roast.

❯ Add the beef broth.

❯ Sprinkle in the oregano and basil getting some on the roast and some in the sauce.

❯ Spread the remaining black pepper on the top of the roast.

❯ Cook on low for 6-8 hours.

❯ Salt to taste. Let rest for at least 10 minutes before carving and serving.

SERVINGS: 6-8

PART TIME PALEO

I highly recommend that people give this whole Paleo thing a committed effort so you can experience the results for yourself. From my own experience and from talking to friends I have found that following Paleo part time is not as effective. Although some people experience some weight loss, many part-timers don't gain other major benefits like increased energy, feeling really healthy, and stabilization of moods. Different studies and books have suggested that gluten can stay in your system for a long time. This may be why cutting back, and not eliminating it altogether, doesn't give our bodies the opportunity to experience a surge in energy. Many of the foods that we are eliminating on the Paleo diet are inflammatory, so if we are still eating inflammatory foods regularly our bodies don't have as much of an opportunity to reduce the inflammation. With all that said, even if you are not fully committed, it is still better to go with the healthier option as often as possible!

WHY GRAINS, LENTILS, CHICKPEAS, SOY AND OTHER LEGUMES ARE NOT PART OF A PALEO LIFESTYLE

The foods that are not part of a Paleo lifestyle contain proteins and/or anti-nutrients that our bodies were not designed to handle. Grains contain large protein molecules called 'lectins.' The digestive system doesn't have the equipment necessary to break down lectins, which means they remain in your gut and cause irritation. These 'loose cannons' have the ability to bind to certain gut receptors and then act as keys, unlocking a gate that lets them out into our bodies. Unfortunately, lectins were born in a barn. They don't close the gate as they leave, and do damage to the gut on the way out. This is how the gut gets 'leaky.' That's not all!! Since lectins are not part of the normal environment, the body doesn't recognize them and the immune system, standing on guard, initiates an attack and creates antibodies against them. Those antibodies have a striking resemblance to other proteins normally found in our system. This leads to an autoimmune response (the body attacking itself). The story is similar for legumes and dairy. They also contain proteins, anti-nutrients and protease inhibitors that irritate the gut in much the same way as lectins.

chapter three

SPICY AND TENDER LAMB FROM THE ANCIENT LANDS

LAMB CONSUMPTION IN THE U.S. IS FAIRLY LOW COMPARED TO OTHER COUNTRIES. However, lamb is a tasty meat to include in our diets, and it can add some variety. Maybe I am just biased because I grew up eating it. Lamb is a huge part of Armenian cuisine.

It is also a very healthy choice. Like cows, lambs are ruminant animals. Their natural diet consists of eating grass, therefore they are a good source of omega-3 fatty acids. Like beef, lamb is also a great source of healthy fats, iron, B vitamins and zinc.

PECAN CRUSTED **RACK OF LAMB**

An impressive dish to serve to guests, it will bowl over people in both presentation and flavor. The mustard adds a nice tangy accent to the sweet-tasting pecans.

INGREDIENTS

1 cup pecans

¼ tsp rock salt

½ tsp black pepper

1 tsp cumin

1 tsp smoked paprika

1 rack of lamb

½ tsp honey

1 tbsp stone ground mustard

Juice of half a lemon

½ cup beef broth

1 sprig of rosemary

Salt and pepper just before serving

COOKING INSTRUCTIONS

❯ Grind the pecans in a food processor or chop finely.

❯ Combine them with the salt, pepper, spices (reserving the rosemary sprig) to make the nut mixture.

❯ In a separate bowl combine the honey, mustard and lemon juice.

❯ Brush lamb with the honey mixture, then the nut mixture.

❯ Place the broth in the slow cooker and then carefully add the rack of lamb.

❯ Put the sprig of rosemary next to the lamb and cook for 6-8 hours.

❯ Salt and pepper to taste and let rest for 5-10 minutes before serving.

SERVINGS: 4-5

BONELESS ROAST LEG OF LAMB
WITH OLIVES AND MINT

The olives and mint give this dish a great and distinctive flavor. It's pretty easy to make, and an impressive dish to serve.

INGREDIENTS

2 lb boneless leg of lamb roasts

1 tbsp ghee

2 cloves garlic, crushed

½ cup green olives

2 tbsp chopped, fresh mint

1 tsp cumin

½ cup white wine

1 tsp fresh ground pepper

¼ tsp cayenne

Salt and pepper just before serving

COOKING INSTRUCTIONS

❯ Preheat a heavy-bottomed pan to medium high.

❯ Add the ghee and brown the lamb roast on all sides, starting on the fat side, about 8 minutes.

❯ Transfer the meat to the slow cooker.

❯ Combine all other ingredients and pour over the meat.

❯ Cook on low for 8 hours.

SERVINGS: 4-6

LAMB WITH POMEGRANATE SAUCE

While this dish isn't the most elegant, the pomegranate juice turns things an odd color, the flavor is absolutely outstanding, and it is something nice and different.

INGREDIENTS

3-4 lbs lamb chops
2 tbsp ghee
4 shallots
1 onion
2 cloves garlic, crushed
1 cup pomegranate juice
½ cup red wine
1 tbsp honey
1 tsp thyme
1 tsp tarragon
Salt and pepper just before serving

COOKING INSTRUCTIONS

> Melt ghee in a heavy-bottomed pan over medium heat.

> Sauté the shallots and onions until translucent, about 5 minutes.

> Add the garlic and cook another 3 minutes until fragrant.

> Add the wine, pomegranate juice and honey and reduce for 5 minutes on medium low.

> Add the lamb to the slow cooker, pour the wine mixture over it and sprinkle with the thyme and tarragon.

> Cook on low for 6-8 hours.

> Salt and pepper to taste, then serve.

SERVINGS: 6-8

PERSIAN STEW WITH EGGPLANT

This is a dish my mom made for me a lot when I was growing up. The dish fills the house with great aromas; none of my childhood friends would refuse dinner if they could smell this cooking.

I want to throw in a quick reminder to always buy and cook with grass-fed meat. The flavor, particularly in lamb, is better and the meat has more nutrients. I try to get my lamb from local farmers, but you can often get grass-fed meats from your butcher.

INGREDIENTS

2 lbs lamb stew meat, 1-inch cubes

3 tbsp ghee

1 large onion, chopped

2 cloves of garlic, crushed

1 tsp turmeric

2 tbsp mint

2 tbsp parsley

½ tsp cinnamon

2 eggplants, peeled and sliced

2 cups of beef broth

4 large tomatoes, peeled and chopped

Juice of 1 lime

Salt and pepper just before serving

COOKING INSTRUCTIONS

❯ Sauté the onions in 1 tablespoon of ghee melted in a heavy-bottomed pan over medium heat for 5 minutes until translucent.

❯ Add the garlic and dried herbs, and cook another 3 minutes until fragrant, then transfer mixture to the slow cooker.

❯ Sauté the eggplant in 1 tablespoon of ghee for 3 minutes and transfer to the slow cooker.

❯ Brown the meat in the remaining ghee in batches, about 5 minutes a batch, and transfer to the slow cooker.

❯ Add the broth, tomatoes and lime juice and cook on low for 6-8 hours.

❯ Salt and pepper to taste, then serve.

SERVINGS: 6-8

WHITE WINE **LAMB CHOPS**

These delicious and decadent little chops are a real crowd pleaser.

INGREDIENTS

2 lbs lamb chops
2 tbsp ghee
1 onion, chopped
2 cloves garlic, crushed
1 cup of dry white wine
2 tomatoes, coarsely chopped
1 tsp cumin
½ tsp paprika
½ tsp thyme
¼ tsp cayenne
Salt and pepper just before serving

COOKING INSTRUCTIONS

❯ In a large heavy-bottomed pan, melt 1 tablespoon of ghee over medium heat and brown the lamb in batches, then transfer to the slow cooker.

❯ Add the remaining ghee and sauté the onions until translucent.

❯ Add the garlic and cook for another 3 minutes until fragrant.

❯ Add the wine and tomatoes to the slow cooker.

❯ Use a spoon to sprinkle in the remaining spices, spreading them evenly over the lamb and sauce.

❯ Cook on low for 6 hours.

❯ Salt and pepper to taste before serving.

SERVINGS: 4-6

ARMENIAN **LAMB AND APRICOT STEW**

Armenians use a lot of lamb in their cooking, and they often incorporate fruit and nuts. Here the apricots add a nice sweet flavor to balance the spiciness of the dish.

INGREDIENTS

1 onion, thinly sliced
2 tbsp coconut oil
2 chili peppers, chopped
2 lbs lamb stew meat, 1-inch cubes
6 oz dried apricots
3 sweet potatoes, peeled and cubed
2 cloves garlic, crushed
1 tbsp fresh ginger, grated
2 cups beef broth
1 tbsp fresh lemon juice
¼ cup brandy (optional)
1 tsp basil
1 tsp dill
1 tbsp parsley
Salt and pepper just before serving

COOKING INSTRUCTIONS

› Melt the coconut oil in a heavy-bottomed pan over medium heat, lightly sauté the onions for about 3 minutes then add the garlic, ginger, chili peppers and apricots, and cook another 3 minutes.

› Transfer mixture to the slow cooker and melt the remaining coconut oil in the pan.

› Brown the lamb in batches, about 6 minutes a batch, and transfer to the slow cooker. (Note that it takes longer to brown in coconut oil).

› Mix the broth, lemon juice, brandy (if using) and dried herbs, and pour over the meat in the slow cooker.

› Cook on low for 6-8 hours.

› Salt and pepper to taste, then serve.

SERVINGS: 4-6

LAMB AND CUMIN CASSEROLE

Armenian markets are known for their great fresh meat, and this Paleo-take on a traditional dish tastes that much better when you use freshly butchered, grass-fed lamb.

INGREDIENTS

2 lbs lamb stew meat, cubed

2 tbsp butter

1 onion, sliced

1 bell pepper, chopped

2 carrots, sliced

3 cloves garlic, chopped

2 tsp cumin

1 tsp allspice

2 tbsp tomato paste

2 sweet potatoes, sliced

4 tomatoes, peeled and chopped

½ cup beef broth

Salt and pepper just before serving

COOKING INSTRUCTIONS

› Brown the lamb in 1 tablespoon of butter in a heavy-bottomed pan over medium heat, about 5 minutes, and transfer to the slow cooker.

› Sauté the onions, bell pepper and carrots until the onions are translucent, about 5 minutes.

› Add the garlic, spices and tomato paste, and cook for another 3 minutes until fragrant, and transfer the mixture to the slow cooker.

› Add the tomatoes to the slow cooker along with the broth and cook for 3 hours.

› Add veggies and cook on low for 3-4 hours.

› Salt and pepper to taste, then serve.

SERVINGS: 6

INDIAN **LAMB**

I love Indian food because of its distinctive flavors. Here the coconut milk not only adds a richness, but is also a good source of fat and a Paleo Diet favorite. Note that this dish requires marinating so it's best to start preparations the day before.

INGREDIENTS

2 lbs lamb cubed
1 tbsp ginger, grated
2 cloves garlic
1 tbsp fresh mint
1 tbsp fresh cilantro
1 tsp coriander
1 tsp garam masala
½ tsp turmeric
½ tsp salt
Juice from a half lemon
1 onion, chopped
2 fresh red chilies, chopped
1 cup coconut milk
Salt and pepper just before serving

COOKING INSTRUCTIONS

› Marinate the lamb for as little as 3 hours, but preferably overnight, in all the ingredients except the coconut milk.

› Add meat mixture with the marinade and the coconut milk to the slow cooker and cook on low for 6-8 hours.

› Salt and pepper to taste, then serve.

SERVINGS: 4-6

HARISSA BRAISED **LAMB SHANKS**

This is a spicy dish, so beware, the faint of heart. But be rewarded, those who like strong flavors. Harrissa paste comes from North Africa and is made from hot peppers and garlic and available in most gourmet food stores.

INGREDIENTS

3 lbs lamb shanks (make sure they fit into your slow cooker)

1 tsp cumin

1 tsp coriander

1 tsp smoked paprika

1 tbsp ghee

¼ tsp allspice

4 cloves garlic, crushed

12 shallots, peeled and whole

8 chopped tomatoes, peeled and chopped or 1 can chopped tomatoes

1 cup chicken stock

1 tbsp Harissa paste (use 2 tbsp if you want more heat)

Salt and pepper just before serving

COOKING INSTRUCTIONS

> Soften ghee in microwave, mix with the cumin, coriander, paprika and rub onto the lamb shanks.

> Brown the shanks in a broiler about 2 minutes a side, being careful not to burn them, and transfer to the slow cooker.

> Add the rest of the ingredients to the slow cooker and cook for 6-8 hours.

> Salt and pepper to taste, then serve.

SERVINGS: 6

GROUND LAMB
WITH PINE NUTS AND MINT

Ground meat is an affordable way to include pasture-raised meat in your diet. This is a really tasty and easy recipe. The pine nuts and mint give a nice light and satisfying flavor.

INGREDIENTS

2 lbs ground lamb

1 tbsp ghee

2 onions, chopped

1 green pepper, chopped

1/8 cup pine nuts

3 cloves garlic, crushed

1 tsp cumin

1 tsp paprika

1/4 cup mint, finely chopped

Salt and pepper just before serving

COOKING INSTRUCTIONS

> Sauté the onions, peppers and pine nuts in the ghee in a heavy-bottomed pan over medium heat for 5 minutes, until the onions are translucent.

> Add the garlic and cook another 3 minutes until fragrant.

> Combine the meat with spices (except the mint) and brown with the onions, breaking up the meat with a wooden spoon, about 8 minutes.

> Transfer everything to the slow cooker.

> Cook on low for 4 hours or high for two hours.

> Add chopped mint 20 minutes before serving.

> Salt and pepper to taste, then serve.

SERVINGS: 4-6

LAMB TAGINE

Strong Moroccan flavors make this dish exotic and delicious.
It warms me up on a cold winter's night.

INGREDIENTS

2 lbs lamb stew meat, cut into 1 ½-inch cubes

2 tbsp ghee

1 medium onion, chopped

3 cloves garlic, crushed

2 tsp paprika

¼ tsp ground turmeric

1 tsp ground cumin

¼ tsp cayenne pepper

1 tsp ground cinnamon

¼ tsp ground cloves

½ tsp ground cardamom

½ tsp coriander

1 small butternut squash, peeled and chopped

6 tomatoes, chopped and peeled

1 cup chicken stock

Juice of 1 lemon

Salt and pepper just before serving

COOKING INSTRUCTIONS

> In a heavy-bottomed pan over medium heat, brown the lamb in 1 tablespoon of ghee in batches, about 5 minutes a batch.

> Transfer the meat to the slow cooker.

> Add the remaining ghee and sauté the onions until translucent.

> Add the garlic and cook another 3 minutes until fragrant.

> Add all the ingredients except butternut squash to the slow cooker and cook for 6-8 hours.

> Add butternut squash last 3 hours to avoid overcooking.

> Salt and pepper to taste, then serve.

SERVINGS: 6

POST WORKOUT NUTRITION

Post workout nutrition protocol depends on several factors; the individual's goals (body composition, performance, health), the type/length/intensity of training, health status and body's response/needs. For those looking to lose weight or lean out with performance playing second fiddle, post workout carbs may not be necessary.

POST-WORKOUT NUTRITION GOALS

1. Maintain and Restore Muscle Glycogen

  • Replenishment is most successful in the post workout period.

  • Plant-based carbohydrates are optimal, including: yams, sweet potatoes, squash, plantains, taro, yucca, cassava, white potatoes with the skin removed, rutabaga, other roots and tubers, bananas, and other fruit.

  • Liquid nutrition like shakes, powders, and other protein supplements should not be relied on. Real food is always the best option!

2. Prevent Muscle Breakdown that Occurs with Exercise

  • Replenishment is most important in the post workout period to reverse muscle catabolism immediately resulting in reduced recovery time and higher workout intensity in the next session.

  • High quality animal-sourced protein is the best choice as it provides the branched chain amino acids (BCAAs) that are key in muscle recovery.

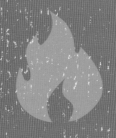

chapter four

PERFECT PORK:
SUCCULENT FROM THE SLOW COOKER

UNLIKE WITH LAMB OR BEEF, IT IS A BIT MORE DIFFICULT TO VERIFY THE DIET OF A PIG SINCE PIGS EAT PRETTY MUCH ANYTHING. Wild pigs have to forage for their food and since they are omnivores, they eat insects, worms, fruits and flowers. Domesticated pigs, even organic ones, are usually given feed from corn, wheat or other grains. However, there are ranchers who raise their pigs on farm scraps and pasture, those are the ones to eat if you can find them.

Pork is a good source of protein. Studies have also shown it to be a good source of vitamins and minerals, such as selenium, thiamin, zinc and B vitamins. Plus, who doesn't love bacon!

I particularly like cooking with pork because it seems to go really well with fruit, and I love incorporating fruit into a main dish.

PEAR GINGER **PORK CHOPS**

I love coming home and smelling the fall flavors in this dish. The ginger adds a nice accent. The pork chops come out succulent and tender.

INGREDIENTS

4 thick cut pork chops

2 tbsp coconut oil

½ tsp cinnamon

1 tsp allspice

2 ripe d'anjou pears, cored and cut into chunks

2 tbsp apple cider vinegar

1 cup white wine (can substitute water or broth)

2 tbsp honey

1 tbsp ginger, minced

Salt and pepper just before serving

COOKING INSTRUCTIONS

❯ Melt 1 tbsp of the coconut oil in a heavy-bottomed pan over medium heat.

❯ Brown the pork chops on both sides (in batches if necessary) for about 5 minutes total and place in the slow cooker.

❯ Sauté the pears and ginger in the remaining coconut oil.

❯ Add the vinegar and wine, turn to medium low and cook for 5 minutes to reduce slightly.

❯ Pour mixture over chops in slow cooker.

❯ Cook on low for 6 hours.

❯ Salt and pepper to taste, then serve.

SERVINGS: 4

SPICY PORK TENDERLOIN
STUFFED WITH PRUNES

The prunes and jalapeños give this dish a great sweet and spicy flavor combination. I recommend you eat this dish fresh from the slow cooker because the prunes can get mushy and make the sauce heavy overnight.

INGREDIENTS

2 lb pork tenderloin

½ tsp black pepper

1 tsp chili powder

1 tsp thyme

1 tsp sage

2 tbsp coconut oil

1 onion, quartered

2 cloves garlic, crushed

2 jalapeños, cut into strips

1 cup prunes, pitted and chopped

2 bay leaves

¼ cup brandy

½ cup chicken broth

Salt and pepper just before serving

COOKING INSTRUCTIONS

❭ Rub the tenderloin with pepper, chili powder and herbs (except the bay leaves) and reserve any extra herbs.

❭ Sauté the onions, garlic and jalapeño in 1 tablespoon of the coconut oil in a heavy-bottomed pan over medium heat for 5 minutes, and transfer to the slow cooker.

❭ Brown the pork in the remaining coconut oil for about 5 minutes and set aside.

❭ Turn the stove to medium-low heat and simmer the prunes in the brandy for 5 minutes.

❭ Create an incision in the pork, and stuff some of the brandied prunes inside along with the sauce. Place the remaining mixture in the slow cooker another with the meat.

❭ Add the broth and remaining herbs.

❭ Cook for 4-6 hours.

❭ Salt and pepper to taste, then serve.

SERVINGS: 4

APPLE CIDER PORK
WITH ROSEMARY

This is another nice fall pork dish that will fill your house with great aromas. Note that often supermarket pork won't taste different than the organic variety. However, organic pork doesn't contain antibiotics so I'd recommend spending money on the organic brands. It's also very important to buy organic apples to avoid the pesticides as well as get better flavor.

INGREDIENTS

3 lb pork roast

2 tbsp coconut oil

1 onion, chopped

2 cloves garlic, crushed

2 apples, peeled, cored and chopped

2 cups hard apple cider

1 tbsp fresh rosemary, minced

1 tsp thyme, minced

Salt and pepper just before serving

COOKING INSTRUCTIONS

❯ Brown the pork in 1 tablespoon of coconut oil in a heavy-bottomed pan over medium-high heat for about 8 minutes, and transfer to the slow cooker.

❯ Turn heat down to medium and sauté the onions in the remaining coconut oil for about 5 minutes.

❯ Add the garlic and apples, cook for another 3 minutes, and then transfer the mixture to the slow cooker.

❯ Add all the other ingredients and cook on low for 6-8 hours.

❯ Salt and pepper to taste, then serve.

SERVINGS: 6

ROASTED **CITRUS PORK**

Can you tell that I love pairing pork with fruit flavors? This dish is more sour than sweet which makes it a bit different than the others.

INGREDIENTS

3-4 lb pork roast

3 tbsp coconut oil

1 tsp orange zest

1 tsp lemon zest

Juice of 1 lemon

½ cup fresh squeezed orange juice

¼ cup broth

3 cloves garlic, crushed

4 whole cloves

½ tsp thyme

Salt and pepper just before serving

COOKING INSTRUCTIONS

> Melt 1 tablespoon of coconut oil in a heavy-bottomed pan over medium-high heat and brown the pork on all sides for about 8 minutes.

> Turn the stove down to medium heat and while the pan cools slightly, poke four whole cloves into the top of the roast evenly spaced, then transfer to the slow cooker.

> Sauté the garlic in the remaining coconut oil for 3 minutes until fragrant being careful to not burn the coconut oil or garlic, and transfer to the slow cooker.

> Pour the remaining spices, juice and wine over the roast and cook on low for 6 hours.

> Salt and pepper to taste, then serve.

SERVINGS: 6-8

PORK CHOPS IN FIG SAUCE

Figs remind me of my childhood. Almost every Armenian family makes fig jam. Now that I don't incorporate a lot of sugar into my diet, I skip the jam and get my fig fix from dishes like this.

INGREDIENTS

4 thick-cut pork chops
1 tbsp coconut oil
½ cup chicken broth or dry white wine
2 tsp apple-cider vinegar
¼ cup finely chopped dried figs
1 tbsp honey
½ tsp fresh thyme
½ tsp fresh sage
Salt and pepper just before serving

COOKING INSTRUCTIONS

❯ Heat the coconut oil in a heavy-bottomed pan over medium heat.

❯ Brown the pork chops in batches, about 5 minutes a batch, and transfer to the slow cooker.

❯ Add the figs with the vinegar, broth, herbs and honey, making sure to stir in the honey so it's not a clump.

❯ Cook for 6-8 hours.

❯ Salt and pepper to taste, then serve

SERVINGS: 4

PORK WITH PINEAPPLE AND PEPPERS

This is a great summertime special the whole family will love.

INGREDIENTS

3 lb pork roast, cut into 1 ½-inch cubes

2 tbsp coconut oil

2 cups fresh-cut pineapple

½ white onion, diced

3 cloves garlic, crushed

2 jalapeño peppers, diced

2 tbsp apple cider vinegar

½ cup dry white wine

Salt and pepper just before serving

COOKING INSTRUCTIONS

❯ Melt 1 tablespoon of coconut oil in a heavy-bottom pan over medium-high heat and brown pork in batches, about 6 minutes a batch, and transfer to the slow cooker.

❯ Lower the stove to medium heat and sauté the onions in the remaining coconut oil for 5 minutes.

❯ Add the garlic and peppers, and cook for another 3 minutes.

❯ Transfer the mixture to the slow cooker with the vinegar and white wine, and cook on low for 6 hours.

❯ Salt and pepper to taste, then serve.

SERVINGS: 6

DIJON **HAM**

Great for a holiday family meal, this dish is really easy and keeps the oven free to make other holiday delights. It also makes great leftovers. Wrapping a piece in butter lettuce with some of the sauce makes a perfect sandwich. We often eat it for breakfast. It's a versatile dish.

INGREDIENTS

5-6 lb ham
¼ cup apple cider vinegar
¼ cup honey
¼ cup coconut oil
1 tsp thyme
2 tbsp Dijon mustard
Zest of 1 orange
Pepper just before serving

COOKING INSTRUCTIONS

❯ Put ham in the slow cooker.

❯ Combine the rest of the ingredients, making sure the honey and mustard are both well incorporated.

❯ Pour over ham in slow cooker.

❯ Cook on low for 6 hours.

❯ Add pepper just before serving.

SERVINGS: 8-10

PORK RIBS IN MANGO BBQ SAUCE

Many tropical fruits like mangos are high in sugar so I don't eat them too much. In this case, incorporating them into an entrée is a good way to satisfy your mango craving since a little goes a long way.

INGREDIENTS

½ onion, minced

1 tbsp fresh ginger, grated

2 garlic cloves, chopped

2 tsp ground mustard

1 red chili, seeded and finely chopped

2 tsp paprika

1 tbsp tomato paste

½ cup apple cider vinegar

Juice of 1 orange

Pinch of ground cloves

1 tbsp honey

1 cup tomato puree

½ cup chicken broth

3-4 lbs pork ribs

2 cups fresh mango, peeled and diced

COOKING INSTRUCTIONS

❯ Mix all the ingredients except the ribs and mango in a bowl and make sure the honey, mustard and tomato are mostly incorporated.

❯ Cut ribs into serving sizes or pieces that will fit your slow cooker (two or three rib sections will probably work).

❯ Place ribs in the slow cooker and pour sauce over them.

❯ Cook on low for 4-5 hours before the meat falls off the bone.

❯ Remove carefully, salt and pepper to taste, then serve.

SERVINGS: 4-6

ASIAN PORK
WITH COCONUT AMINOS

Coconut aminos sounds like a biology term rather than a delicious food. Don't be turned off; it's a good substitute for its soy-based and often wheat-packed brethren, and it delivers nice flavor in this Eastern-inspired dish.

INGREDIENTS

2 lbs boneless pork shoulder, cut into chunks
2 tbsp coconut oil
4 shallots, minced
4 cloves garlic, crushed
3-4 red chilies, sliced
1 tsp dried shrimp paste
¼ cup coconut aminos
2 tsps honey
1 tbsp lime juice
½ cup chicken broth
Pepper just before serving

COOKING INSTRUCTIONS

> Melt the coconut oil in a heavy-bottomed pan over medium heat.

> Brown the pork in batches, about 5 minutes a batch, and transfer to the slow cooker.

> Sauté the shallots in the remaining coconut oil, about five minutes.

> Add the garlic and pepper, cook another 3 minutes, and transfer the mixture to the slow cooker.

> Add the rest of the ingredients to the slow cooker and cook on low for 4-6 hours.

> Add pepper to taste and serve.

SERVINGS: 4-6

ASIAN INSPIRED **RIBS**

My husband thinks this is the best dish I've ever made in a slow cooker. He loves what the five-spice brings to the dish, adding a powerful flavor without overwhelming it.

INGREDIENTS

1 rack of pork ribs, about 12 ribs

½ cup Tamari or coconut aminos

½ cup raw honey

2 tbsp coconut vinegar

1 tsp five-spice blend

½ tbsp fresh ginger, grated

3 cloves garlic, crushed

Juice of 1 lime

Pinch of red pepper flakes

1 tbsp sesame oil 10 minutes before serving

Salt and pepper just before serving

COOKING INSTRUCTIONS

> Cut rack into individual ribs and place in the slow cooker.

> Mix together all ingredients except sesame oil and pour over ribs.

> Add the sesame oil 10 minutes before serving.

> Cook on low for 4-5 hours before the meat falls off the bone.

> Salt and pepper to taste, then serve.

SERVINGS: 4-5

PORK GOULASH RECIPE

Goulash is a traditional Hungarian stew that is nice and hearty and an international favorite of mine.

INGREDIENTS

2 lbs pork roast, cut into cubes

2 slices bacon, diced

1 onion, chopped

3 cloves garlic, crushed

2 tbsp apple-cider vinegar

1 tbsp caraway seeds

2 tbsp, sweet Hungarian paprika

2 cups sauerkraut, without liquid

4 tomatoes, peeled and chopped

2 cups chicken broth

Salt and pepper just before serving

COOKING INSTRUCTIONS

❯ Toss pork with caraway seeds and 1 tablespoon of paprika.

❯ Cook bacon in a large heaby-bottomed pan over medium heat until crispy, about 5 minutes, and reserve.

❯ Brown pork in bacon fat in batches, about 5 minutes a batch, and transfer to the slow cooker with a slotted spoon.

❯ Add the rest of the ingredients and cook on low for 6-8 hours.

❯ Salt and pepper to taste, top with bacon, then serve.

SERVINGS: 4-6

SPICY SAUSAGE AND PEPPER STEW

This hearty and delicious dish is easy to make and a great one to pop into the slow cooker when you are busy.

INGREDIENTS

1½-2 lbs spicy Italian sausage, sliced into ¼-inch coins

1 tsp ghee

2 bell peppers, chopped (I usually use a green and a red one)

1 onion, sliced

3 cloves garlic, crushed

8 tomatoes, blanched and peeled or, a 14-ounce can of stewed tomatoes

2 cups chicken broth

½ tsp oregano

½ tsp thyme

Salt and pepper just before serving

COOKING INSTRUCTIONS

❯ Brown the sausage in a heavy-bottomed pan over medium heat in batches, about 5 minutes a batch.

❯ Add the ghee and sauté the onions until the onions are translucent, about 5 minutes.

❯ Add the garlic and bell peppers, cook another 3 minutes, then transfer the whole mixture to the slow cooker with the rest of the ingredients.

❯ Cook on low for 5-6 hours.

❯ Salt and pepper to taste, then serve.

SERVINGS: 6-8

PORK AND CABBAGE SOUP

This is a hearty winter recipe. The bacon gives the dish the nice smoky flavor I love.

INGREDIENTS

3 strips bacon, diced
1 lb pork loin, cubed
1 tbsp ghee
1 onion, chopped
2 carrots, sliced
2 parsnips, chopped
2-3 cloves garlic, crushed
½ medium head of cabbage, shredded
4 cups chicken or beef broth
6 tomatoes, chopped
1 bay leaf
1 tbsp gluten-free Worcestershire sauce
½ tsp basil
½ tsp oregano
Salt and pepper just before serving

COOKING INSTRUCTIONS

> Cook bacon in a heavy-bottomed pan over medium heat until crispy, about 5 minutes, and reserve for garnish.

> Brown pork in the bacon grease in batches, about 5 minutes a batch, and transfer to the slow cooker.

> Melt the ghee and sauté the onions, carrots and parsnips for 5 minutes until the onions are translucent.

> Add the garlic, cook another 3 minutes and transfer the mixture to the slow cooker.

> Add the rest of the ingredients to the slow cooker and cook on low for 6-8 hours.

> Salt and pepper to taste.

> Garnish with bacon bits, then serve.

SERVINGS: 6

SLIGHTLY SPICY **CARNITAS**

We serve this at our house a lot. We use it throughout the week for other dishes, from lunchtime lettuce-wrap sandwiches to dinner over steamed vegetables.

INGREDIENTS

1 tsp sea salt

1 tbsp cumin

½ tsp oregano

1 tbsp coriander

1 tsp paprika

½ tsp cayenne

3 lb boneless pork shoulder, skin removed, cut into four large chunks

2 tbsp ghee

1 onion, diced

4 cloves garlic, crushed

1 jalapeno, minced

1/4 cup chicken stock

2 bay leaves

Salt and pepper just before serving

COOKING INSTRUCTIONS

❯ Combine the salt, cumin, oregano, coriander, paprika and cayenne pepper, and rub over pork, reserving the extra spices (and being careful not to touch your eyes).

❯ Melt 1 tablespoon of the ghee in a heavy-bottomed pan over medium heat, brown the pork in batches, about 5 minutes a batch, and transfer to the slow cooker.

❯ Sauté the onions in the remaining ghee until the onions are translucent, about 5 minutes.

❯ Add the garlic and jalapeño pepper, cook another 3 minutes, then transfer the mixture to the slow cooker.

❯ Add the chicken broth and bay leaves, and cook on low for 5-6 hours.

❯ Pull the meat apart with 2 forks and cook for an additional hour.

❯ Salt and pepper to taste, then serve.

SERVINGS: 8

SLOW COOKER **STUFFING**

I made this for Thanksgiving, and it was a hit with my non-Paleo in-laws.
The flavors worked well together and you won't miss the starch.
It also saves a spot in the oven, a win-win.

INGREDIENTS

3 Italian sausages, removed from casing (I use 2 hot Italian and 1 mild)

2 tbsp ghee

2 cups of mushrooms, sliced

½ yellow onion, diced

2 stalks celery, diced (about ¾ cup)

3 cloves of garlic, crushed

1 Granny Smith apple, peeled and diced

2 yams, peeled and chopped

6 fresh sage leaves, minced

½ cup pecans, chopped

¼ cup dried cranberries

1 cup beef stock

Salt and pepper just before serving

COOKING INSTRUCTIONS

> Brown sausage in a heavy-bottomed pan over medium heat and transfer to the slow cooker.

> Turn heat to low and melt the ghee.

> Add the rest of dry ingredients to the slow cooker, pour the melted ghee over it and mix with a wooden spoon.

> Add the stock and cook on low for 3-4 hours.

> Salt and pepper to taste, then serve.

SERVINGS: 6-8

INSULIN SENSITIVITY & PALEO

Today's Standard American Diet is a high carb sugar laden nightmare. The heavy carb and sugar load results in high levels of glucose in the blood. This requires the pancreas to make and secrete more insulin which results in high insulin levels in the blood. When insulin levels are high, inflammation increases and insulin sensitivity decreases. The longer these conditions exist the less 'sensitive' our cells become to insulin (think tolerance, like with drugs and alcohol) and the more insulin it requires to get the sugar out of the blood and into the cells. This contributes to further inflammation and even less insulin sensitivity. We've now created a state of insulin resistance. There are other factors that increase inflammation and contribute to insulin resistance; sleep, stress, overall diet composition (grains, dairy, fat type, etc), among other factors all play major roles in the process.

The Paleo diet when followed correctly minimizes many of the dietary causes of inflammation and helps to improve the insulin resistant state. Keep in mind that if the Paleo diet is not implemented correctly and is a diet high in Paleo 'treats' like dried fruit, nuts, smoothies and fruit; the improvements in insulin sensitivity will be drastically reduced. Additionally the Paleo lifestyle calls for smart "not over the top" exercise, adequate and quality sleep, stress reduction and other habits that encourage an anti-inflammatory environment therefore decreasing insulin resistance and increasing insulin sensitivity.

It is often said that certain spices and foods may help increase insulin sensitivity. Cinnamon is one of these magic foods. Several studies have shown that the polyphenols in cinnamon may act as insulin sensitizers. Many of these studies have been conducted in rats and there are few well-controlled, human clinical studies that have been done. This makes it difficult to make a solid conclusion of cinnamon's efficacy as an insulin sensitizer. The research that is available is positive, but at this point inconclusive. Is it worth a shot? It definitely will not hurt you and if you add it to your recipes it's very tasty!

chapter five

SLOW-COOKED
CHICKEN FAVORITES AND OTHER FEATHERED FRIENDS

IT CAN BE DIFFICULT TO VERIFY A CHICKEN'S DIET, as organic and non-organic chickens are often both raised on feed. Organic is always a better option, as organic feed and organic chickens do not contain antibiotics, pesticides, and chemical fertilizers. There are also farmers who put great effort into varying the diets of their chickens with farm scraps, insects and pasture feeding. Pasture-raised chickens have better omega-3 to omega-6 composition, and so do their eggs. If you have access to pasture-raised chicken and eggs from local farmers, this is the best Paleo way to go.

Chicken is a good source of protein, some B vitamins, selenium and choline. It's another protein that goes well with lots of different ingredients, including nuts, fruit and different herbs.

GARLIC TARRAGON **CHICKEN**

I love tarragon and it adds a different twist to a traditional chicken dish. The butter and tons of garlic makes a great basting sauce that I pour over the chicken just before serving, but if you don't tolerate butter well, you should try the slow cooker Chicken Pesto instead, page 142.

INGREDIENTS

1 whole chicken, cut into breasts, whole

legs and wings, skin removed

1 stick of butter

1 whole head of garlic, peeled and minced

½ cup chicken stock

3 tbsp fresh tarragon, minced

Salt and pepper just before serving

COOKING INSTRUCTIONS

> Brown the chicken in 1 tablespoon of the butter in a heavy-bottomed pan over medium-high heat in batches, about 5 minutes a batch.

> Mix the tarragon with 1 tablespoon butter softened in the microwave and a teaspoon of minced garlic cloves.

> Rub this all over the chicken parts and place them in the slow cooker with the chicken stock and remaining butter.

> Cook on low for 4-5 hours.

> Salt and pepper to taste. Pour sauce over the chicken, then serve.

SERVINGS: 6

CHICKEN WITH BUTTERNUT SQUASH AND FIGS

Butternut squash is another one of those foods that I started preparing once I adopted a Paleo diet and became much more adventurous in cooking new vegetables. When I'm working out a lot, I try to include more carbs in my diet and butternut squash is one of my favorites. In this dish, I love how the sweetness of the squash and figs complement the pungent rosemary. If you prefer your butternut squash more crunchy, add it half way through cooking time.

INGREDIENTS

1 onion, diced

2 tbsp coconut oil

3 cloves garlic, crushed

3 lbs chicken breast or boneless thigh (either should be skinless)

½ cup dried figs

½ butternut squash, peeled and cubed

1 cup chicken broth

1 tbsp fresh rosemary, chopped

1 tsp fresh tarragon

1 tsp fresh sage

Salt and pepper just before serving

COOKING INSTRUCTIONS

> In a heavy-bottomed pan, melt the coconut oil and sauté the onions and garlic over medium heat for 5 minutes until translucent.

> Add the chicken in batches and brown for 5 minutes a batch, removing the onions and garlic with the first batch, transferred to the slow cooker.

> Add the figs, squash, broth and spices to the slow cooker.

> Cook on low for 6 hours.

> Salt and pepper to taste, then serve.

SERVINGS: 6

CHICKEN WITH MUSHROOMS AND ARTICHOKES

This is a simple and savory dinner. The combination sounds gourmet while the dish is easy to make.

INGREDIENTS

3 lbs skinless chicken (breast, thighs or any part of choice)

½ tsp paprika

½ onion, chopped

3 tbsp butter

1 cup mushrooms, halved

1 16-oz jar artichoke hearts, drained

½ tsp thyme

½ cup dry white wine

½ cup chicken broth

Salt and pepper just before serving

COOKING INSTRUCTIONS

> Coat the chicken with the paprika.

> Melt the tablespoon of the butter in a heavy-bottom pan over medium heat. Brown the chicken in batches on all sides, about 5 minutes a batch, and transfer to the slow cooker.

> Melt the remaining butter in the pan and sauté the onions for 5 minutes until translucent.

> Add the mushrooms and artichokes and cook another 5-8 minutes until the mushrooms are slightly browned, then transfer the mixture to the slow cooker.

> Combine the herbs, broth and white wine, pour over the chicken in the slow cooker and cook on low for 6 hours.

> Salt and pepper to taste, then serve.

SERVINGS: 6

CHICKEN WITH GINGER AND LEMON

This recipe is a mix of all my favorite ingredients.
The zesty flavors pack quite a punch.

INGREDIENTS

1 onion, thinly sliced

½ tsp ground cinnamon

1 tsp ground cumin

¼ tsp ground turmeric

3 tbsp ghee

3 cloves garlic, crushed

3 lbs skinless chicken (breast, thigh, or any part of choice)

¼ cup fresh grated ginger

¼ cup dried cranberries

2 strands of saffron

Juice of 1 lemon

Zest of 1 lemon

½ cup chicken stock

2 tomatoes coarsely chopped

Salt and pepper just before serving

COOKING INSTRUCTIONS

› Mix cinnamon, cumin and turmeric in a bowl and toss chicken to coat.

› In a heavy-bottomed pan over medium heat, melt 1 tablespoon of ghee and sauté the onions and garlic until translucent, about 5 minutes. Transfer to the slow cooker.

› Melt the remaining ghee and add the chicken breasts. Brown on both sides in batches for about 5 minutes a batch.

› Transfer the chicken and remaining ghee to the slow cooker.

› Add the rest of the ingredients and cook on low for 4-6 hours.

› Salt and pepper to taste, then serve.

SERVINGS: 6

CHICKEN BREASTS STUFFED WITH SUN-DRIED TOMATOES

The already intense flavor of sun-dried tomatoes allows you to make a tasty, yet quick, dish, without having to add too many ingredients. Recipes like this are a must in our house since we both work full-time, have very busy schedules, but love to enjoy delicious homemade meals.

INGREDIENTS

½ onion, chopped

3 garlic cloves

2 tbsp ghee

1 8 oz jar sun dried tomatoes

3 lbs skinless chicken breast

½ cup chicken broth

2 tsp dried oregano

½ tsp basil

Salt and pepper to taste just before serving

COOKING INSTRUCTIONS

❯ In a heavy-bottomed pan over medium heat, sauté the onions and garlic over medium heat until translucent, about 5 minutes.

❯ Meanwhile, cut a big pocket in each chicken breast.

❯ Spoon the onion and garlic into each pocket and follow with two to three dried tomatoes. Carefully transfer stuffed breast into the slow cooker.

❯ Add the broth and sprinkle the herbs over the chicken and broth.

❯ Cook on low for 4-6 hours.

❯ Salt and pepper to taste, then serve.

SERVINGS: 6

HERBED CHICKEN WITH LEMON

Chicken with lemon and herbs is a classic for a reason. It's just great; we cook it all the time. It has a nice light flavor, and is great reheated for easy lunches or dinners during the week. The flavors are basic and not overpowering.

INGREDIENTS

3 lbs skinless chicken legs and thighs or whole chicken cut up

3 tbsp ghee

1 medium onion, chopped

3 cloves garlic, crushed

2 tbsp red wine vinegar

Zest of 1 lemon

Juice of 1 lemon

1 cup chicken broth

1 tbsp fresh rosemary, chopped

½ tsp oregano

½ tsp thyme

COOKING INSTRUCTIONS

> Set a heavy-bottomed pan over medium heat and melt 1 tbsp of ghee.

> Brown the chicken in batches about 5 minutes a batch and transfer to the slow cooker.

> Melt the remaining ghee in the pan and sauté the onions for 5 minutes, until translucent.

> Add the garlic, cook another 3 minutes and transfer mixture to the slow cooker.

> Pour the remaining liquids over the chicken and sprinkle the herbs over the chicken and sauce.

> Cook on low for 4-6 hours.

> Salt and pepper to taste, then serve.

SERVINGS: 6

HONEY **CHICKEN THIGHS**

Growing up I used to go to a restaurant called Rocky Cola Café in our little suburb of Los Angeles. I had many fun times with friends while eating chicken tenders with a honey-mustard dipping sauce. This recipe is inspired by my many memories, but is a much healthier version.

INGREDIENTS

8 skinless and boneless chicken thighs

1 tbsp coconut oil

3 garlic cloves, chopped

2 tbsp stoneground mustard

½ cup chicken broth

¼ cup honey

½ tsp thyme

1 tsp ground cumin

½ tsp paprika

Salt and pepper just before serving

COOKING INSTRUCTIONS

> Melt the ghee in a heavy-bottomed pan over medium heat .

> Coat chicken with thyme, cumin and paprika before browning. Brown the chicken in batches, about 5 minutes a batch and transfer to the slow cooker.

> Add the rest of the ingredients to the slow cooker, making sure the mustard and honey are mixed in, and cook on low for 6 hours.

> Salt and pepper to taste, then serve.

SERVINGS: 4

LEMON **CHICKEN SOUP**

Like many people's moms, my mom always made chicken soup when I was sick. I rarely get sick ever since I went Paleo (honestly!), but we still like to have chicken soup in winter after an exhausting day at work. Plus, homemade broth is a great source of nutrients that give you strength.

INGREDIENTS

1 onion, chopped

2 carrots, sliced

2 ribs celery, chopped

2 tbsp ghee

3 cloves garlic, crushed

3-4 lbs chicken pieces with bone and skin

2 quarts chicken broth

¼ cup lemon juice or juice from 2-3 lemons

½ bunch parsley, tied together

½ tsp fresh ground pepper

2 bay leaves

Salt and pepper just before serving

COOKING INSTRUCTIONS

❯ In a heavy-bottomed pan set over medium heat, sauté the onions, carrots and celery for 5 minutes, until the onions are translucent.

❯ Add the garlic, cook another 3 minutes and transfer the mixture to the slow cooker.

❯ Melt the remaining ghee in the pan and brown the chicken, starting skin side down, in batches, about 5 minutes a batch, and transfer to the slow cooker.

❯ Cook on low for 6 hours.

❯ Remove the chicken, let it cool, then carefully remove and discard the bones and skin.

❯ Chop the chicken and return it to the slow cooker for 1 hour.

❯ Salt and pepper to taste, then serve.

SERVINGS: 6-8

SLOW COOKER CHICKEN PESTO
WITH MACADAMIA NUTS

The readers of my blog loved this dish so much that I had to include it in the book (I repeated only a handful on my favorites). Macadamias are a great option when nuts are called for because they have a very low Omega-6 content compared to their counterparts. They are also a healthy source of magnesium, manganese, thiamine, copper and iron. I make the sauce and brown the chicken at night. Then in the morning all I have to do is take it out of the fridge, put it in the slow cooker and hit "start".

INGREDIENTS

2 lbs skinless chicken thighs

1 tbsp ghee

[Additional ¼ tsp sea salt to be added just before the end of cooking]

PESTO

1 cup flat leaf parsley

2 cups fresh basil

4 cloves garlic

½ cup olive oil

¼ cup macadamia nuts

2 tbsp fresh lemon juice

2 tsp fresh oregano

¼ tsp sea salt

¼ tsp pepper

COOKING INSTRUCTIONS

› To make the pesto, combine all the ingredients (except the chicken and ghee, of course) in a food processor and blend.

› Melt the ghee in a heavy-bottomed pan over medium heat and brown the chicken on all sides for about 5 minutes. If you are cooking for immediate use, transfer the chicken to the slow cooker and pour the pesto over it.

› If you are cooking for later use, transfer the chicken to a bowl, pour pesto over it, cover and refrigerate.

› Place in slow cooker, then cook on low for 5½ hours.

› Sprinkle the additional sea salt over the chicken and cook for another ½ hour, then serve.

› I often reduce any extra sauce in the stove top pan over medium low heat for 5 to 10 minutes to give it extra flavor before pouring it over the chicken.

SERVINGS: 4

CLASSIC CHICKEN CACCIATORE
SLOW COOKER STYLE

I like the traditional Italian flavors of this dish and don't miss the pasta.
It's just great on its own.

INGREDIENTS

2 lbs boneless chicken breast or thighs

3 tbsp butter

1 onion, chopped

1 bell pepper, chopped

2 sticks celery, chopped

½ lb mushrooms, sliced

4 cloves garlic, crushed

8 tomatoes, chopped and peeled

1 tsp paprika

⅛ tsp each basil, oregano, rosemary, thyme and marjoram

Salt and pepper just before serving

COOKING INSTRUCTIONS

> Heat a heavy-bottomed pan over medium heat and melt 1 tablespoon of butter.

> Brown the chicken in batches, about 5 minutes a batch, and transfer to the slow cooker.

> Melt the remaining butter in the pan and sauté the onions, bell pepper, celery and mushrooms for 5 minutes until the onions are translucent.

> Add the garlic, cook for another 3 minutes, and transfer the mixture to the slow cooker.

> Add the tomatoes and spices to the slow cooker and cook on low for 6 hours.

> Salt and pepper to taste, then serve.

SERVINGS: 4-6

CHICKEN IN RED SAUCE

My family loves peppers, especially my mom. She isn't afraid of any amount of spice! My husband loves spicy too, he adds jalapenos to everything. Pretty much any dish heavy on the peppers like this one is a hit at our house. Note that New Mexico chiles have some kick. For a milder yet similar flavor, try dried Anaheim chiles.

INGREDIENTS

6-8 chicken thighs

1 tsp salt

½ tsp ground pepper

1 tsp cumin

½ tsp smoked paprika

1 tsp oregano

1 tsp basil

1 onion, sliced

2 tbsp ghee

4 cloves garlic, sliced

8 dry red New Mexico chiles, seeds removed and cut into small pieces

1 cup chicken broth

1 bay leaf

2 tomatoes, blanched, seeded and chopped

1 tbsp tomato paste

Salt and pepper just before serving

COOKING INSTRUCTIONS

> Rub the chicken with salt, pepper, cumin, paprika, oregano and basil.

> Brown the chicken in 1 tablespoon of ghee on both sides for about 5 minutes in a heavy-bottomed pan over medium heat then transfer to the slow cooker.

> Sauté the onions in the remaining ghee until translucent.

> Add the garlic, cook another 3 minutes until fragrant, then transfer the mixture to the slow cooker.

> Add chiles, broth, bay leave, tomatoes and tomato paste to slow-cooker.

> Cook on low for 4-6 hours.

> Salt and pepper to taste, then serve.

SERVINGS: 6-8

PERSIAN CHICKEN WITH POMEGRANATE & WALNUT (FESENJAN)

This is by far my most favorite Persian dish! We make it just a few times a year. It is very rich and uses large amounts of walnuts, which have a high Omega-6 content. As delicious as this dish is, due to the strong flavor, it is difficult to eat a large portion of it so my mom usually served it for a dinner party, along with a few other main dishes because this is a dish that people either love or hate. Of course, I highly recommend it. This dish is great with cauliflower rice.

INGREDIENTS

3½ lbs bone-in, skinless chicken thigh, breasts and legs

1 tsp sea salt

1 large onion, thinly sliced

4 tbsp ghee

½ tsp cardamom

¼ tsp cinnamon

3 garlic cloves, chopped

2½ cups water

4 cups walnuts, coarsely ground

2 cups pomegranate juice concentrate

1 tbsp honey

¼ tsp, ground saffron

Salt and pepper to taste just before serving

Garnish with fresh pomegranate seeds

COOKING INSTRUCTIONS

> Pat the chicken with the salt.

> In a large heavy-bottomed pan, heat 1 tablespoons of ghee over medium heat, brown the chicken on all sides in batches about 5 minutes a batch and set aside.

> Melt the remaining ghee, and sauté onions until translucent about 5 minutes.

> Add the cardamom, cinnamon and garlic, and cook another 3 minutes.

> Add the water, bring to a boil and simmer for 8-10 minutes on low.

> Add the ground walnuts to pan forming a thick paste.

> Mix in the chicken add pomegranate juice and honey and mix well.

> Place mixture from pan and saffron in slow cooker.

> Cook on low for 4 hours, remove chicken, debone, shred with 2 forks and place back in slow-cooker on high with lid removed for 30 minutes to thicken the sauce.

> Salt and pepper to taste, then serve.

SERVINGS: 6

PALEO **CHICKEN VERDE**

This was one of the first meat dishes I made when I stopped being a vegetarian which had lasted through my teen and college years. Back then, I was a cooking rookie when it came to meat, so if I wasn't able to mess this one up then no one will!

This is really tasty and a go-to recipe if we have friends over for a casual dinner. For guests I usually put out some organic corn tortillas as well as lettuce so guests can choose if they are going to do a Paleo chicken-verde salad or a more traditional taco.

INGREDIENTS

½ pound tomatillos, husked and rinsed

½ onion, chopped

2 cloves garlic, crushed

1 serrano chile pepper, minced

1 large poblano chile pepper

4-6 chicken breasts

¼ cup firmly packed cilantro leaves

½ tsp ground cumin

2 tbsp fresh lime juice

1 head of lettuce

Salt and pepper just before serving

COOKING INSTRUCTIONS

❯ Place oven rack in top position and turn on broiler. Line a baking sheet with foil and place tomatillos and peppers on it.

❯ Broil chilies until charred, about 5-6 minutes a side.

❯ Let stand for a few minutes until the blackened skins loosen and then pull them off (it's okay if a few pieces stay on).

❯ Chop all vegetables and add to the slow cooker with the cumin, cilantro leaves and lime juice.

❯ Place chicken breasts in a slow cooker, pour sauce over them and cook for 5½ hours.

❯ Use 2 forks to shred the chicken and cook another 30 minutes.

❯ Salt and pepper to taste, then serve with avocado and lettuce.

SERVINGS: 4-6

CAMBODIAN **CHICKEN**

Southeast Asia is a part of the world that I have not yet had a chance to visit. But it is at the top of my list of destinations. This dish is certainly one of the attractions.

INGREDIENTS

3 lbs skinless chicken thighs, bone in

1 tbsp coconut oil

3 cloves garlic, crushed

1 tbsp ginger, grated

3 tbsp fish sauce

3 tbsp lime juice

½ cup chicken broth

¼ cup coconut aminos

Salt and pepper just before serving

COOKING INSTRUCTIONS

› Melt the coconut oil in a heavy-bottomed pan over medium heat, brown the chicken on all sides in batches, about 5 minutes a batch, and transfer to the slow cooker.

› Add all the other ingredients to the slow cooker and cook on low for 6 hours.

› Salt and pepper to taste, then serve.

SERVINGS: 6

CHICKEN MOLE

I love a good chicken mole. The best one I have ever had was at a tiny restaurant in Santa Cruz called, Chocolate. I've never been able to break their code. I even know someone who worked there for a long time, but he never got his hands on their amazing recipe. I have been trying many versions throughout the years. Here is one that I've came up with that I really like. Be prepared to be in the kitchen for a while with this one; it take lots of chopping and measuring.

INGREDIENTS

1 tbsp guajillo chili powder

¼ tsp ground black pepper

1 tsp cumin

1 tsp coriander

½ tsp anise seeds

½ tsp cinnamon

⅛ tsp nutmeg

¼ tsp ground cloves

1 tsp oregano

4 tablespoons coconut oil

1 small onion, chopped

3 cloves garlic, crushed

5-6 whole tomatoes, peeled and diced

3 pablano chiles, stemmed, seeded and chopped

2 dried New Mexico chile peppers, stemmed, seeded and chopped

1 dried chipotle chile, stemmed, seeded and chopped

2 tomatillos, husked, rinsed and chopped

2 cups chicken broth

3 tbsp cacao powder

2 tbsp almond butter

¼ cup honey

4-6 chicken breasts

Avocado and cilantro, chopped for garnish

COOKING INSTRUCTIONS

> Heat 3 tablespoons of coconut oil in a heavy-bottomed pan over medium heat, add all the dried spices except the chiles and cacao, and stir for 3 minutes.

> Add the onion and sauté until translucent about 5 minutes.

> Add garlic and cook for another 3 minutes.

> Add the diced tomatoes, chiles, chicken broth, almond butter, cacao and honey, and simmer for 8-10 minutes.

> Allow mixture to cool, puree in a food processor until smooth and reserve.

> Brown the chicken in the remaining coconut oil in a heavy-bottomed pan over medium heat until browned on both sides, about 5 minutes, then transfer to the slow cooker.

> Pour reserved sauce over the chicken and cook on low for 5 hours.

> Use 2 forks to shred the chicken, then replace in the slow cooker for another hour.

> If there is too much liquid, use a strainer to drain the chicken before serving.

SERVINGS: 6

PALEO **CHICKEN ADOBO**

My best friend gave me this recipe. Her husband is from the Philippines and this is practically their national dish. It's also one of my friend's favorite things to eat. It is easy to make and full of tart, savory and garlicky flavor. It's best to marinate the chicken overnight.

INGREDIENTS

4 skinless chicken thighs
4 skinless chicken legs
½ cup white vinegar
½ cup coconut aminos or Tamari
½ cup water
6 cloves garlic, crushed
1 tsp black peppercorns
2 bay leaves
1 tbsp ghee
Salt and pepper just before serving

COOKING INSTRUCTIONS

❯ Put the chicken and all the other ingredients into a bowl, cover and refrigerate for at least 2 hours or, better, overnight.

❯ Place the sauce in the slow cooker.

❯ Set a heavy-bottomed pan over medium heat and brown the chicken in the ghee on all sides in two batches, about 5 minutes a batch, and transfer to the slow cooker.

❯ Cook on low for 6 hours.

❯ Salt and pepper to taste, then serve, spooning the sauce over the chicken.

SERVINGS: 6-8

THAI BASIL **CHICKEN**

This is my favorite Thai dish. Going out for Thai food can be difficult for Paleo dieters because the food is often sautéed in vegetable oils and the soy sauce is not gluten-free. When I went Paleo, I had to find different options. Then I figured out how to make my favorite dish at home!

INGREDIENTS

2 lbs boneless chicken thighs or breasts, cut into cubes

3 Thai red chilies (preferably fresh, but dried is okay too) chopped

2 tbsp fish sauce

1 red bell pepper, sliced

1 tbsp fresh lime juice

¼ cup coconut aminos or Tamari

1 tbsp coconut vinegar

1 tbsp fresh ginger, grated

½ cup firmly packed Asian-basil leaves, coarsely chopped

COOKING INSTRUCTIONS

❯ Add all the ingredients except the basil to the slow cooker and cook on low for 5½ hours.

❯ Add the basil and cook another 30 minutes.

❯ Salt and pepper to taste, then serve.

SERVINGS: 4

THAI CHICKEN SOUP
(TOM KA GAI)

I love this chicken soup because it encompasses every aspect of Thai flavor: spicy, sweet, salty and even sour. My husband and I have had several great memories of going out for a pot of Tom Ka Gai on rainy winter nights so making this at home reminds me of good times out.

INGREDIENTS

3 skinless chicken breasts, cubed

3 cloves garlic, sliced

1 can coconut milk or 2 cups homemade coconut milk

5 cups chicken broth

1 red bell pepper, sliced

1 stalk lemongrass, finely chopped

1 cup mushrooms, sliced

1 tbsp fresh ginger, grated

2 Thai peppers, chopped

2 tbsp fresh lime juice

2 tbsp fish sauce

Salt and pepper just before serving

Cilantro, chopped for garnish

COOKING INSTRUCTIONS

❯ Place all the ingredients in the slow cooker.

❯ Cook on low for 5-6 hours.

❯ Salt and pepper to taste, garnish with cilantro, then serve.

SERVINGS: 6

GREEN **CURRIED CHICKEN**

I am a huge fan of curries of all colors! This green curry uses
Thai green chilies and is packed with flavor.

INGREDIENTS

1 small onion, sliced

4 cloves garlic, minced

2 tbsp coconut oil

2 lbs chicken breast, cut into 1 inch cubes

1 cup coconut milk

3 tbsp green curry paste

2 kaffir lime leaves, chopped

2 tbsp fish sauce

1 red bell pepper, sliced

Serve with fresh Asian-basil leaves

Salt and pepper just before serving

COOKING INSTRUCTIONS

❯ Saute the onions, garlic and chicken in coconut oil in a heavy-bottomed pan over medium heat for 8 minutes, then transfer to slow cooker.

❯ Place all the ingredients in the slow cooker.

❯ Cook on low for 6 hours.

❯ Salt and pepper to taste, garnish, then serve.

SERVINGS: 4

CAULIFLOWER **CHICKEN CURRY**

I love cauliflower and grew up eating it in many ways because it is used in a number of Persian stews, as well as served as part of a "torshi," a Persian dish of pickled vegetables. It lends itself well to Asian flavors too! This dish has it all: sweet, spicy and zesty!

INGREDIENTS

2 lbs chicken breast, cubed
1 tsp cumin
1 tsp coriander
1 pinch of ground cloves
½ tsp turmeric
¼ tsp cayenne
2 tbsp ghee
1 onion, diced
3 cloves garlic, crushed
1 cauliflower, cut into florets
2 sweet potatoes, peeled and cubed
1 green chile
1 can coconut milk or 2 cups homemade coconut milk
1 tbsp fresh ginger, grated
Salt and pepper just before serving

COOKING INSTRUCTIONS

> Combine the dry spices and toss with the chicken to coat it.

> Melt 1 tablespoon of ghee in a heavy-bottomed pan over medium heat, brown the chicken for about 5 minutes and transfer to the slow cooker.

> Add the remaining ghee and sauté the onions until translucent, about 5 minutes.

> Add the garlic and cook another 3 minutes.

> Add the sweet potatoes and then cauliflower to the slow cooker. Place the chicken on top.

> Add the rest of the ingredients and cook on low for 6 hours.

> Salt and pepper to taste, then serve

SERVINGS: 4

HAINANESE CHICKEN WITH CAULIFLOWER RICE

When I first decided to do a cookbook, I was brainstorming recipe ideas with one of my closest friends. This was the first dish she suggested. It is traditionally done on the stove top, but was easy to convert to the slow cooker. The flavors do not come from the chicken, but rather from the strong flavors of garlic and ginger in the rice and chili sauce. One of the benefits is that you end up making a meal, as well as chicken stock, all at once! By the way, this friend and her husband agreed to try the Paleo diet for 30 days and are now full converts to Paleo for several years.

INGREDIENTS

1 whole chicken, 2-3 lbs

6 slices fresh ginger, ¼ inch thick a piece

2 cloves garlic, crushed

1 Serrano chile peppers, chopped

2 tbsp coconut vinegar

1 tbsp coconut aminos or Tamari

1 tsp salt

½ tsp peppercorns

Fresh cilantro for garnish

Enough water to cover the chicken

COOKING INSTRUCTIONS

> Wash the chicken, remove skin and giblets and drain well.

> Stuff cavity with ginger, scallions, garlic and Serrano peppers.

> Rub chicken with coconut aminos.

> Place skin and giblets in slow cooker to add additional flavor.

> Place the chicken in slow cooker and add the water, salt, and peppercorns.

> Cook on high for 1 hour.

> Reduce to low for 3-4 hours until chicken is cooked through.

> Remove the chicken from slow cooker, discard the ginger, scallions, garlic and Serrano pepper from cavity and pat chicken dry.

> When chicken is cool enough to handle, slice into serving-size pieces.

> Garnish with cilantro and serve with chili dipping sauce, cauliflower rice and sliced English cucumbers.

> Put broth through strainer and save for later use.

SERVINGS: 6

GINGER CHILE **DIPPING SAUCE**

INGREDIENTS

6 chopped fresh Thai chiles

3 medium garlic cloves, minced

½ shallot, chopped

2 inches fresh ginger, chopped

1 tbsp fresh lime juice

2 tbsp hot chicken broth (from
the crockpot)

1 tbsp Tamari or
coconut aminos

½ tsp salt

½ tsp honey

COOKING INSTRUCTIONS

> Blend all ingredients in a food processor.

> Add salt to taste

CAULIFLOWER RICE
(NOT A SLOW COOKER RECIPE)

INGREDIENTS

2 tbsp butter

1 medium onion, diced

4 garlic cloves, crushed

1 tbsp fresh ginger, grated

1 head cauliflower, trimmed and coarsely chopped

½ tsp sea salt

1 cup chicken stock from the crockpot (make sure to strain it first)

COOKING INSTRUCTIONS

❯ Place the cauliflower in a food processor and blend until it is the texture of rice.

❯ Melt the butter over medium-high heat, sauté the onions until soft, about 5 minutes.

❯ Add the garlic and ginger, and sauté until fragrant, about another 3 minutes.

❯ Add the cauliflower and salt, and cook for 2 minutes.

❯ Add 1 cup of broth and simmer for about 10 minutes or until all the liquid has evaporated.

INDIAN **GINGER CHICKEN**

The aromas of Indian food are such a delight,
and this dish will fill your house with them.

INGREDIENTS

4 boneless, skinless chicken breasts

2 tbsp coconut oil

1 onion, chopped

2 cloves garlic, crushed

3 Anaheim chiles, chopped

Juice of 1 lemon

1 tsp ground cardamom

1 tsp coriander

½ tsp turmeric

½ tsp paprika

3 cloves

1 stick of cinnamon

4-inches of fresh ginger, chopped

1 bay leaf

2 tomatoes, chopped

1 cup coconut milk

Salt and pepper just before serving

COOKING INSTRUCTIONS

❯ Melt 1 tablespoon of coconut oil in a heavy-bottomed pan over medium heat, brown the chicken on both sides, about 5 minutes, and transfer to the slow cooker.

❯ Sauté the onion in the remaining butter until translucent, about 5 minutes.

❯ Add the garlic and chiles, cook another 3 minutes and transfer the mixture to the slow cooker.

❯ Add the rest of the ingredients and cook on low for 6 hours.

❯ Salt and pepper to taste, then serve.

SERVINGS: 4-6

MULLIGATAWNY

I have founds foods from many parts of the world to be made primarily of whole ingredients and full of flavor. This Indian stew is one of those dishes. It's a little different from the standard curry so offers a great new taste.

INGREDIENTS

2 lbs boneless, skinless chicken thighs

½ tsp ground cinnamon

¼ tsp ground cloves

1 tsp ground coriander seed

1 tsp ground cumin

½ tsp ground turmeric

2 tbsp coconut oil

1 onion, chopped

4 cloves garlic, minced

1 carrot, chopped

2 green chili peppers

1 tbsp fresh ginger, grated

1 apple, peeled, cored and chopped

1 tbsp lemon juice

4 cups chicken broth

Salt and pepper just before serving

COOKING INSTRUCTIONS

❯ Toss the chicken thighs in the dry spices.

❯ Melt 1 tablespoon of the coconut oil in a heavy-bottomed pan over medium heat, brown the chicken on all sides, about 5 minutes, and transfer to the slow cooker.

❯ Add the remaining coconut oil and sauté the onions until translucent, about 5 minutes.

❯ Add the garlic, carrots and chili peppers, cook until fragrant, about 3 minutes and transfer the mixture to the slow cooker.

❯ Add the rest of the ingredients to the slow cooker and cook on low for 6 hours.

❯ Salt and pepper to taste, then serve.

SERVINGS: 4-6

CORNISH HENS
WITH MUSTARD SAUCE

Mustard gives this dish a tangy zip to complement
the classic aroma of rosemary.

INGREDIENTS

2 Cornish hens

1 tbsp butter

Juice of 1 lemon

½ cup chicken stock

1 tbsp fresh rosemary, chopped

1 tsp thyme

2 cloves garlic, crushed

3 tbsp stone-ground mustard

Salt and pepper just before serving

COOKING INSTRUCTIONS

❯ Melt the butter in a heavy-bottomed pan over medium heat.

❯ Brown the hens, about 5 minutes, handling carefully to not tear the skin, and transfer to the slow cooker.

❯ Pour the lemon juice and stock over the meat.

❯ Sprinkle the rosemary and thyme over the meat and sauce, add the garlic and cook on low for 6 hours.

❯ Remove the hens and place the leftover liquid in a sauce pan.

❯ Stir in the mustard, reduce for about 5 minutes and pour over the hens before serving.

❯ Salt and pepper to taste, then serve.

SERVINGS: 2

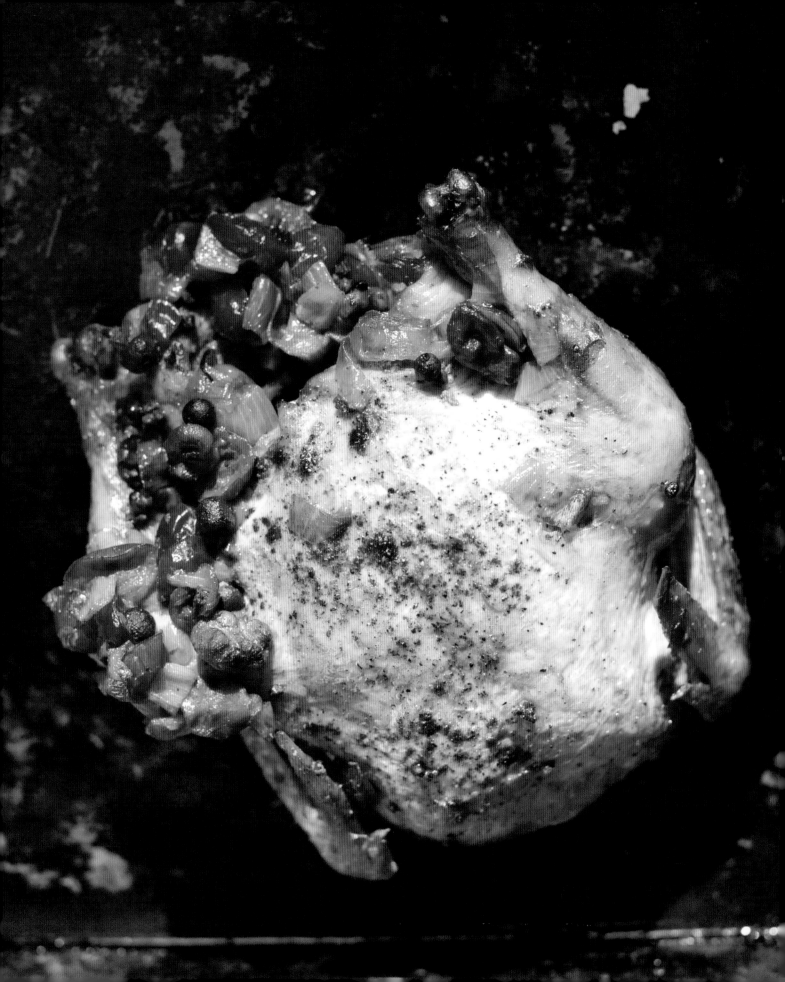

CORNISH HENS WITH WALNUTS AND DRIED CRANBERRIES

This is a great and festive dish for a special dinner for two.
It's like the fall season wrapped up in one dish.

INGREDIENTS

2 Cornish hens

2 tbsp coconut oil

4 shallots, chopped

¼ cup chopped walnuts

¼ cup dried cranberries

½ tsp cardamom

½ tsp cinnamon

¼ tsp nutmeg

½ tsp allspice

Juice of one lemon

½ cup chicken broth or white wine

Salt and pepper just before serving

COOKING INSTRUCTIONS

❯ Heat the coconut oil in a heavy-bottomed pan over medium heat.

❯ Brown each Cornish hen, about 5 minutes, handing them carefully to avoid tearing the skin, then transfer to the slow cooker.

❯ Add the remaining coconut oil and sauté the shallots for 5 minutes until translucent.

❯ Add the nuts, berries and spices, and cook for 2 minutes, until the fruit is softened, and add mixture to the slow cooker, around the meat.

❯ Add the lemon juice, and white wine or broth, and cook on low for 6 hours.

❯ Salt and pepper to taste, then serve.

SERVINGS: 2

TURKEY IN CRANBERRY AND GINGER SAUCE

This is perfect to make around the holidays, especially if you are planning a Thanksgiving dinner for only a few guests! The ginger brightens up the flavor of the traditional cranberry sauce.

INGREDIENTS

2 large skinless turkey breasts, cut into two chunks

1 tbsp ghee

1 lb cranberries

2 pears, peeled and sliced

1 tbsp ginger, grated

¼ cup water

½ cup honey

Salt and pepper just before serving

COOKING INSTRUCTIONS

❯ Brown the turkey breasts in the ghee in a heavy-bottomed pan over medium heat, about 5 minutes, and transfer to the slow cooker.

❯ Add all the remaining ingredients to a saucepan and bring to a boil, stirring occasionally.

❯ Reduce heat to medium, and cook uncovered until most of the cranberries pop and the pears are tender.

❯ Using a wooden spin, crush the pears to create a more saucy consistency.

❯ Pour cranberry sauce over the turkey and cook on low for 4-6 hours.

❯ Salt and pepper to taste, then serve.

SERVINGS: 4

TURKEY CHILI

Paleo chili always reminds me of when I first started following the Paleo diet. It was one of the first dishes I made. I remember thinking if Paleo eating tastes this good, then this diet change will be no problem. It proved to be right!

INGREDIENTS

1½ lbs ground turkey
2 tbsp ghee
1 onion, chopped
1 green pepper, chopped
2 Anaheim chile peppers, chopped
2 tbsp chili powder
1 tsp coriander
½ tsp cumin
1 tsp dried oregano
½ tsp chili pepper flakes
¼ tsp cayenne pepper
½ tsp paprika
2 tbsp tomato paste
1 jalapeño, chopped
2 cups tomatoes, chopped
2 cups beef broth
Salt and pepper just before serving

COOKING INSTRUCTIONS

❯ Melt 1 tablespoon of ghee in a heavy-bottomed pan over medium heat and sauté the onions and all the peppers except the jalapeños about 5 minutes until translucent.

❯ Add the chili powder, coriander, cumin, oregano, pepper flakes, cayenne, paprika and tomato paste, cook until the ground turkey is browned, about 8 minutes, and transfer to the slow cooker.

❯ Add the jalapeños, tomatoes and beef broth to the slow cooker, and cook on low for 6 hours.

❯ Salt and pepper to taste, then serve.

SERVINGS: 6

chapter six

DELICIOUSLY DONE DUCK

I AM PRETTY NEW TO DUCK MYSELF. I just started eating it a couple of years ago. I had it for the first time when eating Thai food and instantly fell in love. Now I order it every chance I get. Like most other farmed animals, most ducks are given feed, so look for free-range ducks raised on pasture with a varied diet. Duck is a great source of protein, vitamins and minerals. And duck fat is great to cook with!

SHREDDED ROASTED DUCK
FOR BREAKFAST OR LUNCH

One of the first times I ever had duck, was with two of my closest girlfriends in San Diego. We were at a terrific little restaurant in Encinitas. They served the duck very simply with lots of fresh thyme and a side of eggs for breakfast which was fantastic. In this recipe, the moist, rich flavor of the duck really stands on its own.

INGREDIENTS

1 duck, quartered and skinned (save skin to render for cooking fat for another dish)

2 tbsp ghee

½ onion, sliced

5 sprigs of fresh thyme, minced plus 2 additional sprigs

¼ cup chicken broth

Salt and pepper just before serving

Boston lettuce leaves

COOKING INSTRUCTIONS

> Lightly coat the chicken with a thin layer of ghee, brown the duck in the broiler, skin side up for 5 minutes, turning once and watching carefully so it doesn't burn, then transfer to the slow cooker.

> Sauté onions in the remaining ghee over medium heat for 5 minutes until translucent and place in the slow cooker.

> Add the broth and thyme, and cook on low for 7-8 hours.

> Shred the duck with forks, add additional thyme.

> Salt and pepper to taste, then serve on Boston lettuce leaves or with eggs for breakfast!

SERVINGS: 4

DUCK WITH BERRY PIQUANT SAUCE

This is another elegant dish, perfect for festivities or guests. The rich flavor of duck can hold its own again strong sweet tastes which makes the duck dishes a little more fun and interesting.

INGREDIENTS

4 duck breasts

4 shallots, finely chopped

2 cloves garlic, crushed

1 tbsp butter

¼ cup red wine

¼ cup apple cider vinegar

½ cup chicken stock

2 tsps tomato paste

1 tsp stone ground mustard

2 sprig tarragon, leaves chopped

1 sprig rosemary leaves, chopped

2 cups red currant

Salt and pepper just before serving

COOKING INSTRUCTIONS

> In a heavy-bottomed pan over medium heat, brown the breasts, skin side down in the butter, about 5 minutes, and transfer to the slow cooker, placing them skin side up.

> Use the remaining fat to sauté the shallots for 5 minutes until translucent.

> Add the garlic and cook another 3 minutes, until fragrant, then transfer the mixture to the slow cooker.

> In a separate bowl, combine the wine, stock, apple cider, tomato paste, mustard, berries, and herbs and stir until the mustard and tomato paste are incorporated, then pour over duck breasts in the slow cooker.

> Cook on low for 6-8 hours.

> Reduce extra liquid on the stovetop for five minutes over medium-low heat and pour over the duck.

> Salt and pepper to taste, then serve.

SERVINGS: 4

ROAST DUCK WITH PEARS

This dish just shouts holiday season to me. I love to cook food that takes our families out of their comfort zones during that time of the year. I am not a huge fan of turkey; I would consider making this instead sometime!

INGREDIENTS

4 duck breasts

2 tbsp ghee

1 onion, sliced

2 pears, sliced

¼ cup dried cranberries

½ cup white wine

¼ tsp ground cinnamon

Salt and pepper just before serving

COOKING INSTRUCTIONS

❯ Melt the ghee in a heavy-bottomed pan over medium heat, brown the duck skin side down for 5 minutes and transfer to the slow cooker, placing them skin side up.

❯ Add the remaining ghee to the pan and sauté the onions for 5 minutes until translucent.

❯ Add the pears and cranberries, cook another 3 minutes, and transfer the mixture to the slow cooker, being careful to not break the pear slices.

❯ Add the white wine and sprinkle the cinnamon over the breasts and sauce.

❯ Cook on low for 6-8 hours.

❯ Salt and pepper to taste, then serve.

SERVINGS: 4

DUCK LEGS WITH YAMS

This simple and delicious one pot meal will impress your friends.
The sweetness of the yams complements the savoriness of the duck.
The wine gives it a nice rich finish.

INGREDIENTS

8 duck legs

1 tbsp ghee

3-4 yams, cubed and peeled

3 sprigs of thyme

2 cloves garlic, clushed

3 shallots, chopped

½ cup chicken stock

½ cup Marsala

2 bay leaves

¼ tsp allspice

Salt and pepper just before serving

COOKING INSTRUCTIONS

❯ Lightly coat the duck legs with ghee, broil skin side up for 5 minutes, watching carefully to not burn the skin

❯ Place the yams at the bottom of the slow cooker and add the rest of the ingredients.

❯ Place the duck on top of the yams and cook on low for 6-8 hours.

❯ Salt and pepper to taste, then serve.

SERVINGS: 4

SPICY **DUCK CURRY**

I think we don't eat enough duck in America. I used to just stick to the typical meats, too, pretty much beef and chicken. The restrictions of the Paleo diet expanded my horizons in a good way. Now I jump at opportunities to try real foods that are out of the ordinary, and duck has become one of my favorites, especially in curry. And this one is a really to make.

INGREDIENTS

4 whole boneless duck breasts, skin removed (and reserved for rendering for a different dish) and cut into large chunks

1 tbsp Thai red curry paste (the instant stuff that you don't have to cook)

¼ tsp cayenne pepper

1 stalk lemongrass, finely chopped

1 tbsp ginger, grated

½ tsp cumin

½ tsp coriander

1 tbsp fish sauce

1 red pepper, chopped

1 red onion sliced

2 tomatoes, chopped and peeled

1 cup coconut milk

1 bunch fresh basil leaves, chopped and added just before serving

Salt and pepper just before serving

COOKING INSTRUCTIONS

❯ Add all the ingredients except the fresh basil to the slow cooker.

❯ Stir to make sure the curry paste is incorporated.

❯ Cook on low for 6-8 hours.

❯ Add the basil, salt and pepper to taste, then serve.

SERVINGS: 4-6

ABOUT INTERMITTENT FASTING

Intermittent fasting is an eating style that alternates between periods of fasting and eating. The fasting is typically longer than the overnight fast we normally do and most often ranges from 12 to 48 hours.

Fasting has been shown to be beneficial in several areas including weight/fat loss, blood lipid and inflammation management, neurological health, appetite and blood sugar control, fighting cancer and may increase overall life span. With all of the pros it may seem that intermittent fasting is the way to go for everyone. This is not necessarily the case and in some situations it may do more harm than good. It is not recommended that one begin fasting unless he/she has all the other details in place. This means clean eating, a smart exercise program, adequate sleep and minimal life stress. If any of these things are out of line, fasting will put you on the 'fast' path to adrenal fatigue and further potential problems. Other situations where fasting may be contraindicated include pregnancy, issues with blood-sugar regulation (diabetes), in small children, and those under a great deal of stress as rigorous training program.

Then who is it good for? If you've got your diet, exercise, sleep and stress well managed and are looking for something to experiment with, then give it a go. Just be smart!

THERE ARE SEVERAL METHODS OF FASTING, WITH THE MOST COMMON PROTOCOLS BEING:

Meal Skipping: This is simply 'missing a meal' - whether it be because you aren't hungry or it's not convenient—say, if you are traveling.

Condensed-Eating Windows: Eating time is limited to a specified number of hours based on schedule and/or preference. The window is usually somewhere between four and seven hours.

24-48 Hour Fast: This is exactly as it sounds, 24-48 hours of no eating followed by resumed normal eating patterns.

Every Other Day Fast: This is usually done for a week or longer and involves alternating between a 24-hour fast followed by a day of eating for a specified period of time.

Personal Protocols: This can also be set up to fit individual needs, goals, and responses. You might fast on Tuesdays and Fridays because of your work schedule, for example. These protocols are tailored to fit what works for your given situation.

chapter seven

FANTASTIC FISH AND SEAFOOD
FOR ANCIENT MARINERS

INCLUDING WILD-CAUGHT FISH IN OUR DIETS is a great way to increase our omega-3 fatty-acid intake. Omega-3s are what are called essential fatty acids; the body doesn't make them so we have to get them from the food we eat. Fish obtain Omega-3s from algae or plankton in their diets. Like other feedlot animals, farmed fish are not given a proper diet, are often treated with antibiotics or given feed that has been treated with pesticides, so are low in Omega-3s. The best sources of Omega-3 fatty acids are oily, cold-water fish, such as salmon, herring, mackerel, anchovies and sardines.

Fish can be cooked in a slow cooker, but fish requires much less cooking time than other proteins. Shellfish is harder. We didn't include too many recipes because the slow cooker often doesn't make cooking seafood more convenient or easy.

LEMON TARRAGON **TILAPIA**

This is a great garlicky and buttery fish dish that's easy to make. The dish contains a lot of butter, if you are sensitive to dairy foods, I would skip this one.

INGREDIENTS

2 sticks butter

6 cloves garlic, crushed

½ cup fresh lemon juice

1 tsp lemon zest

2 lbs tilapia fillets

3 sprigs fresh tarragon, chopped

Salt and pepper just before serving

COOKING INSTRUCTIONS

> Place the butter, garlic, lemon juice and zest in the slow cooker and cook on low for 4 hours.

> Add the tilapia and tarragon, and cook for another 40 minutes until the fish is opaque and cooked through.

> Salt and pepper to taste, then serve.

SERVINGS: 4-6

SLOW COOKED **SALMON**

I eat salmon more than any other fish. I have to admit it's not my favorite fish, but it's so healthy that I buy it often. It's considered by many nutritionists, both Paleo and not, to be a superfood and a great source of Omega-3 fatty acids as well as Vitamin D, which is not found in many foods. It's important to get wild-caught salmon because farmed fish provide less Omega-3s. You can see the difference in the deeper red color of the wild-caught fish. In this dish, the salmon is essentially poached in the slow cooker and white wine.

INGREDIENTS

2 lbs salmon fillets, cut across the fish into 4 pieces

2 cloves garlic, crushed

½ cup white wine

2 tbsp fresh lemon juice

1 tsp lemon zest

4 shallots, sliced

2 tbsp macadamia-nut oil

½ tsp rosemary

½ tsp thyme

Salt and pepper just before serving

COOKING INSTRUCTIONS

❯ Place salmon in the slow cooker skin side down.

❯ Add the garlic, white wine, lemon juice and zest to the slow cooker, making sure the garlic is in the liquid.

❯ Place the sliced shallots on top of the fillets and drizzle the oil over the fish.

❯ Sprinkle the dried herbs over the fillets and sauce, then cook on low for 1½ to 2 hours.

❯ Reduce remaining liquid on the stovetop by half over medium-low heat for about 5 minutes, and pour over the plated salmon.

❯ Salt and pepper to taste, then serve.

SERVINGS: 4

SEAFOOD **BOUILLABAISSE**

Bouillabaisse is another versatile soup dish that has numerous variations all along the Mediterranean coast. I like it because I consider it an easy, throw-together delicious dish packed with herbs and flavor.

INGREDIENTS

2 leeks, chopped

2 carrots, sliced

1 fennel bulb, chopped

2 tbsp ghee

4 cloves garlic, crushed

1 tbsp tomato paste

6 chopped tomatoes (peeled) or can of chopped tomatoes

1 cup fish stock

1 cup dry white wine

A couple of strands of saffron

1 tsp fennel seeds

¼ tsp cayenne pepper

½ lb mussels, scrubbed, debearded

½ lb sea scallops

½ lb shrimp, peeled and deveined

1 lb tilapia cut into 1-inch cubes

Salt and pepper just before serving

COOKING INSTRUCTIONS

❯ Melt the ghee in a heavy-bottomed pan over medium heat and sauté the leeks, carrots and fennel for 5 minutes until the leeks are soft.

❯ Add the garlic and tomato paste, cook another 3 minutes

❯ Add the tomatoes and simmer for 10 minutes, then transfer the mixture into the slow cooker.

❯ Add the stock, wine, saffron, cayenne and fennel seeds to the slow cooker and cook on low for 6-8 hours.

❯ Turn the slow cooker to high and add the seafood in this order; mussels—which should be under the liquid for the most part— scallops, shrimp and last the fish, which should be above the liquid.

❯ Cook on high for 45 minutes until the fish is cooked through and the mussels have opened.

❯ Discard any unopened mussels, salt and pepper to taste, then serve.

SERVINGS: 4-6

CIOPPINO

This fun and fantastic fish stew originated in San Francisco and was made up of local fishermen's typical catch of the day. It thus goes nicely with the Paleo philosophy of cooking what is naturally available.

INGREDIENTS

1 onion, chopped
2 carrots, sliced
1 green bell pepper, chopped
1 tbsp butter
5 cloves garlic, crushed
3 tbsp tomato paste
2 cups white wine
1 cup chicken stock
8 tomatoes, peeled and chopped
2 bay leaves
½ tsp basil
½ tsp marjoram
½ tsp oregano
1 tsp dried thyme
1 spicy pepper, chopped
1 tsp paprika
½ lb clams, scrubbed
½ lb mussels, debearded and scrubbed
½ lb scallops
1 cup crab meat
1 lb shrimp, peeled and deveined
1 lb cod fillets, cubed
½ cup fresh chopped parsley for garnish
Salt and pepper just before serving

COOKING INSTRUCTIONS

❯ Sauté the onions in the butter in a heavy-bottomed pan over medium heat for 5 minutes.

❯ Add the garlic, bell peppers, carrots and tomato paste to the pan, cook another 3 minutes until the garlic is fragrant and transfer the mixture to the slow cooker.

❯ Add the wine, stock, tomatoes, tomato paste, garlic, onion, carrots, peppers and dried herbs to the slow cooker, and cook on low for 6-8 hours.

❯ Turn the slow cooker to high and place the clams and mussels into the liquid.

❯ Add the scallops, crab and shrimp on top, then the fish last above the liquid.

❯ Cook on high for 45 minutes until the fish is opaque and most of the clams and mussels have opened, discarding any unopened shell fish. Garnish with parsley, then serve.

SERVINGS: 6

JAMBALAYA

Here's my Paleo take on a jambalaya. This dish uses a lot of pepper which potentially have health benefits and come with the more obvious advantage of tasting great. It's packed with herbs and different tastes that get combined nicely in the slow cooker. In fact, this is one of the first dishes I made in my slow cooker. Even though it has a lot of ingredients, it's hard to mess up. It's still one of my favorites.

INGREDIENTS

4 slices bacon, cut into 1-inch pieces

1 large onion, chopped

1 large green bell pepper, chopped

1 cup chopped celery

1 tbsp ghee

3 cloves garlic, crushed

1 lb chicken breast, cut into 1-inch cubes

1 lbs spicy sausage like chorizo or hot Italian sausage, casing removed and crumbed

8 tomatoes, peeled and chopped with juices

2 cups chicken broth

½ tsps dried oregano

1 tsps dried parsley

½ tsp dried thyme

2 tsp Cajun seasoning

½ tsp cayenne pepper

½ tsp paprika

1 pound cooked shrimp without tails

COOKING INSTRUCTIONS

> Heat a heavy-bottomed pan over medium heat, add bacon, cook until crisp, about 5 minutes then reserve.

> Add 1 tbsp ghee and onions, bell peppers and celery to the bacon grease, cook until tender, another 5 minutes.

> Add the garlic, cook another 3 minutes and transfer the mixture to the slow cooker.

> Brown the chicken and sausage on all sides in the pan for about 5 minutes and transfer to the slow cooker.

> Add the diced tomatoes, chicken broth and dried spices to the slow cooker and cook on low for 7½ hours.

> Add the shrimp and cook another 30 minutes.

> Add bacon bits, salt and pepper to taste, then serve.

SERVINGS: 12

THAI–INSPIRED
COCONUT PUMPKIN SOUP

I am always looking for new things to do with pumpkin, or in this case an Asian variety called kabocha squash, in the fall season. I love the naturally sweet flavor. Pumpkin/kabocha lends itself well to Asian dishes, and is delicious with coconut milk. The refreshing flavor of the lemongrass is also a great complement.

INGREDIENTS

1 small kabocha squash, peeled and diced

1 yam, peeled and diced

2 small red or green chilies, sliced

3 cups coconut milk

3 cups chicken stock

1 shallot, minced

3 cloves garlic

3 stalks lemongrass, minced

½ cup basil leaves

½ tsp shrimp paste

2 tbsp fish sauce

1 lb cooked prawns, peeled and deveined

Salt just before serving

COOKING INSTRUCTIONS

> Place all ingredients except the shrimp to the slow cooker, starting with the squash and yams.

> Cook for 6-8 hours until the squash and yams are tender.

> Add the shrimp and cook another 30 minutes.

> Salt to taste then serve.

SERVINGS: 4

SWEET AND SOUR **SHRIMP**

I love the flavors in this dish and am a sucker for a light refreshing entrée with some fruit mixed in. The coconut aminos give the dish a nice balance of salty and sweet.

INGREDIENTS

½ cup chicken or fish stock

1 cup fresh pineapple, cut into chunks

1 cup onions, thinly sliced

3 cloves garlic, crushed

2 tsp ginger, minced

2 tbsp apple-cider vinegar

2 tbsp coconut aminos

1 tsp red pepper flakes

1 cup green bell peppers, cut into chunks

1 lb cooked shrimp, peeled

Salt and pepper just before serving

COOKING INSTRUCTIONS

› Place all ingredients except shrimp in the slow cooker.

› Cook on low for 4 hours.

› Add the shrimp and cook for another 30 minutes until the shrimp is cooked through.

› Salt and pepper to taste, then serve.

SERVINGS: 4

IODINE AND THE PALEO DIET

Iodine is an important nutrient, but many Paleo-lifestyle followers do not get a great deal of it. The No. 1 dietary source of iodine for most people is table salt. Kelp and seaweed are also rich in the nutrient and trace amounts are found in many vegetables. When deficient in iodine, thyroid function is compromised, and it is many times taken in supplement form by persons with low thyroid-hormone levels.

We recommend you do not eliminate or avoid table salt. If you are eating any packaged foods like beef jerky, canned tuna, cured meats, bacon or sausage, for example, you are likely getting iodine via the salt used in these products. If a person has a low-functioning thyroid, I often suggest adding a low-dose iodine supplement, especially if they are using non-iodized salt and few processed/salty foods.

WEIGHT LOSS

Losing weight is an $88 billion industry. Surveys show that some people would give up five years of life if they could lose the weight. Losing weight is a goal that nearly everyone at one time or another has had. Weight loss, the ever-sought after dream of having six-pack abs and a perfect body is the stuff that makes news headlines, special products, drugs and surgeries designed to help get the job done. Does it really have to be this difficult? Are we so attached to fast food, soda, refined sugar and processed 'food-like' substances? Sadly, the answer is yes. Fortunately, more and more people are realizing healthy food doesn't have to be 'fat-free' and taste like cardboard.

A Paleo way of life is a great tool for weight loss. There is no feeling hungry, no pills not special foods to buy and everything you need can be found at the grocery store. But how exactly does this 'miracle diet' work?

The standard American diet (SAD) is largely made up of high-calorie, low-nutrient processed foods. Due to the high carbohydrate and sugar content in the SAD, insulin levels are in a constant state of elevation. Insulin is the hormone that turns on the signal for fat storage. The more sugar in our blood, the more insulin we need to take it out. Once muscle and liver glycogen stores are full, all the extra sugar in the blood is stored as fat. The Paleo style of eating eliminates processed, low-nutrient-dense, sugar and carbohydrate-laden foods and replaces them with nutrient-dense vegetables, proteins, and moderate amounts of healthy fats. There is less sugar in the blood and less insulin signaling fat storage.

Vegetables and some fruit are the primary carbohydrate sources in a Paleo diet. Compared to a plate of pasta or a sugary soda, the amount of carbohydrate in vegetables is significantly lower and the vegetables are much more nutritious! It is very difficult to eat too much broccoli; too many potato chips, is a different story. The types of food consumed in the Paleo diet fill us up without filling us out.

Carbohydrates are water-holding molecules. When breads, cereals, soda, pasta and other sugary or carb-laden dishes are removed from the diet and replaced with vegetables and protein, the body loses a great deal of water. This is often the explanation for rapid weight loss in the first week after making the switch to the Paleo diet.

The foods that are part of the Paleo plan, lots of non-starchy vegetables, animal protein, moderate amounts of healthy fats and some fruit, are nutrient-dense without being calorie dense. Eliminating calorie-dense sodas, fast and processed foods, and foods high in carbohydrate results in the body using stored fat for energy instead of carbohydrates.

In addition, many people are sensitive to the food components, chemicals and artificial ingredients in today's food supply. Substances like wheat, dairy, antibiotics and pesticides all have an effect on our body's hormones. Many times these effects result in the development of autoimmune and other conditions that can have a marked effect on hormones that regulate both weight and appetite. A Paleo lifestyle minimizes exposure to foods and agents that may contribute to hormone dysfunction.

Discovering houseplants

GROWING HOUSEPLANTS SHOULD BE A VOYAGE OF DISCOVERY, NOT ONLY ABOUT THE TYPES OF PLANTS THAT WILL OR WON'T GROW WELL IN YOUR HOME, BUT ALSO AN EXPLORATION OF THE PLANT KINGDOM IN ALL ITS DIVERSE MANIFESTATIONS. YOU WILL GET A LOT MORE OUT OF YOUR HOUSE-PLANTS IF YOU INVESTIGATE THE POTENTIAL OF THE VARIOUS TYPES OF PLANTS, AND HOW THEY CAN BE USED IN THE HOME.

Dependable evergreens

CHOOSE SOME OF THE EASIEST AND MOST DEPENDABLE EVERGREENS AS THE BACKBONE OF YOUR DISPLAYS. MANY OF THEM ARE TOUGH ENOUGH FOR THE MORE DIFFICULT POSITIONS AROUND THE HOME, AND MOST OF THOSE SUGGESTED HERE ARE BOLD ENOUGH TO BE FOCAL POINT PLANTS TOO.

The glossy evergreens such as dracaenas, fatsias, ficus, scheffleras, palms and philodendrons generally make excellent stand-alone plants, but they can also be used as the framework plants for groups and arrangements. They will be far more robust than plants with thin or papery leaves, feathery and frondy ferns, or even those with hairy leaves. You need these other leaf textures, as well as flowering plants, to add variety of shape and form, and a touch of colour, but it makes sense to use the toughest evergreens as the basis of your houseplant displays.

Indoor 'trees'

Even the plainest room can be brought to life and given a sense of design and character with a large specimen plant that has the stature of a small tree. Some houseplants grow into real trees in their natural environment, but indoors you need plants that are in proportion with the dimensions of your room, and that won't quickly outgrow their space.

Large palms are ideal for this purpose, but many of the ficus family do just as well. The common *Ficus elastica*, once so popular, but now often passed by as unexciting, is a good choice, and there are many excellent variegated varieties that are far from dull. If you want an all-green one (and these have the merit of growing more quickly than the variegated kinds), 'Robusta' is a good variety to choose. If you don't like the upright and

TOP: Ficus elastica *was once a very popular houseplant, and is still well worth growing. The variety usually grown is 'Robusta', an improvement on the species that used to be grown years ago.*

ABOVE: Ficus lyrata *is a bold 'architectural' plant that can easily reach ceiling height.*

FAR LEFT: Philodendron scandens *is effective both as a trailing plant and grown up a moss pole, as here.*

LEFT: Yucca elephantipes *is a justifiably popular houseplant. It makes a bold focal point and is a really tough plant that should survive for years.*

sometimes leggy appearance of this plant, cut out the tip when it is about 1.5–1.8m (5–6ft) feet high, to stimulate low branching.

Other ficus to look for are *F. lyrata* (very large leaves with a distinctive shape), *F. benghalensis* (though the downy appearance of the leaves can make it a dull-looking plant), and the widely available *Ficus benjamina*. This is especially beautiful because it grows tall with a broad crown and arching branches. There are also beautiful variegated varieties of this species such as 'Starlight'.

Bushy plants that will give height and spread include *Schefflera arboricola* (syn. *Heptapleurum arboricola*) and *Schefflera actinophylla*. Both have finger-like leaflets radiating from a central point.

When a tough plant is needed

If you need a tough, glossy evergreen for a cold or draughty spot, perhaps for a hallway or near the back door, consider using some of the hardy foliage plants that have to cope with frost and gales when planted outdoors!

Fatsia japonica is another glossy evergreen with fingered foliage, rather like the palm of a hand (look for a variegated variety if you don't

like the plain green leaves). Closely related is × *Fatshedera lizei*, a bigeneric hybrid between *Fatsia japonica* and an ivy. Grow it as a shrub by pinching out the growing tips each spring, or let it show its ivy parentage and grow more upright.

Others to look for are variegated varieties of *Aucuba japonica*, and *Euonymus japonicus* varieties such as 'Mediopictus', 'Microphyllus Albovariegatus' and 'Microphyllus Aureovariegatus'.

Ivies are ideal if you need a tough climber or trailer, and there are lots of varieties to choose from, with a wide choice of leaf shape, size and colour.

Philodendron scandens   *P. 'Blue Mink'*   *P. 'Xanadu'*

P. bipinnatifidum   *P. 'Pink Prince'*

Philodendron leaves

Some genera have species and varieties with very different leaves, and they can make an interesting collection. The five philodendron leaves shown here are typical of the variation you can find within one group of plants.

TOP RIGHT: Monstera deliciosa *is one of the most striking focal point foliage plants that you can grow. The leaves are big and shapely, and the plant will grow large.*

ABOVE: Scindapsus aureus, *often sold under its other name of* Epipremnum aureum, *is a useful climber or trailer. This is the golden variety 'Neon'.*

ABOVE RIGHT: *Radermachera combines tough, glossy leaves with a 'loose' and almost ferny appearance; a refreshing change to most of the glossy evergreens.*

RIGHT: Aspidistra elatior *is a tough plant that seems to tolerate all kinds of neglect. If you look after it properly, however, you will have a fine foliage plant. There is also a variegated variety.*

Elegant palms

PALMS ARE THE EPITOME OF ELEGANCE AND WILL ADD A TOUCH OF SOPHIS-
TICATION TO YOUR HOME. THEY BRING TO MIND IMAGES OF A TINKLING
PIANO IN THE PALM COURT OF A GRAND HOTEL, YET SOME CAN LOOK JUST AS
ELEGANT AND IMPOSING IN AN ULTRA-MODERN HOME INTERIOR.

Many palms are slow-growing, and, consequently, large specimens are often expensive. But don't be deterred from trying palms; if you
provide the right conditions, even small plants will gradually become
impressive specimens.

Not all palms grow large, and many are compact enough for a table-top or
for pride of place on a pedestal. Some are even small enough to use in a
bottle garden while young. The box opposite will help you choose a suitable palm for a particular position.

How to grow healthy palms

The most common mistake is to re-
gard all palms as lovers of hot sunshine
and desert-dry air. They often have to
cope with both in countries where they
grow outdoors, but as houseplants you
want them to remain in good condition with unblemished leaves.

- Keep cool in winter, but not less
  than 10°C (50°F).
- Keep out of direct sunshine unless
  you know that your palm revels in
  sunshine (a few do).
- Use a loam-based compost (potting
  soil) and ensure that the drainage is
  good (poor drainage is sure to cause
  problems).
- Only repot when absolutely essential as palms dislike root disturbance. Always ensure that the new
  compost is firmly compacted if you
  do repot.
- Water liberally in spring and summer, sparingly in winter.
- Mist the plants frequently with
  water and sponge the leaves occasionally with water.
- Do not use an aerosol leaf shine.

WHAT WENT WRONG

🐛 **Brown leaf tips** are usually
caused by dry air. Underwatering
and cold are other likely causes.

🐛 **Brown spots on the leaves** are
probably caused by a disease,
encouraged by overwatering or
chills. Cut off all affected leaves.

🐛 **Yellowing leaves** are most likely
to be caused by underwatering,
though they could also indicate that
the plant needs feeding.

🐛 **Brown leaves** are nothing to
worry about if they are few in number
and only the lowest ones are affected.

LEFT: *Washingtonia palms have fan-like
leaves that create a striking effect.*

CHOOSING A PALM

🐾 Tall and tough

Chamaerops humilis Can be grown outdoors where frosts are only mild; suitable for a cold position indoors.
Howeia forsteriana (syn. *Kentia forsteriana*) and *H. belmoreana* (syn. *K. belmoreana*) Associated with the old palm courts. Will survive in a dark situation, but growth is very slow.
Phoenix canariensis This one enjoys full sun (but beware of leaf scorch through glass) and can sit on the patio for the summer. Keep in a cool room – minimum about 7°C(45°F) – in winter.

🐾 Table-top and easy

Chamaedorea elegans (syn. *Neanthe bella*) Can be used in a bottle garden when small. Insignificant flowers often appear on young plants.

🐾 Difficult but worth the effort

Cocos nucifera This is the coconut palm, and it is usually grown as a novelty with the large nut clearly visible at the base. Even a young plant can be 1.8m (6ft) tall, and it is difficult to keep in the home.
Cocos weddeliana A slow-grower. Can be used in a bottle garden.

ABOVE RIGHT: Howeia belmoreana *is sometimes sold under its other name of* Kentia belmoreana.

RIGHT: Cocus nucifera *is a big palm that is quite difficult to keep in the home.*

FAR RIGHT: Chamaedorea elegans *is a palm to choose if you want one that is easy and dependable. It will remain compact enough to use on a table-top.*

Dealing with brown leaves

It is natural for the lower leaves on palms to turn brown and die in time. To keep the plant looking smart, cut these off close to the point of origin (top). Secateurs (floral scissors) are adequate for most palms, but a saw may be required for specimens with very tough leaves. If the tips of the leaves turn brown, trim them off with scissors, but avoid actually cutting into the healthy leaf (above).

Variegated plants

VARIEGATED FOLIAGE PLANTS WILL BRING COLOUR AND A TOUCH OF THE EXOTIC INTO A DULL CORNER OR BRIGHT WINDOWSILL, DEPENDING ON THE TYPE. UNLIKE FLOWERING PLANTS, MOST REMAIN COLOURFUL FOR TWELVE MONTHS OF THE YEAR.

Variegation has evolved for several reasons, and the two main ones are important to understand if you want to grow healthy-looking plants with good variegation.

Many variegated houseplants are derived from forest-floor dwellers in which variegation is useful where they occur in lighter areas, such as on the edge of clearings, because it reduces the area of functional leaf. This type of variegation is frequently white and green, the white areas cutting down the area that is reactive to sunlight. This group of plants often has the best variegation when positioned away from direct light.

Others are light-demanding species and have acquired colours and patterns for other reasons. Red and pink leaves are able to absorb light from different parts of the spectrum to green leaves, for example, and many different colours in the one leaf may make it more efficient. The variegation on these plants is often better if positioned in good light.

A few plants have colourful leaves to attract pollinators. The common poinsettia (*Euphorbia pulcherrima*), and bromeliads such as neoregelia, are able to change the colour of the leaves that surround the insignificant flowers from green to bright colours such as reds and pinks.

There are other reasons for variegation, such as a being a warning to predators, so there can be no simple rules that apply to all colourful foliage plants. Some, such as coleus and crotons (codiaeums) need bright light;

others like fittonias, with their white or pale pink variegation, must be kept out of direct sun.

Potential problems

Some plants lose their strong variegation if the light is too strong, others if it is too weak. If the plant seems unhappy, move it to a lighter or shadier position as appropriate.

If any isolated, all-green shoots appear on an otherwise satisfactorily variegated plant, cut them back to the point of origin. Some plants will 're-vert' and the all-green part of the plant will eventually dominate unless you remove the offending shoots.

Coloured bracts (the modified leaves that frame a cluster of flowers) will lose their colour or intensity of colour outside the flowering period. You can do nothing about this.

Begonia rex leaves
Although they are unlikely to be labelled as specific varieties, you can collect a whole range of *Begonia rex* with different variegations. Two other types of foliage begonias are shown here: *B. masoniana* (top left) and, to the right of this, *B.* 'Tiger'.

GOING FOR A COLLECTION

There are so many variegated houseplants that some people like to start a collection of a particular group of them. This makes it easy to provide the right conditions for all of them, and the searching out of new species or varieties to add to the collection adds another dimension to the hobby.

Good plants to collect are begonias (there are many variations among *B. rex*, but lots of other begonias have interesting variegation), caladiums (if you like a challenge), codiaeums, dracaenas and cordylines, marantas and calatheas, and pileas. Named varieties of vegetatively propagated coleus are difficult to obtain, but a packet of seeds will give you an amazing range of colours and variegation from which to select those to keep.

OPPOSITE TOP: Begonia rex *varies in leaf colouring from one plant to another, but all are attractively variegated and make bold foliage plants.*

OPPOSITE LEFT: Cordyline terminalis, *also sold as* Dracaena terminalis, *comes in many varieties, the difference being in the colouring and variegation.*

OPPOSITE RIGHT: Dracaena marginata *is a popular houseplant, and there are varieties with attractively variegated leaves.*

TOP LEFT: Ficus benjamina 'Starlight' *is an outstanding houseplant with brightly variegated leaves on a plant that will eventually make a tall specimen with attractively arching shoots.*

TOP RIGHT: *Ivies (varieties of* Hedera helix*) are versatile plants that can be used as climbers or trailers.*

RIGHT: *Codiaeums, also known as crotons, can be demanding to grow well, but they make spectacular plants. Leaf hue and shape vary greatly according to variety, but all are bright and colourful.*

Graceful ferns

FERNS ARE FASCINATING PLANTS THAT WILL ADD A SPECIAL CHARM TO ANY

ROOM IN WHICH YOU WANT TO CREATE A FEELING OF COOL TRANQUILLITY

AND GREEN LUSHNESS. THEY BESTOW A RELAXED ATMOSPHERE IN CONTRAST

TO THE VIVID COLOUR OF BRIGHTER FOLIAGE PLANTS AND THE BRASHNESS OF

SOME FLOWERS.

FERN SELECTOR

Good for beginners
Asplenium nidus
Cyrtomium falcatum (syn. *Polystichum falcatum*)
Nephrolepis exaltata
Pellaea rotundifolia

For the more experienced
Adiantum capillus-veneris
Platycerium bifurcatum
Polypodium aureum
Pteris cretica (and its varieties)

Difficult but interesting
Asplenium bulbiferum
Davallia fejeenis

Ferns are grown mainly for the grace and beauty of their fronds, and their elegance compensates for their lack of flowers.

The majority of ferns will thrive in shade or partial shade, conditions that are easily provided in any home. Unfortunately they also require lots of moisture and high humidity, both of which are in short supply in the average living-room. If you want ferns to thrive, you will have to choose easy and tolerant varieties (see the *Fern Selector* above right) or provide them with the humidity and moisture that is so vital. Although most of the ferns

sold as houseplants come from tropical regions and benefit from warmth, central heating spells death to many of them unless you counteract the dry air by taking measures to increase the humidity, at least immediately surrounding the plants.

The ideal place for ferns is in a conservatory, porch or garden room where it is easier to establish a moist atmosphere.

Not all ferns need coddling, however, and some have adapted to dry air or cool temperatures. There are sure to be some ferns that you can grow successfully, and if you are determined to

grow the delicate types with thin, feathery fronds, you can try planting them in a bottle garden or terrarium where they will thrive.

Starting with ferns

If you haven't grown ferns before, start with the easy ones. As you gain experience, add some of the more exotic and difficult species.

The commonest ferns are inexpensive, and even the more unusual kinds are usually cheap if you choose small specimens.

Florists and garden centres sell the most popular houseplant ferns, but you may have to buy the less common ones from a specialist nursery.

Propagating ferns

The simplest way to increase your ferns is to divide a large clump, or to remove offsets. Some, like *Davallia fejeenis*, send out rhizomes that root and can be used to grow new plants,

LEFT: *Most of the aspleniums are much easier to care for than the ferns with very thin and finely divided leaves. Asplenium nidus (left) has broad leaves that radiate from a central well or 'nest' and is a particularly good houseplant.*

others produce small bulbils or even plantlets on the leaves (*Asplenium bulbiferum* is one). These will usually root into moist compost if pressed into the surface. These are interesting and fun ways to grow more ferns.

Growing your own ferns from spores is possible but slow, and you may find it difficult to obtain fresh spores of houseplant species with good germination.

Don't be deceived!

Many plants commonly regarded as ferns simply masquerade under that name. Some, like the selaginellas, are also primitive plants, other such as asparagus 'ferns' are more evolved flowering plants that simply have fine, feathery-looking foliage – an attribute associated with ferns. The asparagus fern is in fact a member of the lily family, though you would hardly recognize the connection from its insignificant flowers.

Selaginellas are pretty, low-growing plants that like the same conditions as indoor ferns: damp shade and moderate warmth. They will happily grow alongside ferns in a bottle garden.

Several asparagus ferns are available as houseplants, all of them tougher and more tolerant of neglect than the majority of true ferns.

Mounting a stag's horn

The *Platycerium bifurcatum* is a native of Australia and unlike most ferns it does not mind a dry atmosphere. One of the most spectacular ways to display it is mounted on bark. Keep the root-ball damp and mist the plant regularly.

1. Find a suitably sized piece of bark. Cork bark is ideal and you can usually buy this from a florist or aquarium shop. Start with a small plant and remove it from the pot. If necessary, remove some of the compost to reduce its bulk, then wrap the roots in damp sphagnum moss. Secure the moss with wire.

2. Bind the mossy root-ball to the cork bark, using florists' wire or plastic-covered wire to hold it securely.

ABOVE: Adiantum capillus-veneris, *like most of the maidenhair ferns, demands a humid atmosphere to do well. However, this is a truly graceful species.*

ABOVE RIGHT: Cyrtomium falcatum *is the one to choose if you find ferns generally too demanding. This one will tolerate a much drier atmosphere than most, and does not need a lot of warmth.*

RIGHT: Nephrolepsis exaltata *is one of the best ferns for a pedestal or table-top display. There are several varieties, with variation in leaf shape, some being more 'ruffled' than others.*

Cacti and succulents

SOME PEOPLE ARE FASCINATED BY CACTI AND THEY BECOME A PASSIONATE
HOBBY, OTHERS DISMISS THEM AS BEING NOT QUITE 'REAL' HOUSEPLANTS.
WHATEVER YOU THINK OF THEM, CACTI AND SUCCULENTS ARE SOME OF THE
EASIEST PLANTS TO LOOK AFTER AND MAKE THE IDEAL CHOICE IF YOU OFTEN
HAVE TO LEAVE YOUR HOUSEPLANTS UNATTENDED.

Cacti can be very beautiful in flower, and a huge epiphyllum bloom
can be almost breath-taking beautiful, but you will probably decide
whether or not to grow cacti depending on whether you like or dislike
their overall shape and form. It has to
be admitted that a few, like the
epiphyllum just mentioned, can be
ungainly and unattractive when out of
bloom, but the vast majority are neat,
compact and in the eyes of most people
have a fascinating beauty of their own.
There are species that creep and cascade, others which have hairy or cylindrical spiny columns, some with flat
jointed pads, and others with globular
or candelabra shapes.

Succulents are just as diverse: some
are grown for their flowers, others for
shape or foliage effect. There are hundreds of them readily available, and
many more can be found in specialist
nurseries.

Flowers of the desert
These need minimal water between
mid-autumn and early spring, but
plenty of sunshine at all times. As a
rule, keep them cool in winter (about
10°C/50°F) to encourage flowering.
Repot annually when young, but later
only repot when really necessary as a
small pot also hastens flowering.

Not all cacti will flower when
young, so if you want some that flower
freely on young plants, look for species
of echinopsis, lobivia, mammillaria,
notocactus, parodia and rebutia.

Forest cacti
The forest cacti, which have flattened,
leaf-like stems, are the most popular
type of cacti. To keep them flowering
well each year remember not to treat
them like ordinary cacti, and follow
these basic guidelines.

Exact treatment depends on the species, but they will require a resting
period, when they are kept cool and
watered only infrequently, usually
mid-autumn to mid-winter or late
winter to early spring, followed by a
period of warmth when they are watered freely. They will also benefit
from spending the summer in a shady
spot outdoors.

LEFT: *Cacti often look better in small groups
rather than as isolated specimens. In the
group shown here, a grafted cactus (to the
left of the arrangement) has been used to add
additional interest.*

BELOW: *Epiphyllums have huge flowers and
are among the most spectacular cacti in
bloom. Unfortunately they look ugly and
ungainly out of flower, so for most of the year
you will want to relegate them to an
inconspicuous spot.*

Succulents

Succulents vary enormously in their requirements – some, such as sempervivums, are tough and frost-tolerant, others are tender and temperamental. Always look up the specific needs for each plant, but as a rule they need very good light and little water in winter.

Displaying and collecting

Few cacti and succulents make good focal point plants – though a large epiphyllum in a porch can be a real stunner – and they are generally best displayed as groups in dish gardens (shallow planters) or troughs. Cascading cacti, however, like the forest cacti already mentioned, are almost always displayed in isolation and look good on a pedestal while they are in bloom. But if you have a conservatory, you can try planting several of them in a hanging basket.

Cacti are very collectable, and you can grow literally hundreds of them in a modest-sized home. A frost-free greenhouse widens the scope considerably, and you can rotate the plants with those indoors, to maintain variety and interest.

Handling cacti

Repotting a cactus can be a prickly job. Make it easier on your hands by folding up a strip of newspaper or brown paper (top). Wrap this around the plant, leaving enough paper at each end to form a handle (above).

CACTUS OR SUCCULENT?

🐛 Succulent simply means a plant that has adapted to dry conditions and can retain moisture with minimal loss from its leaves, which are often plump and fleshy. Cacti are also succulents, but in all except a few primitive species the leaves have become modified to spines or hairs and the stems have taken over the function of leaves – being thick, fleshy and with the ability to photosynthesize.

Although most cacti have their natural home in warm, semi-desert regions of America, some grow as epiphytes on trees in the forests of tropical America. Some of these, such as zygocactus, schlumbergera and rhipsalidopsis, have produced hybrids and varieties that are popular flowering houseplants in winter and spring.

ABOVE: Crassula ovata, *like most succulents, is undemanding and will thrive with just a modicum of care.*

FAR LEFT: Euphorbia trigona *is an easy-to-grow succulent with distinctive three- to four-sided branches.*

LEFT: Sansevieria trifasciata *'Laurentii' is an attractive variegated plant that is really tough and needs minimal attention.*

Bromeliads

BROMELIADS ARE STRANGE PLANTS. SOME HAVE LEAVES THAT FORM WATER-HOLDING VASES, OTHERS HAVE BRIGHTLY COLOURED LEAVES THAT MAKE A SUBSTITUTE FOR COLOURFUL FLOWERS, AND A FEW ACTUALLY GROW ON AIR AND NEED NO SOIL.

Some bromeliads – aechmeas, vrieseas and guzmanias for example – are grown for their attractive flower heads as well as for their foliage. A few – billbergias, for example – have individual flowers that are both strange and beautiful. The vast majority are best considered as foliage plants. Some, such as neoregelias, form a rosette of leaves that becomes brightly coloured in the centre when the plants flower, others like cryptanthus are prettily variegated. The pineapple is the best-known bromeliad, but it is the variegated forms such as *Ananas comosus* 'Variegatus' that are generally grown as houseplants.

Air plants

A large group of tillandsias are known as air plants because they grow without soil. In nature they drape themselves over branches or even wires, or cling to rocks. One of the most attractive ways to display them is on a bromeliad tree (see opposite), but you can buy them displayed in shells, baskets, or even attached to a mirror with glue. You can also improvise with any suitable containers that you have around the house.

- Mist the plants regularly, especially from spring to autumn. This is the only way that they can receive moisture if the air itself is not sufficiently humid.
- Feed by adding a very dilute liquid fertilizer to the misting water, perhaps once a fortnight, when the plants are actively growing.

CARING FOR BROMELIADS

🐾 Bromeliads need special care. The following advice applies to most kinds, but see the separate instructions for air plant tillandsias.

🐾 Most kinds need only moderate warmth (about 10°C/50°F), but some need 24°C/75° to flower.

🐾 Give them good light, out of direct sun (a few, such as cryptanthus and pineapples, will tolerate full sun).

🐾 Grow in small pots as they don't need much compost (potting soil), and water only when the compost becomes almost dry.

🐾 Use a peat-based compost rather than one with loam, and if possible mix in perlite or sphagnum moss.

🐾 For those that form a 'vase', keep this topped up with water (rainwater in hard-water areas).

🐾 Mist the leaves in summer, and add a foliar feed occasionally. Vase types can have a one-third strength fertilizer added to the vase water every couple of weeks.

ABOVE LEFT: *Most tillandsias are popularly known as air plants because they do not need planting in compost (potting soil). They are very ornamental when mounted on a piece of bark or driftwood.*

LEFT: Neoregelia carolinae *is typical of the 'vase' bromeliads. The central leaves colour when the small flowers appear in the central vase formed by the rosette of leaves.*

OPPOSITE LEFT: Ananas bracteatus striatus *is a variegated version of the pineapple that makes a striking houseplant.*

OPPOSITE RIGHT: *Most guzmanias, like* G. lingulata, *have long-lasting flower heads.*

BELOW: *Aechmea fasciata has weird but beautiful flowers, set off by bold, greyish foliage.*

MAKE A BROMELIAD TREE

🌿 The size and shape of your 'tree' will depend on the space that you have available, a suitable container, and the size of your branch. Choose a forked branch from a tree and saw it to size.

Anchor the branch in the container with stones, bricks or beach pebbles – this will add weight and stability as well as holding the branch upright. Then pour in plaster of Paris or a mortar or concrete mix, to within a couple of centimetres (an inch) of the top of the container. You can set a few empty pots into the plaster or concrete to allow for planting into the base later.

When the plaster or concrete has set, wire your bromeliads to the tree. Remove most of the compost (potting soil) from the roots, and pack some sphagnum moss around them. Secure the roots to the tree with plastic-covered or copper wire. Make sure that you take advantage of any forks in the branch to hold an attractive bromeliad.

Air plant tillandsias such as *T. usneoides* can simply be draped over the branches; other species may have to be wired or glued on.

Flowering houseplants

FLOWERING HOUSEPLANTS ARE USUALLY SHORT-LIVED IN THE HOME, BUT THEY BRING A SPLASH OF COLOUR AND VIBRANCY THAT NOT EVEN COLOURED FOLIAGE CAN ACHIEVE. THEY ALSO ADD AN ELEMENT OF SEASONAL VARIATION THAT FOLIAGE PLANTS LACK.

The most rewarding flowering houseplants are those that grow bigger and better each year, with each subsequent blooming crowning another year of good cultivation and care. Flowers that you should be able to keep growing in the home from year to year include beloperones, bougainvilleas, *Campanula isophylla*, clivias, gardenias, hoyas, *Jasminum polyanthum*, *Nerium oleander*, pelargoniums, saintpaulias, spathiphyllums and streptocarpus.

The disposables

Many flowering pot plants are difficult to keep permanently in the home and are best discarded when flowering has finished (or in some cases placed in a greenhouse if you have one). They are no less valuable indoors, and should be

regarded rather like long-lasting cut flowers. A lot of them are annuals and can, therefore, be inexpensively raised from seed: try browallias, calceolarias, cinerarias and exacums, which are all bright and cheerful, inexpensive to buy and not difficult to raise from seed yourself.

Annuals die after flowering and have to be discarded, but others are just not worth the effort of trying to

LEFT: Begonia elatior *hybrids can be in flower for most months of the year, but plants like the dwarf narcissus 'Tete-a-Tete' are especially welcome because of their seasonal nature.*

BELOW LEFT: *Varieties of* Kalanchoe blossfeldiana *are available in flower the year round.*

BELOW: *Pot-grown lilies make striking houseplants, but it is usually better to buy them in flower rather than try to grow your own from bulbs. Commercial growers can ensure that suitable dwarf varieties are used, and chemicals are often employed to keep the plants compact. Plant them in the garden to flower in future years.*

save in home conditions: impatiens are often leggy if saved, and easy to raise or cheap to buy; Hiemalis begonias quickly deteriorate and are difficult to keep healthy, furthermore, they are so cheap to buy that it's hardly worth taking up valuable space with them once flowering is over. Garden bulbs like hyacinths may bloom beautifully if forced for early flowering, but they will fail to give an acceptable repeat performance and are therefore best put out in the garden to recover and give a garden display in future years.

Hardy border plants such as astilbes are sometimes sold as pot plants. They look magnificent in flower, but the pot of large leaves left afterwards is hardly attractive, and the plant is almost sure to deteriorate if kept indoors. By planting it in the garden after flowering you will have enjoyed plumes of beauty for a few weeks after purchase, then years of pleasure in the garden afterwards.

Tricked into flowering

Some plants are tricked into flowering at a particular time, or into blooming on compact plants. You won't be able to reproduce these conditions in the home. Year-round chrysanthemums are made to bloom every month of the

RIGHT: Saintpaulias are among the most popular flowering plants, and there are so many variations in flower shape, size and colour that you can easily form an interesting collection of them.

BELOW LEFT: Hydrangeas make attractive houseplants if bought in flower, but they do not make easy long-term residents in the home. Try planting them in the garden when they have finished flowering.

BELOW RIGHT: Impatiens have always been popular houseplants, but the New Guinea types have bolder foliage than the older types usually grown. Some also have striking variegated leaves, as a bonus to the pretty flowers.

year by having their day length adjusted by special lighting and by blacking out the greenhouse. They will probably be blooming on compact plants because they have been treated with dwarfing chemicals, the effects of which gradually wear off. If you manage to keep them going, they will become taller and probably flower at a different time. Try planting them in the garden – some varieties will thrive as garden plants if the winters are not too severe.

The poinsettia (*Euphorbia pulcherrima*) is another plant that is controlled by manipulating day length and in which height is also chemically controlled. Some people keep them successfully for future years, but they become taller plants, and the colourful bracts are produced at a different time of year unless their day length is controlled. This can be done by covering with a black polythene bag for fourteen hours a day for eight weeks. It is much easier to buy new plants.

Kalanchoes are also induced to flower outside their normal period by adjusting day length in the same way.

BRIGHT BERRIES

Don't overlook plants with bright berries. These will often remain attractive for much longer than flowers; some of the most popular ones are easily raised from seed and are relatively inexpensive if you have to buy them. Annual peppers (*Capsicum annuum*) have cone-shaped fruits in shades of yellow, red, and purple. *Solanum capsicastrum* has orange or red berries shaped like small tomatoes – and with luck you can keep the plant going for another year, placing it outdoors for the summer. Remember to keep the air humid by misting periodically to prevent berries dropping prematurely.

OPPOSITE ABOVE: *Year-round chrysanthemums make excellent short-term houseplants. They are best bought in bud or flower then enjoyed for a few weeks before being discarded.*

OPPOSITE BELOW: *Berries can be as bright as flowers, and often last for much longer. Those of* Solanum capsicastrum *and* S. pseudocapsicum *and their hybrids look like cherry-sized tomatoes. The plants are usually discarded after flowering but can be kept for another year.*

TOP LEFT: Beloperone guttata *is easy to grow, long-lasting in flower, and you should be able to keep it from year to year.*

TOP RIGHT: Primula obconica *is a delightful houseplant when it is in flower. However, some people have an allergic reaction to the leaves.*

CENTRE RIGHT: *The azalea most commonly sold as a pot plant, and sometimes called* Azalea indica, *is botanically* Rhododendron simsii.

RIGHT: Euphorbia pulcherrima, *the so-called poinsettia, has insignificant true flowers, but really spectacular and colourful bracts to surround them.*

GARDEN ANNUALS

If you have a few spare plants after planting out the summer bedding, it might be worth potting some of them up into larger pots to use indoors. Among those that can make attractive short-term house-plants if the position is light enough are ageratums, lobelias, salvias and French marigolds.

Scent in the air

SCENT ADDS ANOTHER DIMENSION TO YOUR PLANTS, AND IT'S NOT ONLY FLOWERS THAT ARE FRAGRANT. TAKE ANOTHER JOURNEY OF DISCOVERY WITH SOME OF THE AROMATIC HOUSEPLANTS THAT WILL MAKE YOU WONDER WHY YOU EVER USED CHEMICAL AIR FRESHENERS.

ABOVE: *The flowers of* Gardenia jasminoides *are pure white in full bloom, darking to a creamy-yellow with age, and are richly fragrant.*

Perception of scent is an individual experience, and one that is more developed in some individuals than in others. Our ability to detect scents can be affected by the way in which our scent receptors are genetically determined. Some people are scent blind in the same way in which some people are colour blind. They can detect most smells but have a deficiency in certain types: someone who can smell a rose or a sweet pea might be unable to appreciate the equally potent perfume of the freesia. This makes it difficult to recommend specific plants to others without qualification: the plants suggested here have a smell readily detected by most people, but you may find a particular scent weak or even indiscernible.

Scent is further complicated by individual reactions to a scent when it is detected. Sometimes this may be for biochemical reasons, but it may even be that some scents are associated with pleasant or unpleasant experiences. There are scented-leaved geraniums (pelargoniums) that might remind one person of the tangy fragrance of lemons while another may detect a thymol smell in them that reminds them of an earlier visit to a dentist.

The only way to discover whether you like the scent of a particular plant

BELOW LEFT: Datura suaveolens *(syn.* Brugmansia suaveolens*) is a large and magnificent plant, with huge bell-like flowers and a strength of scent that matches the size of the blooms. This variety is 'Grand Marnier'.*

is to grow it and sniff it. You will almost certainly like those suggested below, but if you don't, simply cross them off your list for the future.

Placing scented plants

Plants that have a delicate fragrance, which you have to sniff at close quarters, such as an exacum, need to be positioned where sniffing is easy — perhaps on a table or shelf that you pass in the hall, or as a centrepiece for the dining table.

Plants with a dominant scent, like gardenias and hyacinths, can be so potent that one plant will fill the whole room with scent. It doesn't matter where you place these in the room, but avoid other fragrant plants that may conflict with them; place these in another room where you can appreciate their own distinct fragrances in isolation.

ABOVE: Stephanotis floribunda *is a very fragrant climber that can be grown as a pot plant while young.*

ABOVE CENTRE: *A bowl of hyacinths will fill a room with scent. Although they are at their best for perhaps a week, by planting different varieties, and using ordinary bulbs and those specially treated for early flowering, you can enjoy them over a period of months.*

ABOVE RIGHT: *Scented-leaved geraniums (pelargoniums) usually have insignificant flowers. Grow them for their aromatic foliage and position them where you might accidentally brush against them, or can touch the leaves to release their pungent fragrance. This is* Pelargonium graveolens, *with a scent reminiscent of lemons.*

BELOW: *Oranges make superb conservatory plants, and can be brought into the house for short spells.*

FRAGRANT FOLIAGE

Some of the best plants to grow for fragrant foliage are the scented-leaved geraniums (pelargoniums). These are just of few of them:
P. *capitatum* (rose-scented)
P. *crispum* (lemon-scented)
P. *graveolens* (slightly lemony)
P. *odoratissimum* (apple-scented)
P. *tomentosum* (peppermint-scented)

Plants that you have to touch or brush against to release the scent, like scented-leaved geraniums (pelargoniums), should be placed where you might come into contact with them accidentally, or intentionally, as you pass: alcoves or windows by a flight of stairs and on the kitchen table or worktop, for example.

SCENTED FLOWERS

Citrus (fragrant flowers, citrus-scented foliage and fruit)
Datura suaveolens
Exacum affine
Hyacinths
Hymenocallis × *festalis, H. narcissiflora*
Jasminum officinale
Narcissus 'Paperwhite'
Stephanotis floribunda

Orchids and other exotics

ADD A TOUCH OF CLASS TO YOUR COLLECTION OF HOUSEPLANTS BY GROWING
A FEW ORCHIDS, ALONG WITH OTHER EXOTICS, SUCH AS STRELITZIA, THE
'BIRD OF PARADISE FLOWER'.

Orchids have a reputation for being difficult to grow and, consequently, many people are deterred from trying them as houseplants. If you choose the right types, however, they are relatively undemanding and should make larger and more impressive clumps each year.

The drawback to orchids is the contrast between the beauty of their exotic flowers and the rather ungainly foliage with which you have to live for the other ten or eleven months of the year. The best way to grow them is to stand the plants in a sheltered and partially shaded spot in the garden during the summer — or better still in a conservatory if you have one — and then to bring them indoors for the winter or when they are coming into flower.

Easy orchids
The best orchids to start with are cymbidium hybrids, which are easy to grow, readily available and inexpensive to buy if you are not fussy about a particular variety.

Miltonias are a better choice if you want a more compact plant. The large, flat, pansy-like flowers come in a range of brilliant colours, and will often last for a month.

Cypripediums (paphiopedilums) are another group of distinctive and easy orchids to try. Sometimes called slipper orchids, the bottom petals form a slipper-shaped pouch.

Other orchids can be grown indoors, especially if you are able to create a special area for them, perhaps with artificial light, but it is best to gain experience first with the easy genera described above.

Other exotics
Try some of the following exotic-looking flowering plants that will bring some of the brilliance and flamboyance of the tropics to your home.

Anthuriums have vivid pink, red or orange 'flowers' that will never be ignored. The 'flower' is actually a spathe and it is the curly tail-like spadix that contains the true flowers. The 'flowers' are long-lasting and the foliage is attractive too.

Bougainvilleas are at their best climbing into the roof of a conservatory, but you could try one in a porch or light window. The bright 'flowers' are actually papery bracts. Prune after flowering and keep cool but frost-free for the winter.

Grooming orchids
With age, orchid leaves often become blemished. If the damage is towards the end of the leaf, try cutting it away. Angle the cut to make the end a more natural shape than if cut at right-angles.

Daturas are big plants, really at their best in a conservatory, although you can use small plants indoors. The huge bell-like flowers are usually white, pink or yellowish, depending on the species and variety. The heady scent matches the magnificence of the blooms, and even a single flower can almost fill a small house with scent in the evening.

Hibiscus rosa-sinensis grows into quite a large shrub but can be bought as a small plant. The blooms are big and beautiful: 10cm (4in) or more across, in shades of red, yellow and almost orange.

Strelitzias are sometimes called 'bird of paradise flowers' because the orange and blue flowers are thought to resemble the head of an exotic-looking bird. The leaves are often 1m (3ft) or more tall, and a large plant is truly spectacular.

How to Grow Orchids

It is best to check the specific requirements for each species, but the following rules apply to most:

Place them in a very light position, but not in direct, strong sunlight.

Provide plenty of humidity. Stand the pots on a gravel tray, or mist regularly. Small plants do well in an enclosed plant case.

Avoid draughts, but provide plenty of ventilation. Move them away from a cold window at night.

Repot only when the pot is full of roots. Always use a special potting mixture recommended for orchids (you may have to buy it from a specialist nursery).

Feed regularly during the summer.

Stand the plants outdoors in a sheltered position for the summer if you don't have a conservatory to put them in.

Water only when the compost (potting soil) is almost dry.

OPPOSITE TOP: Strelitzia reginae, *the 'bird of paradise flower', never fails to impress with its flamboyant flowers.*

OPPOSITE CENTRE: *The red or pink 'petals' that surround the insignificant proper flowers of the striking anthuriums are in fact modified leaves.*

TOP: *Bougainvilleas have a really exotic look, and although they are climbers can be used as a houseplant while small. Larger plants are best in a conservatory.*

ABOVE: *Phalaenopsis orchids will flower in most months of the year, but they are not easy plants to grow in the home.*

ABOVE RIGHT: *Cymbidiums are among the easiest orchids to grow in the house, but even so they usually benefit from a spell outdoors or in the greenhouse during the summer months.*

RIGHT: Hibiscus rosa-sinensis *blooms are big, bold and bright; they seldom fail to attract attention.*

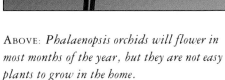

Fun plants

SOME PLANTS ARE ENTERTAINING OR EDUCATIONAL RATHER THAN BEAUTI-

FUL. THEY ARE A GOOD WAY TO INSTILL CHILDREN WITH AN APPRECIATION

OF PLANTS, BUT SOME OF THEM MAKE INTERESTING HOUSEPLANTS TOO.

Carnivorous plants always fascinate children. Few of them are beautiful, though some have quite pretty flowers. *Pinguicula grandiflora* has pretty pink flowers like violets on long stalks that seem to last for weeks. Most have uninteresting flowers, however, and their attraction lies solely in the various forms of trap.

Some cannot be grown satisfactorily in the home, but the following are worth trying: *Dionaea muscipula* (a snap trap), *Drosera capensis* (an adhesive trap), *Pinguicula grandiflora* (a 'fly paper' trap), and *Sarracenia flava* (a pitfall trap). Enthusiasts grow dozens of different kinds, but these represent four different types of trap and all make quite acceptable houseplants, though they must be treated with care if they are not to be short-lived.

Sensitive plants

Several plants are sensitive to touch, collapsing on contact. The most widely available one is *Mimosa pudica*, which makes quite a pretty plant with its sensitive leaflets and attractive flowers like pink balls. It's easy to raise from seed if you can't find plants in local nurseries or garden centres.

Leaves that bear 'babies'

Some plants have the ability to produce small plantlets on the leaves, which eventually fall and root (or you can speed things up by removing them and potting them up).

Two that are quite widely available are *Kalanchoe daigremontiana* (syn. *Bryophyllum daigremontianum*), which has miniature plants all around the edge of the leaf, and *K. tubiflora* (syn.

Bryophyllum tubiflorum), which produces them in clusters at the ends of the leaves.

Other widely available plants that produce ready-made 'babies' are the fern *Asplenium bulbiferum* and *Tolmiea menziesii* (young plantlets form at the base of mature leaves).

Bulbs that flower without soil

For a novelty, try flowering colchicums 'dry'. You can just stand them on the windowsill after purchase, but for stability it is best to place them on a saucer of sand. Usually within weeks, the large crocus-like flowers emerge from the dry bulb.

An unusual bulb called *Sauromatum venosum* (syn. *S. guttatum*) is sometimes sold as a novelty for flowering 'dry' (treat like the colchicums). The tube-like flower that eventually emerges is a sinister greenish-purple. This strange flower will soon make its presence known by the awful stench of carrion – fascinating for children, but not something to have in your living-room for long!

OPPOSITE ABOVE: Colchicum autumnale *can be grown 'dry'. Either stand the corms directly on a windowsill or place them in a saucer of sand or pebbles for stability, and wait just a few weeks for the large crocus-like flowers to emerge.*

OPPOSITE BELOW: Dionaea muscipula *is a carnivorous plant with a snap trap that quickly closes over its prey.*

TOP RIGHT: Sarracenia flava *is a carnivorous plant with a pitfall trap.*

CENTRE RIGHT: Drosera capensis *is an example of an adhesive trap, and makes an interesting addition to a collection of carnivorous plants.*

LEFT AND ABOVE: Kalanchoe daigremontiana *(syn.* Bryophyllum daigremontianum*) produces plantlets along the edges of its leaves (left). These often*

CARING FOR CARNIVOROUS PLANTS

🦋 Don't use an ordinary potting compost. It needs to be acidic and low in soluble minerals. A suitable compost (medium) usually includes peat (peat moss), sand, sphagnum moss, and sometimes perlite or finely chipped bark.

🦋 Grow a collection of them in a plant case or old aquarium. Cover it if possible, to create a humid environment.

🦋 Provide good light.

🦋 Stand the pots on trays of gravel filled with water to provide humidity if not in an enclosed environment.

🦋 Some species prefer a constantly wet compost and you can stand these in a saucer that is kept topped up with water (not advisable for normal houseplants).

🦋 Only ever use soft water (distilled or deionized would do, but rain-water is best).

🦋 It is best not to use a fertilizer. Most may be harmful, and if you think the plants really do need feeding, try misting them with a foliar feed made up at quarter strength, about once a fortnight during the period of active growth.

🦋 These plants catch prey to obtain nutrients, but indoors the number of insects available to them will be limited. Some people release fruit flies near them or feed them with fly maggots (often available from fishing tackle shops).

fall and root into the compost (potting soil) around the parent plant, but you can easily remove them to pot up for a supply of plants to give to friends (above left).

Caring for houseplants

If you want your houseplants to thrive, they need caring for and nurturing. You have to choose and buy wisely, understand the needs of individual plants and make grooming a regular job, just like watering and feeding.

Shopping for houseplants

SHOPPING FOR NEW AND INTERESTING HOUSEPLANTS CAN BE FUN, BUT BE WARY ABOUT WHERE AND WHEN YOU BUY. A PLANT THAT HAS BEEN POORLY TREATED BEFORE YOU BUY IT MAY ONLY REVEAL THE ILL-TREATMENT AFTER YOU GET IT HOME.

Choosing houseplants requires as much thought and care as the purchase of anything else for the home. Indeed, some plants will be with you for much longer than many household items.

You can buy a plant simply because you like the look of it, then try to find a suitable spot; or decide what you need to fill a particular niche in the home, before going out to buy an appropriate plant. The latter is undoubtedly the theoretical ideal, but it overlooks reality.

Except for the most common houseplants, the chances of finding a particular plant, even over several shopping trips, is not great and, more importantly, you may overlook a beautiful plant that you hadn't previously considered. Part of the fun of growing plants is to come across unexpected discoveries, plants that you've never seen before. Although advance planning is desirable, never be deterred from the impulse buy of something interesting or unusual, especially if you are prepared for a few failures along the way.

Where to buy

For everyday houseplants, a garden centre is often the best place to buy: there is likely to be a reasonable selection of 'basic' houseplants, and usually at least a few uncommon kinds. Most importantly, they will almost certainly be in conditions similar to a greenhouse: good light, warmth (ventilated in summer), with a buoyant and humid atmosphere. Staff are also

ABOVE: *Try to buy your houseplants from a nursery or garden centre where they have excellent growing conditions in good light.*

GETTING THEM HOME

🪴 Buy your plants last, immediately before you go home.

🪴 Don't put plants in a hot car boot (trunk), especially if you don't plan to drive straight home, or if the drive is a long one.

🪴 Make sure that they are wrapped in a protective sleeve if carrying them home by public transport. This will protect them from cold and wind, and guard against knocks.

usually knowledgeable, but beware of assuming that part-time or temporary staff know more than you do!

Florists also sell pot plants but, except for the very largest shops, the range is inevitably limited and conditions are seldom good. Some florists have pavement displays outside the shop, in which they include pot plants as well as cut flowers. Avoid these: you run the same risks as with market stalls (outdoor stands), where at least the price is usually cheaper.

Some large stores sell a limited range of plants. At the best of them the quality is excellent, with the plants well looked after and removed from sale if not bought within a certain time. In others they can languish in poor light and with inadequate care, slowly deteriorating until they reach the point of death. The quality and condition of plants sold by ordinary shops or home-improvement stores vary enormously. Go through the *Buyer's checklist* below carefully before buying from these sources.

Market stalls often sell plants at very competitive prices, and they are usually sold quickly, so it is possible to obtain quality plants cheaply if you don't mind the limited range. Beware of buying in cold weather – especially in winter. The chill plants receive, having come out of hot-house conditions, may not be obvious until a few days after you get them home, when the leaves start to drop. Even in the summer, houseplants displayed outdoors can suffer a severe check to growth if the weather is cold or windy.

Buyer's checklist

● Check the compost (potting soil). If it has dried out the plants have been neglected. Don't buy.
● Lift and check the base of the pot. If lots of roots are coming out of the bottom, the plant should have been repotted sooner. A few small roots through the bottom of the pot is not a sign of neglect, and is normal where the plants have been grown on capillary matting.

- If buying a flowering plant, make sure that there are still plenty of buds to open, otherwise the display may be brief.
- Look critically at the shape. If growth is lop-sided, or the plant is bare at the base, choose another.
- Make sure the plant is labelled. A label should tell you how to care for the plant, and unlabelled plants suggest a lack of concern for plants and customers.
- Avoid plants with damaged or broken leaves.
- Don't be afraid to turn the leaves over. Look for signs of pests and diseases. If you find any, leave them in the shop!
- If the plants are displayed in a protective sleeve, don't buy unless you can remove your potential purchase for inspection. Display sleeves can hide all kinds of horrors, such as rots and diseases, pests, and even a sparse or poorly shaped plant.

Protective sleeves
These can be useful: they help to get the plant home with minimum damage and offer some protection from cold winds in winter. But make sure they don't hide damaged or diseased leaves. Be prepared to remove the sleeve to examine a plant if they are displayed in this way.

Root check
It is natural for a few roots to grow through the bottom of the pot, especially if a capillary watering system has been used (which is normal in plant nurseries), but a mass of roots growing through the pot is probably a sign that it needs repotting.

Flowering plants
When buying a flowering plant, make sure that there are plenty of buds still to open. A plant in full flower may be more spectacular initially, but the display will be shorter.

Pests and diseases
Examine the undersides of a few leaves to make sure they are free of pests and diseases before you buy.

Pot sizes

Houseplants look better, and will grow better, if they are in a pot of an appropriate size. The plant in the picture at the top of the page is in a pot that's too large – it dominates the plant. The one shown above is in a pot that's too small; not only is it top-heavy and unstable, but the amount of compost (potting soil) in the pot is unlikely to be sufficient to sustain the plant.

Creating the right environment

IT'S IMPOSSIBLE TO RECREATE THE ATMOSPHERE OF A SOUTH AMERICAN RAINFOREST OR THE SEMI-DESERT CONDITIONS OF THE WORLD'S MORE ARID REGIONS IN OUR HOMES. YET WE EXPECT ORCHIDS AND BROMELIADS TO THRIVE ALONGSIDE CACTI AND SUCCULENTS, PLANTS FROM THE WORLD'S WARMEST REGIONS TO COEXIST WITH HARDY PLANTS SUCH AS IVIES AND AUCUBAS. CREATING THE RIGHT CONDITIONS TO SUIT SUCH A DIVERSITY OF PLANTS, WHILST KEEPING A HOME THAT'S ALSO COMFORTABLE TO LIVE IN, CALLS FOR INGENUITY AND A DASH OF COMPROMISE.

Use the advice on labels and in books as a guide to the best conditions in which to keep your plants. In reality you may not be able to accommodate all the conditions listed as desirable, but most plants will still survive even if they do not thrive. Take recommendations for humidity seriously: a plant that requires very high humidity is likely to die soon in very dry air. Recommendations regarding light and shade are important but if you get this slightly wrong the consequence is more likely to be poor variegation, perhaps scorch marks on the leaves, or drawn and lanky plants, rather than dead ones. You can usually correct the problem by moving the plant.

Temperature is the most flexible requirement, and most plants will tolerate a wide fluctuation above or below the suggested targets.

Temperature
Treat with caution advice in books and on labels that gives a precise temperature range. Most plants will survive temperatures much lower than the ones normally recommended, and, in winter when the light is poor, a high temperature may stimulate growth that can't be supported by the light levels. Upper temperature figures are meaningless unless you have air conditioning. In summer the outside temperature often rises above those recommended for particular plants, and unless you have some way of cooling the air, the plants will have to suffer the heat along with you. They will almost certainly come to no harm if shaded from direct sun and provided that the humidity is high enough.

Once the temperature drops towards freezing, however, most houseplants are at risk. Even in a centrally heated home, temperatures can drop very low if heating is turned off at night.

Light and shade
The best position for most plants is in good light but out of direct sun. Even plants that thrive in sun outdoors may resent the strongly magnified rays through glass, which will often scorch the leaves. Be especially wary of positioning plants behind patterned glass in full sun: the pattern can magnify the sun's rays.

Only plants that normally grow in deserts, on steppes, high mountains and barren moors grow in areas devoid of shade. And even these may not like the sun's rays intensified through glass. If possible, fit shades that you can use for the hottest part of the day. Even net curtains are useful in screening out some of the strongest rays.

The so-called shade plants do not like any direct sun, but that does not necessarily mean that they will grow in gloom. The eye is deceptive when it comes to judging light levels. Use a camera fitted with a light meter, and measure the light in different parts of the room. You might discover that the light is as poor immediately above or below a window as it is in the centre of the room. If the windows are high, experiment with the light meter to see how much better the light might be if

Effects of heat
Leaf scorch (brown marks or blotches that leave the areas looking thin and papery) is a common problem on plants placed on a very sunny windowsill. Unless they are adapted to this kind of intense heat, the tissue of the leaves can be damaged. The problem is most likely if drops of water are left on the foliage in bright sunlight (the water acts like a magnifying glass) or where patterned glass intensifies the sun's rays as it acts like a lens.

KEEPING THEM INSULATED

🐛 The greatest dangers to plants are cold draughts, especially at night when the temperature drops and the heating is turned off, and frost. Take precautions to keep them insulated:

🐛 Move plants into the room when you pull the curtains – don't leave them trapped between curtains and glass, where the temperature can drop dramatically.

🐛 If you have to leave plants by a window on a cold night, try insulating them with sheets of polystyrene (styrofoam) placed against the lower half of the window.

you raised a plant on a pedestal or positioned it on a low table.

Humidity

Humidity – or the amount of moisture present in the air at a given temperature – is important to all plants, but especially those with thin or delicate leaves, such as ferns, selaginellas and caladiums. Grow those plants that need a very humid atmosphere in a bottle garden or plant case, or mist the plants frequently (at least once a day, more often if possible).

For less demanding plants that still need high humidity, grow them in groups to create a microclimate or stand the plants on gravel, pebbles or marbles in a shallow dish containing water. Provided that the bottom of the pot is not in direct contact with the water the air will be humid without the compost becoming waterlogged. Misting is still desirable, but if the plants are in flower shield the blooms while you do so, otherwise the petals may become marked or begin to rot.

Simple humidity trays to place over radiators are inexpensive and help to create a more buoyant atmosphere for houseplants.

ABOVE: *Plants like schizanthus and cinerarias will make a super show if you can provide good light and humid conditions.*

Increasing humidity
It can be difficult to create a humid environment in the home, but a small microclimate can be created around the plant. Standing the plant over a dish containing water will increase the humidity, but the pot must be stood on small pebbles or marbles to keep it above water level and avoid waterlogged compost (potting soil).

Misting foliage plants
The majority of houseplants will benefit from misting with water. If you can do it daily the plants will almost certainly grow better. Delicate ferns that need a very high humidity may need misting several times a day for really good results.

Misting flowering plants
Although the foliage benefits from misting, water can damage delicate flowers. Simply protect the blooms with a piece of paper or cardboard if the plant is in flower.

Windowsill plants

WINDOWSILLS ARE A FAVOURITE POSITION FOR HOUSEPLANTS, BUT YOU NEED TO CHOOSE PLANTS APPROPRIATE TO THE ASPECT. NOT ALL PLANTS APPRECIATE A BAKING IN THE SUNSHINE.

ABOVE: Hoya carnosa *is a pretty climber or trailer for a sunny position. It is usually grown for its white flowers, but the variegated 'Tricolor' also makes an attractive foliage plant.*

It is a good idea to analyse the amount of direct light coming through each window before deciding on the best spots for various plants with different light needs. Large windows obviously let in most light, but it will still be less than outdoors, and the larger the area of glass, the more rapidly temperatures drop at night.

The majority of plants flourish best when placed in good light in a position that is shaded from the direct rays of the sun. There are bound to be some rooms that receive little direct light, but most will receive some sun at least in the morning or evening. Except for shade lovers that are particularly vulnerable to direct sun, the majority of plants will benefit from this as the strength of the sun is generally weaker in the early morning and evening, so leaf scorch is less likely. The compost (potting soil) is also less likely to dry out rapidly if the sun has moved around before its midday peak.

Very sunny windows can still be packed with interest if you select the plants carefully, but be prepared to keep the compost well watered in warm weather. Avoid splashing the leaves when the sun is on them, however, as the droplets of water can act like a further magnifying glass and scorch the leaves.

The lists of suggested plants given here are not definitive, but an example of what can be grown. Be prepared to experiment with many more, especially on a light windowsill that does not receive fierce direct sun.

Where only the genus is mentioned, all the widely available species sold as houseplants should be successful.

You will find some plants listed in more than one group. Many plants will grow in sun or partial shade and a few will do well in both direct sun and indirect light.

Plants for a very sunny window

Ananas, cacti, ceropegia, chlorophytum, coleus, geraniums (pelargoniums), regal, zonal, scented-leaved, gerbera, hippeastrum, *Hoya carnosa*, hypocyrta, impatiens, iresine, *Kalanchoe blossfeldiana* and hybrids, nerium, *Plectranthus fruticosus*, sansevieria, setcreasea, stapelia, succulents (most), yucca and zebrina.

Plants for a window that receives early or late sun

Aechmea, aglaonema, anthurium, aphelandra, begonia, beloperone, billbergia, caladium, calathea, capsicum, chlorophytum, chrysanthemum, cocos, codiaeum, coleus, *Cordyline terminalis* (syn. *C. fruticosa*) and varieties, crossandra, cuphea, ficus (most), gardenia, gynura, hoya, impatiens, maranta, nertera, *Plectranthus oertendahlii*, rhipsalidopsis, saintpaulia, sansevieria, sinningia, solanum, spathiphyllum, tolmiea, tradescantia, zebrina.

Plants for a light window out of direct sunlight

Adiantum, aglaonema, anthurium, asparagus, aspidistra, asplenium, billbergia, calathea, chlorophytum, clivia, dieffenbachia, dracaena, ferns, *Ficus deltoidea*, *Ficus pumila*, hydrangea, maranta, orchids, saintpaulia, sansevieria, selaginella, soleirolia (syn. helxine), spathiphyllum.

ABOVE: Aphelandra squarrosa *needs good light but not direct summer sun. Grow it where it just receives early or late sun in the summer and in the best light possible in winter.*

ABOVE: *Gerberas will tolerate a very sunny position, but if you plan to discard the plant after flowering you can use it to brighten up dull spots too.*

ABOVE: Mammillaria elongata, *like most cacti, will thrive in a hot, sunny position.*

ABOVE: Calathea zebrina *is best in a light position that receives early or late sun, but not direct midday sun.*

ABOVE: Aglaonema *'Silver Queen' grows well in semi-shade or bright light, but avoid direct midday sun.*

ABOVE: Yucca elephantipes *benefits from as much light as possible. It will enjoy a hot, sunny position.*

BELOW: Zygocactus (Schlumbergera) *hybrids are forest cacti, best grown in good light shaded from direct sunlight.*

ABOVE: Aechmea fasciata *is grown mainly for its fascinating flower spike. Because it grows naturally in trees, it is not adapted to life on a very hot, sunny windowsill. Position it where it receives early or late sun.*

ABOVE: Sansevieria trifasciata *'Laurentii' is one of those tough plants that will do well on any windowsill, in shade or full sun.*

RIGHT: Kalanchoe blossfeldiana *hybrids do well on a sunny windowsill.*

Shady spots

PLANTS THAT TOLERATE SHADE ARE PARTICULARLY USEFUL, ESPECIALLY IF YOU NEED FOCAL POINT PLANTS FOR DIFFICULT POSITIONS WITHIN THE ROOM. LARGE SPECIMEN PLANTS ARE USUALLY TOO LARGE FOR A WINDOW-SILL SO THESE HAVE TO COMBINE SIZE WITH SHADE TOLERANCE.

It is a mistake to position a plant purely for decorative effect, and you should always choose a spot that the plant will at least tolerate even if it doesn't thrive. For really inhospitable corners where it's just too dark even for shade lovers, use disposable flowering plants, or even ferns if you are prepared to discard them after a couple of months.

In winter, plants are unlikely to tolerate a light intensity less than 1,000 lux, and 5,000 lux in summer is about the minimum for foliage plants such as aspidistras and *Cissus rhombifolia* (syn. *Rhoicissus rhomboidea*). These are meaningless figures unless you have a way of measuring light, but fortunately there is a simple rough-and-ready way that can be used. Two methods of judging light levels are described in *How to Assess Light* (opposite).

ABOVE: Aglaonema *'Silver Queen' is undemanding and useful for low-light areas.*

ABOVE: Aucuba japonica *varieties are not only shade-tolerant but cold-tolerant too. They are frost-hardy, so choose them for a position that has both low light levels and low temperatures in winter.*

ABOVE: Ficus pumila *is a low-growing trailer that would soon die on a sunny window. The variegated varieties are more attractive than the all-green species.*

ABOVE: Fatsia japonica *is a garden shrub hardy enough to grow outside except in very cold regions, but indoors the variegated form is more attractive. Choose it for a low light area where temperatures also drop in the winter.*

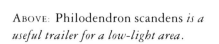

ABOVE: Philodendron scandens *is a useful trailer for a low-light area.*

ABOVE: Helxine soleirolii, *also sold as* Solierolia soleirolii, *is a tough carpeter that will tolerate low light and cool temperatures (it will even stand some frost). There are green, silver and golden forms.*

ABOVE: Adiantum capillus-veneris *will not tolerate a hot, sunny position for long. It will be much happier in a humid and shaded conservatory.*

ABOVE: Ivies (*varieties of* Hedera helix) *grow happily in the wild in sun or shade, and they will do the same in the home. If possible provide bright conditions in winter and avoid direct sunlight in summer.*

ABOVE: Fittonia verschaffeltii *is one of the more difficult foliage plants to try. It will be short-lived in direct sunlight.*

ABOVE: Scindapsus aureus, *also sold as* Epipremnum aureum, *is a trailer or climber that will do well in low-light areas. This golden form is particularly bright, but in time the leaves become more green and less colourful.*

ABOVE: Pellaea rotundifolia *does not demand such a humid atmosphere as most ferns; a light window out of direct sunlight is ideal.*

ABOVE: Asplenium nidus *is one of the easiest ferns to grow.*

HOW TO ASSESS THE LIGHT

Use a camera with a built-in light meter, and set it to a 100 ISO (ASA) film speed and 1/125 second shutter speed. Take the reading at about midday on a bright day in late spring or early summer. Position the camera where you want to place the plant, and point it towards the window.

Read off the aperture setting then use the following as a rough guide to the light level:

f16 or more = Strong light, suitable for those plants that need the best light.

f8–11 = Equivalent to screened daylight, and suitable for those plants that like good light but not strong direct sunlight.

f4–5.6 = Poor light, only suitable for those plants adapted to shade.

f2.8 = Suitable for only the most shade-tolerant species, and plants may not survive in the winter months.

Another test is to try reading a newspaper where you plan to position the plant. Assuming that you have good eyesight, the position is too dark for plants if you can't read the newspaper comfortably.

Plants for poor light
Aglaonema, araucaria, asplenium, aspidistra, aucuba, bulbs (such as hyacinths), but keep in good light until flowering starts, *Cissus rhombifolia* (syn. *Rhoicissus rhomboidea*) × Fatshedera, fatsia, ferns (most), *Ficus pumila*, fittonia, *Hedera helix* (ivy), palms (most), *Philodendron scandens*, pteris, sansevieria, *Scindapsus aureus* (syn. *Epipremnum aureum, Rhaphidophora aurea*), but be prepared for it to lose most of its variegation, *Soleirolia soleirolii* (syn. *Helxine soleirolii*).

Watering

NO PLANT CAN SURVIVE WITHOUT WATER, YET MORE PLANTS PROBABLY DIE
FROM OVERWATERING THAN FROM UNDERWATERING. GETTING TO GRIPS
WITH THIS APPARENTLY SIMPLE PROCEDURE IS ONE OF THE ESSENTIALS OF
GOOD PLANT CARE.

Meters and indicator strips that are pushed into the compost help to put some kind of measurement to the amount of moisture available in the compost, but are impractical if you have a lot of houseplants. You will soon tire of pushing a probe into each pot or reading indicators left in each one. These devices are best used by beginners still gaining experience of how to judge the moisture content by other means.

How much water?
There are no fixed rules about watering. How much a plant needs, and how often, depends not only on the plant but also the kind of pot (clay pots need watering more often than plastic ones), the compost (potting soil), (peat-based composts retain more water than loam-based), and the temperature and humidity.

Watering is an acquired skill, and one that needs to be practised on an almost daily basis, otherwise it is best to switch to self-watering containers or hydroponically grown plants.

Useful techniques
Examine the pots daily if possible, using whichever of the following techniques you find the most convenient:

- Appearance alone can be a guide. Dry, loam-based composts (potting soils) look paler than when they are moist. A dry surface does not mean that the compost is dry lower down, but if it looks damp you know that you don't need to water. If the plant is placed in a saucer, see if there is any standing water. Apart from bog plants, never add more water if there is any trace still left in the saucer.
- The touch test is useful for a peat-based compost. Press a finger gently into the surface – you will know immediately if it feels very dry or very wet.
- The bell test is useful for clay pots, especially large ones containing specimen plants and that hold a large volume of compost. Push a cotton reel onto a short garden cane

Watering from above
A small watering-can is still the most popular way to water houseplants. Choose one that is well-balanced to hold and with a long, narrow spout that makes it easy to direct the water to the compost (potting soil) rather than over the plant.

Compost (potting soil) check
If you use a clay pot, it will ring with a hollow sound if you tap it with a cotton reel on a cane or pencil and the compost is dry. If the compost is still moist the sound will be duller. With a little experience you will be able to detect the difference.

and tap the pot: a dull thud indicates moist compost (although it could also indicate a cracked pot!), a clear ring suggests dry compost. This doesn't work well with peat-based composts, and not at all with plastic pots.
- With practice you can tell when the compost is dry simply by lifting the pot slightly: a pot with dry compost will feel much lighter than one with moist compost.

How to water

When you water, fill the pot to the brim – dribbles are not sufficient. If the root-ball has completely dried out, water may run straight through, down the inside of the pot, in which case stand the pot in a bucket of water until the air bubbles stop rising.

After watering, always check whether surplus water is sitting in the saucer or cache-pot. This will not matter if there are pebbles or marbles to keep the bottom of the pot out of contact with the moisture, but otherwise you must tip out the extra water. *Failure to tip out standing water is the most common cause of failure.* With just a few exceptions, if you leave most ordinary houseplants standing in water for long, they will probably die.

A long-necked watering-can is the most convenient way to water the majority of houseplants. The long neck makes it easy to reach among the leaves, and a narrow spout makes it easier to control the flow, which is also less forceful and unlikely to wash the compost (potting soil) away.

Watering with a can means that you may wet the leaves and crown of ground-hugging plants such as saintpaulias, and unless you are careful this can encourage rotting. For plants like this you may prefer to stand them in a bowl with a few centimetres (inches) of water in the bottom. Remove and allow to drain as soon as the surface of the compost becomes moist. You will probably find it less trouble, however, to be careful with a long-necked watering-can, getting the spout beneath the leaves.

Special needs

Tap water is far from ideal, but the vast majority of houseplants will tolerate it. If the water is hard (has a high calcium or magnesium content), however, you need to make special arrangements for plants that react badly to alkaline soil or compost. These include aphelandras, azaleas, hydrangeas, orchids, rhododendrons and saintpaulias. Rain-water is usually recommended for these plants, but a good supply is not always available throughout the year, and in some areas it can be polluted.

If your tap water is only slightly hard, simply filling the watering cans the day before and allowing the water to stand overnight may be sufficient. For harder water, try boiling it: part of the hardness will be deposited in the form of scale, and you can use the water once it has cooled.

Many water softeners work on a principle that unfortunately does not help the plants: if you want to benefit the plants, a demineralization system is necessary, which removes all the minerals and leaves distilled water. However, it is only worth the expense if you have a lot of plants.

Underwatering

If a plant wilts or collapses like this (top) it can usually be revived by standing the pot in a bowl of water for a few hours, then leaving it in a cool, shady position for a day. By the next day it will probably be as perky as before (above). Always make sure that the compost (potting soil) is dry before doing this, as an overwatered plant will also wilt.

Watering the outer pot
Just a few plants tolerate standing with their roots in water, like this cyperus. With these you can add water to the saucer or outer container, but never do this unless you know the plant grows naturally in marshy places.

Self-watering pots
If you find watering a chore, self-watering pots may be the answer. The moisture is drawn up into the compost (potting soil) through wicks from a reservoir below, and you will need to water much less frequently.

Overwatering
Before an overwatered plant reaches the stage of collapsing, it will probably begin to look sickly. The plant on the left has been overwatered, the one on the right has received the correct amount of water.

Feeding

FEEDING CAN MAKE THE DIFFERENCE BETWEEN A PLANT THAT SIMPLY EXISTS

AND SEEMS TO 'STAND STILL', AND ONE THAT LOOKS HEALTHY AND VIGOROUS

AND REALLY FLOURISHES. MODERN FERTILIZERS HAVE MADE FEEDING REALLY

EASY, AND NOW IT ISN'T EVEN A CHORE THAT YOU HAVE TO REMEMBER ON A

REGULAR BASIS.

Houseplants are handicapped simply by being contained in a pot. The volume of soil or compost that the roots can explore is strictly limited, and sometimes we expect the same compost to support a large plant for many years.

With a few exceptions, your plants will look better if you feed them. You can buy special fertilizers for flowering plants, foliage plants and even special groups such as saintpaulias, but if you want to keep things simple and use one type of feed for all your plants they will still respond better than if they hadn't been fed at all.

When to feed
If in doubt about a particular plant, check the label or look it up in a book. As a general rule, however, plants should be fed only when they are growing actively and when light and temperature are such that they can actually take advantage of the additional nutrients. This generally means between mid-spring and mid-autumn, but there are exceptions – notably with winter-flowering plants.

Cyclamen are fed during the winter as well as before, and the winter- and spring-flowering forest cacti are fed during the winter but rested in summer. The rule of 'active growth' is more important than the time of year.

Controlled-release fertilizers (see top right) are useful for houseplants, but bear in mind that they are influenced by temperature, so they won't stop releasing nutrients in winter as they would outdoors.

How often to apply
Some trial and error is inevitable. Books and plant labels often give advice like 'feed once a fortnight' or 'feed weekly', but with so many different formulations available such advice may be inappropriate. It assumes a typical liquid houseplant feed. Do not follow this advice too closely if you use one of the other types.

Controlled- and slow-release fertilizers
These are widely used commercially, especially for outdoor container-grown plants, and also for pot plants to keep them healthy until sale. Unlike ordinary fertilizers, the nutrients are released slowly over a period of months, so a couple of applications in a year is all that most plants require.

Controlled-release fertilizers are most useful for outdoor plants because they release the nutrients only when the soil temperature is high enough for the plants to make use of them.

Slow-release fertilizers are most useful for houseplants as a compost (potting soil) additive when potting up an established plant.

Why feed?
These two *Rhoicissus rhomboidea* are the same age and were the same size when bought. The plant on the left has been fed regularly and repotted once; the one on the right has not been fed and shows typical signs of starvation.

Slow-release fertilizers
Slow-release fertilizers are worth adding to the compost (potting soil) because they sustain the plants over a period of perhaps six months. The nutrients in many peat-based (peat-moss based) or peat-substitute composts may become depleted within weeks or perhaps a couple of months.

Liquid feeds
Liquid fertilizers are quick-acting, and useful when a plant needs an immediate boost. Strengths and dilutions vary, so *always follow the manufacturer's advice* for rate and frequency of application. Some are weak and designed to be used at almost every watering, others are very strong and should be applied less frequently.

Pellets and sticks
There are various products designed to take the chore out of regular feeding. These will save you a lot of time and trouble in comparison with liquid feeds, although they may work out more expensive in the long run. Some

---

Don't Over-feed
🐾 Because some feeding is good does not mean that more feeding is better. Do not apply more than the manufacturer recommends, otherwise you might kill your plants. Salts build up in the compost (potting soil) and can affect the intake of water and nutrients which, coupled with an over-stimulation of the plant, can end in collapse.

Fertilizer sticks and pellets

Pot-plant fertilizers are also available in sticks (top) and pellets (above) that you push into the compost (potting soil). Many people find these more convenient to use than having to mix and apply liquid feeds.

are tablet-shaped, others stick-shaped, but the principle is always the same: you make a hole in the compost (potting soil), push in the fertilizer stick or pellet, then leave it to release its nutrients slowly over a period of a month or so (check the instructions).

Slow-release sachets
Slow-release fertilizers are available in sachets that you place inside the pot at the bottom. These are most appropriate when repotting.

Soluble powders
These work on the same principle as liquid feeds, but you simply dissolve the powder in water at the appropriate rate. They often work out less expensive than ordinary liquid fertilizers.

Granular fertilizer
If you have to add a granular or powder fertilizer to the compost (potting soil), use a fork to stir it into the surface, then water it in thoroughly.

Benefits of feeding

To appreciate the benefits of feeding try starting with two plants of the same age and size, then feed just one of the plants regularly. The two *Pilea cadierei* (top) are the plants as bought. The same plants (above) show the effect a couple of months later after the one on the right was given just one dose of slow-release fertilizer.

Choosing a compost (potting soil)

YOUR PLANTS WILL ONLY BE AS GOOD AS THE COMPOST THEY GROW IN. FEEDING WILL HELP TO OVERCOME NUTRITIONAL DEFICIENCIES, BUT THE STRUCTURE OF THE COMPOST IS ALSO IMPORTANT IF THE ROOTS ARE TO GET THE RIGHT BALANCE BETWEEN MOISTURE AND AIR, SO VITAL FOR HEALTHY GROWTH. COMMERCIALLY, COMPOSTS ARE CHOSEN THAT MAKE CAPILLARY WATERING EASY, AND THAT ARE LIGHT TO TRANSPORT, BUT IN THE HOME THEY MAY NOT BE THE MOST APPROPRIATE GROWING MEDIUM.

Compost (potting soil) does more than simply anchor the plant, it acts as a reservoir for nutrients and if the structure is right achieves the right balance between moisture and air. It also acts as a host to many beneficial micro-organisms.

Earlier generations of gardeners used to formulate special potting mixtures for different types of plant, but nowadays composts are available that suit the majority of plants, and only a few have special requirements.

The main choice is between loam-based composts and those based on peat (peat moss) or a peat substitute. Most plants will grow well in either type, but there are pros and cons that may make one more or less appropriate for a particular plant.

Loam-based composts use sterilized loam as the main ingredient, with added sand and peat to improve the structure, and fertilizers to supplement the nutrients already present in the loam.

Loam composts have weight, a useful attribute for a large plant with a lot of top growth, such as a big palm, as it provides stability to the pot.

Peat-based composts are light and pleasant to handle, and many plants thrive in them. Sand or other materials are sometimes added, but all of them depend on the addition of fertilizers to support plant growth. Often the fertilizers present in the compost run out quickly, and the plants will almost certainly suffer unless you begin supplementary feeding as soon as the plants show signs of poor growth.

Peat composts are very easy to manage on a commercial scale, with automatic watering systems, but in the home they demand more careful watering than loam composts. They can dry out more completely and become difficult to re-wet, and they are also more easily overwatered.

Some gardeners are reluctant to use peat-based composts on the grounds of depleting wetland areas where peat is excavated. For that reason many alternative products are now being introduced, including composts based on coir (waste from coconuts) and finely pulverized bark. Some use a mixture of materials. Results from these alternative composts can be very variable, depending on the make and formulation. Try a number of plants in several different makes − potting up the same types of plants in each − then decide which is best.

SPECIAL MEDIUMS

A few plants have particular needs that make a general-purpose compost (potting soil) inappropriate. Lime-hating plants, such as azaleas, many begonias, ericas and saintpaulias, are the most common group, and they will grow poorly in ordinary composts. Even peat-based (peat-moss) composts are generally alkaline, because they have lime added to make them suitable for the majority of houseplants. For lime-hating plants you need an 'ericaceous' compost widely available at garden centres.

Bromeliads, cacti and orchids are other groups that have special needs, and you can buy specially formulated composts suitable for these from many specialist nurseries and good garden centres.

Perlite

Gravel

Sphagnum moss

Water-absorbing crystals

Expanded clay
granules

Controlled-release fertilizer

Cactus compost

Ericaceous compost

Peat-based compost

Loam-based compost

Orchid compost

Coir-based compost

ADDITIVES

There are traditional compost (potting soil) additives such as perlite and vermiculite, which keep the compost open and admit plenty of air around the roots while still retaining moisture. These are sometimes used alone to root cuttings, but they contain no significant nutrients. Their contribution is purely structural. You can add them to ordinary composts to make them more moisture-retaining or to keep the compost open so that roots have plenty of oxygen.

Super-absorbent polymers (water-absorbing crystals) have become popular, especially for outdoor containers such as hanging baskets, and by adding them to the compost you will increase the amount of moisture that it will hold. They are no substitute for regular watering, however, and their use for houseplants is fairly limited.

Pots and containers

POTS NEEDN'T JUST BE PRACTICAL, THEY CAN BE PRETTY OR INTERESTING TOO. BUT WHATEVER TYPE YOU CHOOSE, THEIR SIZE AND PROPORTION IN RELATION TO THE PLANTS CONTAINED WILL AFFECT HOW THEY ARE PERCEIVED, AND THE POT CAN MAKE OR MAR A PLANT.

ABOVE: *This zinc container creates just the right atmosphere for an old-fashioned kitchen setting. If a container is large enough, try using a couple of compatible plants, like the adiantum and pellaea ferns used here.*

Ordinary clay or plastic pots lack visual appeal, and most people hide them in a more decorative cache-pot that is slightly larger. If you do this, put gravel, expanded clay granules or a few pebbles in the base to keep the bottom of the pot from contact with the surplus water that collects in the base. Alternatively, pack the space between the inner and outer pots with peat (peat-moss) to absorb most of the moisture, at the same time helping to create a more humid microclimate around the plant. Only use the latter method if you are very methodical about watering and are unlikely to overwater or leave stagnant water sitting at the base of the container. It will be difficult to detect and tip out once the space between the two pots has been filled.

Some plants do look good in clay pots, especially cacti and some succulents. But half-pots are often more appropriate as cacti do not have a large root system, and a shallower pot will usually look more in proportion to the plant. Half-pots have the same diameter as a full pot, but stand only about half the height. Seed pans, which are uncommon now, are similar but shallower; although intended for seed-sowing they can also be used for low or prostrate plants.

Many other plants look better in a half-pot, including azaleas, most begonias, saintpaulias and the majority of bromeliads. Be guided by the type of pot the plant is in when you buy it: if it's a shallow one, use another half-pot when you need to repot.

Some of the better quality plastic pots are coloured and come with a matching saucer, and these can look as attractive as a cache-pot, especially if you choose a colour that is co-ordinated with the room.

You can decorate ordinary clay or plastic pots by painting them freehand or using a stencil. For clay pots use masonry paint (the colours are limited, but you can compensate with a strong design), for plastic pots use acrylic artists' paints.

Square pots are more often used in the greenhouse than indoors, but they are space-saving if you have a collection of small plants such as cacti.

PLASTIC OR CLAY?

The vast majority of the plants on sale are grown in plastic pots: evidence that commercial growers find them satisfactory. Plastic pots are clean, light, easy to handle, remain largely free of algae and are inexpensive. They retain moisture better and the compost (potting soil) is less likely to dry out.

Perhaps surprisingly, clay pots will usually last longer than plastic ones. Plastic pots become brittle with age and even a slight knock is sometimes sufficient to break them. A clay pot won't break unless you actually drop it onto a hard surface. The extra weight of a clay pot will also be of benefit if a plant is large and rather top-heavy.

ABOVE: *Rush baskets can be very effective for small spring bulbs or compact plants like saintpaulias. Always line them or use them simply as a cache-pot.*

ABOVE: *Ceramic pots look stylish, and so much more colourful than an ordinary clay or plastic pot.*

ABOVE: *Bark baskets look good for houseplants that you would normally associate with trees, such as an ivy.*

ABOVE: *In a modern setting you may want a stylish type of container, like this small zinc one. The purple gynura does not detract from the container, which is a feature in its own right.*

ABOVE: *Terracotta hanging pots look more attractive than the plastic versions for a semi-cascading plant like this nephrolepis fern.*

ABOVE: *This china cache-pot picks up the colour of the cyclamen flowers to create a co-ordinated look.*

ABOVE: *Moss baskets make a nice setting for a few spring plants like primroses, and crocuses. Do not plant directly into this type of container unless you can ensure the surface is protected from drips.*

ABOVE: *Keep an eye open for the unlikely or unexpected. This distinctive container is made from dried fungi! The plant in it is a variegated* Ficus pumila.

ABOVE: *Stoneware pots are appropriate for plants in a kitchen. This one has been planted with* Helxine soleirolii *(syn.* Soleirolia soleirolii*), which reflects the rounded shape of the pot.*

ABOVE: *Terracotta wall planters can be used indoors as well as out. This* Philodendron scandens *will have to be trimmed after a few months to retain the container as a feature.*

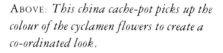

ABOVE: *This metal planter is the kind of container that would look stunning in the right setting. You can line it with moss, rather like a hanging basket.*

ABOVE: *Matching drip trays are useful, and this one is particularly attractive because it takes three ceramic pots.*

ABOVE: *All kinds of decorative cache-pots are available in stores and garden centres, so it should be easy to choose those that appeal to your own tastes.*

ABOVE: *Sometimes old hand-made clay pots can be used effectively. The white deposit that often appears on old pots adds to the impression of age. These have been planted with ivies.*

Potting plants

SOONER OR LATER MOST PLANTS NEED REPOTTING, AND IT CAN GIVE AN AILING PLANT A NEW LEASE OF LIFE. BUT NOT ALL PLANTS RESPOND WELL TO FREQUENT REPOTTING, AND SOME PREFER TO BE IN SMALL POTS. KNOWING WHEN TO REPOT, AND INTO WHICH SIZED POT, IS A SKILL THAT DEVELOPS WITH EXPERIENCE.

Never be in too much of a hurry to pot on a plant into a larger container. Plants do not appreciate having their roots disturbed, and any damage to them will result in some check to growth.

Repotting should never simply be an annual routine. It's a job to be thought about annually, but not actually done unless the plant needs it.

Young plants require potting on much more frequently than older ones. Once a large specimen is in a big pot it may be better to keep it growing by repotting into another pot of the same size, by topdressing, or simply by additional feeding.

When repotting is necessary

The sight of roots growing through the base of the pot is not in it itself a sign that repotting is necessary. If the plants have been watered through a capillary mat, or the pot has been placed in a cache-pot, some roots will inevitably grow through the base to seek the water.

If in doubt, knock the plant out of its pot. To remove the root-ball easily, invert the pot and knock the rim on a hard surface while supporting the plant and compost (potting soil) with your hand. It is normal for a few roots to run around the inside of the pot, but if there is also a solid mass of roots it's time to pot on.

There are several ways to repot a plant, but the two described here are among the best.

When to repot

A mass of thick roots growing through the bottom of the pot (top) is an indication that it's time to move the plant into a large one. Equally, a mass of roots curled around the edge of the pot (above) is another sign that it's time for a larger container.

Pot-in-pot method

1. Prepare the new pot as described in the *Traditional method*, if using a clay pot. However, don't cover the drainage hole at all if using a plastic pot and you intend using a capillary watering mat.

POTTING ON, POTTING UP, REPOTTING

🐾 Although some of these terms are commonly used interchangeably, their true meanings are specific:

🐾 **Potting up** is what happens the first time a seedling or cutting is given its own pot.

🐾 **Potting on** is the action of replanting the root-ball in a larger pot.

🐾 **Repotting** is sometimes taken to mean replacing the plant in a pot of the same size, but with most of the compost replaced. This is only necessary if the plant cannot be moved into a larger pot.

2. Place a little dampened compost (potting soil) over the base material then insert the existing pot (or an empty one the same size), ensuring that the level of the soil surface will be about 1cm (½in) below the top of the new pot when filled.

3. Pack more compost firmly between the inner and outer pots, pressing it down gently with your fingers. This creates a mould when the inner pot is removed.

4. Remove the inner pot, then take the plant from its original container and drop it into the hole formed in the centre of the new compost. Gently firm the compost around the root-ball, and water thoroughly.

Traditional method

1. Prepare a pot that is one or two sizes larger than the original and, if the pot is a clay one, cover the drainage hole with a piece of broken pot or a few pieces of chipped bark.

2. Make sure that the plant has been watered a short time beforehand, and knock the root-ball out of the old pot. Sometimes you can remove it by pulling gently on the plant, otherwise invert the pot and tap the rim on a hard surface.

3. Place a small amount of compost (potting soil) in the base of the new pot, then position the root-ball so that it is at the right height. If too low or too high, adjust the amount of compost in the base.

4. Trickle more compost around the sides, turning the pot as you work. It's a good idea to use the same kind of compost – peat- (peat-moss) or loam-based – as used in the original pot.

5. Gently firm the compost with the fingers. Make sure there is a gap of about 1–2.5cm (½–1in) between the top of the compost and the rim of the pot, to allow space for watering. Water thoroughly.

TOPDRESSING

🌿 Once plants are in large pots, perhaps 25–30cm (10–12in) in diameter, continual potting on into a larger pot may not be practical. Try removing the top few centimetres (inches) of compost (potting soil), loosening it first with a small hand fork. Replace this with fresh potting compost of the same type. This, plus regular feeding, will enable most plants to be grown in the same pot for many years.

Pruning and grooming

GROOMING YOUR PLANTS OCCASIONALLY NOT ONLY KEEPS THEM LOOKING GOOD, IT ALSO ENABLES YOU TO CHECK THEM FOR EARLY SIGNS OF PESTS AND DISEASES BEFORE THESE BECOME A PROBLEM.

Some pruning and grooming tasks simply keep the plants looking fresh and tidy, others actually improve them by encouraging bushier growth or promoting further flowering.

Apart from picking off dead flowers, which is best done whenever you notice them, grooming is only a once-a-week task. Most jobs need doing less frequently than this, but by making a routine of tidying up your plants you will almost certainly detect pest, disease and nutritional problems that much earlier. One also learns to appreciate the plants more by close examination, so you will benefit as well as the plants.

Deadheading

This keeps the plant looking tidy, and in many cases encourages the production of more flowers. It also discourages diseases: fungus infections often start on dead or dying flowers, before spreading to the leaves.

Plants with masses of small flowers, such as fibrous-rooted begonias (*B. semperflorens*) are difficult to deadhead often enough, but unless you make some effort the flowers that fall often make a mess of the furniture or sill that they fall on, as well as spoiling the appearance of the plant itself.

Apart from where the flowers appear in a spike, remove the flower stalks as well as the flowers. Sometimes the stalks are most easily removed by hand, using a pulling and twisting motion at the same time.

If the flowers appear in spikes or large heads, such as a hydrangea, cut the whole head or spike back to just above a pair of leaves when the last blooms have finished.

Leaves

Dust and dirt accumulate on leaves as well as on furniture, but this is not always obvious unless the foliage is naturally glossy. This accumulation not only implies neglect, it also harms the plant slightly by cutting down on the amount of light falling on the leaf and thereby hindering photosynthesis, the process by which the plant produces energy for growth.

Wipe smooth leaves with a soft, damp cloth. Some people add a little milk to the water to produce a shine on glossy foliage. The alternative is to use a commercial leaf shine. Some leaf cleaners come as aerosols or sprays, others as impregnated wipes. If you are using an aerosol, follow the manufacturer's instructions carefully and pay particular attention to the recommended spraying distance.

Cloths and sprays are no use for cleaning hairy leaves. Instead, use a small paintbrush as a duster. You can dust cacti in the same way.

TOOLS FOR THE JOB

🌱 Most of the equipment you need in order to care for houseplants you will probably already have around the home. You might want to try commercial leaf shines or buy secateurs (floral scissors), but a sponge or soft cloth and kitchen scissors will usually do the job just as well.

It is worth keeping a small grooming kit handy, perhaps in a small box that you can carry around during grooming sessions. It should contain:

🌱 Sharp, pointed scissors, or a small pair of secateurs or flower-gathering scissors.

🌱 A supply of split canes for supports.

🌱 A ball of soft garden string, preferably green, or metal split rings. For some jobs, a reel of green plastic-covered wire is useful.

🌱 A sponge for wiping glossy leaves.

🌱 A small paintbrush for cleaning hairy leaves.

Removing leaves
Sooner or later all plants have a few dead leaves. Even evergreens drop old leaves from time to time. Don't let them spoil the appearance of the plant; most are easily removed with a gentle tug, but tough ones may have to be cut off.

Leaf wipes
You might find commercial leaf wipes more convenient to use. They leave large, glossy leaves looking shiny and bright.

Compact non-flowering plants that don't have hairy leaves – aglaonemas for example – can be cleaned by swishing the foliage in a bowl of tepid water. But make sure that the plant dries off out of direct sunlight, otherwise the leaves may be scorched.

Shaping and training
You can improve the shape of many houseplants by pinching out the growing tips to prevent them from becoming tall and leggy. Removing the tips of the shoots makes the plant bushier. Impatiens, hypoestes, pileas and tradescantias are among the many plants that benefit from this treatment. Start when the plants are young, and repeat it whenever the growth looks too thin and long. This is especially useful for trailers such as tradescantias: a dense, bushy cascade about 30cm (1ft) long will look much better than thin, weedy-looking shoots of twice the length.

If any all-green shoots develop on a variegated plant, pinch or prune them back to the point of origin.

Climbers and trailers need regular attention. Tie in any new shoots to the support, and cut off any long shoots that spoil the shape.

Deadheading
Removing dead flowers will keep the plant looking smart, and reduce the chance of dead petals encouraging the growth of moulds and other diseases. Some plants also make a mess of the table or windowsill if the flowers are simply allowed to drop.

Sponging
Glossy-leaved plants like this ficus will look smarter if you wipe over the foliage with slightly soapy water occasionally. The plants also benefit because dust can reduce the amount of light received and also clog some of the pores through which the plant 'breathes'.

Immersing foliage
If the plant is small enough to handle conveniently, try swishing the foliage in a bowl of tepid water. Do not do this if the plant has hairy or delicate leaves.

Brushing leaves
Plants with hairy leaves, like this saintpaulia, should not be sponged or cleaned with a leaf wipe. Instead, brush them occasionally with a soft paintbrush.

Pinching out
If you want a bushy rather than a tall or sprawling plant, pinch out the growing tips a few times while it is still young. This will stimulate the growth of sideshoots that will produce a bushier effect. Most plants will respond to this treatment, but beware of doing it to slow-growing plants.

Holiday care

HOLIDAYS ARE GOOD FOR US, BUT NOT FOR PLANTS. UNLESS YOU HAVE A FRIENDLY NEIGHBOUR WHO CAN PLANT-SIT FOR YOU, YOU WILL HAVE TO DEVISE WAYS OF KEEPING YOUR PLANTS WATERED WHILE YOU ARE AWAY.

Most houseplants will survive in winter for a few days, or even a week, if they are well watered beforehand, especially if the central heating is turned down. In hot summer weather, special arrangements will have to be made for your plants if you are leaving them for anything more than a long weekend.

If you can't arrange for a neighbour to pop in every couple of days to water your houseplants, take the following precautions:

- If it is summer, stand as many as possible outdoors. Choose a shady, sheltered position, and plunge the pots up to their rims in the soil. Then apply a thick mulch of chipped bark or peat over the pots to keep them cool and to conserve moisture. Provided that they are watered well before you leave, most plants will survive a week like this, even without rain.
- Move those that are too delicate to go outdoors into a few large groups in a cool position out of direct sunlight.
- Stand as many as possible on trays of gravel, watered to just below the level of the pot bases. Although this will not moisten the compost (potting soil), the humid air will help to keep the plants in good condition.
- Ensure that all of the most vulnerable plants have some kind of watering system.

Proprietary watering devices

Many kinds of watering devices can be bought, and new ones – usually variations on an old theme – appear each year. Most work on one of the following principles:

Porous reservoirs are pushed into the compost (potting soil) and filled with water. The water slowly seeps though the porous walls over a period of a few days to a week. These are useful for one or two pots for a short period of time, but as you need one for each pot and the reservoir is small, their use is limited.

Ceramic mushrooms work on a similar principle, but the top is sealed and there is a connecting tube for insertion into a large reservoir of water (such as a bucket). As the water seeps through the porous shaft, the pressure in the sealed unit drops and fresh water is drawn from the reservoir. This simple but effective device will keep a plant happy for a couple of weeks, but again, you need one for each pot!

Wicks are sold for insertion into the base of the pot, which is then stood above a reservoir of water. This is a good method if you only have a handful of plants, otherwise too tricky to set up.

Drip feeds, sold for greenhouse and garden use, are a good solution. They can be expensive, and if you use a portable bag reservoir they are not very elegant for the home – but that will not matter while you are away.

Improvising

Two reliable systems use the kitchen sink or bath and capillary matting, which is available at all good garden centres and home improvement stores.

For the sink, cut a length of matting that fits the draining area and is

Short-term holiday care
If you have to leave your plants unattended for a while, try grouping them together in a large container. Place them on wet capillary matting and make sure the compost (potting soil) is moist too. If leaving them for more than a few days, you may need to arrange a system to keep the mat moist.

Improvised wicks
Make your own porous wicks by cutting capillary matting into strips. Make sure the wicks and compost (potting soil) are moist before you leave, and that the wick is pushed well into the compost.

Conserving moisture
Placing a plant in an inflated plastic bag like this will conserve the moisture for quite a long time, but if left too long there is a risk of leaves rotting. Try to keep the bag out of contact with the leaves if possible.

long enough to dip into the basin part. You can fill this with water as a reservoir, or leave the plug out but let the tap drip onto the mat to keep it moist. If you leave the tap dripping, have a trial run beforehand to make sure that it keeps the mat moist without wasting water.

You can set up a similar arrangement in the bath, but if you want to leave water in the bath, place the mat and plants on a plank of wood supported on bricks, to leave space beneath for the water.

Bear in mind that compost (potting soil) in clay pots with broken pots over the drainage holes will not be able to benefit from the capillary action efficiently (though you could insert small wicks though the holes, cut from scraps of the matting). The system works best for houseplants kept in plastic pots, with nothing placed over the drainage holes.

Hardy plants
Many of the tougher houseplants can stand outdoors with their pots plunged in the ground. Choose a shady spot, water the plants thoroughly and cover the tops of the pots with a thick layer of chipped bark.

Porous irrigators
Porous irrigators can be useful if you only leave your plants for a few days. Make sure the compost (potting soil) is moist, then fill the irrigators with water.

Porous wicks
Use a large needle to pull the wicks through the compost (potting soil) and out of the drainage hole at the base of the pot.

Ceramic mushrooms
Ceramic mushrooms can be very effective. As water seeps through the porous container the pressure drops, and more water is sucked up from the reservoir. Provided the reservoir is large enough, you should be able to leave your plant for a week or more.

Using the bath
The bath is a good place to keep plants moist on capillary matting; you can also stand the plants on *porous* bricks without the mat. Have a trial run to make sure the plug retains the water without seepage.

Hydroculture

HYDROCULTURE – ALSO KNOWN AS HYDROPONICS – IS A METHOD OF GROWING PLANTS WITHOUT SOIL OR COMPOST (POTTING SOIL). WATERING IS NORMALLY ONLY NECESSARY EVERY COUPLE OF WEEKS, AND FEEDING IS ONLY A TWICE-YEARLY TASK. HYDROCULTURE WILL GIVE YOU SUCCESSFUL PLANTS WITH THE MINIMUM OF ATTENTION.

Hydroponics can be a highly scientific way to cultivate plants, with nutrient solutions carefully controlled by expensive monitoring equipment. However, the system usually used in homes by amateurs – and generally referred to as hydroculture – is designed to be simple and can be used successfully even by the complete beginner.

You can buy plants that are already growing hydroponically, and these are the best way to start as you would in any case have to buy suitable containers, clay granules and a special fertilizer. But once you realize how easy hydroculture plants are to look after, you will probably want to start off your own plants from scratch.

Routine care

Wait until the water indicator registers minimum, *but do not water immediately.* Allow an interval of two or three days before filling again. Don't keep topping up the water to keep it near the maximum level – it is important that air is allowed to penetrate to the lower levels.

Always use *tap* water because the special ion-exchange fertilizer depends on the chemicals in tap water to function effectively.

Make sure that the water is at room temperature. Because there is no compost (potting soil), cold water has an immediate chilling effect on the plant, and this is a common cause of failure with hydroculture plants.

HOW HYDROCULTURE WORKS

Plants can grow different kinds of roots: ground roots and water roots. If you root a cutting in water it will produce water roots, but once you pot it into compost (potting soil) it almost has to start again by producing ground roots. This makes the transition between compost and water cultivation tricky in either direction. But once the plant has passed through the transitional phase, a hydroculture plant can draw its moisture and nutrients from the solution at the base of the container, while those above can absorb the essential oxygen.

The level of the nutrient solution is crucial. If you fill the tank with too much water there will not be enough air spaces left for the roots to absorb sufficient oxygen and the plant will die.

Make a note of when you replace the fertilizer, and renew it every six months. Some systems use the fertilizer in a 'battery' fitted within the special hydroculture pot, but otherwise you can just sprinkle it on to be washed in with a little water.

Just like plants in compost, hydroculture plants gradually grow larger. Because the roots do not have to

Starting off a new plant

1. Choose a young plant and wash the roots free of all traces of compost (potting soil), being careful not to damage them. Then place the plant in a container with slatted or mesh sides.

5. Pack with more clay granules to secure the inner pot and water indicator.

search for moisture and nutrients the root system is usually smaller than for a comparable plant in compost, but in time the plant will need repotting, especially if the top growth looks out of proportion with the container.

Remove the plant as carefully as possible. It may be necessary to cut the inner container to minimize damage to the roots, but sometimes you can leave the plant in the inner container and just use a larger outer one. If a very large and tangled root system has formed, some judicious pruning may be called for. Both roots and top growth can often be trimmed back

2. Pack expanded clay granules around the roots, being careful to damage them as little as possible.

3. Insert the inner pot into a larger, watertight container, first placing a layer of clay granules on the base to raise the inner pot to the correct level of about 1cm (½in) below the rim.

4. Insert the water level tube. If you cannot find one specially designed to indicate the actual water level, use one that indicates how moist the roots are – those designed for other systems using aggregates are suitable.

6. Sprinkle the special hydroculture fertilizer over the clay granules.

7. Wash the fertilizer down as you water to the maximum level on the indicator. If the indicator does not show an actual level, add a volume of water equal to one-quarter the capacity of the container – and only water again when the indicator shows dry. Always fill with tap water.

8. A few months on and the houseplant is flourishing.

successfully, but much depends on the type of plant.

Suitable plants

Not all plants respond well to hydroculture, so some experimentation may be necessary. The range is surprisingly wide, however, and includes cacti and succulents (with these it is essential to ensure an adequate 'dry period' before topping up with more water, and not to let the water level rise too high), as well as orchids.

As a starting point, try some plants from the following list, or be guided by what you see planted in commercially-produced hydroculture units. Then experiment further as you gain more experience – *Aechmea fasciata*, aglaonema, amaryllis, anthurium, asparagus, aspidistra, beaucarnea, *Begonia manicata*, *Begonia rex*, cacti*, cissus, clivia, codiaeum, dieffenbachia, dizygotheca, dracaena, *Euphorbia pulcherrima*, ficus, gynura, hedera, hibiscus, hoya, maranta, monstera, nephrolepis, philodendron, saintpaulia, sansevieria, schefflera, *Spathiphyllum wallisii*, stephanotis, streptocarpus, tradescantia, *Vriesea splendens*, yucca.

* Most cacti can be grown hydroponically, but it is essential that the water level is regulated carefully. If the water level is too high the plants will soon die.

Simple multiplication

A PLANT THAT YOU HAVE RAISED YOURSELF, FROM SEED OR A CUTTING, ALWAYS SEEMS MORE SPECIAL THAN ONE THAT YOU HAVE BOUGHT. PROPAGATION IS ONE OF THE MOST DEEPLY SATISFYING ASPECTS OF GARDENING, AND ONCE YOU HAVE ENOUGH PLANTS FOR YOUR OWN NEEDS YOU WILL STILL HAVE PLENTY TO EXCHANGE WITH FRIENDS.

Growing from seed

IT CAN BE PARTICULARLY GRATIFYING TO TELL ADMIRING FRIENDS THAT YOU RAISED YOUR ABUTILON OR VENUS FLY TRAP FROM SEED, BUT PERENNIALS CAN BE QUITE A CHALLENGE AND, IN THE CASE OF MIXTURES, NOT ALL THE PLANTS WILL BE AS GOOD AS NAMED VARIETIES. ANNUALS, ON THE OTHER HAND, ARE VERY EASY TO GROW AND SELDOM DISAPPOINT.

If you haven't grown houseplants from seed before, start with easy annuals, which will bring quick and reliable results. This spurs most people to try the trickier or more interesting plants like cacti, cycads and ferns (which are actually grown from spores and not true seeds), as well as favourites like saintpaulias.

As a general rule, those houseplants offered by seed merchants that normally deal in the more common and 'everyday' plants are likely to be the

How to sow in a tray

1. Fill the tray loosely with a seed compost (medium) – loam- and peat-based (peat-moss based) are equally satisfactory for the majority of seeds. Do not use a potting compost as the higher level of nutrients these contain can inhibit germination.

2. Level off the compost, using a piece of wood or rigid cardboard, then firm it gently with a 'presser' or piece of wood that will fit within the tray. Make sure that the compost is still level.

3. Sprinkle the seeds as carefully and as evenly as possible over the surface. A good way to do this with small seeds is in a folded piece of paper that you tap gently with a finger as you move it over the surface.

4. Unless the seed is very fine, or the packet says that the seeds should be left exposed to light, sprinkle a little more compost over the top of the seeds. As a guide, cover with a layer of compost that is about the thickness of the seeds themselves. Use an old kitchen sieve to sift the compost over. This keeps back large pieces and makes it easier to spread evenly.

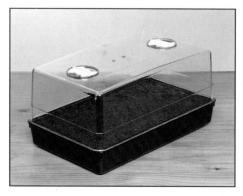

5. Water carefully, using a watering-can fitted with a very fine rose (fine-mist head) – take the tray outdoors to do this. Otherwise stand it in a bowl of water as described for pots opposite. Place the tray in a propagator, or cover it with a sheet of glass. Follow the instructions on the seed packet regarding the required level of light or darkness, and temperature.

SOWING VERY FINE SEED

Some seeds are very tiny, almost like dust, making them difficult to sow evenly. Mix seed that is this small with a little silver sand in the palm of one hand, then use the finger and thumb of the other to sprinkle the mixture over the surface of your seed tray. If the seed and sand have been well combined, distribution of the seed should be even, especially as the sand will help you judge how evenly you are sowing the seed.

easiest to grow. Those offered by seed merchants specializing in the uncommon or unusual are often more difficult to germinate, but the very fact that they are demanding explains part of their appeal to many enthusiasts.

Many perennial houseplants can be slow to germinate and they may take a couple of years to reach a respectable size. If you have a heated greenhouse or conservatory it makes sense to grow them on in there until they are large enough to be used for indoor display.

Sow in trays if you need a lot of plants, otherwise use pots, as these take up less space.

Pricking out

As soon as the seedlings are large enough to handle, prick them out, either into individual pots or into seed trays, to grow on until large enough for their own pots.

Use a potting compost (medium) for this, and always lift the seedlings carefully by their leaves rather than by the fragile stem.

AVOID THE CONDENSATION PROBLEM

🐾 Condensation will form inside a propagator or on the sheet of glass covering the tray or pot. If this is so heavy that drips start to fall on the germinating seedlings, ventilate the propagator or wipe the glass.

How to sow in a pot

1. Fill the pot with a seed compost (medium), but this time use a round presser to firm and level it gently. Make a presser from wood, or simply use a jam-jar.

2. Sow the seeds as evenly as possible. The easiest way to sow over the small area of a pot is to sprinkle the seeds between finger and thumb, as you might sprinkle salt. Sprinkle more compost over the sown seeds unless they are very fine, or the instructions on the packet advise otherwise. Most seeds should be covered with approximately their own depth of compost.

3. Water by the immersion method. Stand the pot in a bowl of water, making sure that the water level remains below the top of the compost. Remove the pot to drain once the surface of the compost has become moist. Using this method, even the smallest seeds will not be disturbed.

4. Place in a propagator or cover with a sheet of glass.

RIGHT: Exacum affine *is one of the easiest houseplants to try raising from seed. Sow in spring to flower in summer and autumn, or in autumn to flower the following spring.*

Stem cuttings

MOST HOUSEPLANTS CAN BE RAISED FROM STEM CUTTINGS, AND SOME ARE SO

EASY THAT THEY WILL EVEN ROOT IN WATER. OTHERS ARE MORE CHALLENG-

ING, REQUIRING ROOTING HORMONES AND A PROPAGATOR.

Impatiens
Impatiens are often grown from seed, but they root readily from softwood cuttings. As old plants often lose their compact shape, take a few cuttings periodically.

Geraniums
Geranium (pelargonium) softwood cuttings root readily. You can use this technique for zonal geraniums, regal geraniums like these, and scented-leaved geraniums.

Most houseplants can be propagated from softwood cuttings taken in spring, and many of the shrubby plants root from semi-ripe cuttings taken later in the year.

Softwood cuttings
This method of taking cuttings is similar to semi-ripe cuttings, but choose the ends of new shoots. Take softwood cuttings after the first flush of spring but before the shoots have become hard. Now follow the same procedure as for semi-ripe cuttings.

Cuttings in water
Softwood cuttings can often be rooted in water, especially easy ones like coleus and impatiens.

Almost fill a jam-jar with water and fold a piece of wire-netting (chicken wire) over the top, or use a piece of aluminium foil with holes pierced in it. Take the cuttings in the normal way but, instead of inserting them into compost (potting soil), rest them on the netting or foil, with the end of the stem in water.

Top up the water as necessary. When roots have formed, pot the cuttings up into individual pots using a sandy potting compost. Keep the plants out of direct sunlight for at least a week to give them a chance to become established in the pot.

HORMONES HELP ROOTING

Some plants, such as impatiens and some tradescantias, root readily even without help from a rooting hormone. Others, and especially semi-ripe cuttings, will benefit from the use of a rooting hormone. Rooting hormones are available as powders or liquids, and their use usually results in more rapid rooting and, in the case of the trickier kinds of plants, a higher success rate.

How to take semi-ripe cuttings

1. Fill a pot with a cuttings compost (medium) or use a seed compost, and firm it to remove large pockets of air.

2. Make the cuttings 10–15cm (4–6in) long (they may have to be shorter on very compact plants), choosing the current season's growth after the first flush of growth but before the whole shoot has become hard. They should be firm yet flexible, and offer some resistance when bent.

3. Trim the cutting just below a leaf joint, using a sharp knife, and remove the lower leaves to produce a clear stem to insert into the compost.

4. Dip the cut end of the cutting into a rooting hormone. If using a powder, moisten the end in water first so that it adheres.

5. Make a hole in the compost with a small dibber or a pencil, and insert the cutting so that the bottom leaves are just above the compost. Firm the compost gently around the stem to remove large air pockets. You can usually insert several cuttings around the edge of a pot.

6. Water the cuttings (adding a fungicide to the water will help to reduce the risk of the cuttings rotting), then label and place in a propagator. If you don't have a propagator, cover the pot with a clear plastic bag, making sure it does not touch the leaves. Keep in a light place, but *out of direct sunlight*.

If a lot of condensation forms, reverse the bag or ventilate the propagator until excess condensation ceases to form. Do not allow the compost to dry out.

Pot up the cuttings individually once they have formed a good root system.

Leaf cuttings

LEAF CUTTINGS ALWAYS SEEM MORE FASCINATING TO ROOT THAN STEM CUTTINGS, AND THERE ARE PLENTY OF HOUSEPLANTS THAT YOU CAN PROPAGATE THIS WAY. THE TECHNIQUES ARE EASY AS WELL AS FUN, AND SOME OF THE MOST POPULAR PLANTS, SUCH AS SAINTPAULIAS, FOLIAGE BEGONIAS, STREPTOCARPUS AND SANSEVIERIAS, CAN BE RAISED FROM LEAF CUTTINGS.

Square leaf cuttings

1. First cut the leaf into strips about 3cm (1¼in) wide, in the general direction of the main veins, using a sharp knife or razor-blade.

There are several types of leaf cuttings described here. For leaf petiole cuttings you need to remove the leaves with a length of stalk attached. Some leaves form new plants from the leaf blades, especially from points where the veins have been injured. For square leaf cuttings, instead of placing a whole leaf on the compost (medium), you can cut it into squares and insert these individually. With leaf midrib cuttings, the long, narrow leaves of plants such as streptocarpus can simply be sliced into sections and treated like square leaf cuttings.

Leaf petiole cuttings

1. Use only healthy leaves that are mature but not old. Remove the leaf with about 5cm (2in) of stalk, using a sharp knife or razorblade.

3. Insert the stalk into the hole, angling the cutting slightly, then press the compost gently around the stalk to firm it in. The base of the blade of the leaf should sit on the surface of the compost. You should be able to accommodate a number of cuttings in a seed tray or large pot. Water well, preferably with a fungicide, and allow surplus moisture to drain.

2. Fill a tray or pot with a suitable rooting compost (medium), then make a hole with a dibber or pencil.

4. Place the cuttings in a propagator, or cover with a clear plastic bag. Make sure that the leaves do not touch the glass or plastic, and remove condensation periodically.

Keep the cuttings warm and moist, in a light place out of direct sunlight. Young plants usually develop within a month or two, but leave them until they are large enough to be handled easily.

PLANTS TO GROW FROM LEAF CUTTINGS

🌿 **Leaf petiole cuttings**
Begonias (other than *B. rex*)
Peperomia caperata
Peperomia metallica
Saintpaulia

🌿 **Leaf blade cuttings**
Begonia rex

🌿 **Leaf midrib cuttings**
Gesneria
Sansevieria*
Sinningia speciosa (gloxinia)
Streptocarpus

* If you use this method for the variegated *S. trifasciata* 'Laurentii' the plantlets will not be variegated.

2. Next cut across the strips to form small squares of leaf.

3. Fill a tray with a rooting compost (medium), then insert the squares on edge, making sure that the edge that was nearest to the leaf stalk faces downwards.

4. After a month or two you should have plenty of young plants that have grown from the leaf squares. Once these are well established, pot them up individually.

Leaf midrib cuttings

1. Remove a healthy, undamaged leaf from the parent plant, ideally one that has only recently fully expanded.

2. Place the leaf face down on a firm, clean surface, such as a sheet of glass. Cut the leaf into strips, no wider than 5cm (2in).

> ### LONGITUDINAL LEAF CUTTINGS
>
> An alternative method of propagating streptocarpus:
>
> Lay the leaf on a hard surface, and cut it twice along the length of the leaf, on both sides of the main vein. Discard the main vein.
>
> Insert these halves into the compost, so that they stand on edge with about one-third in the compost.

3. Fill a tray or large pot with a rooting compost (medium), and insert the cuttings into this about 2.5cm (1in) apart. Insert the end that was nearest the stalk into the compost. About one-third of the cutting should be in the compost.

Young plants will eventually appear from the compost. Pot these up individually when they are large enough to handle safely.

Leaf blade cuttings

1. Select a healthy leaf, and sever it close to the base of the main stalk.

2. Cut off the attached stalk close to the blade.

3. Cut across the main and secondary veins on the underside of the leaf, using a sharp knife or razor-blade. Make the cuts about 2.5cm (1in) apart.

4. Fill a seed tray with a rooting compost (medium), then peg the leaf so that the back is in contact with the compost. Make several small U-shaped 'staples' from pieces of galvanized wire, to act as anchors.

5. Alternatively, instead of using wire staples, you can hold the leaf in contact with the compost by using small stones as weights.

6. Keep in a propagator, or in a warm place, in a light position but out of direct sunlight. Do not allow the compost to become dry.

New plants will eventually grow, and once these look well established, pot them up individually. Often the old leaf has disintegrated by this time, but if not, just cut the new plants free of the old leaf.

LEFT: Begonia rex *should be propagated using leaf-blade cuttings, rather than other methods.*

Easy division

DIVISION IS THE QUICKEST AND EASIEST OF ALL METHODS OF PROPAGATION.
THE RESULTS ARE INSTANT, AND MOST PLANTS WITH A CROWN OR THAT
FORM A CLUMP CAN BE PROPAGATED THIS WAY.

Many ferns can be divided, including adiantum, phyllitis, and *Pteris cretica*. Marantas, and related genera such as calathea, also form a clump and lend themselves to division. Other popular houseplants to try are anthuriums and aspidistras.

Water the plant about an hour before you divide it. If the roots are thick and fleshy, have a sharp knife handy to cut though them.

Dividing a plant

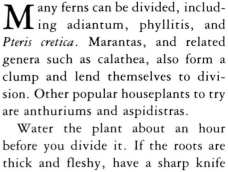

1. Knock the plant out of its pot. If the plant is large and the pot full of roots, you may need to invert the pot and tap the rim on a hard surface. Place a hand over the root-ball to catch it as it falls free.

2. Pull away some of the compost (potting soil) from the bottom and sides, freeing some of the roots in the process.

3. Try pulling the plant apart with your hands, first into two pieces, and then into smaller ones if you need a lot of new plants.

4. Sometimes the tough or fleshy roots make this difficult: chlorophytums are an example. If this is the case, prise the roots apart with a hand fork and separate the clump into smaller pieces with a sharp knife.

5. Replant healthy young pieces of the root clump, using a smaller pot and a good potting compost (medium). It may be necessary to trim back some of the largest roots with a knife, but try to leave the small, fibrous ones intact.

After watering, keep the plants in good light but out of direct sun, at least until they have become established and started to grow again.

Layering

LAYERING IS A USEFUL TECHNIQUE IF YOU REQUIRE JUST A FEW EXTRA OR REPLACEMENT PLANTS. ORDINARY LAYERING IS ONLY PRACTICAL FOR A FEW PLANTS INDOORS, BUT AIR LAYERING IS A POPULAR WAY TO IMPROVE AN OLD FICUS THAT HAS BECOME BARE AT THE BASE.

Ordinary layering is most appropriate for climbers or trailers with long and flexible shoots that can easily be pegged down into pots close to the parent plant. Ivies and *Philodendron scandens* are plants that readily lend themselves to this form of propagation.

Air layering is most often used for large ficus, such as *F. elastica*, but the method can also be used for other plants, such as dracaenas. Normally plants are air layered on an area of bare stem just below the leafy part, but if a few old leaves are in the way cut these off flush with the stem.

Ordinary layering

1. Fill a few small pots with a seed or cuttings compost (medium), and position them close to the parent plant.

2. Choose long, healthy shoots with young growth, and untangle them from the rest of the plant so that they can be pegged down into the pots.

3. Use pieces of bent wire to hold the stem in contact with the compost where there is a leaf joint. It does not matter if the stem is slightly covered by the compost.

4. When the roots have formed – usually after about four weeks – and new shoots begin to grow, sever the new plant from its parent. Keep the newly severed plant in a light position out of direct sunlight, and pay special attention to watering, until it is well established and obviously growing away strongly.

ABOVE: Philodendron scandens *is one of the few plants which you can successfully propagate by ordinary layering.*

ABOVE: *Try air layering a leggy* Ficus elastica *'Robusta' and you will once more have a plant like this.*

Air layering

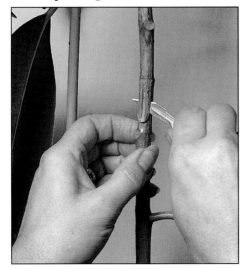

1. Make a sleeve out of a piece of clear plastic and secure it below the point where the layer is to be made, using a plastic-covered twist-tie or adhesive tape. Then, using a sharp knife or blade, make an upward-facing cut about 2.5cm (1in) long, finishing just below a leaf joint. Make sure that you do not cut more than about one-third of the way through the stem, otherwise the top may break.

2. Brush inside the wound with a rooting hormone. A small paintbrush is useful for this. To hold the wound open, insert some moist sphagnum moss into the incision, or use a small piece of matchstick.

3. Pack plenty of moist sphagnum moss around the area, then bring up the plastic sleeve to hold it in place.

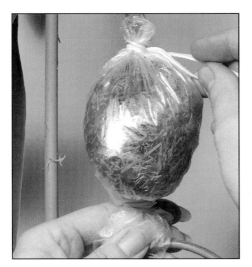

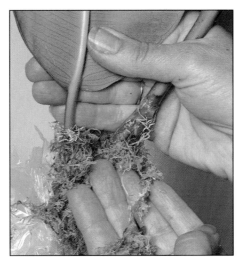

4. Secure the top of the sleeve with another twist-tie or some adhesive tape.

5. Check the moss occasionally to make sure that it is still moist, and to see if any roots have formed.

6. Once new roots are visible through the sleeve, cut off the stem just below the root-ball. Loosen the ball of moss slightly, but do not attempt to remove the moss when you pot up the plant. As the root system will still be small at this stage, it may be necessary to provide a stake for a few weeks.

Offsets and plantlets

OFFSETS AND PLANTLETS PROVIDE YOU WITH NEW PLANTS FOR THE MINIMUM

OF EFFORT – AND YOU DON'T HAVE TO SACRIFICE THE PARENT PLANT.

A few plants obligingly grow 'babies' on their leaves – just waiting to root when they come into contact with the compost (potting soil). Others produce plantlets on runners and raising new plants from these is as simple as pegging them down. Many plants – such as bromeliads – produce new shoots clustered around the old ones. These are easily detached and potted up.

Plantlets

Two succulents popularly grown as curiosities carry baby plants on their leaves: *Kalanchoe daigremontiana* (syn. *Bryophyllum daigremontianum*) and *K. Tubiflora* (syn. *B. tubiflorum*). The plantlets often fall off and can be found growing in the compost (potting soil) at the base of the parent plant. Just lift these up carefully after loosening the compost, and pot them up individually. Alternatively, remove the largest of the plantlets from the leaves before they fall, and gently press them into the surface of a cuttings compost (medium). Other viviparous plants like this, such as *Asplenium bulbiferum*, can be treated in the same way.

Tolmiea menziesii has young plantlets at the base of its leaves. Just detach a parent leaf, cut off the surplus leaf blade around the plantlet, and bury it just below the compost, with the plantlet still visible.

Runners

Some popular houseplants, such as *Saxifraga stolonifera*, produce plantlets on long runners, others, like *Chlorophytum comosum*, produce them at the ends of arching stems. All of these are very easy to propagate.

Place small pots filled with a cuttings compost (medium) around the parent plant and peg down the plantlets into them using pieces of bent wire or hairpins, to hold them in close

1. Bromeliads produce offsets around the edge of the main flowering part of the plant, which later dies. Pot up these offsets when they are about a third the height of the parent plant.

contact with the compost. Keep well watered and sever the plantlets from the parent plant once plenty of roots have formed and the new plant has started to grow.

Offsets

Some plants produce offsets – new growth close to the old that can be separated and grown on independently – and this is normal with bromeliads.

Runners

1. *Chlorophytum comosum* is easy to propagate from plantlets produced at the ends of long, arching stems.

2. Peg the plantlets down into small pots, using pieces of bent wire to hold them in position.

3. Sever the plants from their parent once they have rooted well and are growing strongly.

2. They can usually be pulled away easily, but if necessary cut them away with a knife.

3. Pot the offsets up individually.

4. Firm the plants in, then water and keep in a warm, humid position, out of hot direct sunlight, until they show signs of new growth.

Many epiphytic bromeliads (those that in nature grow in trees or on rocks) have flowering rosettes that die after blooming. Before these plants die, they produce plenty of offsets around the old mature rosette. Leave these on until they are about one-third of the size of the parent plant, then detach them and pot up individually. Most can simply be pulled off by hand, but the tough ones will have to be severed with a sharp knife.

Some terrestrial bromeliads, such as ananas, produce offsets on stolons (short horizontal stems). Remove the plant from its container and cut off the offsets without causing too much damage to the parent.

Pot up the offsets without delay, and keep moist. Position them in good light but out of direct sunlight. They will soon start to grow independently and should then be treated normally.

Propagating from plantlets

1. *Kalanchoe tubiflora* (syn. *Bryophyllum tubiflorum*) produces plenty of plantlets at the ends of its leaves. Remove the plantlets with a gentle tug, and avoid holding the roots.

2. Plant them in a free-draining cuttings compost (medium), where they will soon grow away as young plants.

3. *Kalanchoe daigremontiana* (syn. *Bryophyllum daigremontianum*) produces plantlets around the edges of its leaves. Treat like the previous species, or simply peg down a whole leaf.

4. The ensuing plantlets can be potted up singly when they are larger.

Special techniques

SPECIAL TECHNIQUES LIKE CANE CUTTINGS, LEAF-BUD CUTTINGS, CACTI CUTTINGS AND CACTI GRAFTING ARE USEFUL SKILLS TO ACQUIRE. EVEN IF YOU DON'T USE THE METHODS OFTEN, THEY ARE INVALUABLE FOR PROPAGATING CERTAIN PLANTS.

Some houseplants with thick and erect stems, such as cordylines, dracaenas and dieffenbachias, can be propagated by a technique known as cane cuttings. This is a good method to try if a plant has lost most of its leaves and you are left with a long length of bare stem. In this case, you might as well use the leggy shoots for cane cuttings.

Leaf-bud cuttings are sometimes used for *Ficus elastica*, especially where more plants are required than you could achieve with air layering. You can also use this method of propagation for *Aphelandra squarrosa*, dracaenas, epipremnums, *Monstera deliciosa* and philodendrons.

The majority of cacti will root fairly easily from cuttings, but their odd shapes, as well as their prickles, call for special techniques.

If the cactus has rounded pads (like opuntias), just cut new pads off making a straight cut across the joint. Leave the cutting exposed for about 48 hours for the wound to form a callus. Then insert the cutting into a mixture of grit or coarse sand and peat (peat moss) or peat substitute. Once the cutting has rooted and started to grow, pot it up into a normal cactus compost (medium).

Columnar cacti can often be propagated if the top 5–10cm (2–4in) of stem is removed. Dry off as described above, before inserting the cutting.

Flat-stemmed cacti such as epiphyllums can be cut into lengths about 5cm (2in) long. Dry off as usual then insert upright in the compost.

Cane cuttings

1. Cut the thick stem into pieces about 5–7.5cm (2–3in) long, making sure that each piece has at least one node (the area between two points where leaves were attached).

2. You can insert them vertically, but they are usually laid horizontally with the lower half pressed into the compost. Make sure that the leaf buds are pointing upwards.

Leaf-bud cuttings

1. Select a young stem in spring or summer, and cut it into 1–2.5cm (½–1in) sections, each with one leaf and its bud.

BLEEDING WOUNDS

Some succulents, such as euphorbias, produce a milky latex when cut. If this happens, dip the cutting into tepid water for a few seconds to stop the flow. Hold a damp cloth over the cut surface on the parent plant to stop the bleeding. As the sap of some is an irritant, be careful not to get it near your eyes or on your skin.

HANDLING PRICKLY CACTI

Thick gloves make it possible to handle some spiny cacti while taking cuttings, as you do not have to grip the plant hard, but many will simply pierce the gloves. To handle these, fold a newspaper over several times to form a thick band a couple of centimetres (about an inch) wide, then grip the plant with this, holding the 'handles' formed by the ends. A flexible piece of cardboard can be used in a similar way, but be careful not to use anything so hard that the spines are damaged.

2. Dip the base of each cutting in a rooting hormone, then insert it in a 7.5cm (3in) pot filled with a cuttings compost (medium).

3. To reduce moisture loss from the leaf, curl the leaf so that it is rolled up, and hold in place with an elastic band. This also saves space as you can pack the pots closer together than if the leaves were spread horizontally.

4. Once roots have formed, often after about a month if you have used a propagator, remove the elastic band and give the plant more space. Pot on into a normal potting compost (medium) a few weeks later.

Cacti cuttings

1. Cacti and succulents like this are easy to raise from cuttings. Just remove a stem of suitable length.

2. Leave the cutting exposed for about 48 hours to allow the wound to form a callus.

3. Insert the cuttings like those of any other plant. A rooting hormone should not be necessary.

4. Columnar cacti often have only a single stem, so waiting for separate young shoots can be a problem. However, they can often be propagated if the top 5–10cm (2–4in) of the stem is removed. Allow the cut surface to dry for 48 hours before inserting the cutting.

5. Cacti with flat pads are easy to root but need careful handling (see *Handling Prickly Cacti*, opposite). Treat as the other types, once removed.

6. These two cuttings have been taken from a columnar cactus (left) and one with flat pads (right).

Sometimes cacti are grafted for fun, or to make them flower more quickly than they would on their own roots, but a few that have stem colours other than green, such as some orange-red gymnocalycium species and varieties, have to be grafted onto a green stem because they are incapable of supporting themselves without the green chlorophyll found there. For these, flat grafting is the easiest method.

Some orchids, such as cymbidiums, have back-bulbs (a kind of bulb that sits on the surface of the compost). These can be removed and potted separately to produce new plants. Orchids can also be propagated using the division technique.

Fern spores can be used to propagate new plants; they resemble dust-like seeds, but they are not the equivalent of seeds. The fern plant is just an asexual stage in the life cycle, and the spores are another asexual stage. When they germinate they produce the sexual stage, the prothallus, which is green and prostrate or scale-like and carries both male and female organs. When fertilization takes place, the fern as we know it begins to grow.

Propagating orchids

1. Orchids can produce large clumps and may need dividing. Remove growth from the outer edge to repot. Some produce back-bulbs (old bulbs without leaves) that can be used for repotting.

2. Pot up individually, and always use a special orchid compost (medium). Back-bulbs (which may have no leaves) are treated in the same way. Plant to one side of the pot, as new growth will expand in front of the old growth.

Grafting cacti

1. Slice the top off the rootstock using a sharp knife to produce a flat surface.

2. Slightly bevel the edges of the cut with a knife.

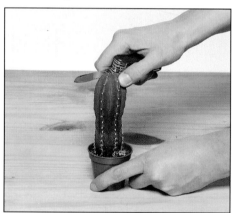

3. Slice off the part to be grafted onto the rootstock, again cutting it cleanly.

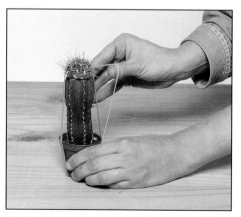

4. Place the two parts together and hold in place with a couple of elastic bands looped over the top of the grafted cacti and under the bottom of the pot.

5. Label and keep in a warm, light place. The elastic bands can be removed as soon as new growth is noticed. The grafted cactus on the left is *Gymnocalycium* 'Black Cap'.

Ferns from spores

1. Fill a shallow pot with a peaty compost (peat-moss potting soil). Some people then sprinkle a thin layer of brick dust over the top. Firm it gently so that it is lightly compacted and level.

2. Sprinkle the spores over the surface as evenly as possible.

3. Cover the pot with a piece of glass and stand it in a saucer of water (rain or soft water is best). Keep in a warm, shaded position, and make sure that there is some water in the saucer.

4. In about a month the tiny prothalli will start to grow and gradually cover the surface. It is essential that the compost remains moist at this stage. It is also worth keeping the glass over the pot.

5. A month or two later the ferns proper should begin to appear. At this stage, remove the glass but still keep out of direct hot sunlight. When large enough to handle, prick out the little clumps of ferns into a seed tray.

When the small ferns are large enough to handle easily and a suitable size for their own pot, prick them out into individual pots.

BELOW: *Fern spores are usually sold to amateurs as mixtures of either hardy or tropical species. This* Asplenium nidus *is one fern that a mixture might include, but if you want to propagate a particular species it is worth saving and sowing the spores from your own plants.*

Trouble-shooting

No matter how circumspect you are in selecting new plants, how carefully you check them for signs of ill-health, or how well you care for them, pests and diseases arrive unannounced. However, they should never be allowed to spoil your enjoyment of houseplants and with a little vigilance most should be easily kept under control.

Eliminating pests

EVERYONE GETS PESTS ON THEIR HOUSEPLANTS: BEGINNERS, EXPERTS AND

EVEN PROFESSIONALS. SOME, LIKE APHIDS, READILY ATTACK A WHOLE RANGE

OF PLANTS, OTHERS ARE MORE SELECTIVE AND TEND TO BE A PROBLEM ONLY

ON CERTAIN TYPES OF PLANT, OR IN PARTICULAR CONDITIONS. ALL NEED TO

BE DEALT WITH QUICKLY AND EFFECTIVELY.

Red spider mites
Red spider mites are so small that you can
hardly see them without a magnifying glass,
but, as this sick *Fatsia japonica* shows, an
infestation can be serious.

Aphids
Aphids are perhaps the most common and
troublesome pest, but are relatively easy to
control provided you act as soon as they are
detected.

Whitefly
Whitefly look like tiny white moths that often
rise up like a cloud when the plant is moved.
Although tiny, they gradually weaken the
plant, as this radermachera shows.

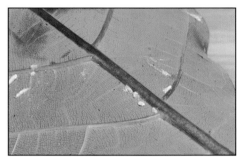

Mealy bugs
Mealy bugs are slow-moving and multiply less
rapidly than aphids, but they still weaken the
plant and can spread diseases.

Most pests fall into one of the three categories given below, so even if you do encounter a pest that you don't immediately recognize, you should be able to decide from this information which group it falls in, and choose an appropriate control.

Sap-suckers

The ubiquitous aphids are the biggest problem, and even if you win the first battle when you realize that an attack is under way, never let your guard down because there will always be new armies of aphids to take their place.

Aphids, and all sap-sucking insects, are important not only for the immediate damage they do, but also because of the long-term health risk to your plants. When aphids cluster on buds or the tips of shoots, leaves and flowers will often be distorted when they open, and because they tap into

the veins and 'blood' supply of the plant, they can easily transmit virus diseases from one plant to another. Always take aphids seriously, and take action before the population rapidly increases, as they can reproduce at a phenomenal rate.

Whitefly look like tiny moths and rise up in a cloud when disturbed. The nymphs (immature insects) are green to white and scale-like, turning yellow before emerging as an adult fly.

Red spider mites are tiny and the actual insects are easily missed, but you will notice their fine webs and yellowing, mottled leaves.

Control: almost all houseplant insecticides will control aphids, so choose one that is convenient to use, and has the right persistence taking into account your personal views on garden chemicals. You can buy some insecti-

cides that kill only aphids and leave beneficial insects unharmed, but in the home this is of marginal benefit. You don't have to worry about pollinating insects or natural predators as you might outdoors. Many strong insecticides are not suitable for use indoors, but you can take your plant outside to spray it. Alternatively, use one of the milder and less persistent ones – often based on natural substances like pyrethrum – more often.

Systemic insecticides that you water into the soil, or that are contained in impregnated sticks pushed into the compost, are easy to use indoors and protect the plant for weeks.

Pests like whitefly need repeated spraying with ordinary contact insecticides, so don't give up too soon.

Red spider mites dislike a humid atmosphere. Once you've used the chemical control, regular misting to

Caterpillar damage
Caterpillars can be a problem on indoor plants as well as in the garden. Here one has attacked a pereskia.

Biological controls
A predatory mite – *Phytoseiulus persimilis* – can be used for red spider mite as a biological control. Here a leaf containing the parasite is being placed on a houseplant.

Nematode weevil control
There is now a natural control for vine weevil grubs – a microscopic parasitic nematode. Mix the culture with water and apply to the plants. Here a cyclamen is being dosed.

Vine weevil grubs
Vine weevil grubs are particularly troublesome because they eat the roots and the first you may know of the problem is when the plant collapses.

Using systemic insecticides
These special 'pins' release a systemic insecticide that is absorbed by the plant's roots, making the plant toxic to sap-sucking insects for weeks.

Controlling aphids
You may be able to reduce the population of insects such as aphids simply by swishing the plant in water.

create a humid atmosphere will please the plants and deter the mites.

Mealy bugs and other relatively stationary sap-sucking insects can be treated by dabbing them with a cotton swab dipped in alcohol. This will penetrate the waxy coat that protects them from most contact insectides. Otherwise try using a systemic insectide that will be carried in the sap.

Leaf eaters
Leaf eaters give themselves away soon after arrival, by the tell-tale chunks missing from leaves. Fortunately, most of the these pests are large and easily seen, and on the whole control is relatively simple.

Control: large pests that remain on the plant, such as caterpillars, slugs and snails, can usually be picked off by hand (remove the whole leaf if in-fested). Chemical control is hardly ever necessary indoors, but in a conservatory you may want to use slug bait (protect it under pieces of broken pot if you have pets).

Those insects that feed at night and hide during the day, such as earwigs, present a bigger problem. Most household crawling insect powders and sprays will control these if you use them around the area where the plants are. If you don't want to use an insecticide, leave small traps made from matchboxes, left slightly open and filled with litter such as chopped straw. Check these each morning and destroy any pests that you find.

Root chewers
The problem with root pests is that you are unlikely to know of their existence until the plant collapses, by which time it's often too late.

A number of pests affect the roots, from some types of aphids to the grubs of insects such as weevils. If a plant looks sick, fails to grow properly, or starts to collapse, and there is no obvious cause such as overwatering or underwatering, remove the plant from its pot and shake off the compost (potting soil). Examine the roots: if there are grubs or other pests, that's the likely cause; if you find none but the roots are sparse or rotting, a fungus disease is the more likely cause.

Control: if you have taken the plant out of its pot for examination, shake the compost off the roots and dip them into an insecticidal solution before repotting in fresh compost. Your plant may then recover. Drench the compost in nearby pots with an insecticidal solution as a further precaution, though results may be variable.

Dealing with diseases

PLANT DISEASES CAN BE DISFIGURING AND EVEN FATAL, SO ALWAYS TAKE THEM SERIOUSLY. IF YOU CAN'T CONTROL THEM BY PICKING OFF THE AFFECTED LEAVES, RAPID RESORT TO A FUNGICIDE MAY BE THE BEST SOLUTION. IF A VIRUS STRIKES, IT MAY BE BETTER TO SACRIFICE THE PLANT TO THE BIN RATHER THAN RISK THE INFECTION SPREADING TO OTHER PLANTS.

Leaf spot

Leaf spots are quite common, and are caused by various fungi. If just a few leaves are affected, pick them off then spray the rest of the plant as a precaution.

Fungus diseases are often difficult to identify accurately and many different species of fungi can cause similar symptoms. Fortunately, a scientific identification of the exact fungus is not necessary in order to go about controlling it. The chemicals used to control each main group of diseases are largely effective against all the organisms likely to be responsible – but don't assume that all fungicides are equally effective against all fungus diseases. Always read the label to check what disease a particular chemical is most effective against.

Leaf spots

Various fungi and bacteria cause leaf spots. If tiny black specks can be seen on the affected surface, they are likely to be the spore-bearing bodies of a fungus, so a fungicide is likely to be effective. If no specks can be detected it might be a bacterial problem, though a fungicide might still be of some help.

Control: prune off and destroy the affected leaves. Water with a systemic fungicide, and avoid misting too frequently. Increase ventilation if the weather permits.

Root rots

The first sign of a root rot is usually the sudden collapse of a seemingly healthy plant. The leaves turn brown or black, and curl up. The entire plant may wilt. This is almost always the result of overwatering.

Control: if the plant has not already deteriorated too far, try drying it out. However, there is usually little that can be done at this stage.

Sooty mould

The fungus covers the leaves, often the back but sometimes the front, with a black growth that looks like soot. It does not directly harm the plants but looks unsightly.

Fungal diseases

The protective sleeve of this newly purchased saintpaulia disguised the fact that it is infected with *Botrytis cinerea*. This grey-brown mould develops on dead or damaged plants, and can be caused by lack of ventilation.

Sooty mould

Sooty mould is a fungus that grows on the sugary substance excreted by aphids and other sap-suckers. If you control the pests you will eliminate the disease, which is unsightly but not particularly harmful.

Mildew

Various kinds of mildew affect houseplants, and begonias are particularly prone to them. Control is difficult once the disease is well established, but various fungicides are useful for early and preventative treatment.

Control: sooty mould is a fungus that lives on the 'honeydew' (excrement) left by aphids and whitefly. When this food disappears so will the sooty mould, so eliminate the insects that are the prime cause.

Mildews

There are various kinds of mildew, the powdery types being the most common. Evidence of the disease is seen as a white, powdery deposit, almost as if the leaf has been sprinkled with flour. The problem starts in one or two areas but quickly radiates out and can soon engulf the whole leaf. Some plants, such as begonias, are more prone to mildew than others.

Control: pick off the affected leaves at an early stage, then use a fungicide to limit its spread. Increase ventilation, and reduce the humidity around the plant – at least until the disease is under control.

Using fungicides

If you need to use a fungicide, you can use those developed for outdoor plants by mixing a small amount and using it in a hand-pumped mister.

Viruses

The main symptoms of virus diseases are stunted or distorted growth, irregular yellow blotches on foliage and streaked petals on flowering plants. They are easily transmitted by sap-sucking insects such as aphids, and can even be carried on the knives used to take cuttings.

There is no effective control and, apart from the rare cases where the plants are cultivated for the variegation caused by the virus, the plants are best destroyed.

Disorders and deficiencies

NOT ALL TROUBLES ARE CAUSED BY PESTS AND DISEASES. SOMETIMES PHY-SIOLOGICAL PROBLEMS SUCH AS CHILLS AND COLD DRAUGHTS, OR NUTRI-TIONAL DEFICIENCIES, CAN BE THE CAUSE.

Tracking down a physiological problem calls for a bit of detective work. The descriptions of some common problems described here will help to pinpoint some potential causes, but be prepared to look for anything that has disturbed the usual routine – has the plant been moved, watered more or less heavily, has the weather become much colder, have you turned the central heating on but not increased humidity or ventilation? By piecing together the various clues you can often deduce probable causes, and thereby work out what you can do to avoid a repetition.

Temperature
Most houseplants will tolerate cool but frost-free temperatures if they have to. It is sudden changes of temperature or icy draughts in a warm room that cause most problems.

If leaves drop it may be due to low temperature. This often happens with newly bought plants that have been on display outdoors or chilled on the way home. Leaves that look shrivelled and slightly translucent may have been touched by frost.

Hardy plants like *Euonymus japonicus* may drop their leaves if kept too warm in winter. Berries are also likely to fall prematurely if the temperature is kept too high.

Light and sun
Plants that need a high light intensity will become elongated and drawn if the illumination is poor, and leaves and flower stalks will be drawn towards the window. Lop-sided growth is another indication of inadequate

Neglect
This plant is clearly showing signs of stress and lack of nutrients. It may be best to discard a plant in this state.

Sun scorch
Plants that are not adapted to grow in very strong light are easily scorched by strong sunlight intensified by a glass window. This dieffenbachia is suffering from scorch.

light. If you can't move the plant into a lighter position, try turning the pot round by 45 degrees each day (put a tiny mark on the pot as a reminder of whether you've turned it).

Light is usually a good thing, but direct sunlight, intensified through glass, will often scorch leaves – the effect will be brown, papery areas on the leaf. Patterned glass is a particular problem as it can act like a magnifying glass, causing dry brown patches where the rays have been concentrated.

Humidity
Dry air can cause leaf tips to go brown and papery on vulnerable plants.

Watering
Too little water is the most likely cause of wilting and collapse, if the compost (potting soil) feels very dry to the touch. If the plant collapses and the compost feels very wet, or water is standing in the saucer or cache-pot, suspect overwatering.

Feeding
Pale leaves and short, stunted growth may be due to lack of fertilizer in the

Effects of overwatering
Yellowing lower leaves are often a sign of overwatering, but may also be due to a chill if it happens in winter. This is a *Fatshedera lizei* beginning to show signs of overwatering.

Aerosol scorch

A plant can also be damaged by aerosol sprays (even one containing an insecticide intended for houseplants). This dieffenbachia has dropped many of its leaves, and others are scorched, because an insecticidal aerosol was used too close to the plant.

Effects of dry air

Dry air is a particular problem for most ferns. This adiantum is showing the signs of low humidity.

compost (potting soil). Try liquid feeding for a quick boost. Specific plants, such as citrus fruits and rhododendrons, may show signs of iron deficiency (yellowing leaves) if grown in an alkaline compost. Feed with a chelated (sequestered) iron and next time you repot use an ericaceous compost (specially developed for lime-hating plants).

Bud drop

Bud drop is often caused by dry compost (potting soil) or dry air, but sometimes it is due to the plant being moved to a different position or turned once the buds have formed. (Zygocactus is an example of a plant that resents having to re-orientate its buds to light from a different direction.)

Dehydration

This thunbergia shows the classic symptoms of a dehydrated plant. The very dry compost (potting soil) is confirmation of the cause. The best treatment is to stand the pot in a bowl of water for several hours, until the compost is thoroughly wet. Peat (peat moss) composts are particularly difficult to rewet once they have dried out completely, but a few drops of mild household detergent added to the water will help to rewet it.

Bud drop

Bud drop is often caused by dry root, overwatering, or by moving a plant once the flower buds have formed.

Wilting and worse

WHEN A PLANT WILTS OR APPEARS TO COLLAPSE, IT'S TIME TO TAKE DRASTIC ACTION. THE FIRST PRIORITY IS TO DECIDE WHAT'S WRONG, THEN, IF POSSIBLE, TO APPLY FIRST AID MEASURES WITHOUT DELAY TO BRING THE PLANT BACK TO HEALTH.

First aid for a dry plant

1. If the leaves of a plant have started to wilt like this, the compost (potting soil) is probably too dry. Feel it first – overwatering also causes wilting.

2. Stand the pot in a bowl or bucket of water and leave it until the air bubbles have ceased to rise.

3. It will take some hours for the water to revive the plant. In the meantime, help the plant further by misting the leaves with water from time to time.

4. Once the plant has revived, remove it from the bowl and stand it in a cool place out of direct sunlight for at least a day.

Wilting and collapse are a signal that something is drastically wrong. If you ignore this warning, you may lose the plant. Plants usually wilt for one of three reasons:

- Too much water.
- Too little water.
- Insects or a disease affecting the roots.

The first two will usually be obvious: if the compost (potting soil) is hard and dry, underwatering is the likely cause: if there is water standing in the cache-pot or saucer, or if the compost oozes water, overwatering is almost certainly the cause.

If the compost seems neither overwatered nor underwatered, check the base of the plant just above compost level. If the stem looks black or rotten, a fungus disease is the likely cause and the plant is best discarded.

If none of the above symptoms are present, remove the plant from its pot and shake off some of the soil. If many of the roots are soft or black and decaying, a root disease is the likely cause. Look also for grubs or other insects around the roots. The larvae of beetles such as weevils can sometimes cause a plant to collapse.

First aid for root pests or diseases
It will be very difficult to revive a plant with a severe root rot, but you can try drenching the compost with a fungicide, then after a couple of hours letting it dry out on absorbent paper. If the root system is badly damaged it may be worth repotting it in sterilized compost first, after removing as much of the old soil as possible.

Some soil pests, such as root aphids, can be controlled if drenched with an insecticide. Wine weevil grubs and other serious soil pests are not so easy to control. Try shaking the old soil off the roots, dusting them with an insecticidal powder, then repotting in fresh, sterilized compost. If the damage is not too extensive the plant may survive once it has had time to make new growth.

First aid for a wet plant

1. Knock the plant out of its pot. If it does not come out easily, invert the plant while holding the compost (potting soil) in with one hand, and knock the rim of the pot on a hard surface.

2. Wrap the root-ball in several layers of absorbent paper.

3. Stand the plant in a warm place, out of direct sunlight, with more absorbent paper wrapped around the root-ball. Change the paper periodically if it is still drawing moisture from the compost.

OTHER POSSIBLE CAUSES OF COLLAPSE

Plants may collapse for physiological reasons:

Cold air at night, especially in winter, may cause some plants to collapse, especially if they have been kept warm during the day.

Strong, hot sunshine through glass will make many plants wilt. Usually they recover when given cooler, shadier conditions.

Hot, dry air will have a similar effect on some plants, such as the more delicate ferns.

Poor light will eventually cause a plant to exhaust itself. But this is likely to be a gradual process, much less rapid than collapse caused by watering problems or pests.

4. Continue until the compost has dried out, but do not let it become completely dry. Repot and water only very cautiously for the next week.

Creative displays

WHETHER YOU COLLECT HOUSE-PLANTS AS A PHILATELIST COLLECTS STAMPS, OR WHETHER YOU CHOOSE THEM IN THE SAME WAY AS AN INTERIOR DESIGNER SELECTS A PAINTING, YOU HAVE TO FIND POSITIONS THAT WILL NOT ONLY PLEASE THE PLANT, BUT ALSO SUIT THE DÉCOR.

Interior design

THE WAY IN WHICH YOU FURNISH AND DECORATE YOUR HOME IS AN EXPRESSION OF YOUR OWN PERSONALITY. YOU MAY NOT BE ABLE TO INFLUENCE THE WORLD OUTSIDE, OR EVEN YOUR WORKPLACE, BUT IN YOUR OWN HOME YOU CAN MAKE THE KIND OF STATEMENTS THAT PLEASE YOU PERSONALLY. HOUSEPLANTS CAN HELP YOU TO CREATE YOUR CHOSEN IMAGE: WHETHER WARM AND 'COTTAGEY', BOLD AND CLINICAL, STYLISH AND ELEGANT, OR SIMPLY PROVOCATIVE. IT DOES NOT MATTER WHETHER YOU HAVE A COUNTRY COTTAGE, CITY FLAT, OR SUBURBAN HOUSE, YOU CAN USE PLANTS TO COMPLEMENT YOUR CHOSEN DÉCOR.

A room without plants is rather like a meal without any seasoning. It serves its purpose and can even look good, but it lacks spice and that extra ingredient that would make it interesting. Not everyone wants to be strangled by an over-exuberant ivy as they mount the stairs, or grapple with a monstera in order to place a coffee cup on the sideboard, but a few well-chosen plants will transform a bare or dull room into something special in the same way as a carefully chosen picture or ornament.

Plants can also serve a functional purpose when used to screen off part of a room in a natural and much less obtrusive way than furniture or normal room dividers.

Establishing a style
Decide on the image and style that you intend to create, then buy plants that will help you to achieve it. Be prepared to invest in one or two really good specimens if necessary: they may cost no more than half a dozen mediocre plants yet will have far more impact. To create an old-fashioned cottage atmosphere, however, a collection of traditional plants on the win-

dowsill and a large aspidistra or sansevieria in an attractive cache-pot are more likely to achieve the right ambience than some big, bold 'architectural' plants that would create a strong statement in a large modern room, office, or foyer.

Groups or single specimens?
Most plants prefer to grow in groups as they benefit from the microclimate produced, and three or five quite ordinary houseplants grouped in a large container will make a far greater impact than they would if dotted around the room individually. Grouping plants usually means you have to use a large container rather than ordinary plant pots, and this also adds to the sense of purpose and design.

Large plants can usually be used in isolation, and many of the tall-

ABOVE AND LEFT: *A good way to learn about the best ways to arrange plants in the home is to place the same plants in different containers or groups to see the very different effects you can create with the same plants. Here three cyclamen have been placed in separate containers (above) then grouped together in a single cache-pot (left). Both displays look elegant, but strikingly different.*

growers, such as yuccas, philo-dendrons, and ficus such as *F. benjamina* and *F. lyrata*, often have enough presence to stand alone as focal point. If they become rather tall and bare at the base, however, you could try planting some flowering plants, or even small trailing ivies, in the same container to hide the stem.

Backgrounds and backdrops

Most plants are best viewed against a plain background. If you have a highly patterned wall covering, especially if it includes leaves or floral motifs, the plants you choose need to have big, bold foliage. This is where plain green has a definite advantage over varie-gated foliage: visual chaos will result from a boldly coloured and variegated plant placed against a brightly deco-rated wall covering.

Making the most of height

If all your plants are on tables or windowsills, they will look attractive but predictable. Use a few large speci-mens on the floor, or consider hanging containers in light corners of the room that seem devoid of decoration at a higher level. Use trailers from the

TOP: *Plants usually make a bolder feature if grouped, and they benefit from the microclimate produced. Here, the plants have been graded in height to provide an attractive foliage screen between the eating and working areas of the kitchen.*

ABOVE: *A disused fireplace can become a focal point if used to frame plants. Use taller plants in the hearth and smaller plants and trailers on the mantelpiece.*

mantelpiece if you do not use the fireplace, and make the most of pedes-tals for attractive containers with trail-ers like *Scindapsus aureus*, spiky up-right plants like dracaenas or arching plants like nephrolepsis ferns.

Choosing containers

Containers should never dominate, but they can make a mediocre plant look special, and many are ornaments in their own right. Try using an attractive ornament as a cache-pot for a plant, or if you have an interesting container, like an old kettle or coal-scuttle, plant it up with a flowering or foliage plant that makes a happy mar-riage and which does not dominate the container.

A question of scale

The relationship between the size of the plant and its required function in the room should not be overlooked. A solitary saintpaulia, even if it is set on an attractive table, will make no im-pact in the overall composition; like-wise, a large *Ficus benjamina* in a tiny room in a cottage will certainly be noticed, but not for its contribution to the interior design.

Table-top displays

A BEAUTIFUL FLOWERING PLANT OR AN ARRANGEMENT OF FOLIAGE PLANTS MAKES A SUPERB CENTREPIECE FOR A TABLE, WHETHER YOU USE IT AS A FOCAL POINT ON A BARE TABLE OR AS THE CROWNING GLORY TO A TABLE-SETTING FOR A DINNER PARTY. UNFORTUNATELY SUCH POSITIONS SUIT FEW PLANTS, MOST OF WHICH PREFER A LIGHTER SPOT NEAR THE WINDOW, SO CHOOSE YOUR PLANTS CAREFULLY AND BE PREPARED TO CHANGE THEM FREQUENTLY.

Flowering plants

Give your table display a designer look by choosing a flowering plant that is colour co-ordinated with the table-cloth. This can look particularly pleasing if you are using the plant as part of a table-setting for a meal, and even a small plant will look effective if it appears to have been chosen and displayed with care.

A cloth can be used to good effect on a table used purely for display, especially if the table itself is mediocre. By choosing a patterned or plain cloth that is light in colour, you can draw attention to the feature, and make even more of a focal point with your plant. A cyclamen may look nice but uninspiring if placed on a bare table. But if you put it on a pink tablecloth to match the shade of the flower, it becomes something special.

Try positioning a bright flowering plant with blooms on long stems, such as a gerbera, on a side table with a mirror behind. It will reflect the tall blooms and appear to multiply the number of flowers.

Gerberas are good examples of flowering pot plants that are suitable for a table display. They are usually sold in bloom and are difficult to keep for more than one year, so you might treat them like a long-lasting display of cut flowers. It will not matter that

the light is poor if the plant is to be discarded after flowering, which should continue for weeks.

Other flowering pot plants that will bring colour and cheer to a dull corner and that are usually discarded after flowering include year-round chrysanthemums, cinerarias, *Erica* × *hyemalis* and *E. gracilis*, and small annuals like *Exacum affine*. In winter and spring, bowls of bulbs such as hyacinths can be used if you keep them in good light until they come into flower and do not try to force them to flower indoors the following year.

Foliage plants

It is among the foliage plants that the most shade-tolerant types are to be found, but most are unsuitable for table-tops. Most species of ficus, for example, grow too large, while others, such as ivies, have a sprawling habit. Choose something tough and variegated, with a neat shape, such as *Sansevieria trifasciata gigantea* 'Laurentii', or variegated aglaonemas.

For a cool position, such as an unheated bedroom, or a hall that is not too stuffy, varieties of *Aucuba japonica* are useful.

POT-ET-FLEUR

A *pot-et-fleur* arrangement makes an ideal centre piece, giving plenty of scope for artistic presentation. Anyone keen on floral art will find plenty of scope for expressing their talent.

To make a classic *pot-et-fleur* arrangement, choose an attractive planter (some self-watering pots are suitable), and plant a group of three or five foliage plants (you can plant more but the container needs to be large). As you plant them, insert a glass tube or metal florist's tube into the compost (potting soil), either at the centre of the arrangement or a little to one side.

Fill the tube with water and insert a few cut flowers (and cut foliage if you want). You won't need many flowers, yet they will bring a touch of colour to the arrangement, and because you have to replace them regularly the composition will be constantly changing. If one or two of the foliage plants begin to deteriorate in time, just replace them with fresh ones.

OPPOSITE ABOVE: *Colour co-ordinate your plants for a really tasteful effect. Here a pink cyclamen harmonizes with the tablecloth and wallpaper border.*

OPPOSITE LEFT: *Try placing a plant, like this gerbera, in front of a mirror where the reflection can make even a small plant look larger and more imposing.*

RIGHT: *This* pot-et-fleur *arrangement uses floral foam to hold the cut flowers, which makes it particularly flexible in the way you can arrange the blooms. Lilies, freesias, cut fern leaves and ivies were used to create the arrangement, here displayed in a hearth.*

Creating a pot-et-fleur with foam

1. If using a basket like this, line it first to ensure that it is waterproof.

2. Position your foliage plants first, preferably in shallow pots.

3. Cut floral foam to size to pack between the pots.

4. Insert your flowers (and additional cut foliage if wished) into the moist floral foam.

Pedestals and hanging pots and baskets

HANGING AND CASCADING PLANTS ARE ESPECIALLY USEFUL IF YOU WANT TO MAKE THE MOST OF A VERTICAL SPACE OR CREATE A FEELING OF LUSHNESS IN A GARDEN ROOM. WHERE SPACE IS LIMITED AND THE FLOOR ALREADY HAS ITS BURDEN OF PLANTS, HANGING CONTAINERS CAN MAKE THE MOST OF THE AVAILABLE SPACE. USE THEM TO CREATE CASCADING CURTAINS OF FOLIAGE.

Pedestals

Many pedestals are extremely ornate, and make focal points in themselves. If you have an attractive pedestal, don't cover it with long trailers that mask its beauty. Use short trailers that will cascade over the pot but won't completely hide the pedestal under a curtain of leaves. Good plants to choose for this effect include *Asparagus densiflorus* 'Sprengeri', *Campanula isophylla* and flowering hybrids of zygocactus and rhipsalidopsis.

Plants with an arching rather than a cascading habit are also ideal for a pedestal where you want to show off both pot and pedestal: chlorophytums

ABOVE: *Chlorophytums look good displayed on a pedestal or in a hanging basket, where the arching effect can be seen to advantage. Hanging baskets are much more successful in a conservatory than indoors.*

LEFT: *The nephrolepis fern is a popular choice for a pedestal, as it makes a neat mound of growth with enough 'droop' to take the eye down to the pedestal. Here an attractive table has been used, and the opportunity taken to place another fern on the shelf beneath.*

OPPOSITE LEFT: *Hanging baskets should always be placed in a bright position, as the light near the ceiling is almost always poorer than lower down the window. This one contains a rhoicissus.*

and nephrolepis ferns are especially attractive used in this way.

For a pedestal that is functional rather than decorative, go for tumbling curtains of growth, with plants like ivies, *Plectranthus oertendahlii* and *P. coleoides* 'Marginatus', or a golden *Epipremnum aureum* 'Neon' (syn. *Scindapsus aureus*).

Hanging pots and baskets

Ordinary hanging baskets are unsuitable for using indoors, although you can of course use them in a conservatory. Unless you are prepared to take great care with the watering, and take precautions to avoid drips over your carpets and furniture, choose a hanging pot with a drip tray, or a specially designed indoor 'basket' (in effect a basket-shaped pot, sometimes with a water reservoir).

Hanging containers are difficult to position: they shouldn't be hung where they can be a hazard to anyone walking by, and in addition many plants suitable for baskets need to be near good light. If the room is not large enough for hanging baskets, try the same plants in half baskets or wall pots. Many trailing or arching plants look magnificent when positioned against the background of a plain or pale wall.

PRACTICAL POINTS

🐾 Pedestals are far more practical than hanging pots. The plants will usually be in better light (because sunlight generally shines downwards, the upper part of the room is generally gloomier than the lower part), and watering is much easier if the plants are grown in ordinary pots. Baskets are difficult to water, and need to be hung where the baskets and their trailing contents do not cause an obstruction to anyone walking by.

TRAILERS AND CASCADERS TO TRY

🐾 **Flowering plants**
Aeschynanthus, *Aporocactus flagelliformis*, *Campanula isophylla*, columnea, *Rhipsalidopsis gaertneri* and *Zygocactus truncatus*.

🐾 **Foliage plants**
Asparagus densiflorus 'Sprengeri', *Chlorophytum comosum* 'Variegatum', *Epipremnum aureum* (syn. *Scindapsus aureus*), *Hedera helix* (ivies), small-leaved varieties, plectranthus and *Rhoicissus rhomboidea* (syn. *Cissus rhombifolia*).

Planting a pedestal arrangement

1. A wide, shallow container, which is more stable and detracts less from the pedestal itself, has been chosen here.

2. Choose a mixture of flowering and foliage plants for a spectacular display. You can try them for position while still in their pots, until you are happy with the arrangement.

3. Remove them from their pots for final planting. Try setting those at the edge at a slight angle so that they tend to grow outwards and tumble over the side.

RIGHT: *Don't just think of single specimens when choosing plants for a pedestal. A group can be arranged rather like a hanging basket, but planted in a pot.*

Grouping large plants

SOMETIMES A LARGE PLANT IS BEST VIEWED IN ISOLATION: ITS VERY SIZE AND

IMPORTANCE WILL THEN BE EMPHASIZED. MORE OFTEN, HOWEVER, THEY

LOOK BETTER WHEN POSITIONED AS PART OF A GROUP, PERHAPS WITH

SMALLER PLANTS IN FRONT.

Group plants together in places that might otherwise look bare. A disused fireplace can be improved with perhaps a single, elegant fern, provided that it is large enough. The whole fireplace and hearth area can be the ideal place for a group of plants — tall ones positioned mantelpiece height at the back, smaller ones in front at the bottom of the hearth, and arching or trailing plants sitting on the mantelpiece.

If you have a really magnificent plant, perhaps a yucca 1.8m (6ft) tall or more, or a beautiful variegated *Ficus benjamina* that almost reaches the ceiling, show it off in splendid isolation. These plants deserve to act as focal points in their own right. Less imposing plants usually look better arranged in small groups, where they will make a greater impact than they would individually. You can create the effect of a garden brought indoors by positioning plants in this way. Plants standing shoulder to shoulder always look more convincing than those dotted around the room wherever there seems to be space to put a plant.

Small plants are easily grouped in a large planter, but this is not suitable for large specimens. The huge planters used in offices and hotel foyers are not practical for the home, and the plants are best left in their own pots and arranged in close proximity with the largest at the back and smaller ones in front.

The majority of large houseplants are grown for their foliage, but many are variegated or boldly coloured. It's a good idea to mix a few plants with coloured or variegated foliage among the greens, although you may sometimes need an all-green group to produce a cool, tranquil effect. Variegated plants also require higher light levels than all-green ones because a smaller area of the leaf is able to photosynthesize with what light is available, so it's best to avoid these for plant groupings in the darkest parts of the home.

Group policy

The natural way to group large house-plants is with the tallest at the back, with bushier, lower ones at the front. Take into account their position in the room. If the group is placed halfway down a long room with windows at each end, so that the plants act almost as a divider, include more plants in the arrangement, with smaller ones at each side and the tallest in the centre. In a corner of a room, a group of plants consisting of a single big specimen at the back, with smaller ones spilling forwards to fill out the corner, can look quite stunning.

If the plants in your group lack sufficient variation in height, try standing some on a low table or raise them in some other way.

To protect the floor, stand each pot on a saucer – those designed to match the pot look good and are perfectly practical. It is difficult to water plants at the back of a group, so the risk of a little water overflowing will be that much greater.

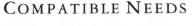

COMPATIBLE NEEDS

🌺 Wherever practical, group together those plants with similar needs. Yuccas and palms will tolerate a dry atmosphere and will be happy together, but most philodendrons and dracaenas prefer a humid atmosphere. For the short term you can mix any plants together, but if you plan to keep them in good condition, it's worth grouping plants with similar requirements so that they receive the most appropriate care.

OPPOSITE: *Plants often look better in groups, but choose ones appropriate to the setting. A group of small plants would look out of proportion in this hearth. The large specimens used here fill the space and give the setting a sense of design.*

TOP: *If this nephrolepis fern on a pedestal had been displayed on its own, it would probably have looked too isolated. By using it with other plants it looks interesting yet integrated.*

ABOVE: *Add one or two flowering plants to a group. Even a little colour will draw the eye.*

ABOVE: *Tall plants are always impressive, but they can look bare towards the base. By surrounding them with smaller bold plants in front, you can create a well-planned group. A selection of all-green and variegated plants with a wide array of leaf size and shape have been selected here for maximum visual interest.*

Grouping small plants

SMALL PLANTS CAN BE DISPLAYED MORE CREATIVELY THAN JUST IN INDI-
VIDUAL POTS. PLANT THEM IN GROUPS IN PLANTERS OR SELF-WATERING
POTS. YOU CAN EVEN CREATE MINIATURE GARDENS.

Grouping plants together often makes them easier to care for, and they usually look more attractive as an arrangement rather than as individual plants.

The overall effect of a group is usually bolder than that of individual specimens, and by placing taller ones at the back of the arrangement the effect is more 'landscaped'. Small-leaved prostrate plants such as *Ficus pumila* and *Helxine soleirolii* (syn. *Soleirolia soleirolii*) assume a new role in a group and are less insignificant than when they are grown as prostrate plants in an individual pot. In a group they become ground-cover plants, which is their natural state. Another advantage of grouping plants is that you can get away with less than perfect specimens: a plant with lop-sided growth, or one that is bare at the base, can be arranged so that its defects are hidden by other plants.

Grouped plants benefit from the microclimate created when plants are grown together. The local humidity is likely to be a little higher as the leaves tend to protect each other from drying air and cold draughts, and it is easier to keep the compost (potting soil) evenly moist in a large container than a small one. Groupings are ideal for self-watering containers and for plants grown hydroponically, and simply ensuring a steady and even supply of moisture almost always produces better growth.

Group styles

There are no hard and fast rules about how to group plants – whatever pleases you is right provided that the plants are also happy (avoid placing together plants with totally different needs). The suggestions for grouping styles described here work well for most plants, and generally look attractive, but be prepared to experiment. A group of plants arranged in an old coalscuttle in the hearth, for example, may look more attractive than any of the more traditional styles if the setting is right.

Collections of pots have the advantage of being infinitely flexible. You can rearrange and remove plants at will, and use transient flowering plants such as chrysanthemums and poinsettias more easily than in a permanent planting. A group of five or six plants in their individual pots will look cheery and bold if you mix different types of foliage plants (stiff and upright, arching, feathery or trailing) with a couple of flowering plants. You can space them out as necessary to fill the space, but make sure that they are close enough to overlap a little and look like a group.

Pebble trays are ideal for plants that like a lot of humidity. Use a tray

Grouping plants in a planter

1. A bowl without drainage holes will protect the table, but place a drainage layer at the bottom and be *very* careful not to overwater.

2. Place a little compost (potting soil) in the bowl first, then insert the plants. Try to achieve a good balance between flowering and foliage plants.

3. Firm the plants in, and pack more compost around the roots if necessary. Water, but be careful not to waterlog the compost.

ABOVE: *Pot up several plants in a bowl to make an attractive group; a* Begonia rex, *a cyclamen and ivies were used here.*

that will fit on a table or windowsill, and fill it with pebbles. Stand the pots on the pebbles. It does not matter if water stands in the tray provided that the bottoms of the pots are not in direct contact with it.

Planters and self-watering pots will usually accommodate at least three plants if you choose a suitable size. These look elegant, and are ideal if you find regular watering difficult. Choose plants that will not need frequent repotting or removing, and plant directly into the compost (potting soil).

WATCH OUT FOR PROBLEMS

🐛 Growing plants in groups has some drawbacks. Pests and diseases can spread more easily and rapidly, and you may be less likely to notice the early symptoms on leaves that are hidden by other plants. If grooming is a regular routine, however, this should be only a minor drawback, and one that is easily overcome.

ABOVE: *Grouping small plants is particularly effective if you need to use them in a low position, where they are viewed from above. Add some flowering plants (here gerberas and begonias) to bring a foliage group to life.*

TOP: *Small plants benefit from grouping as much as large ones. You can often group small plants in one large container, but by keeping them in individual containers you can ring the changes more easily. This is especially important if you use flowering plants that may look attractive for only a relatively short time.*

ABOVE: *Grouping plants in a shallow dish keeps them happy and looks good too. Because these plants are raised on expanded clay granules (you could use small gravel), some water can be kept in the bottom without waterlogging the compost (potting soil) – providing invaluable humidity for the ferns.*

Garden rooms and conservatories

WITH A GARDEN ROOM OR CONSERVATORY YOU CAN GROW ALMOST ANY HOUSEPLANT SUCCESSFULLY, AS WELL AS MANY MORE FOR WHICH YOU WOULD NORMALLY NEED A GREENHOUSE. HOWEVER, YOU WILL HAVE TO RESOLVE THE CONFLICT BETWEEN THE NEEDS OF PLANTS AND HUMANS, FOR WHAT IS A COMFORTABLE ENVIRONMENT FOR TROPICAL PLANTS MAY NOT BE COMFORTABLE FOR YOU WITH CAREFUL PLANNING, HOWEVER, YOU CAN MAKE THE GARDEN ROOM AN EXTENSION OF THE LIVING AREA, WHERE YOU CAN ENJOY HOUSEPLANTS AT THEIR VERY BEST.

Many conservatories and garden rooms are built on as a home extension or a sun room where the garden can be enjoyed when the weather is pleasant but not warm, and in which the plants are merely decorative accessories. You can, however, create a veritable jungle atmosphere, with plants from floor to roof, and hot and humid air to match.

Mainly for people

If a sun room or conservatory is to be a comfortable place to sit for long periods and enjoy the view of the garden, a few attractive chairs, a coffee table and a few elegant pot plants dotted around are all that's required. It just becomes another room.

Paint the back wall white or cream, plant a bougainvillea against it, buy a few big palms and add one or two flowering shrubs such as *Nerium oleander*, and perhaps an orange or lemon in an attractive tub, and you will have a room with instant charm.

Mainly for plants

If your conservatory was bought mainly to increase the number and type of houseplants that you can grow, treat it like a greenhouse. Indeed the distinction between some modern lean-to greenhouses and garden rooms can be a little blurred.

Make the most of climbers; these will clothe the wall and cover the roof space if you secure galvanized wires at about 30–60cm (1–2ft) intervals for support. The roof cover will provide welcome shade in the summer, and if you choose deciduous climbers such as a grapevine or a passiflora, the other inhabitants will receive full light at the time of year when they most need it. Even so, climbers such as grapes may still need to be cut back periodically during the summer to prevent them from dominating and casting too much shade.

Plant climbers and wall shrubs in the ground if possible, by lifting the paving and making planting pits. Use special display shelves, or improvise your own. Don't just arrange plants around the edge of the structure, create islands of plants, or use them as a backdrop for seats, which can be almost surrounded with plants.

Hanging baskets should thrive, so use plenty of them and be adventurous with what you plant. Although traditional bedding plants can be used in a conservatory, cascading fuchsias or curtains of columneas are usually much more spectacular.

For healthy houseplants, lay a floor that won't come to harm if you splash water about. Use a humidifier if possible, so that the air is aways moist in warm weather, and provide heating for the winter. A minimum of 7°C (45°F) is sufficient to keep most houseplants alive, while the majority of tender types will survive the winter at 13°C (55°F) minimum.

ABOVE: *Bold, tall plants, like this palm, can be used as an eye-catching feature in a conservatory. It also emphasizes the vertical line of the magnificent wrought-iron staircase.*

OPPOSITE: *Citrus fruits, such as oranges, do not do well indoors, but they make excellent conservatory plants. Try painting your conservatory wall white to reflect light and to make an attractive backdrop against which to view your plants.*

TOP RIGHT: *By keeping most of the planting around the edge, and using plenty of hanging baskets, you can give the impression of lush plant growth while still retaining an attractive sitting area.*

ABOVE RIGHT: *Make the most of available space. Plant climbers against the house wall, and use hanging baskets, which will do much better in the improved light than indoors.*

RIGHT: *Plants should thrive in a conservatory, and you can use bold all-green foliage groups like this. With a tiled floor you can provide plenty of moisture and humidity without worrying about drips or splashed water.*

Bottle gardens

BOTTLE GARDENS, CREATED IN SEALED BOTTLES WITH MOISTURE RECIRCU-
LATING AS IT CONDENSES AND RUNS DOWN THE GLASS, MAKE AN IDEAL HOME
FOR MANY SMALL BUT DEMANDING PLANTS THAT ARE DIFFICULT TO KEEP IN
A NORMAL ROOM ENVIRONMENT. THEY ALSO MAKE A VERY DECORATIVE WAY
OF DISPLAYING PLANTS AND ONE THAT IS SURE TO BECOME A TALKING POINT
WITH VISITORS.

The still, protected and humid environment of a sealed bottle garden makes it possible to grow many small jungle and rain forest type plants that would soon die in a dry living-room. Yet if you leave the top off and water very carefully, a bottle garden can also be a pretty way to display those that enjoy less humid conditions. Even flowering plants can be used if you are careful to deadhead them regularly to prevent the rotting flowers becoming a source of diseases.

Sealed bottles will thrive for months without attention, and you can go on

How to plant a bottle garden

1. Place a layer of charcoal and gravel or expanded clay granules in the bottom of a thoroughly clean bottle, then add compost (potting soil). Use a funnel or cone made from thick paper or thin cardboard as a guide.

2. Use small plants, and if necessary remove some of the compost to make insertion easier. Unless the neck is very narrow you should be able to insert the plants without difficulty.

3. After tamping the compost around the roots (use a cotton reel on the end of a cane if necessary), mist the plants and compost. If necessary, direct the spray to remove compost adhering to the sides.

LEFT: *An open-topped bottle like this will require regular careful watering, but as it contains some quick growing plants the ready access makes routine grooming and pruning much easier.*

holiday confident that even tricky ferns and selaginellas will be safe until you return. Unsealed containers require careful watering, and if you use flowering or fast-growing plants in them, regular grooming and pruning are essential.

Bottle gardens can be difficult to display. The plants need good light, and if you choose a bottle with coloured glass (many of those readily available are green) it is important to remember that much of the useful light will be filtered out. A sunny window is as undesirable as a gloomy corner: temperatures can soar as the sun's rays penetrate two layers of glass. The best place is by a window that does not receive direct sunlight, or on a table just below a sunny window, where it will receive good light but little direct sun.

Metal display stands make more of a feature of a bottle that would otherwise be placed on the floor, and help by raising it a little towards the light.

Sealed or open?

If you have a container with a stopper, a sealed environment will mean that you can leave it for months without watering, *once the atmosphere has been balanced*. But these are not suitable for plants with flowers, or fast-growing foliage plants. Any plant used in a sealed bottle must be able to tolerate constantly damp, humid conditions, and poor light.

Tip
If you can't get your hand into the bottle, use a spoon tied to a cane to make the planting hole, and a fork tied to another one to hold the plant while you lower it into position.

BALANCING A SEALED BOTTLE

If you add too much water to a sealed bottle, the plants may rot and condensation on the glass will be a constant problem. If you add too little, the plants will not grow. You can only achieve the correct balance by trial and error.

If the compost (potting soil) looks or feels too wet, leave the stopper off for a few days until it begins to dry out.

It is normal for the bottle to mist up inside when the outside temperature drops, so a 'steamed up' bottle in the morning is not abnormal. If the condensation does not clear during the morning, the compost is too moist (leave the stopper off for a day). If there is no condensation when the room temperature drops significantly, the compost may be too dry.

ABOVE LEFT: *A large kitchen jar makes an interesting bottle garden. This one contains a miniature saintpaulia. Open the jar regularly to remove dead flowers, which will otherwise start to decay and cause the other plants to rot.*

FAR LEFT AND LEFT: *Bottle gardens can be used to display a variety of foliage plants, such as selaginella, variegated ivy and a colourful dracaena (far left). A collection of just one kind of plant, such as three different pileas (left), can also make an interesting group.*

Terrariums and other plant cases

TERRARIUMS AND PLANT CASES ARE USUALLY USED AS A DECORATIVE ORNA-MENT, PERHAPS ON A SIDE TABLE WITH ADEQUATE ARTIFICIAL LIGHTING TO SHOW OFF THE CONTAINER AND TO STIMULATE PLANT GROWTH, OR ON A TABLE IN FRONT OF A WINDOW KEEP THE PLANTS SIMPLE AND UNCLUT-TERED IF YOU WANT TO MAKE THE MOST OF AN ATTRACTIVE CONTAINER; CONCENTRATE ON A LUSH PLANTING IF THE CASE IS PRACTICAL RATHER THAN PLEASING.

Terrariums and plants cases encompass those containers that are not bottles, but the advantages and challenges are exactly the same as for a bottle garden. With a terrarium you can let your imagination roam wider in search of suitable containers. The old-fashioned Wardian cases (now rare and expensive, though replicas can be found) are especially attractive, but a second-hand aquarium will do just as well and you may be able to obtain one quite cheaply as it does not even have to be watertight.

Some glass cases can be sealed, in the same way as a bottle garden, but most are left open. The plants are protected from draughts on all sides, and this helps to keep the atmosphere warm and moist around the plants.

SUITABLE CONTAINERS

Elaborate terrariums are available from garden centres and shops, but you can sometimes buy kits to make your own. Designs vary from plain to ornate, but most are assembled with glass cut to shape and held together with strips of lead. Inexpensive, improvised containers are often just as successful if your interest lies in the plants rather than in the container.

Aquariums offer plenty of scope for 'landscaping'. On the one hand they can be used without a top and kept fairly dry for a cactus garden, complete with a suitably arid setting of stones and stone chippings; on the other they will make an ideal home for delicate ferns if you create a humid atmosphere by covering with a glass top. You can buy aquarium covers that include a light, enabling you to make a feature of it even in a dark corner. But be sure to use the type of fluorescent tube sold for aquariums, as these are balanced to produce a quality of light that is suitable for plant growth.

Goldfish bowls can be used for just one or two plants. A single plant like a saintpaulia will look good, or choose a spreading small-leaved carpeter such as *Helxine soleirolii* (syn. *Soleirolia soleirolii*) that will gradually creep up the sides and then spill over the rim.

Specimen jars, originally used to preserve biological specimens, can be attractive, but they are more difficult to obtain (try a laboratory equipment supplier).

LEFT: *Miniature kalanchoes and miniature saintpaulias can be depended on to provide colour in any terrarium, but a contrasting foliage plant, like the selaginella in this one, will improve the arrangement.*

Planting a terrarium

1. Always place a drainage layer at the bottom of the terrarium. Use gravel and charcoal or expanded clay granules to counter the effects of standing water.

2. Plants that are a little too tall for the terrarium, such as this palm, can be trimmed to size, but do not use fast-growing plants that would quickly dominate the smaller specimens.

3. If necessary, remove some of the compost (potting soil) from the root-ball and firm the plant in well.

Many containers used for terrariums have more room than bottles or preserving jars, so larger plants can be grown, and you don't have to worry so much if a vigorous member of the group tries to pop its head above the rim. Long or deep containers, such as an aquarium, also offer much more scope for 'landscaping', with small rocks, even miniature pools.

Follow the watering advice for bottle gardens and take care with preparation and planting:

- Place a layer of charcoal and gravel at least 1cm (½in) thick on the bottom.
- Use a sterilized potting or seed compost (medium), but avoid feeding or using a compost high in nutrients, otherwise the plants will soon outgrow their space.
- Add small rocks or pebbles if you want to 'landscape' the terrarium, but avoid wood as this may rot and encourage diseases.
- Cover the container with a sheet of close-fitting glass if appropriate, and if you want to create an enclosed environment.

ABOVE: *An attractive terrarium like this can be expensive to buy, but some people make their own, and you may be able to buy one in kit form to assemble yourself.*

RIGHT: *Saintpaulias are a good choice for a container with easy access for removing dead flowers. They benefit from the protected and humid atmosphere. Instead of planting them alone, use them with a carpet of moss or low-growing selaginellas.*

Specimen plants

EVERY HOME NEEDS AT LEAST A COUPLE OF SPECIMEN PLANTS TO PROVIDE ATTRACTIVE FOCAL POINTS. THEY DO NOT NEED TO BE LARGE SPECIMENS LIKE SMALL TREES, PROVIDED THAT THEY ARE IMPOSING. A WELL-ESTABLISHED CLIMBER THAT FORMS PART OF A ROOM DIVIDER, OR A REALLY LARGE ASPIDISTRA OR *NEPHROLEPIS EXALTATA* ON A PEDESTAL, FOR EXAMPLE, WILL SERVE THE SAME PURPOSE AS A LARGE *FICUS BENJAMINA* THAT ALMOST TOUCHES THE CEILING.

The purpose of a specimen plant is to catch the eye and be admired. This can be achieved by a really well-grown chlorophytum in a hanging container with cascading shoots carrying their small plantlets, as effectively as by an large, expensive palm. It just needs to be a superb example of the plant, well displayed, against a suitable background.

A large plant with a bold profile or outline, often called an 'architectural' plant, will transform a bare wall in a large room, add character to an otherwise uninspiring hallway, or give a sense of design and purpose if placed at the end of a long passage. If necessary, use spotlights to highlight the plant. If you use lights balanced for good plant growth the plant will benefit too. It is difficult to grow such large specimens yourself simply by starting with a small plant. It may take years and in the poor light and dry atmosphere indoors it will be extremely difficult to grow a plant to a large size without blemishes. Large specimens are expensive, however, so be sure that you can provide conditions that will maintain your investment.

Background and lighting
A bold plant requires a suitable background to show off its size and shape to advantage. A plain background is usually best, and a light-coloured wall will make most plants look good. If the background is colourful or confused, choose a plant with bold plain green leaves, such as a *Ficus lyrata*.

Once natural light fails, use spotlights to draw attention to key plants, but make sure that the bulbs are not so close that the heat generated damages the plant.

Containers
Choose a container that does justice to the plant. An ordinary large plastic or clay pot will let down a magnificent palm or large weeping fig. If you want an ordinary terracotta pot, choose one that is large and ornately decorated (you don't have to worry about whether it is frostproof for indoors). If the décor demands something more modern, there are many very attractive planters and coloured plastic plant holders available.

Make sure that the colour of your chosen container goes with your décor and that the size is in proportion to the plant. A pot that is too large or too small will mar the effect.

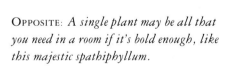

OPPOSITE: *A single plant may be all that you need in a room if it's bold enough, like this majestic spathiphyllum.*

TOP LEFT: *You don't need to buy expensive or exotic plants for a specimen with real impact. The commonplace chlorophytum is so easy to grow and propagate that many plants are acquired as gifts from friends with surplus plants. If you keep a young plant for long enough, repot it annually, and are generous with the feeding and watering, you can end up with a magnificent specimen.*

ABOVE LEFT: Monstera deliciosa *is a firm favourite as a specimen plant, and this picture shows why. Here the clever use of a mirror not only makes the most of an attractive clock, but also reflects the bold leaves of the monstera.*

ABOVE RIGHT: *A large window or patio door with no sill needs a big floor-standing plant to create instant impact. Yuccas, and palms like this one, are ideal.*

PLANTS TO TRY

Architectural plants
Araucaria heterophylla (syn. *A. excelsa*), *Fatsia japonica*, *Ficus benjamina*, *Ficus elastica* varieties, *Ficus lyrata*, palms, *Philodendron bipinnatifidum* and yucca.

Climbing plants
Cissus antarctica, *Monstera deliciosa* and *Philodendron domesticum* (syn. *P. hastatum*).

Choosing a container

BESIDES FULFILLING AN ESSENTIAL FUNCTION, CONTAINERS CAN ALSO BE DECORATIVE IN THEIR OWN RIGHT AND FORM PART OF THE ROOM DÉCOR JUST LIKE A VASE OR ORNAMENT. THE RIGHT CONTAINER WILL ENHANCE AN ATTRACTIVE PLANT AND CAN OFTEN COMPENSATE FOR A MEDIOCRE ONE. THE CHOICE OF CONTAINER CAN DEMONSTRATE YOUR ARTISTIC FLAIR AND EVEN YOUR SENSE OF HUMOUR.

Ordinary plant pots have a place in the greenhouse, but not in the home. Some plants, especially large palms, benefit from the weight of a large clay pot, which gives them stability if filled with a loam-based compost (potting soil), but indoors an ornate one with an attractive pattern will always look nicer than a plain one. As a general rule, all other houseplants look better in especially designed indoor containers.

Cache-pots
Repotting into a new container is not always necessary. A cache-pot (an outer container in which you hide the pot containing the plant) creates the right illusion and avoids the need to repot. This technique is especially useful for flowering plants that will probably only be in the home for a short time, and for fast-growing plants that are likely to need frequent repotting.

Any decorative container can be used as a cache-pot. Attractive ones are available in shops and garden centres, but a search around the home often provides something suitable. Even old kitchenware, such as a teapot or copper saucepan, can look appropriate for a plant in the kitchen.

If you are an amateur potter, making your own cache-pots can be particularly rewarding, and the plants provide a good opportunity to display your talents around the home.

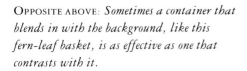

OPPOSITE ABOVE: *Sometimes a container that blends in with the background, like this fern-leaf basket, is as effective as one that contrasts with it.*

OPPOSITE BELOW: *If you don't have matching decorative containers for a group arrangement, improvise. Ordinary plastic pots and saucers have here been wrapped in strips of white cotton fabric for an eye-catching effect.*

ABOVE LEFT: *A metal container like this ornamental bucket adds to the crisp, clean look of a plant like* Asplenium nidus.

ABOVE CENTRE: *If you have a container with lots of character, like this antique 'self-watering' planter, choose a plant that does not detract from it. This* Asparagus plumosus *(syn.* A. setaceus*), has a feathery appearance that clothes the container without masking it.*

ABOVE RIGHT: *Containers like this decorative milk churn are great for kitchen herbs, such as parsley, but water very cautiously unless you can make drainage holes in the base.*

RIGHT: *This beautifully rounded container made from a hollowed-out pumpkin reflects the rounded shape and colour of the begonia it contains. As a finishing touch, moss has been draped around the plant and allowed to tumble over the rim of the container.*

Plastic and ceramic containers

A visit to any good garden centre will give you an idea of the huge choice of pretty yet practical containers that you can use. Whenever possible, choose one with drainage holes, otherwise you will have to treat it like a cache-pot or be *very* careful with watering. It is never a good idea to plant directly into any container without drainage holes. Even if you are careful about watering, sooner or later the roots will find themselves standing in water and, as a result of oxygen starvation, they will start to die.

Don't dismiss modern plastic containers. Some of them are bright, clean-looking and appropriate for a modern décor, or perhaps an office setting. Otherwise the choice of material and design must reflect your own taste and home décor.

Planters and self-watering containers

Planters are generally taken to mean containers that are large enough to hold several plants rather than individual specimens. These are ideal for displaying a group of plants.

Some planters are self-watering, with a reservoir at the bottom. Plants will generally thrive in these, and you can leave them for a few days with no problem. Although more expensive than ordinary containers, they are strongly recommended if plastic containers do not look incongruous in your home.

Think small as well as big
Very small plants are sometimes difficult to display, and a prostrate plant such as *Nertera depressa* can look slightly ridiculous grown in a normal pot — you will see more of the pot than of the plant. Try growing plants like these in small, decorative or fun containers, such as a collection of ducks or hens with a planting space in their backs. If you have a group of perhaps three such containers, planted with

WARNING WORDS

🌿 Cache-pots usually lack a drainage hole. This means that you don't have to bother with a saucer beneath the pot, but the plant inside will be standing in water and will soon die unless you are very careful about watering.

🌿 Place a few pebbles or marbles in the bottom, to raise the inner pot off the bottom of the container. If a little surplus water drains through, the compost (potting soil) should not remain soaked. But always check that the bottom of the inner pot is clear of any standing water.

🌿 If planting in any container without drainage holes, be *extremely careful* when watering. It's almost impossible to know whether there is standing water in the bottom of a container. You may want to risk it for a short-term plant that you know will have to be discarded soon, otherwise just use the container as a cache-pot or choose a different one.

TOP LEFT: *Glass containers can look very stylish. A lining of moss will look more attractive than exposed compost (potting soil). Careful watering is essential if you plant straight into any container without drainage holes.*

CENTRE LEFT: *Ornamental cabbages and kales are usually sold for outdoor decoration, but you can use them indoors for a few weeks. For a table-top display, try wrapping the plastic pot in a crisp white napkin.*

BELOW LEFT: *Sometimes the colour of a variegated leaf can pick up and extend the colour of the container. Here a variegated ivy tumbles out of a white teapot.*

BELOW RIGHT: *Low, mound-forming or carpeting plants such as* Helxine soleirolii *(syn.* Soleirolia soleirolii*) need a small container in proportion to the plant.*

OPPOSITE ABOVE: *Moss baskets make unusual containers for the right plants. This spathiphyllum looks right because the flower is taller than the handle.*

OPPOSITE BELOW: *Use a bit of lateral thinking in the kitchen. Try displaying some of your fruit with the flowers. Here oranges and apples share an interesting wooden container with* Streptocarpus saxorum.

matching or different prostrate plants, they will bring a touch of humour to your home, and should not seem to be in poor taste.

Baskets

Many foliage and flowering plants look especially attractive in wicker and moss-covered baskets, but if using a basket not specifically intended for plants, be sure to line it with a protective sheet. If you simply place pots into the basket, or replant into compost (potting soil) placed directly into the basket, moisture will seep through, mar any surface beneath, and in time rot or damage the basket.

Line the basket with a sheet of flexible plastic or any other waterproof membrane (a large piece of kitchen foil will do if you have nothing more suitable to hand). The protective liner can be taped down and should not be visible once the basket has been filled with compost and planted.

Small plants can look especially pretty in a basket with a handle, but taller plants can look awkward if the plant is very leafy or its height coincides with the top of the handle.

Search out the unusual

The container that is just right for a particular plant, or a special position, may be one that you will only recognize when you see it. Part of the fun of growing houseplants lies in using them creatively, and displaying them with imagination. Searching out fun or interesting containers can become part of the hobby.

Garden centres often have a useful range of containers to start with, but for the more stylish plant holders you may have to visit the kind of shop that sells well-designed furniture, stores that specialize in modern home accessories, and even antique shops. But you might find something just as good, and far less expensive, in a junk shop or even a jumble or garage sale. One person's throw-away may be a source of inspiration to a flower arranger or houseplant enthusiast.

Porch plants

USE YOUR PORCH TO GROW THE TOUGHER HOUSEPLANTS THAT NEED PLENTY

OF SPACE AND GOOD LIGHT. YOU CAN EVEN MAKE IT LOOK LIKE A SMALL

CONSERVATORY.

A porch influences the visitor's first impression of your home, so one that is well clothed with plants rather than bare and bleak will make a warmer welcome. An enclosed porch can be awash with colour the year round, but with an open porch in an exposed or cold position you will have to be content with hardy foliage plants for the cold months.

Enclosed porches

An enclosed porch can be like a mini lean-to greenhouse, and you can enjoy lush foliage and colourful flowers every month of the year. However, try to avoid using plants that will resent the sudden, icy blasts of air that occur when the outer door is opened in cold weather. Intolerant plants will soon drop their leaves and probably die.

Choose mainly plants recommended for cool temperatures, such as primulas, bowls of bulbs such as hyacinths and tulips, or cyclamen and azaleas for the winter. During the summer, regal and zonal geraniums (pelargoniums) do well in the hot atmosphere of such a small enclosed space, and cacti and succulents usually thrive. Provided that the porch can be maintained above freezing temperature, most cacti and succulents will benefit from being left there during the winter. The majority of cacti flower better if they have experienced a cold period during the winter.

Make use of climbers against at least one of the walls: passifloras would do well, but are generally too rampant. Choose something that is more easily restrained, such as *Hoya carnosa* or *Jasminum polyanthum* (be prepared to

ABOVE: *Porches can be bright or gloomy, protected or exposed. Choose plants appropriate to the conditions. This large* Ficus benajamina *will be happy in this position for the summer months, but will have to be brought indoors once the weather turns cold.*

keep it cut back once well established), or even a bougainvillea. Or go for foliage effect with *Cissus antarctica* or *Rhoicissus rhomboidea* (syn. *Cissus rhombifolia*).

If the porch is large, you can use plenty of big plants in floor-standing pots, such as *Fatsia japonica* (a variegated variety will look brighter in a porch), or perhaps an oleander (*Nerium oleander*).

Shelves will be needed to display small plants. If there are no built-in shelves, use the small free-standing display units sold for greenhouses, or special plant stands.

Open porches

Even an open porch can be made attractive. Group plenty of pots of hardy evergreens such as *Aucuba japonica* varieties, *Fatsia japonica*, skimmias (most have attractive berries in winter), and ivies if you want a trailer or climber. If you have pot-grown camellias and rhododendrons, for example, you can bring them into the porch for extra colour when they are in bloom.

Erica × *hyemalis*, *E. gracilis*, *Solanum capsicastrum* and its hybrids, even year-round chrysanthemums, will all provide colour for weeks or even months before having to be discarded.

During the summer, many of the tougher indoor plants can be placed in your porch. Yuccas will do well, and the variegated chlorophytums are reliable, but you can use plants as diverse as the brightly coloured coleus and flowering bougainvilleas. Don't be afraid to add a few unusual hardy foliage plants, such as rhubarb, to create a talking point.

PRACTICAL PROBLEMS

🐦 Most houseplants will thrive in an enclosed porch if you avoid extremely high or low temperatures.

🐦 A small electric heater coupled to a thermostat will keep it frostproof at little cost, and a fan heater will warm the air rapidly when the door is open. But blasts of cold are hard to avoid, so don't persevere with plants that seem to resent the position.

🐦 Too much heat is the main problem in summer. Unlike a greenhouse or conservatory, ventilation is often inadequate. If the porch is in a position where it receives a lot of direct sun, be sure to fit at least one automatic ventilator and, whenever possible, open all the windows before the temperature rises. However, bear in mind that these solutions may affect the security of your property.

🐦 Shading will help, and you may find the shade offered by a climber more acceptable than blinds or shading paints.

OPPOSITE: *This large regal pelargonium is kept indoors as a houseplant, but moved to the porch in full flower so that it can be shared with passers-by.*

ABOVE: *This indoor yucca is happy to stand outdoors for the summer in a sheltered position, and it gives height and 'presence' to the rest of the group, which is made up of tough houseplants that will also tolerate cold conditions.*

RIGHT: *The porch is where indoor plants can rub shoulders with hardy plants. Here, a tender begonia has been used with hardy miniature daffodils grown in a pot, and a pot-grown rosemary. The miniature roses were bought as houseplants but will later be planted in the garden. The rhododendron is totally hardy.*

Living-rooms

THE LIVING-ROOM IS THE PLACE WHERE MOST PEOPLE GROW THEIR HOUSE-

PLANTS. IT IS LIKELY TO BE WARM AND LIGHT, WITH PLENTY OF SPACE TO

DISPLAY PLANTS CREATIVELY.

The living-room is probably the best room for houseplants. There are usually large windows – often ceiling to floor patio doors at one end – plenty of standing places such as windowsills, tables and ledges or alcoves, and usually ample space for large floor-standing specimens. It is also the room that most people make an effort to decorate attractively, and where they spend most of their leisure time.

Just as the appearance of a room can be changed by moving the furniture around, so the positioning of plants can radically alter how a room looks. This is especially true for large specimen plants that act as focal points, and for groups of large plants used to screen areas.

In living-rooms, the colour and texture of plants can play important roles, especially the way in which they blend or contrast with the background. Try to use the juxtaposition of contrasting forms, shapes and colours to emphasize the visual impact of the plants.

Colour always needs to be considered. A foliage or flower colour that blends with an accompanying pot or ornament will look tasteful, but the wall behind will look best if it is neutral, or plain and contrasting. But for a special effect you may want to blend the colours of your plants with a more decorative background – perhaps white daisy-like flowers with green ferns, and green-and-white dieffenbachia against white net curtains, all set off on a white table.

Texture adds variety. The long purple hairs of a gynura will be best emphasized by a smooth pale background, a prickly cactus may look more in keeping with the colour and texture of rough bricks behind. The papery, wing-like leaves of caladiums will need a colour behind that brings out the beauty of these exotic-looking leaves (as they vary from white and green to bright red, the best background depends on the variety). But above all, the leaves of caladiums need to be illuminated well, either from behind or in front, to show off their delicate texture. The puckered leaves of the *Begonia masoniana* have a texture that you want to touch, adding tactile to visual stimulation.

Shape will compensate for lack of colour. Most philodendrons have large and interestingly shaped leaves, like the fingered and fringed *P. bipinnatifidum* and the more deeply cut *P. selloum*, and among the large-leaved ficus, *F. lyrata* has enormous, waxy leaves the shape of an upside-down violin. Plants like this will create as much interest as those with bright flowers or brilliant foliage, and they do it in a restrained way that creates the right mood for an elegant and sophisticated living-room.

Making a mini cactus garden

1. Make sure there are adequate drainage holes. Cover these with pieces of broken pot.

2. Although a cactus compost (potting soil) is preferable, you can use an ordinary compost.

3. If you have a very prickly cactus to plant, hold it in a strip of folded paper like this.

LEFT: *Cacti and succulents often look best in small groups, and a half-pot or shallow clay container is particularly appropriate.*

ABOVE: *Living rooms are usually light and spacious. Plants like aglaonemas, which like bright light but not direct sunlight, often do well by a window with net curtains. White net curtains make an excellent backdrop for many plants.*

RIGHT: *The living room is where you might want to use an especially beautiful container as a cache-pot for an appropriately impressive plant, like this azalea. As the blooms on one flowering plant die, replace with another, so that your special corner of the room always looks fresh and colourful.*

FAR RIGHT: *Succulents like this crassula are undemanding provided you can give them a position near the window. As they lack colour, try using a bright pot.*

Kitchens

IN THE DAYS WHEN KITCHENS WERE DARK AND DINGY AND COOKING WAS DONE WITH COAL GAS, OR EVEN AN OPEN RANGE, THE KITCHEN WAS A PLACE FOR ONLY THE TOUGHEST OF PLANTS. MODERN KITCHENS ARE USUALLY LIGHT, BRIGHT AND RELATIVELY SPACIOUS. PLANTS SHOULD THRIVE HERE, AND THERE ARE PLENTY OF OPPORTUNITIES TO USE THEM.

PROBLEM SPOTS

🐾 Bear in mind that heat rises, so do not place any plants where the heat from cooking will make life uncomfortable – on shelves or cupboards near the cooker for example.

🐾 Few houseplants will be happy with icy blasts from an open back door in winter. If possible, keep your plants well away from the door.

As always, the windowsill is the first place to fill with plants. Here you can grow those that need good light, but if the room receives direct sun at the hottest part of the day you will be restricted to those that tolerate the sun's rays intensified by the glass, such as cacti and succulents, geraniums (pelargoniums) and tradescantias.

Make the most of the tops of cupboards near the window for trailing plants. Although watering can be difficult, and the light near the ceiling will be poor, as the plants trail and tumble they enter the zone of better light and most will thrive. If they become thin and straggly, keep pinching back the long shoots to keep the growth bushy and compact.

Avoid trailing or cascading plants on or near work surfaces or eating areas. Choose plants with upright growth that will not get in the way. *Sansevieria trifasciata* 'Laurentii', upright dracaenas, especially those on a mini trunk, clivias and aglaonemas are among the plants that look good and won't get in the way of normal kitchen activities.

Practical pot plants
Many cooks like the idea of having culinary herbs on hand to pluck straight from pot to pot. Unfortunately, if you use herbs a great deal in your cooking, your herb plants will not remain attractive for long! So don't

expect your indoor herbs to keep the kitchen supplied, but they will create the right mood and aromas, and you can raid the plants for a leaf or two in an emergency. Nearly all herbs need good light, and the best place for them is by a bright window.

You can place individual pots on the windowsill, but it is more effective, and better for the plants, if you stand them all on a tray covering the length of the window and filled with gravel on which to stand the pots. Some, such as basil and pot marjoram, will need turning regularly to even up the growth, and regular pinching out of the growing tips is essential for many herbs. Unless you pinch out the growing tip, and later subsequent main shoots, basil will grow tall, flower and then deteriorate before you can harvest much of a crop. Marjoram needs to be pinched back regularly to keep it compact: the flowers are pretty, but an untamed plant will be too big and bushy for a windowsill.

Young plants of shrubs such as sage (*Salvia officinalis*) and rosemary (*Rosmarinus officinalis*) are inexpensive to buy and are worth growing as young pot plants. They will deteriorate indoors long before they become the large shrubs that you see in gardens, but they will enhance the kitchen for a season. If they are still alive and healthy the following spring, plant them in the garden, and buy another small plant for indoors.

Planting a herb windowbox

1. For an inexpensive improvised windowbox, use a polystyrene (styrofoam) trough. You can paint it to suit the decor.

2. Always insert a layer of drainage material, such as gravel and charcoal or expanded clay granules, before filling with potting compost (medium).

3. Choose small, bushy plants wherever possible. Some will eventually grow too tall, but you can usually restrict the height by repeatedly pinching out the growing tips.

OPPOSITE ABOVE: *Windowsill space is often limited, but kitchen shelves provide scope for many more plants, and a white-painted wall will reflect the available light and encourage growth.*

OPPOSITE BELOW: *Use trailers like this* Philodendron scandens *where its cascading stems won't get in the way. Near working surfaces, choose compact plants like this variegated* Tolmiea menziesii.

CENTRE RIGHT: *An indoor or outdoor windowbox full of herbs will not keep you supplied with all you need for culinary use, but it's a fun feature and may extend the season of fresh herbs when those outdoors are no longer available. This windowbox contains (from left to right) basil, thyme, parsley, rosemary and variegated apple mint.*

BELOW RIGHT: *The vacant space on top of cupboards can be used for low-growing or trailing plants, but bear in mind that light levels are often low, trailers may interfere with opening doors and watering can be difficult.*

BELOW FAR RIGHT: Codiaeums *usually do well in a kitchen provided you avoid a position exposed to cold draughts.*

Bedrooms

IF YOUR ENTHUSIASM FOR PLANTS OUTGROWS THE SPACE AVAILABLE IN

TRADITIONAL DISPLAY AREAS SUCH AS THE LIVING-ROOM AND KITCHEN,

OVERCOME PREJUDICE AND MAKE YOUR BEDROOM MORE BEAUTIFUL, TOO.

Many people are deterred from placing plants in their bedroom on the grounds that they are 'unhealthy'. However, plants will not deprive you of oxygen, and the reluctance to use them in the bedroom is no more than prejudice. You will probably find it a more restful place with the added greenery of a few plants, and you can even wake up to the perfume of stephanotis or hyacinths.

Bedrooms are often kept cooler than living-rooms, and this is an advantage for many plants. Winter-flowering plants, in particular, often last much longer in a cool atmosphere.

Suitable plants

Plants in bedrooms are probably viewed less than those in other parts of the house. Although we spend many hours there, most of them will be spent asleep, which means the plants are sometimes neglected.

Bedrooms are an excellent place for a collection of cacti and succulents, and for large individual specimens of tolerant foliage plants such as aspidistras and scindapsus (epipremnums), which are unlikely to become stressed if forgotten for a day or two.

If you can discipline yourself to water and mist them regularly, however, even delicate ferns will often do well because the air is usually more humid than in a hot living-room.

Fragrant plants can be especially pleasing, and the strongest scents will be appreciated beyond the bedroom itself if you leave the door open.

Bedside tables and dressing tables

Plants can add the finishing touch to a dressing table or a bedside table, but these are usually areas where natural light levels are low. Table lamps can display the plant to advantage after dark, but these do little for plant growth (and if too near, may scorch the plant). Be prepared to move your plants around, giving them a week or

two at most in these positions, then rotate them with other plants that have had a spell in better light.

A place for plants to rest

Although you will want your bedroom to look well-designed and furnished with pretty or attractive plants, you may want to use a spare bedroom as a resting place for all those plants that are so perfect for a short time but border on the unattractive for the rest of the year. 'Resting' orchids and ephiphyllums, and tender primulas that have finished flowering, for example, are among the candidates for a light position in a bedroom. You can move them into a prominent position when they come into bloom again.

OPPOSITE ABOVE: *Instead of using air fresheners, wake up to the fragrance of real flowers, provided by plants such as this* Stephanotis floribunda.

OPPOSITE BELOW: *Enjoy the delicate perfume of* Jasminum polyanthum *as you sit at your dressing table. Dressing-table plants should be used at their prime, then moved to a lighter and more appropriate position to recuperate.*

ABOVE RIGHT: *If you adore the heady scent of gardenias, try one on your bedside table. When flowering has finished, move it to a lighter position.*

RIGHT: *Many bromeliads bought in bloom are discarded after flowering, so they can be used on a table well away from the window. This one is* Vriesea splendens, *with a distinctive flower spike that can be 60cm (2ft) long. The yellow* Celosia plumosa *is an inexpensive annual which can be used as a short-term houseplant for a few weeks.*

Halls and landings

HALLS AND LANDINGS PRESENT BOTH PROBLEMS AND OPPORTUNITIES. THE
LIGHT IS OFTEN POOR, SPACE SOMETIMES CRAMPED AND COLD BLASTS FROM
THE OPEN FRONT DOOR IN WINTER ALL PROVIDE UNPROMISING CONDITIONS
FOR PLANTS. BUT THERE ARE STILL SOME THAT WILL THRIVE AND EVEN LOOK
GOOD ENOUGH TO MAKE YOU LINGER TO ADMIRE THEM. IF YOU ARE A
HOUSEPLANT ENTHUSIAST YOU'LL WANT TO MAKE THE MOST OF ALL THE
GROWING SPACE AVAILABLE.

In some centrally heated homes, halls and stairways are as warm as any other part of the house, in others they are often cold and lack sufficient natural light. Despite these drawbacks one survey showed that more than a third of people who grow houseplants have at least some of them in the hall, and probably many more would if they could find plants that would thrive there. The plants suggested here are tough enough to grow even where these imperfect conditions exist, but in any place where there is enough winter warmth, conditions can be improved by using plenty of artificial light to make a feature of your plants.

It is always better to have one or two well-displayed, tough evergreens that look really lush and healthy, than to struggle with lots of colourful exotics that end up looking sickly.

Large plants

One or two specimen plants used as focal points will impress visitors on their arrival. Depending on the layout of your hallway, place one at the end of the passage leading to the door, in the vestibule where the doors opens, or on the landing or top of the stairs if there is space. Good plants for this purpose are large specimens of *Ficus benjamina* (a variegated variety is especially effective in this situation), *Monstera*

ABOVE: *Plants on stairs must always be used with caution, but where you have space, as with this turn in the stairs, a few plants will transform what would otherwise be a featureless part of the house.*

deliciosa, Dracaena deremensis, Schefflera actinophylla, Yucca elephantipes, or a tough palm such as *Howeia forsteriana* (syn. *Kentia forsteriana*). If the position is gloomy during the day, use fluorescent lights balanced for plant growth, or spotlights recommended for plants.

Make sure that your décor shows off specimen plants to their best advantage: a plain, light-coloured wall is particularly effective, and a mirror placed behind a plant will deflect the light, perhaps making the hall look larger, as well as reflecting the plant itself. A white or cream-coloured ceiling will also help to reflect light.

Climbers and trailers

Provided that using plants will never become a danger to anyone in this area, stairwells provide a great opportunity for luxuriant climbers and trailers to grow freely.

Troughs filled with trailers, placed on a balcony along the stairwell, will enable the plants to tumble over the edge to provide a living curtain. A climber in the hall or at the bottom of the stairs can sometimes be trained to grow along the banister.

Climbers that often thrive in hall conditions include *Rhoicissus rhomboidea* (syn. *Cissus rhombifolia*) and the small-leaved varieties of the ordinary ivy (varieties of *Hedera helix*).

You can let ivies trail too, but more interesting are *Philodendron scandens*, and *Epipremnum aureum* 'Neon', both of which will produce long trails of growth. *Plectranthus australis* and *P. coleoides* 'Marginatus' are also vigorous trailers that will soon produce a hanging curtain of foliage.

Table plants

One of the most popular positions for a hall plant is on a small table near the front door. If the door and the surrounding area are solid you might find cut flowers more successful here, but if they are mainly glass, conditions will be ideal for a plant that does not object to cold draughts. Be warned, however: the patterned glass sometimes used in this situation can act like a magnifying glass and scorch leaves directly in the sun's rays.

Dependable plants for a hall table with reasonable light are chlorophytums, and two tough ferns: *Cyrtomium falcatum* and *Asplenium nidus*.

ABOVE: *If you have a hall with an old-fashioned look or an ambience associated with antiques, choose a large plant for the entrance, such as a palm, large ficus, or even a tall bamboo, but make sure it will cope with blasts of cold air in the winter.*

RIGHT: *If you use white or pale walls to reflect the light, some plants will do quite well even away from a window. Here a fern makes a statement of elegance in an area that could otherwise look bare.*

FAR RIGHT: *Floor-standing plants for landings must be chosen with care. Although height is useful, it is important that the plant does not cause an obstruction. Try to position the plant in a corner. The white walls of this landing help to reflect light and show the plant off to advantage.*

Bathrooms

BATHROOMS ARE NOT THE PARADISE FOR PLANTS THAT SOME PEOPLE THINK.

ALTHOUGH THE HUMIDITY IS OFTEN HIGH, THERE ARE DRAWBACKS TOO, SO

CHOOSE YOUR PLANTS WITH CARE.

The average bathroom has conditions that prevail nowhere else in the home: short periods of high temperature and high humidity contrasting with much longer spells of quite cool conditions (especially if the central heating is not kept on permanently), and because the windows are often small, poor natural light. The plants may also have to contend with the use of aerosols and sprays containing a variety of chemicals for personal care, and often a liberal dusting of talcum powder too. These are not conditions in which the majority of houseplants will thrive.

Good positions

Try to keep foliage out of reach of splashes from the bath and washbasin. Pots perched on the edge or back of the bath are in a precarious position, and the chances are that the light will also be poor.

Make the most of the windowsill, especially for flowering plants. Further into the room, use tough foliage plants such as aspidistras and asparagus ferns, perhaps in front of a mirror, where they will receive reflected light and the mirror will make the plants look larger.

Tolerant trailers such as ivies and *Philodendron scandens* look good hanging from a high shelf, perhaps framing a mirror.

CARING FOR YOUR PLANTS

Bathroom plants need more regular grooming than those growing elsewhere. Leaf cleaning in particular should be done at least once a week. It is difficult to remove powder from plants with hairy leaves, so it is best to avoid these. If other plants become very coated with sprays or powder, try submerging the leaves briefly in water especially if there is so much foliage that it is tiring or impractical to wipe each leaf individually. If you splash soap, shampoo or toothpaste over a leaf, wipe it off immediately. If poor light is causing growth to arch towards the window, turn the plant regularly.

As soon as a plant appears to look unhappy, change it for another one. When the first one has recovered after a month or two in better conditions, rotate them again.

LEFT: *Plants may have to be concentrated near the window as bathrooms are not usually well illuminated with natural light, but by using plenty of plants on all available surfaces, the effect can be particularly pleasing.*

Use small flowering plants such as saintpaulias and kalanchoes on a make-up table or vanity unit, using attractive cache-pots that suit the setting. These will not make long-term bathroom plants, but they will look good for weeks before you have to move them on.

SUITABLE PLANTS

The following plants generally do well:

Large plants
Fatsia japonica, *Monstera deliciosa* and *Philodendron bipinnatifidum*.

Trailers
Epipremnum aureum (syn. *Scindapsus aureus*), *Philodendron scandens* and small-leaved ivies.

Bushy plants
Aglaonema species and varieties, *Aspidistra elatior* and *Chamaedorea elegans* (syn. *Neanthe bella*).

Short-term flowering plants
Chrysanthemum, cyclamen and exacum.

ABOVE RIGHT: *Plants as diverse as the hardy ivy and tricky* Asplenium capillus-veneris *can thrive in a bathroom. The ivy is good for low light levels, and the fern will appreciate the frequent spells of high humidity.*

RIGHT: Philodendron scandens *is a good choice for a trailer, while a spathiphyllum always looks elegant with its glossy green leaves and white sail-like flowers. Flowering plants, such as the cyclamen, can be brought in as short-term plants.*

FAR RIGHT: *Use trailers with imagination. Bathrooms usually have small windows and tend to be relatively gloomy, but by rotating the plants between rooms periodically you can feature attractive plant displays in all areas of the home.*

A–Z directory of houseplants

Browse through this parade of houseplants to choose those that appeal, then check their requirements to make sure you can provide suitable conditions.

The following pages contain most of the houseplants that you are likely to find in garden centres and shops, and even many specialist nurseries. If you have a plant that you can't identify, the chances are you will find it here . . . though the nature of the houseplant trade means that from time to time you are likely to find a plant that may not be in the books.

Introduction

Most of the houseplants in the following pages can be found in garden centres and shops, and the many illustrations will allow you to use the book for identification as well as for practical advice. No book can be totally comprehensive, of course, and if you begin to collect particular groups of plants such as bromeliads, cacti or orchids, you will find many more varieties at specialist nurseries. In most cases, these varieties are likely to prefer similar conditions and care to those mentioned in this book.

Finding the right name

Sometimes botanists change the names of old favourites, and it is not unknown for other botanists to change them again – even back to the original name! Sometimes new names are taken up quickly, but often it is many years, even decades, before a new name becomes accepted by nurserymen and gardeners.

In this book the up-to-date names are mentioned to make the book as complete as possible, but the entry is likely to be found under the name by which the plant is commonly sold. Wherever applicable the names have been cross-referenced, so you should be able to find the plant whether you normally use the 'old' or 'new' name.

In common with many books, we have used the word 'variety' in its colloquial sense, rather than the more botanically correct 'cultivar', 'variety' or 'varietas', and 'forma', which makes for difficult reading and is of no practical value to the gardener. The typographical presentation of the names is, however, correct.

If you know a plant only by its common name, look it up in the common name index. This will give you the Latin name under which you will find the entry.

OPPOSITE: *A selection of houseplants*

ABOVE: Columnea gloriosa

Reading the entries

Genus This is equivalent to a surname, identifying the group of plants with common characteristics.

Species This is equivalent to a forename, identifying an individual plant within the genus. Sometimes there is only one species in a genus, but usually there are many – sometimes hundreds. Those listed are the species you are most likely to encounter when buying houseplants.

Temperature Except where a plant is frost-sensitive (when it is very important to prevent the plant freezing), the temperatures given are target minima. But the majority of plants will not come to any harm if the temperature drops lower – they may not thrive or grow as well, but they are unlikely to die. Maximum temperatures are not given, as in most households it is not practical to reduce the summer air temperature significantly. When a high winter temperature caused by central heating may be detrimental – perhaps shortening the flowering period – a suggested maximum has been given.

Humidity The amount of moisture in the air can be crucial. Plants from tropical rain forests may demand very moist or humid air, yet desert plants will often tolerate air drier than you are likely to find in the home. Avoid those that require high humidity unless you can provide it . . . or are prepared to treat the plant simply as a short-term decoration for the home.

Position This can be crucial – if the light is bad many plants grow poorly and fail to thrive. Other plants will be scorched (develop brown burn marks on the leaves) or even die if placed in a hot and sunny spot.

Watering and feeding Never water by the calendar alone, and always use your own discretion when deciding whether a plant requires more water. This book indicates periods of high or low water needs. Feeding should never be neglected, but the advice here is based on periods of need rather than frequency of feeding. Frequency depends on the type of fertilizer being used – follow the instructions on the fertilizer label.

Care Useful hints and tips that will help you get the best from your plant.

Propagation Detailed propagation techniques are beyond the scope of this book, but the main methods used are given for guidance. If sowing seed, follow the information on the packet or in the catalogue. Cuttings are likely to require a heated propagator during cold months, but should root at air temperature during the summer. The best type of cutting may depend on the time of year it is taken, so consult a propagation book for the trickier subjects if in doubt.

Abutilon

These versatile evergreen shrubs are usually grown as foliage plants, but some are chosen primarily for their striking flowers. *A. megapotamicum* is grown as an outdoor wall shrub in mild areas.

Abutilon × hybridum

Most hybrid varieties, such as 'Canary Bird' or 'Yellow Belle', and 'Golden Fleece' or 'Moonchimer' (both yellow), are grown for their bell-like flowers. A few, such as 'Savitzii' (white and green blotched leaves) are attractive foliage plants. In a conservatory, plants may grow to 1.5m (5ft) or more, but smaller plants also flower well.

Abutilon megapotamicum

Small, pendent, red and yellow bell-like flowers for most of the summer. The plant will trail from a large hanging basket or can be trained against a conservatory wall. 'Variegatum' has yellow-splashed leaves.

Abutilon striatum

Although correctly known as *A. pictum*, you are more likely to find it sold under its traditional name. It is often grown in its variegated form 'Thompsonii', which has yellow-blotched leaves and pale orange flowers.

TOP: Abutilon *hybrid*

ABOVE: Abutilon striatum *'Thompsonii'*

Temperature Aim for 12–15°C (53–59°F) from early autumn to late winter. Avoid high winter temperatures.
Humidity Mist occasionally.
Position Good light, but avoid exposing to direct sun.
Watering and feeding Water freely in summer, sparingly in winter. Feed regularly in summer.
Care Repot each spring, but use a pot only one size larger as the plant flowers best if the roots are constrained. If the plant has lost its beauty by spring, cut back long shoots at the same time to encourage new bushy growth. Tie in the shoots of *A. megapotamicum* in spring and summer if grown against a conservatory wall. Ventilate freely. The plant can stand in the garden for the summer.
Propagation Cuttings. Seed if you do not want a particular colour or variegation.

Acacia

Acacias are grown mainly for their feathery foliage and pretty yellow flowers. In their native habitat most make large trees, but many can be grown in a large pot and will make a bush about 1–1.5m (3–5ft) tall. They are more suitable for a conservatory than the home.

Acacia armata

Pale yellow, fragrant flowers, like small balls clustered along the stems, freely produced between mid winter and early spring. It makes a branching shrub to about 1.5m (5ft). More correctly known as *A. paradoxa* now, but usually found under its old name.

Acacia dealbata

Sulphur-yellow flowers, often sold by florists as mimosa, from mid winter to early spring. Attractive feathery foliage. This species is cold tolerant.

LEFT: Abutilon megapotamicum *'Variegatum'*

ABOVE: Acacia dealbata

HELPFUL HINTS

Temperature Aim for a minimum 10°C (50°F). Avoid high winter temperatures.

Humidity Undemanding.

Position As much light as possible.

Watering and feeding Water sparingly in winter, freely at other times. Feed during the summer (generous feeding may stimulate too much growth).

Care To keep the plant compact, cut back shoots that have become too long when flowering is over. Repot every second year, after flowering. If you don't have a conservatory, stand the plant ouside for the summer.

Propagation Seed; cuttings.

Acalypha

The acalyphas are a diverse group of plants, some grown for their bright coleus-like foliage, others for their spectacular drooping flowers.

Acalypha hispida

Red tassel-like flowers up to 50cm (20in) long. 'Alba' has whitish flowers. In a warm conservatory it can grow to a height of 1.8m (6ft) or more; in the home it is unlikely to grow to more than half this size.

Acalypha wilkesiana

Brightly coloured oval leaves about 15cm (6in) long. Most are attractively variegated in shades of red, and there are named varieties such as 'Godseffiana' (pale green), and 'Musaica' (patches of bronze, red and orange).

HELPFUL HINTS

Temperature Winter minimum 15°C (59°F).

Humidity High humidity is essential. Does best in a conservatory; if in a room, mist frequently (especially *A. hispida*).

Position Good light, but avoid exposing to direct sun.

Watering and feeding Keep the compost (potting soil) moist at all times, but avoid waterlogging. Feed from spring to autumn.

Care To keep compact, prune back by half in early spring or late summer. Repot in spring (topdress if the pot is already large). Deadhead *A. hispida* as the flowers die. Pinch out any flowers on *A. wilkesiana* before they open, and remove the tips of long shoots as necessary, to keep the plant compact and bushy.

Propagation Cuttings.

ABOVE: Acalypha wilkesiana 'Ceylon'
BELOW: Acalypha hispida

ABOVE: Achimenes *hybrid*

Adiantum

These delicate-looking ferns include a few species that are frost-tolerant, but most are delicate plants that need warmth and high humidity and they can be difficult to keep for long in a living-room. The small ones do well in a bottle garden.

Adiantum capillus-veneris
Thin, feathery-looking fronds on dark stems. This fern is the toughest of those described. In some countries this is known commercially as *A. chilense*, though there is a distinct plant with this name.

Adiantum chilense *see A. capillus-veneris*.

Adiantum cuneatum *see A. raddianum*.

Adiantum hispidulum
A coarser-looking fern than most adiantums, although the new fronds are a delicate pinkish-bronze.

BELOW: Adiantum hispidulum

Achimenes

True species are sometimes grown, but the plants you are most likely to find are hybrids. Specialist nurseries offer a large range of named varieties, and the rhizomes are often sold by bulb merchants and seedsmen.

Achimenes hybrids
The short-lived flowers, in shades of pink, purple, yellow, red, and white, are produced in abundance from early summer to autumn. The plants die down in winter but grow again the following spring.

HELPFUL HINTS
Temperature Undemanding as the plant dies down for the winter. Aim for a minimum 13°C (55°F) while growing.
Humidity Mist frequently when the flower buds are developing, then provide humidity without spraying by standing the pot on a tray of pebbles.
Position Good light, but avoid exposing to direct sun.
Watering and feeding Water with tepid, soft water during the growing season. Never allow the compost (potting soil) to dry out. Feed regularly.
Care Grow in a hanging pot if you want its weak stems to cascade, otherwise support them with thin canes. Stop watering when the plant begins to drop its leaves in autumn. Leave the rhizomes in the pot or remove and store in peat (moss peat) or sand in a frost-free place. Start into growth or replant in late winter or early spring.
Propagation Division of rhizomes; cuttings; seed (not named varieties).

ABOVE: Adiantum raddianum *'Fragrantissimum', also known as 'Fragrans' (left), and 'Fritz Luthii' (right)*
LEFT: Adiantum capillus-veneris

Care Most problems arise from dry or cool air. Never let the compost (potting soil) dry out, but do not leave the pot standing in water.
Propagation Division is the easiest method, but spores can be sown in spring.

Adiantum raddianum

One of the most popular species, with erect young fronds that later curve. If conditions suit, it will make a medium-sized pot plant. There are many varieties, with slight variations in leaf shape or colour and growth habit. 'Fragrantissimum' is slightly aromatic. 'Fritz-Luthii' has bright green fronds. Also known as *A. cuneatum.*

HELPFUL HINTS
Temperature A winter minimum of 18°C (64°F) is generally advisable for most species.
Humidity High humidity is essential for good results.
Position Shaded from direct sun and away from cold draughts.
Watering and feeding Water freely throughout the year. Apply a weak fertilizer from spring to early autumn.

Aechmea

The most widely grown species, *A. fasciata*, is one of the best-known of the bromeliads, with attactive foliage and a spectacular and long-lasting flower head.

Aechmea fasciata

Large green leaves, banded silvery-grey, form an urn-like rosette. The spiky-looking flower head has pink bracts and small blue flowers that fade to lilac. The main flowering season is mid summer to early winter; individual heads can remain attractive for months, but the rosette dies afterwards. The plant is sometimes seen under its old name of *A. rhodocyanea.*

Aechmea rhodocyanea *see A. fasciata.*

HELPFUL HINTS
Temperature Winter minimum 15°C (59°F), unless you intend to discard the plant after flowering.
Humidity Undemanding.
Position Good light, but avoid exposing to direct sun.
Watering and feeding Keep roots moist at all times, top up water in funnel in summer, but empty it in winter unless the temperature is above 18°C (64°F). Feed with a weak fertilizer in summer.
Care Young plants raised at home will not flower for several years, but to stimulate flowering on a mature plant, enclose in a plastic bag with a couple of ripe apples for a few days. The gasses released may induce flowering. Mist only on hot days. After flowering, that part of the plant will die, but offsets will be produced that can be used for propagation.
Propagation Remove the young rosettes when about half the height of the parent. Pot up, retaining as much of the root system as possible.

BELOW: Aechmea fasciata

Aeschynanthus

Several species may be grown as house-plants, but the one described is among the most successful. Even this is better in a conservatory than a living-room. All have trailing stems with leathery leaves and clusters of red or orange flowers.

Aeschynanthus lobbianus

Dark green, fleshy leaves on trailing stems, with terminal clusters of bright flowers with brownish-purple calyces and red flowers lightly flushed with yellow. Flowering time is usually early summer.

HELPFUL HINTS

Temperature Warm in summer, cool in winter, but with a minimum of 13°C (55°F).
Humidity Mist frequently all year round, especially in hot weather.
Position Good light, but not direct sun.
Watering and feeding Water freely from spring to autumn, sparingly at other times. Use soft, tepid water if possible. Feed in summer.

Care After flowering, shorten the stems to prevent the plant becoming too straggly. Moving a plant in flower to a different position may sometimes cause the blooms to drop. It is a good

ABOVE: Aeschynanthus *hybrid 'Mona'*

idea to repot the plants every second or third year.
Propagation Cuttings.

Agave

Although often regarded as succulents, agaves are xerophytes (plants able to survive in areas with scanty water supplies). Some have magnificent flower spikes where they are able to grow outdoors, but they are regarded as foliage plants indoors. *A. americana* is often used in a tub as a patio plant, and in mild areas can sometimes be overwintered successfully outdoors.

Agave americana

Large grey-green or blue-grey, strap-like leaves, often 1–1.2m (3–4ft) long in favourable conditions, and with sharp spines. As a pot plant it is

LEFT: Agave americana
OPPOSITE TOP: Agave victoriae-reginae

usually grown in one of its variegated forms such as 'Marginata', 'Mediopicta' or 'Variegata'.

Agave filifera

A rounded rosette of stiff, fleshy, pointed leaves that curve upwards, with thread-like growths.

Agave victoriae-reginae

Dull-green, white-edged triangular leaves, forming an almost spherical rosette. One of the best agaves as a houseplant.

HELPFUL HINTS

Temperature Winter minimum 10°C (50°F) is adequate for all species. Some will tolerate lower temperatures but keep frost-free.
Humidity Tolerates dry air.
Position Full sun.
Watering and feeding Water as required in summer, but keep almost dry in winter (water occasionally if the light is good). Feed occasionally during the summer.
Care Stand large plants such as *A. americana* outdoors for the summer (but beware of any spines if placing on a patio). Repot each spring.
Propagation Root the runners or separate the young plants that form around the bases of some species. Can be raised from seed, but growth tends to be slow.

Aglaonema

Clump-forming plants with spear-shaped leaves on short stems arising from the base. The plain green ones lack interest, but the variegated species and varieties make attractive and tolerant houseplants.

Aglaonema crispum

Green leaves with silvery-grey patches. 'Marie' has particularly good variegation.

Aglaonema commutatum

Green leaves crossed with silvery bands. Inconspicuous greenish-white flowers are sometimes followed by red berries.

Aglaonema hybrids

Some of the best aglaonemas to use as houseplants are hybrids. 'Silver Queen' has silver and green leaves, 'Silver King' has leaves almost entirely silvery-grey and spotted leaf stalks.

The nomenclature of aglaonemas has been confused, and you will sometimes find these listed as varieties of *A. treubii*.

HELPFUL HINTS

Temperature Aim for a winter minimum of 15°C (59°F), although plants will continue to grow at 10°C (50°F).
Humidity Needs high humidity. Mist regularly.
Position All-green aglaonemas tolerate low light levels, but variegated forms need only light shade. Avoid direct sun.
Watering and feeding Water freely spring to autumn, sparingly in winter. Feed from spring to autumn.
Care Best in shallow pots. The plants are slow-growing so repot only when necessary.
Propagation Cuttings. Division.

BELOW LEFT: Aglaonema crispum *'Marie'*

Aloe

Aloes are trouble-free succulents with a dramatic appearance, which makes them useful as specimen houseplants for a sunny windowsill.

Aloe arborescens
Erect growth with tentacle-like fleshy leaves, edged with sharp thorns. May produce spikes of attractive orange-red flowers. Will make a tall plant in time, but growth is relatively slow if restricted in a pot.

Aloe ferox
Thick, fleshy leaves with reddish-brown spines over the surface that give the plant a warty appearance. Mature plants produce branching red flower spikes. Grows to about 45cm (1½ft).

Aloe mitriformis
Fleshy blue-green leaves, conspicuously spined around the edge and on the back. Dull scarlet flowers in summer.

Aloe variegata
Forms a rosette of triangular, dark green, purple-tinged leaves with V-shaped white bands. Red flowers are sometimes produced. Makes a compact plant that grows to about 15–30cm (6–12in) tall.

HELPFUL HINTS
Temperature Cool but frost-free in winter. Aim for about 5°C (41°F).
Humidity Tolerates dry air.
Position Full sun. Can stand in the garden in summer.
Watering and feeding Water a couple of times a week in summer, sparingly in winter. Feed occasionally in summer.
Routine care Repot in spring every second or third year.
Propagation Offsets (sever carefully with as much root system as possible). Seed in spring.

LEFT: Aloe ferox
BELOW: Aloe variegata

Ananas

The ornamental pineapples grown as houseplants sometimes have small inedible fruits. These are an interesting bonus, but ananas are grown primarily as foliage plants indoors.

Ananas bracteatus striatus
Brightly striped, spiky leaves in green, cream and pink. Although this plant is often found under this name, you may also see it as the more correct *A. b. tricolor*.

Ananas comosus variegatus
This is a variegated form of the edible pineapple. The plain green species is an unattractive houseplant, but this variegated form with lengthwise cream banding is more compact and appealing.

HELPFUL HINTS
Temperature Aim for 15–18°C (59–64°F) in winter.

Anthurium

Some species, such as *A. crystallinum* and *A. magnificum*, are grown as foliage plants, but the ones you are most likely to find are sold as flowering plants. They are difficult to keep indoors, but their distinctive flowers make them popular where a dramatic effect is required.

Anthurium andreanum
The plants sold under this name are almost always hybrids. One may also find the name with its more correct spelling of *A. andaeanum*. Heart-shaped leaves are produced on long stalks. The flowers have a large, shiny, red, pink, or white spathe and generally a straight spadix. Flowering is between spring and later summer, and the blooms last for several weeks.

Anthurium scherzerianum
The plants sold under this name are almost always hybrids. The leaves are

Humidity Undemanding, but mist in very hot weather.

Position Good light. The variegation is often better in sun. If placing on a windowsill, beware of the spines, which tend to catch on net curtains.

Watering and feeding Water freely in summer, cautiously in winter, and allow the soil to dry out a little before watering. Feed from late spring to early autumn.

Care In summer, occasionally add a little water to the vase formed by the rosette of leaves. Mature plants can be encouraged to flower by placing them in a plastic bag together with a few ripe apples or bananas for a few days.

Propagation Commercially, plants are often raised from seed, but for just a few plants it is quicker to use the crown of leaves on top of the fruit.

RIGHT: Ananas bracteatus striatus

lance- rather than heart-shaped and the spadix is curled. Flowering time for these plants is the same as for the previous species.

HELPFUL HINTS

Temperature Winter minimum 16°C (60°F).

Humidity Needs high humidity. Mist frequently, but avoid spraying the flowers.

Position Good light, but avoid exposing to direct summer sun.

Watering and feeding Water freely in summer, sparingly in winter. If possible use soft water. Feed with a weak fertilizer during summer.

Care Repot every second year, in spring, using a fibrous compost (potting mixture), and avoid over-firming.

Propagation Division. Stem cuttings and seeds are possible methods, but much more difficult.

LEFT: Anthurium scherzerianum

Aphelandra

The only species widely grown is a useful dual-purpose plant with attractive foliage and flowers.

Aphelandra squarrosa

Large, glossy, dark green leaves striped white along the veins. Conspicuous flower spike with long-lasting yellow bracts surrounding shorter-lived yellow flowers. The bracts overlap, giving a tiled effect, and remain attractive for a month or more. Flowering is usually in the autumn, but plants may bloom from late spring onwards and are sometimes available in flower in winter. The true species is not usually grown, and you are most likely to find more compact varieties such as 'Dania' and 'Louisae'.

HELPFUL HINTS

Temperature Winter minimum 13°C (55°F).
Humidity Needs high humidity. Mist frequently.
Position Good light; not direct sun. Good light induces flowering.
Watering and feeding Water freely in summer, less often in winter, but never let the compost become dry. Use soft water if possible. Feed regularly from spring to autumn.
Care Deadhead when flowering has finished. To prevent the leaves falling keep warm and humid, and away from cold draughts.
Propagation Stem cuttings in a propagator, in spring. Stem sections with a single eye can also be used.

BELOW: Aphelandra squarrosa

Aporocactus

A small group of undemanding cacti, the species described here being the ones most usually found. Of these, A. *flagelliformis* is most common. Although these trailing plants can be grafted on a taller rootstock, they are usually grown on their own roots and cascade over the edge of the pot.

Aporocactus flagelliformis

Circular trailing stems, with sharp spines. The red or pink flowers, large in relation to the size of the plant, are produced in spring.

Aporocactus flagriformis

Stronger and thornier stems than the previous species (although this is not always regarded as a distinct species).

Araucaria

The species described is the only one normally grown as a pot plant, and is one of the few conifers used indoors. It makes a very large tree in the wild, but indoors grows into a majestic specimen plant of about 1.5m (5ft) after a few years. It needs space to grow symmetrically.

Araucaria excelsa *see A. heterophylla.*

Araucaria heterophylla
Tiers of stiff branches covered with prickly conifer needles about 1.5cm (⅝in) long. It is still sometimes sold under its old name of *A. excelsa*.

HELPFUL HINTS
Temperature Aim for 5–10°C (41–50°F) in winter.

Humidity Needs high humidity. Does not do well in a dry, centrally-heated room without regular misting.
Position Good light; not direct sun. Stand plant in the garden in summer.
Watering and feeding Water freely from spring to autumn, sparingly in winter. Never let the soil dry out. Use soft water if possible. Feed with a weak fertilizer in summer.
Care Try to avoid a hot room in winter. Repot only every third or fourth year to prevent the plant becoming too large.
Propagation Tip cuttings in a propagator, but amateurs usually have a low success rate.

BELOW: Araucaria heterophylla

ABOVE: Aporocactus flagelliformis

Flowers are yellowish-red in bud and scarlet edged with violet when open.

HELPFUL HINTS
Temperature Winter minimum 5°C (41°F).
Humidity Tolerates dry air, but mist in very hot weather.
Position Full sun, but avoid intense afternoon sun. The plant can stand in the garden for the summer.
Watering and feeding Water freely in spring and summer, sparingly at other times.
Care Never move the plant once the buds have started to form, as this often causes them to drop. Keep in a cool, well-lit position in winter.
Propagation Cuttings; seed.

Asparagus

Although popularly called ferns, these useful houseplants belong to the lily family and are not true ferns at all. The feathery-looking foliage, reduced to needle-like scales in many species, gives some of them a ferny appearance and they are a useful choice for a position that demands a tougher plant than most ferns. The species below are the most common, but others are sometimes available.

Asparagus densiflorus
The 'leaves' (technically cladophylls and not true leaves) are a fresh green and larger than those of *A. setaceus*, creating a more striking plant. The thread-like stems arch and become more pendulous as the plant grows older. Small white or pink flowers are sometimes produced and may be followed by red berries. The variety usually grown is 'Sprengeri'. 'Meyeri', sometimes listed as a separate species and more correctly spelt 'Myersii', is more erect and compact in habit.

Asparagus meyeri *see A. densiflorus* 'Meyeri' (syn. 'Myersii').

Asparagus plumosus *see A. setaceus.*

ABOVE: Asparagus densiflorus *'Sprengeri' (syn.* A. sprengeri)

Asparagus setaceus
Thread-like pale green 'leaves' (phyllodes) produce a feathery and ferny effect. Young plants are compact, but as they mature, long climbing shoots are produced. The plant is still widely known as *A. plumosus.*

Asparagus sprengeri *see A. densiflorus* 'Sprengeri'.

HELPFUL HINTS
Temperature Winter minimum 7°C (45°F). *A. setaceus* is best kept at a minimum 13°C (55°F).
Humidity Mist occasionally, especially in a centrally-heated room in winter. Mist *A. setaceus* in winter.
Position Good light or partial shade, but avoid exposing to direct sun.
Watering and feeding Water from spring to autumn, sparingly in winter. Feed from spring to early autumn.
Care Cut back by half a plant that has started to turn yellow or grown too large: it will often produce new shoots from lower down. Repot young plants every spring, older ones every second year.
Propagation Division; seed.

Aspidistra

Evergreen herbaceous plants with leaves that grow directly from soil level. The one species grown as a houseplant was once very popular because of its tough constitution and tolerance of poor growing conditions.

Aspidistra elatior
Large, dark green leaves about 45–60cm (1½-2ft) long, arising from the base. 'Variegata' has irregular creamy-white longitudinal stripes. Small purplish flowers sometimes appear at soil level in late winter or early spring, but usually go unnoticed.

HELPFUL HINTS
Temperature Keep cool but frost-free in winter, 7–10°C (45–50°F) is ideal.
Humidity Tolerates dry air.
Position Light or shade, but avoid exposing to direct sun.
Watering and feeding Water moderately from spring to autumn, sparingly in winter. Avoid waterlogging.
Care Wash or sponge the leaves occasionally to remove dust and improve light penetration. Repot only when really necessary – usually every four years or so.
Propagation Division.

BELOW: Aspidistra elatior

Asplenium

Of the many hundreds of species of this fern, including some that are hardy, only a few are regularly grown as houseplants. *Asplenium nidus* is especially popular because its thick, leathery leaves make it a much more tolerant houseplant than ferns with thinner and more delicate foliage.

Asplenium bulbiferum

Typical fern fronds, usually about 45–60cm (1½-2ft) tall. Small plantlets develop on the upper surfaces of mature leaves, which can be potted up to provide new plants.

Asplenium nidus

An epiphytic fern with glossy, undivided leaves that form a vase-like rosette. Mature plants may have brown spore cases on the undersides of the leaves.

HELPFUL HINTS

Temperature Winter minimum 13°C (55°F) for *A. bulbiferum*, 16°C (60°F) for *A. nidus*.
Humidity High humidity is essential.

ABOVE: Asplenium bulbiferum

Position Light or shade, but avoid exposing to direct sun.
Watering and feeding Water freely from spring to autumn, moderately in winter. Use soft water whenever possible.

Care Dust *A. nidus* leaves periodically. If brown or disfigured edges form on the leaves of *A. nidus*, these can often be successfully trimmed off with scissors — but avoid cutting into the green area.
Propagation Spores (difficult) or division. Pot up the plantlets of *A. bulbiferum*.

Aucuba

Frost-hardy shrubs widely planted in gardens, and often used as a houseplant for difficult situations where more tender plants would not thrive. You can plant them out in the garden if they grow too large, but acclimatize them first.

Aucuba japonica

Large, dark green, leathery leaves, blotched or spotted yellow in the varieties usually used as houseplants. There are many varieties, differing mainly in the amount of variegation. Popular ones, though often not identified on the label, are 'Crotonifolia' (boldly spotted and blotched gold), and 'Variegata' (speckled yellow). The inconspicuous flowers and red berries are seldom produced on indoor plants.

Although a large shrub of 1.5–1.8m (5–6ft) in the garden, it seldom grows to more than half this height when grown indoors in a pot.

HELPFUL HINTS

Temperature Undemanding and tolerates frost. Avoid high winter temperatures.
Humidity Tolerates dry air, but mist regularly in a warm room in winter.
Position Useful for shade but will grow in a light position. Avoid direct summer sun.
Watering and feeding Water freely spring to autumn, sparingly in winter.
Care Repot every second spring. Prune any over-long or sparse shoots at the same time.
Propagation Cuttings.

RIGHT: Aucuba japonica *variety*

Azalea

See Rhododendron.

Begonia – Foliage

Foliage begonias are attractive all year round. Although most foliage begonias will flower, the blooms are generally inconspicuous.

Begonia bowerae

Compact growth to about 15–23cm (6–9in), with small, bright green, brown-edged leaves, which are slightly serrated and hairy. Grows from a creeping rhizome. Single white flowers, tinged pink, in winter. Attractive hybrids include 'Tiger', heavily blotched bronze and green. Also spelled *B. boweri*.

Begonia listada

Lobed, dark green, softly hairy leaves with bright emerald green markings. A few white flowers in autumn and winter.

Begonia masoniana

Very distinctive, large, bright green, puckered leaves with a central brownish 'cross'. The flowers are insignificant.

Begonia rex

It is the hybrids of this important species that are now widely grown. There are named varieties, but the plants are usually sold as mixtures or unnamed. The asymmetrical leaves are about 23cm (9in) long and brightly variegated in shades of green, silver, brown, red, pink, and purple.

Helpful hints

Temperature Winter minimum 16°C (60°F).

Humidity Provide high humidity, but avoid spraying water directly onto the leaves.

Position Good light, but not direct sun.

Watering and feeding Water freely from spring to autumn, sparingly in winter.

Care Repot annually in spring.

Propagation Division; leaf cuttings.

Begonia – Flowering

Many begonias are grown for the beauty of their flowers – some for the prolific mass of small flowers over a long period (such as *B. semperflorens*, a very popular choice for a summer display in the garden); others, such as some of the tuberous hybrids, are grown for their less numerous, but larger, blooms.

Begonia × cheimantha *see B. lorraine hybrids.*

Begonia elatior hybrids
Single or double flowers in a wide colour range mainly in shades of red, pink, yellow, orange, and white. They are derived from crosses between *B. socotrana* and tuberous species from South America. The Rieger begonias belong to this group of hybrids, and these varieties are generally superior because they are less prone to mildew and bud-drop. The natural flowering period is winter, but commercial growers induce them to flower at all seasons. There are many named varieties.

This group of begonias is also known as *B. × hiemalis.*

Begonia × hiemalis *see B. elatior hybrids.*

Begonia lorraine hybrids
A cross between *B. socotrana* and *B. dregei*, and now botanically described as *B. × cheimantha,* this winter-flowering begonia has clusters of small pink or white flowers. 'Gloire de Lorraine', with its pink flowers, is one of the best-known varieties.

Begonia semperflorens
Low, mound-forming plant covered with small flowers all summer. Colours include shades of pink and red, as well as white, some with bronze foliage. Many varieties are offered by seed companies.

Begonia sutherlandii
Trailer with small lance-shaped leaves and a profusion of single orange flowers in loose clusters in summer.

Begonia × tuberhybrida
A group that includes large-flowered, double begonias used as both pot plants and for garden display. There are many varieties, including single and double Pendula trailers for hanging baskets, and Multifloras with masses of single, semi-double and double flowers. Colours include many shades of red, orange, pink, and yellow. All flower for many months during the summer.

HELPFUL HINTS
Temperature Aim for 13–21°C (55–70°F) for winter-flowering types. Tuberous types that die back need to be protected from frost, but only for the tubers.
Humidity High humidity is beneficial but not critical.
Position Good light, but out of direct summer sun. Provide the best possible light in winter.
Watering and feeding Water freely while the plants are in flower, cautiously at other times. Gradually withhold water from those that die

ABOVE: Begonia sutherlandii
OPPOSITE ABOVE: Begonia rex
OPPOSITE BELOW: *A group of foliage begonias. 'Cleopatra' (top left), 'Tiger' (top right)*, B. listada *(centre)*, B. masoniana *(bottom left)*, 'Red Planet' *(bottom right)*

back and have a resting period once the foliage begins to yellow with age. Begonias are sensitive to over- and under-watering. Feed with a weak fertilizer while in bud and flowering.
Care Many types of begonia are prone to mildew. Spray at first sign of the disease and keep in a well-ventilated position. Pick off any affected leaves. If growing large-flowered tuberous begonias as specimen pot plants, pick off the small female flowers behind the larger and showier male blooms. Deadhead regularly except small-flowered species, which make it impractical. Tuberous varieties can be saved and overwintered in a frost-free place, but other kinds are usually discarded after flowering.
Propagation *B. semperflorens* is raised from seed. Tuberous species can be raised from cuttings in spring or by dividing old tubers (some can also be raised from seed). Winter-flowering lorraine and elatior hybrids can be propagated by leaf or tip cuttings.

Beloperone

See Justicia.

Billbergia

Terrestrial bromeliads grown for their exotic-looking flowers. The plants described are easy houseplants, and *B. nutans* is especially tolerant. Flowering time depends on the growing conditions — spring is the normal season, but if subjected to cool temperatures they may not flower until late summer.

Billbergia nutans
Arching, pendulous clusters of yellow and green, blue-edged flowers hang from conspicuous pink bracts. Foliage grows in clusters of narrow, funnel-shaped rosettes.

Billbergia × windii
A hybrid between *B. nutans* and *B. decora*. Similar to the previous species but with larger flowers and particularly conspicuous pink bracts.

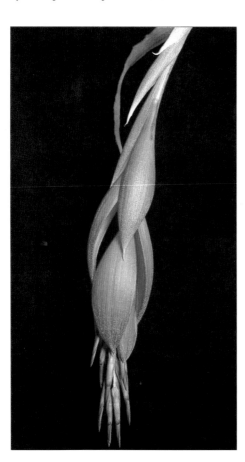

ABOVE: Billbergia nutans
BELOW LEFT: Billbergia × windii

HELPFUL HINTS
Temperature Winter minimum 13°C (55°F). Lower but frost-free temperatures are unlikely to kill the plant, but it may not grow or flower so well.
Humidity Tolerates dry air if necessary.
Position Good light, but not direct sun.
Watering and feeding Water freely from spring to autumn, sparingly in winter. In summer, pour some water into the leaf rosettes, but leave these dry at other times. Feed from spring to autumn.
Care Do not discard after flowering — often the case with flowering bromeliads grown as houseplants — as new offsets flower quickly. After a few years it will make a large clump that flowers reliably every year. Repot when the clump has filled the pot.
Propagation Offsets that form around the old rosette that has flowered. Separate from the parent when the new shoots are half as tall as the parent plant.

Blechnum

Distinctive ferns with a creeping rhizome or short stem or 'trunk' (on mature plants). The leaves are arranged in a funnel-shaped rosette.

Blechnum brasiliense
Rosette of reddish-brown young fronds, maturing to green. Makes a plant up to 1m (3ft) tall.

Blechnum gibbum
Rosette of large fronds that can be up to 1m (3ft) long on a mature plant. A distinct trunk develops with age.

HELPFUL HINTS
Temperature Aim for 13–18°C (55–64°F) in winter. High winter temperatures are detrimental.
Humidity Moderate humidity.
Position Light or partial shade. Avoid exposing to direct sun.
Watering and feeding Water freely in spring and summer, moderately at other times. Never let the roots dry out. Feed with a weak fertilizer in spring and summer.
Care Remove any dead or marked fronds to keep the plant looking attractive.
Propagation Division or spores.

BELOW: Blechnum gibbum

Bougainvillea

Climbing shrubs grown for their colourful papery bracts rather than their true flowers, which are insignificant. Because of their size — 3m (10ft) or more in a border — they are better suited to a conservatory than indoors, although they can be grown successfully around hoops or supports in a small container for several years in a living-room. Besides the species and hybrids listed you will find many sold simply under varietal names, which may be varieties of the following species or be hybrids with others. They are all treated in the same way.

Bougainvillea × buttiana

A hybrid between *B. glabra* and *B. peruviana*. 'Mrs Butt' or 'Crimson Lake' are the best-known varieties, with scarlet, long-lasting, papery bracts in spring and summer. Other varieties sometimes offered include 'Miss Manila' (reddish-pink bracts), 'Mrs Helen McLean' (apricot to amber), and 'Scarlet O'Hara' (scarlet).

Bougainvillea glabra

Vigorous climber with thorny stems. Rose-red bracts in summer. There are varieties with purple to violet bracts, and 'Variegata' has variegated foliage. Varieties sometimes seen include 'Magnifica' (vivid purple), 'Rainbow' (coral red bracts becoming multicoloured as they fade), and 'Snow White' (white).

Bougainvillea spectabilis

A thorny, vigorous species, seldom grown as a houseplant. Reddish-purple bracts, but there are also varieties that are red, pink, white, and yellowish-orange.

HELPFUL HINTS

Temperature Winter minimum 13°C (55°F).
Humidity Mist regularly if in a heated room, and on hot summer days.
Position Good light. Tolerates direct sun if not too fierce, but avoid exposing

to direct midday sun through glass.
Watering and feeding Water freely in summer, sparingly at other times. Avoid over-watering in spring when the new growth starts, as this may retard flowering. Feed regularly during the summer months.
Care Repot in spring if necessary. The plant rarely flowers for a second season if kept in living-room conditions, so move to a conservatory or greenhouse if possible when not in flower. Shorten the shoots in autumn to keep the plant compact, training new shoots to the support.
Propagation Cuttings.

LEFT: Bougainvillea *hybrid*
BELOW: Boungainvillea glabra *'Alexandra'*

Browallia

A small group of mainly herbaceous plants, but the one most often grown is a semi-shrubby plant usually treated like an annual and discarded when it deteriorates.

Browallia speciosa

Pale or deep blue, or white or purple flowers on bushy plants about 30cm (1ft) tall. Its varieties, rather than the species itself, are usually grown. These vary in colour and compactness, and have larger flowers than the species. Can be had in flower for most of the year by staggering the sowings.

HELPFUL HINTS
Temperature Aim for 10–15°C (50–59°F). Plants flower for longer if the temperature is not too high.

Humidity Undemanding, but mist the leaves occasionally.
Position Good light. Tolerates some direct sun, but avoid direct sun through glass during the hottest part of the day.
Watering and feeding Water freely at all times. Feed regularly.
Care Grow one plant in a 10cm (4in) pot or three in a 15cm (6in) pot. Pinch out the growing tips periodically – especially when young – to encourage bushiness. Deadhead regularly. Discard the plant when flowering has finished.
Propagation Seed in late winter or early spring for summer and autumn flowering, and in summer for winter and spring flowering.

BELOW: Browallia speciosa

Brugmansia

Likely to be found under this name or its previous name datura. The species and hybrids likely to be grown as indoor or patio plants are large shrubs. Their large size – often 1.8m (6ft) or more even if pruned back each year – makes them more appropriate for a conservatory than a living-room. All parts of these plants are potentially poisonous, so they are not a good choice if there are small children in the home.

Brugmansia × candida

Large leaves, often 30cm (1ft) or more long, and huge, bell-shaped flowers up to 20cm (8in) deep. 'Plena' has double flowers. Very fragrant. Can be in bloom throughout the year if conditions are suitable, but summer is the main flowering period. Also sold as *Datura × candida*.

Brugmansia suaveolens

Similar to the above species, with even

larger white flowers. There is a double form. Very fragrant. Also sold as *Datura suaveolens*.

HELPFUL HINTS
Temperature Winter minimum 7°C (45°F).
Humidity Undemanding, but mist the leaves occasionally.
Position Good light, preferably with some direct sun.
Watering and feeding Water freely from spring to autumn, sparingly in winter. Feed regularly from spring to autumn.
Care Prune back hard at the end of the flowering season to keep the shrub compact. If possible, grow in a tub that can be moved out to the patio for the summer and brought back indoors for the cold months.
Propagation Cuttings.

RIGHT: Brugmansia suaveolens (*syn.* Datura suaveolens)

Bryophyllum

The two viviparous species described are grown as curiosities rather than plants of beauty. They become tall and leggy with age and their appeal lies in their ability to produce plantlets along the edges or at the tips of their leaves. These can be potted up to produce new plants. If you propagate these plants frequently and discard old specimens, they make interesting plants which are easy to grow. They also make ideal houseplants for children to grow. Like other bryophyllums, they are now more correctly called *Kalanchoe*, but you will still see them sold under their old name.

Bryophyllum daigremontianum
An erect, unbranching plant to about 75cm (2½ft), with succulent leaves blotched purple beneath and plantlets around the serrated leaf edges. Also known as *Kalanchoe daigremontiana*.

Bryophyllum tubiflorum
Erect growth with cylindrical, pale reen leaves with darker markings. Plantlets are formed at the toothed ends. Also known as *Kalanchoe tubiflora*; now botanically named *K. dalagonensis*.

HELPFUL HINTS
Temperature Winter minimum 5°C (41°F).
Humidity Tolerates dry air.
Position Good light, but avoid exposing to direct summer sun.
Watering and feeding Water sparingly at all times, with enough moisture only to prevent the soil becoming completely dry in winter. Feed regularly in summer for a large plant: do no feed for a compact plant.
Care Remove plantlets that drop before they root.
Propagation Pot up the plantlets.

LEFT: Bryophyllum tubiflorum (*syn.* Kalanchoe tubiflora)

ABOVE: Bryophyllum daigremontianum (*syn.* Kalanchoe daigremontiana)

Calathea

Calatheas are exotic-looking rainforest plants, popular for their striking variegated foliage. They are demanding plants to grow in a living-room and are short-lived unless provided with sufficient warmth and humidity.

Calathea crocata
Dark green foliage with a reddish bloom, almost purple beneath the leaf. Long-lasting orange flowers.

Calathea insignis *see C. lancifolia.*

Calathea lancifolia
Lance-shaped leaves about 45cm (1½ft) long with alternating small and large darker green blotches along each side of the main vein. The reverse side is purple. This plant is also known as *C. insignis.*

Calathea lietzei
Slightly wavy oblong leaves about 15cm (6in) long, green with olive stripes above, reddish-purple beneath.

Calathea lubbersii
Large green leaves irregularly splashed with flashes of yellow along each side of the main vein.

Calathea makoyana
Long stalks bearing oval papery leaves, with feathery streaks of silver and dark green blotches running from the central vein. The reverse of the leaves is purple with similar markings. This plant is also known as *Maranta makoyana.*

Calathea medio-picta
Pointed oblong leaves about 15–20cm (6–8in) long, the upper surface dark

green with a whitish band along the central vein.

Calathea picturata

Oval, dark green leaves with white and yellowish-green streaks along the midrib and near the margins. 'Vandenheckei' has silvery streaks in the centre and on either side.

Calathea roseopicta

Large oval leaves about 20cm (8in) long, streaked pink and later fading to silvery-white. Red central vein and purplish reverse.

Calathea zebrina

Lance-shaped leaves 30–45cm (1–1½ft) long with dark green patches each side of the main vein. Grey-green or reddish-purple reverse.

HELPFUL HINTS

Temperature Winter minimum 16°C (60°F). Avoid sudden fluctuations in temperature.
Humidity Needs high humidity.
Position Partial shade or good light out of direct sun. Good light in winter, but avoid exposing to direct sun.
Watering and feeding Water freely,

FAR LEFT: Calathea crocata
OPPOSITE ABOVE: Calathea lubbersii
OPPOSITE BELOW: Calathea zebrina
ABOVE: Calathea picturata
'Vandenheckei' (left) and Calathea lancifolia (right)

using soft water if possible, from spring to autumn; sparingly in winter. Feed with a weak fertilizer in summer.
Care Repot annually in spring. Sponge the leaves occasionally.
Propagation Division.

Calceolaria

The only calceolarias widely grown as houseplants are hybrids, sometimes listed as *C. × herbeohybrida*. They are annuals that have to be discarded after flowering.

Calceolaria hybrids

Pouch-shaped flowers in shades of red, orange, yellow, pink, and white, usually attractively blotched or spotted. Height about 23–45cm (9–18in) according to variety. 'Grandiflora' varieties have flowers up to 6cm (2½in) across; 'Multiflora' varieties have flowers about 4cm (1½in) across. Seed companies offer many varieties.

HELPFUL HINTS
Temperature Aim for 10–15°C (50–59°F). Avoid high temperatures as much as possible.
Humidity Moderate humidity, but avoid wetting the blooms when the plant is in flower.
Position Good light, but avoid exposing to direct sun. Avoid draughts.
Watering and feeding Water freely. Never allow the plant to become dry.
Care Be alert for aphids, and spray promptly to control them if necessary. If possible, grow in a conservatory or greenhouse until just coming into flower. Discard the plant when flowering is over.
Propagation Seed in early summer. If you do not have a greenhouse or conservatory to raise plants, it is best to buy them ready-grown.

RIGHT: Calceolaria herbeo hybrida

Campanula

Most of this large group of plants are used in the herbaceous border or rock garden. *C. carpatica* is frost-hardy and best planted outdoors when flowering has finished. The other species listed here are trailing plants for the greenhouse or conservatory, but useful for short-term decoration indoors.

Campanula carpatica

Compact plant 15–23cm (6–9in) tall, covered with upward-facing, blue or white, cup-shaped flowers in summer. Often sold as a pot plant, but best planted in the garden after flowering.

Campanula fragilis

Trailing stems about 30cm (1ft) long, with blue flowers in early and mid summer.

Campanula isophylla

Trailing stems with soft blue, star-like flowers in mid and late summer. 'Mayi' has slightly larger flowers, 'Alba' is white.

HELPFUL HINTS
Temperature Winter minimum 7°C (45°F) for *C. fragilis* and *C. isophylla*. *C. carpatica* is hardy.
Humidity Undemanding, but mist the leaves occasionally.
Position Good light, but not direct summer sun.
Watering and feeding Water freely from spring to autumn, sparingly in winter.
Care Deadhead regularly. Plant *C. carpatica* in the garden when flowering is over. Cut the stems back to 5–7½cm (2–3in) at the end of the growing season to keep the plant compact and well clothed.
Propagation Seed; cuttings.

BELOW: Campanula isophylla

Capsicum

Only one species is used as a house-plant, an annual grown for its colour-ful fruits. Some varieties have round fruits, but most are cone-shaped.

Capsicum annuum

White, inconspicuous flowers in spring or summer, followed by green fruits that ripen to shades of yellow, orange, red, or purple; at their most attractive in early and mid winter.

Helpful hints

Temperature Winter minimum 13°C (55°F).
Humidity Mist the leaves regularly.
Position Good light with some direct sun.
Watering and feeding Water freely. Never allow the plant to become dry.

Care As the plant is uninteresting until the fruits ripen, keep in a green-house or conservatory if possible, and bring indoors as the fruits develop their colour. The fruits will be held for longer if kept in cool, humid conditions. Hot, dry air causes them to drop prematurely.
Propagation Seed.

Below: Capsicum annuum

Catharanthus

A small genus with a few species, only one of which is usually grown as a houseplant. Although perennial, this species is often grown as an annual.

Catharanthus roseus
Pink or white flowers about 2.5cm (1in) across with a dark eye, on compact plants that resemble the popular impatiens at a glance. Leaves have a prominent white vein. Catharanthus flower mainly between early summer and late autumn although they can be in bloom almost the year round. May also be sold as *Vinca rosea*.

HELPFUL HINTS
Temperature Minimum 10°C (50°F).
Humidity Moderate humidity.
Position Good light, but not direct sun during the hottest part of the day.
Watering and feeding Water freely at all times. Feed regularly.
Care The plant is easily raised from seed and is best discarded once it deteriorates. If you want to overwinter plants, cuttings taken in late summer will take up less space. Never let the roots become dry. Pinch out the growing tips of young plants to encourage a bushy shape.
Propagation Seed; cuttings.

BELOW: Catharanthus roseus

Caryota

ABOVE: Caryota mitis

Palms with distinctive fronds that look ragged and torn at the ends. Most caryotas make large plants given good conditions, but indoors they rarely grow to more than 1.2m (4ft).

Caryota mitis
Large fronds with individual leaflets about 15cm (6in) long and 10cm (4in) wide on a mature plant. The ends are ragged, giving a fishtail effect.

HELPFUL HINTS
Temperature Winter minimum 13°C (55°F).

Humidity Moderate humidity. Mist regularly in a centrally-heated room.
Position Good light, but avoid exposing to direct summer sun.
Watering and feeding Water freely from spring to autumn, sparingly in winter but always keep the roots slightly moist. Feed in summer.
Care Repot only when the roots have filled the pot and growth is beginning to suffer. Always ensure there is very good drainage when repotting. Sponge the leaves occasionally.
Propagation Suckers. Seed (can be difficult).

Celosia

Easy-to-grow, colourful flowering plants, often used for summer bedding outdoors but useful as a pot plant. Although strictly perennial they are almost always grown as annuals. Celosias are happier in a conservatory than in a living-room.

Celosia argentea *see C. cristata.*

Celosia cristata
Crested 'cockscomb' flowers, deeply crenated and ruffled, in shades of red, yellow, orange, and pink, in summer and early autumn. The Plumosa group has feathery flower plumes. Lance-shaped pale green leaves. The nomenclature has become confused, and you may find them listed as separate species (*C. cristata*, and *C. plumosa*) or as varieties of *C. argentea*.

Celosia plumosa *see C. cristata.*

HELPFUL HINTS
Temperature Aim for 10–15°C (50–59°F) if possible, although in summer the temperature will inevitably be

higher. Plants last better indoors than outside, and often have stronger colours if kept cool.
Humidity Moderate humidity.
Position Good light, but avoid exposing to direct summer sun through glass.
Watering and feeding Water moderately. The plant is vulnerable to both under- and over-watering. Feed regularly but cautiously: too much fertilizer with a high nitrogen content

ABOVE: Celosia cristata (*syn.* C. argentea). *These are the cockscomb type.*

may produce healthy leaves but poor flowers.
Care Discard after flowering. Best raised in a greenhouse to produce sturdy plants, but can usually be bought as young plants coming into flower.
Propagation Seed.

Cephalocereus

Ribbed, columnar cacti that rarely branch, grown mainly for the eye-catching profusion of long white hairs that they produce.

Cephalocereus chrysacanthus
Forms a large column with a green body and woolly top clothed with yellow hairs. Nine to fourteen ribs clothed with amber thorns. Red flowers are occasionally produced. Now more correctly called *Pilosocereus chrysacanthus*.

Cephalocereus senilis
Columnar growth that rarely branches, covered with long grey or white, slightly twisted hairs. Pink flowers, but these only produced on very large plants.

HELPFUL HINTS
Temperature Winter minimum 16°C (60°F).
Humidity Tolerates dry air but benefits from misting occasionally in summer.
Position Lightest possible position, benefits from direct sun.
Watering and feeding Water moderately in summer, keep almost dry in winter. Feed in spring and summer.
Care Repot only when necessary, and move into a pot only slightly larger. It may be necessary to support a tall plant with thin canes for a month or two after repotting.
Propagation Seed.

RIGHT: Cephalocereus senilis

ABOVE: Cereus peruvianus

Cereus

Columnar cacti, although in some varieties there is a disturbance of the growth point that gives them a congested and malformed appearance. In many species the flesh is covered with a whitish, green or bluish waxy layer that helps to minimize water loss through evaporation. Most are vigorous growers, and are sometimes used as rootstocks for other grafted cacti.

Cereus azureus
Upright habit with slender stems, the young ones covered with a bluish waxy bloom. The columnar stems have six or seven ribs. The large white flowers are brownish on the outside.

Cereus chalybaeus
Upright-growing columns that can be tall and 10cm (4in) across in suitable conditions, with a blue bloom. There are usually six ribs. The large flowers

are pink to red on the outside and white inside.

Cereus jamacaru
Fast-growing species with four to six ribs and stong yellowish-brown thorns. A blue waxy bloom is often noticeable. 'Monstrosus' has malformed growth that produces a mass of congested stems. Cup-shaped white flowers which open at night appear on mature plants.

Cereus peruvianus
Columnar growth with blue bloom and five to eight ribs. Clusters of sharp brown thorns, the central one up to 2cm (¾in) long. 'Monstrosus' develops a congested head of shoots that makes the plant look malformed. Old plants – often over 1m (3ft) tall – may produce flowers of 10–15cm (4–6in), red outside, white inside. The plant

sold as *C. peruvianus* is botanically considered to be *C. uruguayanus*.

HELPFUL HINTS
Temperature Winter minimum 5°C (41°F).
Humidity Tolerates dry air.
Position Lightest possible position, benefits from direct sun.
Watering and feeding Water moderately in spring and summer, very sparingly in winter.
Care Repot only when necessary. Mist occasionally to help keep the plant looking clean and fresh. The plant can be stood in the garden in summer.
Propagation Seed; cuttings (for the branching species).

Ceropegia

Over 150 species are known but only a handful are cultivated. Some species have fleshy, erect-growing stems that may be leafless, but the best-known ones are succulent trailers.

Ceropegia radicans
Creeping succulent stems that root readily, with oval to oblong succulent leaves and long, tubular flowers striped green, white, and purple-red.

Ceropegia stapeliiformis
Upright, shrubby growth with succulent stems mottled grey-brown, and only rudimentary, scale-like. Funnel-shaped greenish-white flowers blotched purple-black.

Ceropegia woodii
Wiry purplish stems, up to 1m (3ft) long, with sparse small, heart-shaped, silver-mottled leaves. Inconspicuous 1–2cm (½-¾in) pinkish tubular flowers in summer. Small tubers sometimes form on the stems. Now considered to be *C. linearis woodii*.

HELPFUL HINTS
Temperature Winter minimum 10°C (50°F).
Humidity Tolerates dry air.

species of *Echinopsis* and has been called *E. chamaecereus*.

Chamaecereus silvestrii

Clump-forming, with finger-like, densely spined stems that are often decumbent and tend to trail over the edge of the pot. Funnel-shaped bright red flowers in early summer. One of the most reliable cacti for flowering.

HELPFUL HINTS

Temperature Keep cool in winter. Aim for a minimum 3°C (37°F), although it will not be killed if a couple of degrees lower.
Humidity Tolerates dry air.
Position Good light, but not direct summer sun.
Watering and feeding Water freely from spring to autumn; keep practically dry in winter. Feed regularly with a weak fertilizer from mid spring to late summer.
Care Do not over-pamper in winter. If kept cold and dry the plant may shrivel but will probably bloom all the more prolifically afterwards.
Propagation Seed; cuttings.

BELOW: Chamaecereus silvestrii

ABOVE: Ceropegia woodii

Position Good light. Tolerates both full sun and partial shade.
Watering and feeding Water sparingly at all times, especially in winter. Feed regularly with a weak fertilizer in summer.
Care Shorten spindly stems that have become bare in spring.
Propagation Seed; layering; cuttings from sections of stem containing a stem tuber.

Chamaecereus

A genus of just one species, an easy-to-grow cactus that flowers readily. It is now considered by botanists to be a

Chamaedorea

A genus of more than 100 species, but only one is widely grown as a houseplant. *C. elegans* is widely popular because of its compact size and undemanding nature.

Chamaedorea elegans
Bright green arching leaves growing from the base. On small plants these may be only 15–30cm (6–12in) long, but on a mature plant can be 60cm (2ft) or more. Flowers, like tiny yellow balls, may appear on quite young plants. Still sometimes listed under the name *Neanthe bella*.

RIGHT: Chamaedorea elegans

HELPFUL HINTS
Temperature Aim for 12–15°C (53–59°F) in winter.
Humidity Mist the leaves occasionally, even in winter if the room is centrally-heated.
Position Good light, but avoid exposing to direct sun.
Watering and feeding Water generously from spring to autumn, but keep only just moist in winter. Feed regularly with a weak fertilizer in spring and summer.
Care Repot when its roots start to grow through the bottom of the pot. Avoid high winter temperatures as *C. elegans* benefits from a winter resting period.
Propagation Seed; division.

Chamaerops

Palms with large fan-shaped leaves. Although older specimens may be sizeable if given ideal conditions, in a large pot or tub they rarely exceed 1m (3ft). Only one species is widely grown indoors as a houseplant.

Chamaerops humilis
Fan-shaped leaves on spiny stalks on top of a short trunk on an old specimen, but in most plants of houseplant size the trunk is missing.

HELPFUL HINTS
Temperature Aim for 3–10°C (37–50°F) in winter. Avoid high winter temperatures. Will even tolerate a few degrees of frost if the roots are dry, although this is not recommended.
Humidity Benefits from high humidity. Mist the leaves regularly, especially in a centrally-heated room.
Position Good light, but avoid exposing to direct summer sun.
Watering and feeding Water generously from spring to autumn. Keep fairly moist in winter if the temperature is high, almost dry if cold. Feed regularly in summer.
Care Can be stood outside for the summer, after careful acclimatization. Sponge the leaves occasionally. Trim off any brown leaf tips, but do not cut into the green area. Repot young plants every two or three years.
Propagation Seed.

BELOW: Chamaerops humilis

Chlorophytum

A genus of about 200 or so species, but only a few are commonly grown as houseplants. *Chlorophytum comosum* is a native of South Africa, and it is the variegated forms that are almost exclusively used as pot plants.

Chlorophytum comosum

Linear leaves up to 2cm (¾in) wide and 30–60cm (1–2ft) long, arching to form a cascading habit. The flower stalk gradually curves as it lengthens, and as well as small star-shaped white flowers it usually bears small rosettes of leaves that form plantlets. 'Variegatum' and 'Vittatum' have white and green striped leaves.

LEFT: Chlorophytum comosum *'Vittatum'*

HELPFUL HINTS

Temperature Winter minimum 7°C (45°F). Will withstand temperatures just above freezing, but for strong, healthy plants keep them above the recommended minimum.
Humidity Undemanding, but mist the leaves occasionally.
Position Good light, but avoid exposing to direct sun.
Watering and feeding Water generously from spring to autumn, sparingly in winter. Feed regularly from spring to autumn.
Care Repot young plants annually in spring, more mature ones only when the strong, fleshy roots show signs of cracking the pot or pushing the plant from its container.
Propagation Plantlets that form on the flowering stems. Large plants can be divided.

Chrysanthemum

The florist's year-round pot chrysanthemums need no introduction. By adjusting the day length and using dwarfing chemicals, commercial growers are able to produce compact plants in flower for every season. The correct botanical name for these plants is dendranthema, but you are unlikely to find them for sale under that name. The varieties used for year-round pot chrysanthemums are derived from many species, and although named varieties are used these are seldom specified at the point of sale. There may be several plants in a single pot to produce a better display.

Year-round pot chrysanthemums

Usually less than 30cm (1ft) high when grown as a houseplant. Single and double flowers in shades of red, pink, purple, yellow, and white. Grown normally, most of these make tall plants that flower in the autumn.

HELPFUL HINTS

Temperature Aim for 10–15°C (50–59°F). Plants tolerate a warm room but the display of flowers will be much shorter-lived.
Humidity Undemanding, but mist the leaves occasionally.
Position Undemanding. As you will probably discard the plant afterwards, place in any position.
Watering and feeding Keep moist at all times. Feeding is unnecessary.
Care Deadhead to keep the plant looking tidy. Discard after flowering unless you want to try them as garden plants in which case plant out in spring or summer. Some varieties will make good tall garden plants for autumn colour, others will die – so this is a gamble.
Propagation Cuttings, although it is not practical to raise your own indoor pot chrysanthemums year-round.

BELOW: *Chrysanthemum, year-round type*

Cineraria

See Senecio cruentus.

Cissus

A large genus of tropical plants with about 350 species, some succulents, others woody. Those used most often as houseplants are vigorous climbers grown for their foliage. Any flowers that appear in summer are usually green and inconspicuous.

Cissus antarctica
Climber with woody stems and shiny oval, dark green leaves up to 10cm (4in) long. Will grow rapidly to about 3m (10ft) and needs plenty of space.

Cissus discolor
Climber with red tendrils and stems, and heart-shaped, pointed leaves that combine violet-red with silvery-grey and olive-green variegation. Flushed purplish-red beneath.

Cissus rhombifolia
Vigorous climber with dark green leaves, the undersides covered in reddish hairs. Leaves have three leaflets, the central one larger than the two behind. Still widely sold under the name *Rhoicissus rhomboidea*. 'Ellen Danica' is a widely grown variety with more deeply lobed leaflets.

HELPFUL HINTS
Temperature Aim for 7–13°C (45–55°F) in winter, with a minimum of 16°C (60°F) for *C. discolor*.
Humidity Undemanding, but mist occasionally, especially in summer.
Position Good light, but avoid exposing to direct summer sun. Provide light shade for *C. discolor*.
Watering and feeding Water generously from spring to autumn, more sparingly in winter.
Care Pinch out growing tips on young plants to stimulate new growth from low down. Keep new shoots tied to the support. Thin out overcrowded stems in spring. Spray or sponge the leaves of *C. antarctica* periodically to keep them bright and dust-free. Other species also benefit from occasional leaf-cleaning.
Propagation Cuttings.

TOP: Cissus rhombifolia
ABOVE: Cissus antarctica

× Citrofortunella

A hybrid genus (*Citrus × Fortunella*) of evergreen shrubs and trees grown mainly for their fruit. × *C. microcarpa* (syn. *Citrus mitis*) is a popular pot plant producing miniature oranges on compact plants suitable for growing indoors where larger citrus fruits would be unsuitable.

× Citrofortunella microcarpa

Glossy, dark green foliage. Small clusters of fragant white flowers, produced even on young plants, followed by miniature orange fruits about 4cm (1½in) across. These are rather bitter to taste. Summer is the usual flowering period, but both flowers and fruit may be produced almost all year round. It will reach about 1.2m (4ft) in time. May be seen under its older name of *Citrus mitis*.

× Citrofortunella mitis *see* × *C. microcarpa*.

HELPFUL HINTS
Temperature Winter minimum 10°C (50°F).
Humidity Undemanding, but mist the leaves occasionally.
Position Good light, but avoid direct summer sun through glass.
Watering and feeding Water freely in summer, sparingly in winter. Feed regularly in summer. A fertilizer containing magnesium and iron may be necessary as the plants are prone to a deficiency of these elements.
Care Stand the plants outside for the summer, afer careful acclimatization. Pollinate the flowers by dabbing with cotton wool or a small paintbrush.
Propagation Cuttings.

RIGHT: × Citrofortunella microcarpa (*syn.* Citrus mitis)

Citrus mitis

See × *Citrofortunella microcarpa.*

Clerodendrum

A large genus of about 400 mainly woody trees, shrubs and climbers, including a few that are hardy. Only *C. thomsoniae* is widely used as a houseplant, and even that is likely to prefer the conditions in a conservatory to the living-room.

Clerodendrum philippinum

Broad oval leaves up to 25cm (10in) long, and covered in hairs at the back. Fragrant white or pink flowers, at almost any time of the year.

Clerodendrum splendens

Wavy-edged, heart-shaped leaves up to 15cm (6in) long, dark green above, paler beneath. Pendulous red flower plumes between early winter and late spring.

Clerodendrum thomsoniae

Climbing stems that reach 2.4m (8ft) or more in a conservatory or greenhouse. Dark green, heart-shaped leaves. Distinctive red and white flowers in summer. The red corolla soon drops but the white calyx remains for many weeks.

HELPFUL HINTS
Temperature Aim for 13–15°C (55–59°F) in winter.
Humidity Mist the leaves regularly.
Position Good light, but not direct summer sun.
Watering and feeding Water freely spring to autumn, sparingly in winter. Feed regularly in spring and summer.
Care If required as a hanging or small bushy plant, cut back the stems by about half to two-thirds in late winter (by which time most of the foliage has probably dropped). Pinch out the growing tips of young plants if a bushy shape is required. Trail long stems around an upright support.
Propagation Cuttings; seed.

RIGHT: Clerodendrum thomsoniae

Clivia

A genus of evergreen perennials grown for their large heads of funnel-shaped flowers. Although belonging to the amaryllis family, they have fleshy, rhizomatous roots rather than a bulb. *C. miniata* is most often grown.

Clivia miniata

Large strap-shaped leaves often more than 5cm (2in) wide growing on opposite sides to create a fan-like effect. Large flower heads made of up 10–20 smaller, funnel-shaped orange or yellow flowers, in early spring.

HELPFUL HINTS
Temperature Winter minimum 10°C (50°F). Avoid warm winter temperatures.
Humidity Undemanding.
Position Good light, but avoid exposing to direct summer sun.

Watering and feeding Requires careful watering for regular blooming. Water moderately from spring to autumn, but sparingly in winter until the flower stalk is at least 15cm (6in) tall. If you water freely too soon, the leaves will grow rapidly while the flower stalk remains stunted. Be careful never to overwater as the roots are prone to rotting. Feed from flowering time to early autumn.
Care Sponge the leaves occasionally. Remove the old flower stems cutting them back as low as possible. Repot mature plants only when the roots are beginning to push the plant out from its container, and as soon as flowering is over.
Propagation Division, removing offsets with at least four leaves, after flowering.

BELOW: Clivia miniata

Cocos

A small genus, with only a couple of species that are grown as houseplants. One, the coconut palm (*C. nucifera*) is a large plant, even when young. The other (*C. weddeliana*) is a miniature palm, small enough for a table-top. Both species are difficult to keep for long periods in a living-room.

Cocos nucifera

The large seed, usually still visible when you buy the plant, indicates the large size that this palm can reach. Even indoors it will grow to 3m (10ft), but growth is slow. The fronds on a mature plant are feathery and very large, but on a young one are shaped almost like fish-tails.

Cocos weddeliana

A small palm with gracefully arching fronds of thin leaflets. It is small enough and sufficiently slow-growing to be used in a bottle garden while small. Many name changes surround this palm, and you may also find it listed or sold as *Lytocaryum weddeliana*,

ABOVE: Cocos weddeliana
LEFT: Cocos nucifera

Microcoelum weddelianum, and *Syagrus weddeliana.* Some experts now consider that it should be called *Syagrus cocoides.*

HELPFUL HINTS
Temperature Winter mimimum 18°C (64°F).
Humidity Needs high humidity.
Position Good light, ideally with some full sun, but avoid exposing to direct sun through glass during the hottest part of the day.
Watering and feeding Water freely in summer, moderately in winter. Never allow the roots to dry out. Feed with a weak fertilizer in summer.
Care Sponge the leaves occasionally, but do not use a leaf shine. Repot young plants in spring.
Propagation Seed, but this is best done by a professional grower.

Codiaeum

A small genus containing colourful evergreen trees and shrubs. Most of the plants now grown are the results of many crosses and the plants are usually classified as *C. variegatum pictum.*

There are hundreds of hybrids and varieties grouped under this name, but individual names are rarely seen on specimens sold as houseplants. Typical of the range available are 'Goldfinger' (narrow pale green leaves flushed yellow along the centre) and 'Mrs Iceton' (oval leaves, very dark and heavily marked with red and pink between the veins). 'Gold Ring' has twisted, distorted leaves.

Codiaeum variegatum pictum
Many varieties available, some with narrow, finger-like leaves, others with broad foliage; some have spiralling leaves while others are deeply lobed.

All foliage is thick, glossy, and brightly coloured or variegated; colours include green, pink, orange, red, brown, and near-black. Inconspicuous flowers, like small whitish balls, sometimes appear in summer.

HELPFUL HINTS
Temperature Winter minimum 16°C (60°F).
Humidity Needs high humidity. Mist the leaves regularly.
Position Good light, but avoid exposing to direct summer sun.
Watering and feeding Water generously from spring to autumn, sparingly in winter. Feed regularly in spring and summer.
Care Avoid cold draughts. Repot in spring, only when the plants have outgrown their existing container.
Propagation Cuttings.

BELOW: Codiaeum variegatum pictum

Colchicum

Corms with the ability to flower without soil, sometimes grown as a fun plant to flower on a windowsill in the late summer or early autumn. They are planted in the garden to grow normally once flowering indoors is over. The species described is the most common, but several other species can be treated in the same way.

Colchicum autumnale

Large crocus-shaped flowers in early autumn, usually in shades of pink. The colours are almost always paler when flowered dry indoors than when planted in the garden. The leaves do not appear until spring. Note that the corms and leaves are poisonous.

HELPFUL HINTS
Temperature Undemanding, as the plants are hardy and can be planted in the garden after flowering.
Humidity Undemanding. No special care needed.
Position A light windowsill, preferably out of strong direct sunlight.
Watering and feeding No watering or feeding necessary.
Care Place the dry corms in a saucer of sand or tray of dry pebbles to keep them upright. Set in a light position and leave the corms to flower — no water is needed. After flowering, plant in the garden in light shade, and cover with about 10cm (4in) of soil. Buy new corms each year rather than use the same ones again.
Propagation Seed; division of a large clump, but it is usually easier to buy new corms.

RIGHT: Colchicum autumnale

Coleus

A large genus of about 200 species, including perennials, annuals and evergreen sub-shrubs, many with bright and colourful foliage, but only one is widely grown. These are almost always listed as *C. blumei* hybrids, but botanists now list them as *Solenostemon* instead of coleus. However, you will almost always find them under their traditional name.

Coleus blumei hybrids

Perennial sub-shrub, but usually treated as an annual. Most have oval leaves that are gently serrated around the edge, but a few have deeply lobed foliage. Variegation varies enormously in colour and pattern, many incorporating shades of red, yellow, and green. There are named varieties, some of which have to be propagated from cuttings, but most seed mixtures produce a pleasing range of colours and patterns. Plants or cuttings are best overwintered in a greenhouse or conservatory if new stock is not to be raised from seed.

HELPFUL HINTS
Temperature Winter minimum 10°C (50°F).
Humidity Needs high humidity. Mist the leaves frequently.
Position Good light, but avoid exposing to direct summer sun during the hottest part of the day.
Watering and feeding Water freely from spring to autumn, keep the roots just moist in winter, and use soft water. Feed from spring to autumn.
Care Pinch out the growing tips of young plants to promote bushy growth. Pinch out several times more for really bushy plants. If an old plant has been overwintered, cut back hard and repot in spring to stimulate new growth from low down.

If you have raised your own plants from seed, you will probably have many, as they germinate easily. Once the plants are large enough to show their variegation clearly, retain the most appealing and discard the rest.
Propagation Seed in spring; stem cuttings in spring or summer.

RIGHT: Coleus *hybrids*

Columnea

A genus of creeping or trailing ever-green perennials or sub-shrubs, from the rain forests of Central America.

Columnea × banksii

Creeping or trailing stems with small, glossy leaves, green above and reddish beneath. Orange-red, two-lipped flowers, about 6cm (2½in) long, usually in winter and spring.

Columnea gloriosa

Long, limp, trailing stems with small leaves covered in red hairs. Scarlet flowers about 8cm (3in) long, with a yellow spot in the throat, usually in winter or spring.

Columnea hirta

Creeping or trailing stems that root readily. Red flowers about 10cm (4in) long in spring. The entire plant is covered with short, stiff hairs.

Columnea microphylla

Long, thin, trailing stems up to 1m (3ft) in length, with small almost circular leaves. Orange-red flowers in spring or summer.

HELPFUL HINTS

Temperature Winter minimum 13°C (55°F).

Humidity Needs high humidity. Mist the leaves regularly.

Position Good light, but avoid exposing to direct summer sun.

Watering and feeding Water freely from spring to autumn, sparingly in winter. Feed regularly in spring and summer months.

Care Shorten the stems once flowering is over to keep the plant compact. Repot every second or third year.

Columneas do best planted in the humus-rich fibrous compost (potting soil) sold for bromeliads and orchids.
Propagation Cuttings.

TOP: Columnea microphylla
BOTTOM: Columnea gloriosa
MIDDLE: Columnea hirta

Cordyline

Evergreen shrubs and trees grown mainly for their foliage. Some of the species are sometimes sold as dracaenas, and there is often confusion between these two genera. If in doubt about whether a particular plant is a cordyline or a dracaena, check the roots. Cordylines have creeping roots that are knobbly and white when cut, while dracaenas have non-creeping roots that are smooth and yellow or orange if cut.

Cordyline australis
Sword-shaped green leaves that can be 1m (3ft) long. Some varieties are variegated, with red or yellow stripes along the green leaves. C. a. 'Purpurea' has reddish-purple leaves. Young plants grown indoors usually lack a distinctive trunk, which only develops on older plants. Young plants in the home are unlikely to flower.

Cordyline fruticosa
Old plants develop a clear stem or trunk, and grow large, but the young specimens usually sold as houseplants are leafy down to the base and remain compact for a long time. The species itself has plain green leaves, but there

ABOVE LEFT: Cordyline australis
ABOVE: Cordyline terminalis (*syn.* C. fruticosa) '*Kiwi*'

are many variegated varieties, heavily marked with red, pink, or cream, and sometimes a combination of these colours. Some have broad leaves, others narrower ones. Treat them all in the same way. This plant can be sold as *C. terminalis* or *Dracaena terminalis*.

Cordyline terminalis *see C. fruticosa.*

HELPFUL HINTS
Temperature Winter minimum 13°C (55°F) for tender species such as *C. fruticosa*, 3°C (37°F) for tough species such as *C. australis*.
Humidity *C. australis* is undemanding. Tropical species such as *C. fruticosa* require high humidity and should be misted regularly.
Position Good light, but avoid exposing to direct sun. *C. australis* will tolerate direct sun, but avoid summer sun through glass during the hottest part of the day.
Watering and feeding Water freely from spring to autumn, sparingly in winter. Feed tropical species regularly in spring and summer, *C. australis* less frequently.

Care Sponge leaves occasionally to remove dust and make them look brighter. Repot every second spring. *C. australis* and its varieties make attractive patio plants for the summer, but acclimatize them to outdoor conditions first. In mild areas where frosts are never severe they are sometimes successful when planted permanently in the garden, but they are best regarded as frost-tender, especially young plants.
Propagation Cuttings and stem sections with an eye, rooted in a propagator, are the best ways to increase the number of plants. An old specimen that has become leggy where leaves have fallen can be air layered.

Crassula

A large genus of about 300 succulents, ranging from dwarfs of less than 2.5cm (1in) to tall species over 5m (16ft). The species listed are just a selection of those sometimes grown as house and conservatory plants.

Crassula arborescens
Tree-shaped and will grow to about

BELOW: Crassula argentea

ABOVE: Crassula lycopodiodes
RIGHT: Crassula arborescens

1.8m (6ft) if conditions are suitable. Thick, greyish leaves edged with a red margin. White flowers, fading to pink, may appear in early and mid summer on a mature plant.

Crassula argentea *see C. portulacea.*

Crassula ovata *see C. portulacea.*

Crassula portulacea

Tree-shaped with a short 'trunk'. May grow to 1m (3ft) or more. Thick dark green succulent leaves about 2.5–5cm (1–2in) across, edged red. You may also find the plant under two other names: *C. argentea* and *C. ovata.*

Crassula lycopodioides

Distinctive fleshy stems forming an upright cluster, completely covered with minute fleshy, scale-like leaves arranged in four rows. Tiny greenish-yellow flowers in spring. The correct botanical name for this plant is now *C. mucosa.*

HELPFUL HINTS
Temperature Aim for 7–10°C (45–50°F) in winter. Avoid high temperatures in winter, otherwise the plants become lanky and leaves may fall.
Humidity Tolerates dry air.
Position Good light, in sun if possible. Species with very pale green leaves or a white bloom are best protected from strong direct sunlight through glass.

Watering and feeding Water sparingly at all times, and keep almost dry in winter. Feed with a weak fertilizer occasionally in summer.
Care Repot annually in spring while the plants are still young. Restrict watering for a while after repotting, otherwise the roots may rot.
Propagation Leaf and tip cuttings. Seed is an option but seldom used.

Crocus

Mainly spring-flowering corms, but some bloom in the autumn. It is the popular spring-flowering kinds that are almost exclusively used indoors.

Crocus chrysanthus

Typical crocus-shaped flowers, but smaller and earlier than the large-flowered varieties. The true species is seldom grown, but there are many varieties in a range of colours available for autumn planting. They bloom indoors in late winter. The grass-like leaves have a white central stripe.

Crocus, large-flowered

The typical large-flowered crocuses of spring, botanically derived from *C. vernus.* Grass-like leaves with a white central stripe. There are many varieties to plant in autumn for late winter and early spring blooming.

HELPFUL HINTS
Temperature Keep cool. Leave in the garden until mid winter but protect from excessive freezing in cold climates, also rain that might waterlog the pots or containers. Maintain in cool conditions indoors until at least a third of the developing flower bud is visible.
Humidity Undemanding.
Position Good light once brought indoors. A sunny position will encourage the flowers to open fully.
Watering and feeding Water cautiously so that the corms do not start to rot.
Care After flowering, plant in the garden. Do not attempt to force the same corms for a second time – buy new ones each year.
Propagation Small offset corms; seed. Crocuses are seldom propagated by amateurs because it takes several years to produce plants of flowering size. It is more convenient to buy flowering-sized corms.

BELOW: Crocus, *large-flowered hybrid*

ABOVE: Crossandra infundibuliformis

Crossandra

A genus of tropical evergreen sub-shrubs with long-lasting, attractive flowers. Several species are grown as houseplants, but the one described here is the most commonly found.

Crossandra infundibuliformis
Bright heads of tubular soft orange flowers about 2.5cm (1in) across above glossy, dark green, oval to lance-shaped leaves. The plants flower while still young and may be in bloom from mid spring to autumn if conditions suit. Most plants reach about 30–60cm (1–2ft) indoors. Sometimes sold under its old name of *C. undulifolia*.

Crossandra undulifolia *see C. infundibuliformis*.

HELPFUL HINTS
Temperature Winter minimum 13°C (55°F).
Humidity High humidity is essential. Mist the leaves regularly.
Position Good light, but avoid exposing to direct summer sun.
Watering and feeding Water gener-

ously in summer, less often in winter.
Care Deadhead regularly to prolong season of flowering. Repot in spring if necessary.
Propagation Stem cuttings; seed (used commercially but difficult in the home).

Cryptanthus

Genus of rosette-forming bromeliads, grown for their attractive foliage. The colouring often varies according to the light intensity.

Cryptanthus acaulis
Low-growing rosette of green, narrow, pointed leaves about 10–15cm (4–6in) long, the edges wavy and slightly serrated. Fragrant tubular white flowers sometimes appear from the centre of each rosette in summer.

Cryptanthus bromelioides
Large rosettes about 20cm (8in) or more tall, with strap-shaped and finely toothed green leaves. White flowers are occasionally produced, usually in summer. More decorative is *C. b. tricolor*, which is suffused with carmine and striped white.

Cryptanthus zonatus
Flattish rosettes of wavy leaves about 20cm (8in) long, cross-banded dark sepia-green and silvery-white. A clus-

BELOW: Cryptanthus bromeliodes tricolor

ter of white flowers may be produced from the centre of rosettes in summer.

Temperature Winter minimum 18°C (64°F).
Humidity Needs high humidity.
Position Good light, but not direct summer sun.
Watering and feeding Water freely in spring and summer, cautiously in autumn and sparingly in winter. Never allow the roots to dry out. Pour water into the rosettes in summer, but not in winter. Try to use tepid water. Feed regularly with a weak fertilizer in summer.
Care If the plant has to be repotted, choose a shallow container as cryptanthus have a shallow root system. Can also be grown as epiphytes in a basket or on a piece of bark. Old rosettes die once they have flowered, but young ones (offsets) will have formed around the centre of the old plants.
Propagation Offsets or plantlets which grow from the centre of the old plant in these species.

Ctenanthe

Evergreen perennials, mainly from Brazil, grown for their attractive foliage. The two species listed here are the ones most likely to be sold as houseplants.

Ctenanthe lubbersiana
Clump-forming with almost oblong leaves, about 20–25cm (8–10in) long, and on long stalks that end in an abrupt point. The leaves are irregularly splashed with pale yellow above, pale green below. Grows to about 60–75cm (2–2½ft) as a houseplant.

Ctenanthe oppenheimiana
Densely leaved, clump-forming plant with leaves usually more than 30cm (1ft) long, on tall stems that produce a plant about 1m (3ft) tall. The foliage is dark green above with irregular silvery-white bands each side of the

ABOVE: Ctenanthe lubbersiana
RIGHT: Ctenanthe oppenheimiana

midribs, and reddish-purple beneath. 'Tricolor' has large cream blotches over the green leaves.

Temperature Winter minimum 16°C (60°F).
Humidity Needs high humidity.
Position Good light, but avoid exposing to direct sun.
Watering and feeding Water moderately at all times. Do not water if the surface is still damp, but never let the roots dry out. Use soft water if possible – for watering and misting. Feed in summer.
Care Sponge leaves occasionally to remove dust and to keep them looking bright. Cut out any leaves that have deteriorated.
Propagation Division.

ABOVE: Cyclamen, *large-flowered hybrid*

Watering and feeding Water freely while the plants are growing actively. Gradually reduce the amount of water given once flowering has finished. During the resting period give just a little water occasionally to prevent the corm shrivelling. Feed regularly during the active growing and flowering periods.

Care Deadhead regularly, trying not to leave any stumps of flower stalk as these will be prone to rotting. Once the leaves have died, the corm goes into a dormant period, so keep the pot in a cool place (perhaps outside) and almost dry until mid summer. Then start watering again (repot if necessary, burying the tuber to half its depth), and bring indoors if the plant has been in the garden during the summer months.

Propagation Seed. Most varieties take 15–18 months to flower, but miniature cyclamen can be in flower in about 8 months.

Cyclamen

A small genus that includes hardy species with tiny flowers as well as the more popular florist's cyclamen. Those grown as pot plants are derived from *C. persicum*, which is native to the Middle East.

Cyclamen persicum

The species itself is not grown, but its hybrids and varieties are available in a range of pinks, reds, purples, salmon and white. The wide, reflexed petals are sometimes frilled or ruffled, and some of the varieties are fragrant. Leaf patterning is also variable, and often marbled or zoned white or silver. The main flowering time is autumn to early spring. Standard varieties grow to about 30cm (1ft), intermediate ones to about 23cm (9in), and miniatures to 15cm (6in) or less.

HELPFUL HINTS
Temperature Aim for 10–15°C (50–59°F) in winter. High temperatures will shorten the flowering period.
Humidity Moderate humidity. Plants benefit from misting when only foliage is present, but be careful not to spray the flowers. Humidity is best provided by standing the pot on pebbles over water.
Position Good light, but avoid exposing to direct sun.

Cymbidium

A genus of 45 or so species, including both epiphytes and semi-terrestrial orchids. There are a great many hybrids, and it is these that are normally grown in the home, where they are among the most reliable orchids to grow as houseplants.

Cymbidium hybrids

Upright spikes of large waxy-looking flowers, in colours such as green, yellow, pink, and white, usually attractively speckled or marked. Flowering time is usually between autumn and spring. Many named hybrids are grown by specialist orchid nurseries, but variety names may not be identified if you buy from a garden centre or superstore. However, all those widely sold as pot plants can be treated in the same way.

HELPFUL HINTS
Temperature Aim for 7–13°C (45–55°F) in winter.

Humidity Mist the leaves regularly. Humidity is best provided by standing the pot on pebbles over water.

Position Good light, but avoid exposing to direct sun.

Watering and feeding Water freely in spring and summer, sparingly in autumn and winter. Never let the roots dry out. Use soft, tepid water if possible. Feed during the flowering period.

Care Avoid a stuffy position and provide ventilation whenever it is warm enough. The plants – which are uninteresting out of flower – can be stood in a sheltered position outdoors for the summer. Repot only when the existing pot is full of roots, and use a special orchid mixture if possible.

Propagation Commercial growers use micropropagation but the easiest method for an amateur is division of an established clump, ideally after flowering.

BELOW: Cymbidium *hybrid*

Cyperus

A large genus with more than 600 species of rush-like plants, a few of which are grown as houseplants. They are a good choice for anyone who tends to overwater their plants, as they will actually thrive if the pot stands in a little water.

Cyperus albostriatus

Sedge with grass-like leaves, radiating out like the ribs of an opened umbrella, at the top of stems about 60cm (2ft) tall. This is the plant often grown as *C. diffusus*. 'Variegatus' has white-striped leaves.

Cyperus alternifolius

Grass-like leaves radiate from stiff stalks, resembling the ribs of an open umbrella. 'Variegatus' has white stripes along the length of its leaves. Height about 1m (3ft). Now more correctly called *C. involucratus*, but the name under which it is listed here is

ABOVE: Cyperus alternifolius

the one by which you are likely to purchase it.

Cyperus diffusus *see C. albostriatus*.

Cyperus involucratus *see C. alternifolius*.

HELPFUL HINTS
Temperature Winter minimum 7°C (45°F).
Humidity Mist the leaves regularly.
Position Good light, but not direct summer sun.
Watering and feeding Water freely at all times. Keep the roots moist. It will not matter if the pot stands in a little water. Feed from mid spring to early autumn.
Care Cut out any yellowing stems. Repot every spring.
Propagation Division.

Cypripedium

See Paphiopedilum.

Datura

See Brugmansia.

Davallia

A genus of evergreen or semi-evergreen, often epiphytic, ferns from tropical areas of Asia and Australia.

Davillia bullata

Divided fronds about 30cm (12in) long, sometimes with a puckered appearance.

Davallia fejeensis

A small to medium-sized fern with layers of delicate lacy fronds. Creeping rhizomes on the surface often grow over the edge of the pot.

HELPFUL HINTS

Temperature Winter minimum 7°C (45°F).
Humidity Mist the leaves regularly.
Position Partial shade or good light without direct sun.
Watering and feeding Water freely from spring to autumn, more sparingly in winter.
Care Remove dying or fading fronds.
Propagation Division; spores.

BELOW: Davallia bullata

Dendranthema

See Chrysanthemum.

Dieffenbachia

Bold foliage plants with poisonous or irritant sap that should be kept away from mouth, eyes and skin. The nomenclature of some dieffenbachias has become very confused, and you may find them sold under several synonyms. Many of the hybrids are listed simply under varietal name. As they can all be treated in the same way, this is not especially important horticulturally.

Dieffenbachia amoena

Large oblong leaves, often 60cm (2ft) long, on a thick stem. Dark green foliage with cream or white marbling along the side veins. 'Tropic Snow' is an example of a variety with heavier white variegation. You might find *D. amoena* listed as a variety of *D. seguine*, which is where some botanists now prefer to place it.

Dieffenbachia × bausei

Yellowish-green leaves about 30cm (1ft) long, marbled dark green with white patches.

Dieffenbachia bowmannii

Varieties of this species have dark and light flecks on the body of the leaves, overlaid with white or cream. The leaves can be up to 75cm (2½ft) long. There are varieties with bolder white variegation.

Dieffenbachia maculata

Large oval leaves up to 60cm (2ft) long and 20cm (8in) wide with ivory or cream blotches and markings – the variegation depending on the variety. 'Camilla' and 'Exotica' are popular varieties. For many years this species has been considered synonymous with *D. picta*.

Dieffenbachia picta *see D. maculata.*

TOP: Dieffenbachia maculata *'Camilla'*
ABOVE: Dieffenbachia maculata *'Exotica'*

Dieffenbachia seguine *see D. amoena.*

HELPFUL HINTS

Temperature Winter minimum 16°C (60°F).
Humidity Mist the leaves regularly.
Position Partial shade or good light without direct summer sun. Good light without direct sun in winter.
Watering and feeding Water freely from spring to autumn, sparingly in winter.
Care Wash leaves occasionally. Repot each spring. If the plant has become

bare at the base, try pruning back to leave a stump of about 15cm (6in) – it will often respond by producing new shoots.

Propagation Cane cuttings or stem cuttings. Air layering is a useful method for plants that have become bare at the base.

Dionaea

Insectivorous, rosette-forming perennials. The species described here is most widely sold as a fun plant. It does not make a good houseplant, however, and will probably die in a short time in a living-room.

Dionaea muscipula
Rosettes of modified hinged leaves fringed with large hairs along the edges. Insects landing on the plant can trigger the trap, which snaps closed. The two halves open again when the insect has been digested.

HELPFUL HINTS
Temperature Aim for 3–10°C (37–50°F) in winter. Keep plants frost-free, but avoid exposing to high temperatures.
Humidity High humidity is essen-

BELOW: Dionaea muscipula

ABOVE: Dizygotheca elegantissima

tial. Mist regularly, and if possible provide additional humidity by other methods.
Position Good light, even direct sunlight, provided plants are screened from sun through glass during the hottest part of the day in summer. Best possible light in winter – supplementary artificial lighting can be beneficial, but should be of the type specially designed for use with plants.
Watering and feeding Keep constantly moist. Do not feed.
Care Repot, if necessary, in spring but use an ericaceous compost (potting soil) (one for acid-loving plants) and mix with an equal volume of chopped sphagnum moss (the type used to line hanging baskets). Cover the surface with more moss.
Propagation Seed; division.

Dizygotheca

A genus of small evergreen trees and shrubs, the species below being the only one widely used as a houseplant.

Dizygotheca elegantissima
Graceful plant with dark green,

almost black, leaves divided into seven to eleven finger-like serrated leaflets. On mature plants the leaflets tend to be broader, which alters their appearance slightly. In the home it will often make a plant 1–1.2m (3–4ft) tall. The plant used to be known as *Aralia elegantissima*, and some experts consider there is confusion among the plants in cultivation between this species and *Schefflera elegantissima*. However, you are most likely to find it sold as a dizygotheca.

HELPFUL HINTS
Temperature Winter minimum 13°C (55°F).
Humidity Mist the leaves regularly.
Position Good light; not direct summer sun at the hottest part of the day.
Watering and feeding Water moderately from spring to autumn, sparingly in winter.
Care Repot every second spring. If the plant becomes leggy, try cutting it down to about 10cm (4in) – it may be stimulated into producing new shoots from the base.
Propagation Seed or air layering in spring. Tip cuttings in summer.

Dracaena

The genus dracaena contains many species of palm-like plants from Africa and Asia, most of them creating the impression of an exotic plant while actually being quite tough. This has made them very popular indoor plants. The genus is sometimes confused with cordylines, but the dracaenas on the whole have less spectacularly coloured leaves and they rely on simple but very striking variegation and bold outline for their attraction. *D. godseffiana* is the odd one out, being distinctly shrubby and bearing oval rather than strap-shaped leaves.

Dracaena deremensis

Stalkless sword-shaped leaves growing directly from an upright stem. 'Janet Craig' is an all-green variety, but mostly the variegated varieties are grown. These include varieties with light or dark green leaves, and white, silver, yellow, or green stripes. Two well-known examples are 'Bausei' (white stripes on a dark green background), and 'Warneckii' (green and white central band and narrow white lines along the margins).

Dracaena fragrans

Similar to the previous species but the leaves are longer and broader and a distinct trunk forms even on young plants. The attractively variegated varieties are usually grown, such as 'Massangeana' (yellowish-green stripes along the centre of the leaf). The heavily scented flowers are unlikely to form on small plants in the home.

Dracaena godseffiana

Shrubby growth with pointed oval leaves on thin stems. The glossy green foliage is splashed and mottled with cream, but the colouring and extent of the variegation depends on the variety. Makes a bushy plant about 60cm (2ft) high, and flowers at an early age. These flowers are yellowish-green and fragrant, and may be followed by attractive red berries.

Dracaena marginata

Narrow trunk, often twisted; unbranched on young plants but in time may become branched and tall (perhaps to ceiling height). Narrow green leaves, edged purplish-red, 30–45cm (1–1½ft) or more long. More brightly coloured varieties include 'Colorama' (broad red band along each edge) and 'Tricolor' (green, cream, and red).

Dracaena sanderiana

Oval to lance-shaped leaves about 23cm (9in) long, edged with a broad creamy-white band.

Dracaena surculosa *see D. godseffiana*.

Dracaena terminalis *see Cordyline fruticosa*.

HELPFUL HINTS

Temperature Winter minimum 13°C (55°F); 10°C (50°F) for *D. godseffiana* and *D. sanderiana*.

Humidity Mist the leaves regularly. *D. godseffiana* tolerates dry air.

Position Good light, but avoid exposing to direct sun.

Watering and feeding Water freely from spring to autumn, sparingly in winter. Never let the roots dry out. Feed regularly in spring and summer.

Care Sponge the leaves occasionally to keep them clean and bright. Cease feeding by autumn to help give the plant a resting period of less active growth. Repot in spring if necessary.

Propagation Tip cuttings; air layering (for a leggy plant); cane cuttings.

BELOW: Dracaena deremensis *(right)*, *and two of its varieties:* 'Yellow Stripe' *(centre) and* 'White Stripe' *(left)*
OPPOSITE ABOVE: Dracaena sanderiana
OPPOSITE MIDDLE: Dracaena fragrans *(right) and* D.f. 'Massageana' *(left)*
OPPOSITE BELOW: Dracaena godseffiana
FAR RIGHT: Dracaena marginata *(right)* *and* D.m. 'Tricolor' *(left)*

Echeveria

Rosette-forming succulents, grown mainly for their often attractive shape and colouring. Most species will flower, and although the flowers are not especially beautiful they are sufficiently appealing in most species to be a bonus. Of the more than 150 species and many hybrids, the ones listed below are just examples.

Echeveria elegans

Rosettes of fleshy bluish-white leaves up to 15cm (6in) across. Pink or red flowers, tipped yellow, from early spring to mid summer. Its correct botanical name is *E. secunda glanca*.

Echeveria glauca

Rosettes of waxy, spoon-shaped, blue-grey leaves. Yellow flowers tinged red in spring and early summer.

HELPFUL HINTS
Temperature Aim for 5–10°C (41–50°F) in winter.
Humidity Tolerates dry air.
Position Best possible light throughout the year. Will tolerate full sun.
Watering and feeding Water moderately from spring to autumn. Give enough water in winter to prevent the leaves shrivelling. Feed in spring and summer using a weak fertilizer.
Care Avoid getting water on the leaves if possible (it may damage the waxy layer and lead to rotting). Avoid high winter temperatures. If most of the lower leaves drop in winter, use the tips as cuttings and start again.
Propagation Tip cuttings; leaf cuttings; offsets (if the rosette produces them); seed.

LEFT: Echeveria elegans
BELOW LEFT: Echeveria glauca

Echinocactus

Slow-growing spherical to cylindrical cacti, usually with fierce but attractive spines. The plants rarely flower in cultivation.

Echinocactus grusonii

The best-known species, spherical when young, slightly more cylindrical

BELOW: Echinocactus grusonii

with age. Very old specimens in botanic gardens can be 1m (3ft) across, but in the home they usually remain small.

HELPFUL HINTS
Temperature Aim for 5–10°C (41–50°F) in winter.
Humidity Tolerates dry air.
Position Best possible light throughout the year. Tolerates full sun.
Watering and feeding Water moderately from spring to autumn, keep practically dry in winter. Feed with a weak fertilizer in spring and summer.
Care Repot only as necessary, and always use a special cactus mixture. Be careful because the roots are easily damaged.
Propagation Seed.

Echinocereus

Spherical to columnar cacti, freely branched with age. Different species vary considerably in appearance — some are practically bare, others are densely thorned or hairy.

Echinocereus pectinatus
Columnar growth with numerous ribs and small spines that are yellow at first but later become grey. Sometimes sparsely branched. Flowers freely in spring, with trumpet-shaped purple,

BELOW: Echinocereus salm-dyckianus

ABOVE: Echinocereus pectinatus

pink, or yellow blooms about 12cm (5in) across.

Echinocereus salm-dyckianus
Dark green stems, branching at the base, covered with yellowish thorns tipped red. Produces its orange flowers freely in spring. This is now considered by botanists to be more correctly named *E. scheeri*.

HELPFUL HINTS
Temperature Aim for 10–13°C (50–55°F) in winter.
Humidity Tolerates dry air, but appreciates higher humidity than most cacti.
Position Best possible light throughout the year. Tolerates full sun.
Watering and feeding Water moderately from spring to autumn. Keep practically dry in winter. Feed regularly in spring and summer with a weak fertilizer.
Care Repot only when necessary, using a cactus mixture.
Propagation Cuttings if the species produces a sideshoot; seed.

Echinopsis

Spherical cacti, sometimes slightly columnar; generally freely branching.

Echinopsis eyriesii
Spherical at first, becoming more columnar with age. Numerous ribs with dark brown spines. Large, tubular, greenish-white scented flowers in spring or summer.

Echinopsis rhodotricha
Globular or columnar stems with 2.5cm (1in) long pale yellow spines tipped brown. Large white flowers in summer.

HELPFUL HINTS
Temperature Aim for 5–10°C (41–50°F) in winter.
Humidity Tolerates dry air.
Position Good light, but screen from very intense direct sunlight.
Watering and feeding Water moderately from spring to autumn. Keep practically dry in winter. Feed with a weak fertilizer in spring and summer.
Care Repot as necessary, using a cactus mixture. Avoid turning the plant when coming into flower (after flowering it does not matter). It is common for the flowers to develop on the shady side.
Propagation Seed; cuttings.

BELOW: Echinopsis eyriesii

Epiphyllum

Genus of cacti with strap-shaped leaves, mainly from Central and South America and especially Mexico. The plants that are grown in the home, however, are almost always hybrids.

Epiphyllum hybrids

Erect, flattened, or triangular stems, sometimes winged or with a wavy edge, spreading outwards with age and often requiring support. Very large funnel-shaped flowers with a wide-flared mouth, in spring and early summer. Mainly in shades of red and pink, as well as white.

HELPFUL HINTS
Temperature Aim for 7–10°C (45– 50°F) in winter. Avoid high winter temperatures.
Humidity Undemanding, but benefits from misting in spring and summer.
Position Good light, but avoid exposing to direct sun.
Watering and feeding Water freely from spring to autumn, sparingly in winter. Use soft water if possible. Feed regularly in spring and summer.
Care The plants are uninteresting out of flower so you may prefer to stand them in the garden for the summer. Avoid moving the plants once buds form, otherwise they may drop.
Propagation Cuttings.

BELOW: Epiphyllum *hybrids*

ABOVE: Epipremnum aureum (*syn.* Scindapsus aureus)

Epipremnum

Woody climbers. The most popular species, described below, is often used in the home as a trailing plant.

Epipremnum aureum

Climber with aerial roots and heart-shaped glossy leaves, blotched or streaked with yellow. There are attractive variegated varieties such as 'Marble Queen' (white and green), and golden forms such as 'Neon'. This plant has been subject to several name-changes, and although you will find it in some shops and garden centres under the name given here, you will also find it sold as *Scindapsus aureus,* and it is sometimes listed as *Rhaphidophora aurea.*

HELPFUL HINTS
Temperature Winter minimum 13°C (55°F).
Humidity Undemanding, but benefits from occasional misting.
Position Good light, but avoid exposing to direct sun. Usually does well in poor light, but variegation is much improved in good light.
Watering and feeding Water freely from spring to autumn, sparingly in

winter. Feed in spring and summer.
Care Repot in spring if necessary. Long shoots can be shortened to keep the plant compact.
Propagation Leaf bud or stem tip cuttings; layering.

Erica

A very large genus of over 500 species, many of them hardy plants used in the garden, but only the two described here are the ones most commonly used as houseplants.

BELOW: Erica gracilis
BOTTOM: Erica hiemalis

Erica gracilis
Leafy spike of urn-shaped pink flowers with white tips, in winter. The plant grows to about 30cm (1ft). Needle-like foliage.

Erica hyemalis
Small white, pink, or reddish bell-shaped flowers on spikes with needle-like leaves, in winter. Grows to about 30cm (1ft).

HELPFUL HINTS
Temperature Aim for 5–13°C (41–55°F) during flowering period.
Humidity Mist the leaves regularly.
Position Good light. Will benefit from winter sun.
Watering and feeding Water freely at all times. Never allow the roots to dry out. Use soft water if possible.
Care These are not practical plants to keep in the home long-term, and are usually bought in flower. Cool temperatures will prolong flowering, after which the plants are usually discarded. They can sometimes be kept successfully for another year by trimming back the shoots after flowering and keeping in a cool, light position until early summer. Stand the pot outdoors for the summer and bring in again before the first frost.
Propagation Cuttings.

Euonymus

A genus that includes many hardy trees and shrubs, and the species sometimes grown as a houseplant is a common hardy garden shrub. The variegated varieties make acceptable pot plants for an unheated room or for a cold porch, and these varieties can be planted in the garden once they become too large.

Euonymus japonicus
Oval leaves on upright stems, the upper surface dark green and glossy, the underside paler. The more attractive and less vigorous variegated varieties are the ones usually grown indoors, such as the small-leaved 'Microphyllus Albovariegatus' (white variegation), and 'Microphyllus Aureovariegatus' (gold and green).

HELPFUL HINTS
Temperature Aim for 3–7°C (37–45°F) in winter, although plants should survive even if it drops below freezing.
Humidity Undemanding, but mist the leaves occasionally.
Position Good light, with or without direct sun.
Watering and feeding Water freely from spring to autumn, sparingly in winter. Feed regularly in spring and summer.
Care It is a good idea to stand the plants in the garden for the summer months, to keep the growth sturdy and the variegation strong.
Propagation Cuttings.

BELOW: Euonymus japonicus
'Mediopictus'

Euphorbia

There are about 2,000 species of euphorbia ranging from annuals to shrubs, hardy border plants to tender houseplants including the poinsettia (*E. pulcherrima*). Others, such as *E. milii,* are succulents.

Euphorbia milii
Succulent shrub with woody and very thorny stems, bearing inconspicuous true flowers surrounded by bold, bright red bracts. Flowering time is spring to mid summer. The plant can grow to about 1m (3ft), but it will remain compact for many years. The sap is poisonous. May also be found under its old name of *E. splendens.*

Euphorbia obesa
Unusual-looking spherical succulent, dark green often chequered with light green, with eight flat ribs dividing the body in sections from top to bottom. A crown of cup-shaped, greenish-yellow flowers in summer.

Euphorbia pulcherrima
Erect shrubby plant grown for its colourful red, pink, or white bracts in winter (the true flowers are insignificant). Most plants bought in flower are a compact 30–60cm (1–2ft) but dwarfing chemicals will have been used. If you keep the plant for another season it will be taller.

Euphorbia splendens *see E. milii.*

Euphorbia trigona
Candelabrum-shaped succulent with triangular or winged stems. Pale green stem markings. Small oval leaves that are deciduous.

HELPFUL HINTS
Temperature Winter minimum 13°C (55°F) for most species, although the succulent kinds will usually tolerate temperatures of 10°C (50°F) quite happily.
Humidity High humidity for *E. pulcherrima* – mist the leaves regularly.

ABOVE: Euphorbia milii
ABOVE LEFT: Euphorbia trigona
LEFT: Euphorbia obesa

Succulent species tolerate dry air, but mist *E. milii* occasionally in spring and summer.
Position Best possible light for all species in winter, but avoid direct summer sun for *E. pulcherrima.* Succulent species tolerate direct sun.
Watering and feeding Water succulent species freely from spring to autumn, sparingly in winter. Water *E. pulcherrima* freely when in flower and in summer, moderately at other times but never let the roots dry out. Feed succulent species with a weak fertilizer in summer; feed *E. pulcherrima* in summer and until it is in full flower.
Care Succulent varieties need little extra care apart from repotting when it becomes necessary. *E. pulcherrima* needs careful cultivation if it is to flower another year. Cut back the stems to leave 10cm (4in) stumps when flowering is over, and keep the roots only just moist, to induce a resting period. Repot in late spring and start watering more freely, feeding regularly as new growth is stimulated. Thin excess stems to leave about four or five on each plant. To induce flowering in early winter again, control the amount of light received from early or mid autumn. Eliminate light (using a black plastic sack, for instance) for 14 hours each day. Put the cover on in the evening and remove the next morning. Continue this treatment for eight weeks, then grow the plant on normally.
Propagation Cuttings of *E. pulcherrima* and *E. milii.* Seed is the best method for the other succulent species mentioned.

Eustoma

A genus of annuals and perennials with poppy-like flowers. The species listed is often grown as a cut flower but can also be found as a pot plant.

Eustoma grandiflorum

Open, poppy-like flowers in shades of blue, pink, and white, in summer. There are also double varieties. Small lance-shaped green leaves, about 5cm (2in) long. Compact varieties that grow to about 30–45cm (1–1½ft) are best for pots. Other names are *Lisianthus russellianus* and *E. russellianum*.

BELOW: Eustoma grandiflorum (*syn.* Lisianthus russellianus)

HELPFUL HINTS
Temperature Winter minimum 7°C (45°C).
Humidity Mist occasionally.
Position Good light, but avoid direct summer sun.
Watering and feeding Water with care at all times, making sure the compost (potting soil) never becomes dry or waterlogged. Feed regularly once the nutrients in the initial potting soil become depleted.
Care Although technically perennials, these plants are treated as annuals and discarded when flowering has finished.
Propagation Seed. Plants can be divided in autumn, but it is more satisfactory to raise fresh ones from seed.

ABOVE: Exacum affine

Exacum

A genus of about 40 species, including annuals, biennials and perennials. Only one species, however, is now widely grown, mainly because it is so easy to raise from seed and because it flowers well in a pot.

Exacum affine

Masses of small, pale purple (sometimes white), slightly fragrant flowers with yellow centres. The main flowering period is from mid summer to late autumn. Small, fresh green leaves 2–4cm (¾–1½in) long.

HELPFUL HINTS
Temperature Aim for 10–21°C (50–70°F).
Humidity Mist the leaves regularly.
Position Good light, but avoid exposing to direct summer sun.
Watering and feeding Water freely at all times. Feed regularly once the nutrients in the initial potting soil become depleted.
Care Deadhead regularly. Discard after flowering (although they can sometimes be kept growing into the second year, it is best to start with new plants).
Propagation Seed.

✕ Fatshedera

A bigeneric hybrid from a cross between *Fatsia japonica* and *Hedera helix* 'Hibernica'.

✕ Fatshedera lizei

Shiny, five-fingered, hand-shaped leaves. The shoots grow upwards initially, then tend to become decumbent. Rounded heads of creamy-white flowers are sometimes produced in autumn on mature plants. Will grow to 1.8m (6ft) or more if conditions are suitable, and is hardy enough to grow outside where frosts are not severe. The variegated varieties, such as 'Variegata', are slower-growing and more attractive as houseplants.

HELPFUL HINTS
Temperature Winter minimum 3°C (37°F). Keep below 21°C (70°F) if possible.
Humidity Undemanding in a cool position, mist the leaves occasionally in a warm room.
Position Good light, but avoid exposing to direct summer sun. Best possible light in winter.
Watering and feeding Water freely from spring to autumn, sparingly in winter. Feed in spring and summer.
Care Repot each spring. Provide a support if you want to grow it like an ivy, but pinch out the growing tips each spring if you prefer a more bushy plant.
Propagation Cuttings.

RIGHT: ✕ Fatshedera lizei *'Pia'*
BELOW: ✕ Fatshedera lizei *'Anne Mieke'*

Fatsia

A genus with only one species, a useful evergreen for the garden where winters are not harsh and a good houseplant for a cool and shady position.

Fatsia japonica

Deeply lobed, glossy dark green leaves, 20–40cm (8–16in) across. Variegated varieties make less vigorous and more attractive houseplants.

HELPFUL HINTS
Temperature Winter minimum 3°C (37°F), although it is not critical if the plants are exposed to a little frost. Variegated varieties are more cold-sensitive and are best in a winter minimum of about 13°C (55°F). Keep below 21°C (70°F) if possible.
Humidity Moderate humidity.
Position Good light, but not direct summer sun. Tolerates shade well.
Watering and feeding Water freely from spring to autumn, sparingly in winter. Feed in spring and summer.
Care Sponge the leaves once a month.
Propagation Cuttings; air layering; seed (for the green form).

ABOVE: Fatsia japonica

Faucaria

South African succulents with semi-cylindrical or angled fleshy leaves, and golden-yellow, daisy-like flowers in autumn.

Faucaria tigrina
Fleshy green leaves about 5cm (2in) long, speckled white and with deeply-toothed edges that create a jaw-like appearance.

HELPFUL HINTS
Temperature Winter minimum 5°C (41°F). Avoid high winter temperatures, if possible.
Humidity Tolerates dry air.
Position Brightest possible position, benefits from direct sun.
Watering and feeding Water freely in summer, sparingly in autumn and spring, and keep practically dry in winter. Feed regularly with a weak fertilizer in summer.
Care Rest the plant once the leaves begin to shrivel in autumn, and keep the compost (potting soil) and air dry

BELOW: Faucaria tigrina

to reduce the risk of rotting. Repot the plant every third year, using a cactus mixture.
Propagation Cuttings; seed.

Ferocactus

Slow-growing spherical cacti that become columnar with age. Curved, colourful spines. Specialist nurseries will offer several species, but the one described here is among those most commonly grown as houseplants.

Ferocactus latispinus
Blue-green body, spherical on small plants, with about 20 prominent ribs that bear large hooked spines. The red flowers rarely appear on specimens kept as houseplants.

HELPFUL HINTS
Temperature Winter minimum 5°C (41°F).
Humidity Tolerates dry air.
Position Brightest possible position, benefits from direct sun.
Watering and feeding Water moderately from spring to autumn. Keep practically dry in winter. Use soft water if possible.
Care Repot in spring, using a cactus mixture.
Propagation Seed; offsets.

BELOW: Ferocactus latispinus

Ficus

A huge genus with more than 800 species, most of them originating in Asia and Africa, and including the edible fig. Those used as houseplants are grown for foliage effect, and for many years *F. elastica* was one of the most popular of all houseplants. The larger species still make some of the finest focal-point plants for a room, while the trailers make useful plants for hanging pots and bottle gardens.

Ficus benghalensis

Resembles the more popular *F. elastica* but the 20cm (8in) leathery leaves are hairy. They make immense trees in the wild, and in the home will reach ceiling height after a few years if conditions are suitable.

Ficus benjamina

A tall tree with a broad crown and trailing branches in the wild, but as a pot plant the pendulous shoots give the whole plant the appearance of a small weeping tree and will seldom grow to more than 2.4m (8ft) indoors. In the species the 10cm (4in) long, pointed leaves are green, but the variegated varieties are more popular. 'Starlight' is a variety with particularly bold white markings.

Ficus deltoidea

Dark green, leathery leaves about 6–8cm (2½–3in) long, tapering towards the base and blunt at the tip. Makes a branching shrub to about 75cm (2½ft) in cultivation. May also be found under the name *F. diversifolia*.

Ficus diversifolia *see F. deltoidea.*

Ficus elastica

Large oval leaves about 30cm (1ft) long, glossy and dark green. The young leaves are sheathed in red stipules, which drop as the leaf opens. The species itself is seldom grown, and the green varieties usually sold are 'Decora' and 'Robusta', which have broader leaves, often more densely spaced. Variegated varieties include 'Doescheri' and 'Tricolor'. 'Black Prince' has very dark foliage.

Ficus lyrata

Large, waxy leaves shaped like an upside-down violin, about 50cm (20in) long. A tall plant, usually reluctant to branch, that will reach ceiling height after a few years.

Ficus pumila

Trailing plant with thin wiry stems and heart-shaped leaves about 2.5cm (1in) long. The foliage on mature plants has thicker and longer leaves, but it is almost always seen as a houseplant with its juvenile foliage. Will also climb by means of clinging roots. 'Minima' has smaller leaves and more compact growth. There are variegated varieties such as 'Variegata'. May also be found as *F. repens*.

Ficus radicans

Trailing, wiry stems with pointed leaves about 7.5–10cm (3–4in) long. The limp stems will trail or climb by rooting at the leaf joints. 'Variegata' has narrower leaves marked with white. More correctly known as *F. sagittata*.

Ficus religiosa

A large tree in the wild, with prop roots growing from the branches. Dull green 10–15cm (4–6in) leaves with long, slender, almost thread-like tips.

Ficus repens *see F. pumila.*

Ficus sagittata *see F. radicans.*

Helpful hints
Temperature Winter minimum 13°C (55°F).
Humidity Mist the leaves occasionally. *F. lyrata*, *F. pumila* and *F. radicans* benefit from regular misting.
Position Good light for tree and shrub types, but avoid direct summer sun through glass during the hottest part of the day. Partial shade for creeping and climbing types.
Watering and feeding Water all varieties freely from spring to autumn, but sparingly in winter. Use tepid water if possible, especially in winter. Feed in spring and summer.
Care Repot young plants every second year. Occasionally sponge the leaves of species with large, glossy foliage.
Propagation Cuttings; air layering of woody species.

Left: Ficus lyrata
Opposite above: *Three varieties of* Ficus elastica: *'Belgica' (left), 'Robusta' (centre), 'Black Prince' (right)*
Opposite below: *Three varieties of* Ficus benjamina: *'Exotica' (left), 'Starlight' (centre), 'Reginald' (right)*
Far right above: Ficus benghalensis
Far right below: Ficus deltoidea

ABOVE: Fittonia verschaffeltii

Fittonia

Non-woody, creeping ground cover plants that originate from the tropical rain forests of Peru. Although small yellowish flowers may appear in spring they are inconspicuous and the plants are grown for foliage effect.

Fittonia argyroneura *see F. verschaffeltii.*

Fittonia verschaffeltii

This species has olive green leaves about 5cm (2in) long, with deep pink veins. *F. v. argyroneura* (often sold simply as *F. argyroneura*) has pale green leaves with white veins. *F. v. argyroneura nana* (frequently sold as *F. argyroneura nana*) also has white veins on light green leaves, but these are only about 2.5cm (1in) long. Large-leaved forms grow to about 10cm (4in), the small-leaved variety only half this height.

HELPFUL HINTS
Temperature Winter minimum 16°C (60°F).
Humidity Needs high humidity.
Position Partial shade. Avoid direct sunlight.
Watering and feeding Water freely from spring to autumn, sparingly in winter. Use tepid water if possible. Feed from spring to autumn with a weak fertilizer.
Care Pinch back long, straggly shoots to keep the plant compact. Repot each spring. Difficult to keep unless the humidity is high, but plants do well in a bottle garden.
Propagation Division; cuttings; or just pot up plants where the creeping stems have rooted.

Fuchsia

A genus of evergreen and deciduous trees and shrubs, grown mainly for their attractive pendent flowers.

Fuchsia hybrids

The hybrid fuchsias need little description as their usually bell-shaped flowers with flared 'skirts' are so well known as garden and greenhouse plants. There are single, semi-double and double varieties in a wide range of colours, but mainly pinks, reds, purples and white. The ones likely to be grown as pot plants will be hybrids, most of which will make a compact plant about 45–60cm (1½-2ft) tall. Old specimens are best discarded unless trained as a standard, when they should be repotted each spring.

HELPFUL HINTS
Temperature Aim for 10–16°C (50–60°F) in winter. Avoid high winter temperatures.
Humidity Mist the leaves occasionally when the plant has foliage.
Position Good light, but not direct summer sun.
Watering and feeding Water freely from spring to autumn while the plant is growing vigorously, sparingly early and late in the season. Water very sparingly in winter if the plants are dormant – just enough to prevent the soil drying out completely. Continue to water cuttings in leaf sufficiently to sustain growth. Feed from late spring to late summer.
Care It is natural for the leaves to fall in autumn. If possible, keep the plants in a cool, light position for the winter. New growth will appear in spring. Shorten the old shoots just before, or as, new growth starts, to keep the plant compact and bushy. The pruning can be severe as the flowers form on new growth, which is freely produced.
Propagation Cuttings.

RIGHT: Fuchsia *hybrid*

Gardenia

Evergreen shrubs and small trees. The shrub described here is widely grown for its fragrant flowers.

G. augusta *see G. jasminoides.*

Gardenia jasminoides
Fragrant semi-double to double white flowers about 5cm (2in) across, usually borne in summer although there are varieties that flower in winter. Glossy green leaves up to 10cm (4in) long. Will make a shrub of about 1.5m (5ft) in a conservatory, but as a houseplant grows no taller than 45cm (1½ft).

HELPFUL HINTS
Temperature Winter minimum 16°C (60°F).
Humidity Mist the leaves regularly.
Position Good light, but not direct summer sun during the hottest part of the day.
Watering and feeding Water freely from spring to autumn, sparingly in winter, but never let the roots become dry. Use soft water if possible. Feed

ABOVE: Gardenia jasminoides

from spring to autumn.
Care Avoid widely fluctuating temperatures when the buds are forming, as this may cause them to drop. Deadhead regularly – the blooms turn yellowish with age. After flowering the plant can be placed in a sheltered spot outside for the summer. Repot every second or third year, using an ericaceous (lime-free) compost (potting soil).
Propagation Cuttings.

Gerbera

Herbaceous perennials with daisy-like flowers. There are about 45 species but only one is grown as a pot plant.

Gerbera jamesonii
Single or double, daisy-type flowers about 5cm (2in) across, in bright colours such as red, orange, pink, yellow, and white, with a yellow centre. Main flowering time is early summer to late autumn, but they are sometimes sold

in flower in winter. Lobed hairy leaves about 15cm (6in) long arise from the base. Some grow to about 60cm (2ft) tall, but compact varieties about 25–30cm (10–12in) tall are more suitable as houseplants.

HELPFUL HINTS
Temperature Aim for 10–21°C (50–70°F) during flowering.
Humidity Mist the leaves regularly.
Position Good light, with direct sun for at least part of the day.
Watering and feeding Water freely while the plant is growing actively, more cautiously when it is resting, but never allow the roots to dry out. Feed regularly while the plant is in active growth.
Care It is difficult to keep the plant for another year when flowering has finished, unless you have a conservatory. As old plants tend to flower poorly, they are usually discarded.
Propagation Seed is the usual method, but division is an easy technique if you have an old plant.

BELOW: Gerbera jamesonii *hybrid*

Gloxinia

See Sinningia speciosa.

Guzmania

Epiphytic bromeliads, mainly from the tropical rain forests of South America. They are usually grown for their showy flower heads. The species described here is one of the most popular, but others are also sold as pot plants.

Guzmania lingulata
Rosette of foliage with strap-shaped leaves about 15–20cm (6–8in) long. The flower stalk, up to about 30cm (1ft) long, is topped by bright red or orange bracts with small yellowish-white flowers in the centre, and usual-ly blooms in summer, although commercial growers can produce plants in flower throughout the year. *G. l. minor* is a smaller plant, often only about 15cm (6in) tall.

HELPFUL HINTS
Temperature Winter minimum 16°C (60°F).
Humidity Mist occasionally in winter, regularly in summer.
Position Light shade in summer, good light in winter.
Watering and feeding Water freely from spring to autumn, sparingly in winter. Feed with a weak fertilizer in spring and summer.
Care In summer pour water into the 'vase' formed by the rosette of leaves.
Propagation Offsets; seed.

BELOW: Guzmania lingulata

Gymnocalycium

A genus of cacti with about 50 species. Many of them will produce their funnel-shaped flowers at an early age, but the ones most often sold are grafted forms that lack enough chlorophyll to thrive on their own roots. The grafted forms are grown for their curious appearance rather than their flowers, which tend to be less freely produced.

Gymnocalycium mihanovichii
Normally has a grey-green ribbed body with small curved thorns, and yellowish-green flowers. *G. m. friedrichii* has pink flowers. The 'curiosity' varieties have yellow, orange, red, or almost black bodies, and these are sold grafted onto a green stem from a different cactus.

ABOVE: Gymnocalycium mihanovichii

HELPFUL HINTS

Temperature Aim for a winter temperature of 5–10°C (41–50°F).
Humidity Tolerates dry air.
Position Good light, full sun in winter, but avoid direct summer sun during the hottest part of the day for coloured grafted varieties.
Watering and feeding Water moderately in summer, very sparingly at other times (just enough to prevent the body shrivelling). Feed with a weak fertilizer in summer.
Care Use a special cactus mixture if repotting.
Propagation Offsets from those species that produce them freely; coloured varieties that lack chlorophyll are best grafted.

Gynura

A genus of about 25 herbaceous or shrubby plants, from tropical areas of Asia, but only the species with attractive purple hairs are usually grown as houseplants.

Gynura aurantiaca
Dark green leaves about 15cm (6in) long, covered with purple hairs that create a velvety appearance. Upright growth to about 45–90cm (1½-3ft). Orange flowers with an unpleasant smell in winter.

Gynura procumbens *see G. sarmentosa.*

Gynura sarmentosa
Similar to previous species but smaller leaves about 7.5cm (3in) long on trailing or climbing stems. Will reach 60cm (2ft) or more with a support. May also be listed as *G. procumbens.* The plant grown as *G. sarmentosa* in cultivation is likely to be the variety *G. 'Purple Passion'.*

HELPFUL HINTS
Temperature Winter minimum 10°C (50°F).
Humidity Mist occasionally.
Position Good light, but not direct summer sun.
Watering and feeding Water freely from spring to autumn, more sparingly in winter.
Care Pinch out the growing tips periodically if you want to keep the

ABOVE: Gynura sarmentosa
BELOW: Gynura *'Purple Passion'*

plant compact and bushy. Pinch out any flowers as soon as the buds appear, as they smell unpleasant.
Propagation Cuttings.

Haworthia

A genus of clump-forming succulents with a basal rosette of warty leaves.

Haworthia fasciata
Rosette of thick, slightly incurving, finely-pointed leaves with pearly warts on the lower surface. These appear to form crosswise white bands.

Haworthia margaritifera
Similar to the previous species, but with broader rosettes, about 13cm (5in) across; the warts are arranged more randomly and do not appear to form bands.

Temperature Aim for 10–13°C (50–55°F) in winter.
Humidity Tolerates dry air.
Position Brightest possible position, benefits from full sun.
Watering and feeding Water moderately from spring to autumn, very sparingly in winter. Feed with a weak fertilizer or a cactus food while plant is growing actively.
Care Repot in spring, but only when the rosette has grown too large for the pot.
Propagation Offsets; seed.

Below: Haworthia margaritifera

Hedera

A small genus of self-clinging climbers, but with many varieties. Plants will climb or trail, depending on how you grow them.

Hedera algeriensis *see H. canariensis.*

Hedera canariensis
Large, slightly lobed leaves, with white margins in 'Variegata', often sold under its other name of 'Gloire de Marengo'. Botanists now consider the correct name for this plant to be *H. algeriensis* 'Gloire de Marengo', but you are unlikely to find it sold under this name.

Hedera helix
This plant – the common ivy – needs no description. The leaves are much smaller than those of the previous species, and varieties are available with foliage of many different shapes and markings.

Temperature Cool but frost-free is ideal, although plants are frost-hardy if suitably acclimatized. Avoid warm rooms in winter – plants are more likely to thrive in an unheated room.
Humidity Mist the leaves occasionally, regularly in summer if possible.
Position Good light or some shade.

OPPOSITE ABOVE: Hedera helix
'Goldchild'
ABOVE: Hedera canariensis
'Variegata'

Will tolerate poor light for short periods. Benefits from good light in winter, but avoid direct summer sun.
Watering and feeding Water freely in warm weather, moderately in cool temperatures. Never allow the roots to dry out. Feed regularly from spring to autumn.
Care Repot each spring unless the plant is already in a large pot. Pinch out the growing tips periodically if you want a bushy plant.
Propagation Cuttings.

Helxine

See Soleirolia.

Heptapleurum

See Schefflera.

Hibiscus

A genus that contains evergreen and deciduous trees and shrubs, herbaceous perennials, and annuals. Just one species is widely grown as a houseplant, a shrubby plant widely grown in gardens in subtropical regions.

Hibiscus rosa-sinensis
Large, double or single showy flowers about 10–13cm (4–5in) across, with stamens on a prominent central column. Colours include red, pink, orange, yellow, and white. 'Cooperi' has variegated foliage and red flowers. The main flowering time is summer, but commercial growers are able to extend the season considerably. Individual blooms are short-lived but there is a constant succession of them. Will make a shrub of 1.5m (5ft) or more given suitable conditions, but more often seen as a compact plant less than half this height indoors.

HELPFUL HINTS
Temperature Winter minimum 13°C (55°F).
Humidity Mist occasionally.
Position Good light, but not direct summer sun through glass during the hottest part of the day.
Watering and feeding Water freely from spring to autumn, sparingly in winter, but never allow the roots to dry out. Feed regularly in summer.
Care Deadhead regularly. Shorten long shoots after flowering, or in late winter. Do not turn or move the plant once buds have formed as this may cause the buds to drop. Repot each spring. The plant can be placed in a sheltered spot outdoors for the summer months.
Propagation Cuttings; seed.

BELOW: Hibiscus rosa-sinensis

Hippeastrum

A genus of about 70 bulbous species from tropical and subtropical parts of America, but the plants with huge trumpet-shaped flowers grown as pot plants are hybrids. Although these are popularly known as amaryllis, this is really the botanical name of a different plant that is sometimes grown in the garden.

Hippeastrum hybrids

Clusters of three to six huge, trumpet-shaped flowers on strong stems about 60cm (2ft) tall. Colours include shades of red, pink, and white, some bicoloured. There are a few semi-double varieties. The large, strap-shaped leaves usually emerge once the flowers have started to open. It can be forced into flower in winter without the need for a period in the dark.

HELPFUL HINTS

Temperature Needs warmth to start into growth (*see* Care), but the flowers will last for longer in a cool room.
Humidity Undemanding.
Position Good light.
Watering and feeding Water moderately when the bulbs are growing, keep almost dry when resting. Feed regularly once the leaves start to grow, and cease when the resting period is due (*see* Care).
Care Bulbs prepared for early flowering should be planted when available, and they will bloom in winter. Unprepared bulbs planted at the same time will flower later. Bulbs planted in late winter or early spring will flower in mid or late spring. A soil temperature of 21°C (70°F) is required to start dormant bulbs into growth. If the roots look very dry, soak the bulbs for a few hours before potting up, burying only about half the bulb.

As soon as the flower stalk is 15–20cm (6–8in) tall, keep in a very light position. Cut off the flower stalk when blooming is over. The plant will then look unattractive and is best

ABOVE: Hippeastrum *hybrid*

placed in a conservatory or greenhouse, or outdoors for the summer once there is no risk of frost. Reduce watering in early autumn and allow the leaves to die back. Start into growth again by resuming watering a month or two later.
Propagation Offsets (which may bloom after three years); seed (unpredictable results and flowering even slower).

Howea

Evergreen palms, also occasionally seen under their old name of kentia.

Howea belmoreana

Thin green stems and arching pinnate foliage, the edges covered in woolly hairs. Will eventually grow to ceiling height indoors if conditions suit. May also be listed as *Kentia belmoreana*.

Howea forsteriana

Similar to previous species, but with broader leaflets and less arching fronds. May also be listed as *Kentia forsteriana*.

HELPFUL HINTS
Temperature Winter minimum for

RIGHT: Hôwea belmoreana (*syn.* Kentia belmoreana)
ABOVE RIGHT: Howea forsteriana (*syn.* Kentia forsteriana)

H. belmoreana 16°C (60°F), for *H. forsteriana* 10°C (50°F).

Humidity Mist the leaves regularly.

Position Good light, but not direct summer sun through glass during the hottest part of the day. Tolerates some shade. Good light in winter.

Watering and feeding Water moderately in summer, sparingly in winter. Keep the soil just moist. Feed in summer.

Care Sponge the leaves occasionally. The plant benefits from being stood outside in a light summer shower. Avoid using leaf shines, as some can damage the fronds.

Propagation Seed (difficult).

Hoya

Evergreen climbers, trailers, or lax shrubs, but only three out of over 200 species are grown as houseplants. The two listed are the ones most commonly grown.

Hoya bella

Fleshy leaves about 2.5cm (1in) long. Pendulous clusters of fragrant white, waxy-looking, star-shaped flowers with purplish-red centres. Flowering time is usually between late spring and early autumn. The correct botanical name for this plant is *Hoya lanceolata bella*, although you are unlikely to find it under this name.

Hoya carnosa

Similar to the previous species but with slightly larger, pale pink flowers, which are also fragrant. Leaves about 7.5cm (3in) long. There is a variegated variety.

HELPFUL HINTS

Temperature Aim for 10–13°C (50–55°F) in winter for *H. carnosa,* and a winter minimum of 18°C (64°F) for *H. bella.*

Humidity Mist the leaves regularly, but not when plant is in bloom.

Position Good light. Some direct sun is beneficial, but avoid summer sun

ABOVE: Hoya bella

through glass during the hottest part of the day.

Watering and feeding Water freely from spring to autumn, sparingly in winter. Feed sparingly when the plant is in flower as over-feeding can inhibit flowering.

Care Provide suitable support if the plant is to be grown as a climber. A trellis or moss pole is suitable, but *H. bella* can also be grown in a hanging basket. Do not move the plant once flower buds form. Do not repot until absolutely necessary as root disturbance is resented.

Propagation Semi-ripe tip cuttings or eye cuttings. *H. bella* is sometimes grafted onto *H. carnosa.*

Hyacinthus

A small genus of bulbous plants, from Asia Minor and around the Mediterranean. Only one is widely grown, but its varieties are among the most popular indoor bulbs for winter colour and fragrance.

Hyacinthus orientalis

The dense spikes of the hyacinth need no description. There are many varieties in shades of red, pink, mauve, blue, yellow, and white. Multiflora varieties produce several small spikes from each bulb instead of one large one. Flowering time ranges from early winter to mid spring, depending on variety, planting time, and

whether the bulb has been specially prepared for early flowering. Consult a bulb catalogue for specific varieties, planting and flowering times.

HELPFUL HINTS

Temperature Hardy. Keep as cool as possible unless advancing flowering, and then only force once the bud has emerged. Once in bloom, the cooler the room, the longer the flowers will last.

Humidity Undemanding.

Position Good light once flower buds start to show colour. Once in full flower, can be positioned anywhere as a short-term houseplant.

Watering and feeding Ensure the roots do not dry out at any time. Feeding is not necessary unless you want to save the bulbs to plant in the garden.

Care Hyacinths should be regarded as short-term houseplants. If you want to plant the bulbs in the garden after flowering, continue to water and feed regularly until the leaves begin to die down. At this stage, place in a garden frame to acclimatize to outside conditions and then plant in the garden. Do not use again indoors.

Propagation Offset bulbs can be grown on, but this is not practical for propagating houseplants. Buy fresh bulbs each year.

BELOW: Hyacinthus orientalis *variety*

Hydrangea

A genus of over 20 deciduous shrubs and deciduous and evergreen climbers, but only the species below is used as a pot plant.

Hydrangea macrophylla

Shrub with broad oval, coarsely toothed deciduous leaves about 15cm (6in) long, and ball-shaped flower heads in shades of blue, pink, and white. Mop-head varieties have rounded heads of flowers that all look the same; Lacecap varieties have an outer ring of open flowers. Although they make shrubs of at least 1.5m (5ft) in the garden, these plants are only used indoors while small. Hydrangeas are usually sold as flowering pot plants in flower in spring, but specially-treated plants may be available in bloom at other times of year.

HELPFUL HINTS

Temperature Frost-hardy, but indoors these plants are best in a winter minimum of 7°C (45°F). Move them to a warm, bright position in mid winter, when you can increase watering. If possible, avoid a very warm room.

Humidity Mist occasionally.

Position Good light or light shade. Some direct sun is beneficial in winter but avoid hot summer sun.

Watering and feeding Water freely from spring to autumn, sparingly in early winter. Use soft water if possible. Feed regularly while plants are growing actively.

Care Flower colour can be affected by the acidity of the compost (potting soil). Use an ericaceous (acidic, humusy, lime-free) mixture if you want blue flowers. You can also buy proprietary blueing compounds but plants must be treated before they flower. Never allow the roots to dry out during the growing season. Cut back the stems to half their height after flowering. The plants are not particularly attractive when flowering has finished, so stand in the garden for the summer.

Propagation Semi-ripe cuttings.

ABOVE: Hymenocallis × festalis

Hymenocallis

A genus of about 40 bulbous plants, only a few of which are sometimes grown as pot plants. You can buy the bulbs from specialist bulb suppliers.

Hymenocallis × festalis

Large white central cup surrounded by backward-curving petals, in late spring or summer. Fragrant. Strap-shaped leaves die down in autumn. A hybrid between *H. narcissiflora* and *H. longipetala*.

Hymenocallis narcissiflora

Clusters of three to six pendulous white flowers with a white funnel-shaped fringed cup surrounded by backward-curving slender petals. Fragrant. Leaves die down in autumn.

HELPFUL HINTS

Temperature Winter minimum 15°C (59°F), although the plant may be dormant for most of that time.

Humidity Undemanding.

Position Good light, but avoid direct summer sun through glass during the hottest part of the day.

Watering and feeding Water freely during the growing season. Keep the

BELOW: Hydrangea macrophylla

species that die back practically dry in winter and water those that retain their foliage cautiously. Feed regularly when active growth starts.

Care More likely to be available as dry bulbs than growing plants. Start the bulbs into growth in late winter or early spring.

Propagation Offsets.

Hypocyrta

A small genus of about nine species, which has since been divided by botanists into other varieties. Only one of these is widely grown.

Hypocyrta glabra

Shiny dark green, leathery leaves, about 3cm (1¼in) long on compact plants 15–23cm (6–9in) tall. Small orange, waxy-looking flowers appear along the stems in summer. Now considered by botanists to be more correctly *Nematanthus*, although you are much more likely to find it sold under the name used here.

BELOW: Hypocyrta glabra

HELPFUL HINTS
Temperature Winter minimum 10°C (50°F).
Humidity Mist the leaves regularly.
Position Good light, but do not expose to direct summer sun during the hottest part of the day. Best possible light in winter.
Watering and feeding Water moderately from spring to autumn, sparingly in winter.
Care Cut back after flowering, shortening the shoots by about a third. Avoid high winter temperatures as the plant benefits from a rest at this time.
Propagation Cuttings; division; seed.

Hypoestes

A genus of mainly evergreen perennials and sub-shrubs, only two of which are grown as houseplants. The one described here is the species most commonly seen.

Hypoestes phyllostachya

Pointed, oval leaves about 6cm (2½in)

ABOVE: Hypoestes phyllostachya (*syn.* H. sanguinolenta)

long, covered with red or pink spots and blotches. The intensity of variegation depends on variety and growing conditions: some appear mainly pink, red or white, with areas of green, others are mainly green with more distinct spots of pink or white. Colouring is usually more vivid with some direct sunlight. Can be kept to 30–60cm (1–2ft) by regular pruning. Also sold as *H. sanguinolenta*, although strictly this is a different plant.

Hypoestes sanguinolenta *see H. phyllostachya*.

HELPFUL HINTS
Temperature Winter minimum 13°C (55°F).
Humidity Mist the leaves regularly.
Position Good light, but avoid direct summer sun through glass during the hottest part of the day.
Watering and feeding Water freely from spring to autumn, sparingly in winter. Feed regularly in summer. Over-feeding may encourage tall, spindly growth.
Care Pinch out the growing tips and cut back straggly shoots from time to time to keep the plant compact. If it becomes tall and straggly, cut it back – shoots will regrow from near the base. Pinch out flowers as they will spoil the plant's compact shape.
Propagation Cuttings; seed.

Impatiens

A large genus of about 850 species, but those used as houseplants are mainly derived from the single species *I. walleriana*. These plants have been subject to intensive breeding; apart from compact and floriferous varieties (used for summer bedding as well as pot plants), foliage plants such as the New Guinea hybrids have extended the range of impatiens that are suitable for the home.

Impatiens hybrids

Masses of spurred, flat flowers, 2.5–5cm (1–2in) across, at any time of the year if the temperature can be maintained above 16°C (60°F). Blooms are mostly in shades of red, orange, pink, and white, of which many are multi-coloured and some double. Small pale green leaves on brittle stems. The New Guinea hybrids have large, more lance-shaped, bronze or variegated leaves and generally make taller plants, of 30–60cm (1–2ft). The blooms on New Guinea hybrids are usually fewer but larger.

HELPFUL HINTS

Temperature Winter minimum 13°C (55°F); 16°C (60°F) if you want to keep plants flowering.

Humidity Mist the leaves occasionally, but try to keep water away from the flowers.

Position Good light, but not direct summer sun during the hottest part of the day. Will tolerate shade, but the plants will be taller and lankier and the blooms less prolific.

Watering and feeding Water freely from spring to autumn, sparingly in winter.

Care If an old plant has become tall and lanky, cut it back to within a few inches of the base – it will usually regrow. Repot old plants in spring if necessary. As impatiens are so easy to grow from cuttings and seed, however, it is generally preferable to raise new plants regularly and to discard old ones.

TOP: Impatiens *hybrid*
ABOVE: Impatiens, *a New Guinea hybrid*

Propagation Seed; cuttings. Most New Guinea hybrids can only be raised from cuttings, although a few varieties can be grown from seed.

Iresine

A genus of evergreen perennials grown for their colourful foliage, widely used as formal bedding in countries where frosts do not occur.

Iresine herbstii

Spatula-shaped leaves about 7.5cm (3in) long, dark reddish-brown with carmine veins. 'Aureoreticulata' has green leaves with yellow veins, on red stems. Grows to about 60cm (2ft), but is kept smaller by pruning.

Iresine lindenii

Narrow, glossy deep red leaves with prominent veins. Uncommon.

HELPFUL HINTS

Temperature Winter minimum 13°C (55°F).

Humidity Mist the leaves regularly.

Position Good light, but not direct summer sun through glass during the hottest part of the day.

Watering and feeding Water freely from spring to autumn, sparingly in winter. Feed from spring to autumn.
Care Pinch out the growing tips occasionally to encourage compact and bushy growth. Will tolerate regular clipping if necessary. Can be stood outdoors for the summer. Overwintered plants often look unhappy by spring, but cuttings root easily and it may be more practical to start again with new plants.
Propagation Cuttings.

BELOW: Iresine lindenii

Iris

A large group of plants that includes hardy border plants with rhizomes and some that form bulbs. Those sometimes used as short-term houseplants are hardy dwarf bulbous species useful for providing spring colour indoors.

Iris danfordiae
Fragrant yellow flowers on stems about 10cm (4in) tall appear before the leaves. The grass-like foliage grows to twice this height, but plants are normally placed outside before the foliage becomes obtrusive.

Iris reticulata hybrids
Slightly fragrant blue or purple flowers (depending on variety) with yellow markings. About 15cm (6in) tall in flower, although the grass-like foliage later grows taller.

HELPFUL HINTS
Temperature Frost-hardy. Keep cool to prolong flower life.
Humidity Undemanding.
Position Good light once the buds begin to open.

RIGHT: Iris reticulata *'Harmony'*
BELOW: Iris danfordiae

Watering and feeding Keep the potting mixture moist but not wet.
Care Plant the bulbs in early or mid autumn, in pots or bowls, and place outside or in a garden frame. Once the shoots are through bring the bulbs indoors and keep in a light place. Discard or plant out in the garden once flowering is over. Do not reuse the bulbs indoors.
Propagation Offsets, but for growing in pots or bowls it is best to buy fresh bulbs each year.

Jasminum

A genus of about 200 species, mainly deciduous and evergreen woody climbers. Being vigorous climbers, they are more suitable for a conservatory than a living-room, especially if you want to keep them as long-term plants.

Jasminum officinale
Deciduous climber with divided leaves and loose sprays of fragrant white flowers about 2.5cm (1in) across in summer. 'Grandiflorum' (which may also be seen as *J. o. affine*), with larger flowers tinged pink on the outside, is a form commonly sold. Can be grown outdoors where winters are mild.

Jasminum polyanthum
Similar to the previous species, but usually pink in bud, with plumes of

ABOVE: Jasminum polyanthum

fragrant white flowers in winter.

HELPFUL HINTS
Temperature Winter minimum 7°C (45°F).
Humidity Mist the leaves regularly.
Position Good light with some direct sun.
Watering and feeding Water freely from spring to autumn, but in winter keep compost (potting soil) only moist enough to prevent it from completely drying out. Feed regularly during periods of active growth.
Care Grow in a large pot with a suitable support. Prune back to contain size if necessary – jasminums will soon reach 3m (10ft) or more if left to grow unchecked. Avoid high winter temperatures. Can be stood outside in summer.
Propagation Cuttings.

Justicia

Genus of evergreen perennials, shrubs and sub-shrubs, from tropical and sub-tropical regions, but only the species described here is widely grown as a pot plant. You are just as likely to find it sold under its other name of *Beloperone guttata*.

Justicia brandegeana
Small white flowers surrounded by reddish-brown bracts that overlap like roof tiles. These bracts are the main reason for growing the plant, as they

Kalanchoe

A genus of about 125 perennial succulents or shrubs with fleshy leaves, which includes a number of popular and undemanding houseplants.

Kalanchoe blossfeldiana hybrids
Small, leathery, serrated oval leaves, which often turn reddish in strong sunlight. Clusters of long-lasting, short-stalked small flowers in shades of red, orange, yellow, and lilac. Although naturally spring-flowering plants, commercial growers are able to produce flowering specimens throughout the year.

Only hybrids are grown, and most of these make compact plants 15–30cm (6–12in) tall. There are also miniatures.

Although there are many named varieties, they are usually sold simply by colour.

Kalanchoe daigremontiana *see Bryophyllum daigremontianum*.

Kalanchoe manginii
Lance- or spatula-shaped leaves about 2.5cm (1in) long, on upright stems that gradually arch over. Larger, pendent, bell-like orange-red flowers in arching sprays.

Kalanchoe tubiflora *see Bryophyllum tubiflorum*.

remain attractive for a long period. The plants can be bought in flower every month of the year. Old plants can reach 90cm (3ft) or more, but in the home they tend to be discarded before they reach this size and are usually only half this height.

HELPFUL HINTS
Temperature Aim for 10–16°C (50–60°F) in winter.
Humidity Mist occasionally.
Position Good light, including some direct sun, but not direct summer sun through glass during the hottest part of the day.
Watering and feeding Water freely from spring to autumn, sparingly in winter. Feed regularly from spring to autumn.
Care Repot each spring. At the same time, prune the shoots back by one-third to half to keep the plant a compact shape.
Propagation Cuttings.

LEFT: Justicia brandegeana

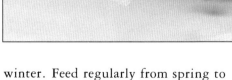

ABOVE: Kalanchoe blossfeldiana *hybrid*
RIGHT: Kalanchoe manginii

HELPFUL HINTS
Temperature Winter minimum 10°C (50°F).
Humidity Tolerates dry air.
Position Good light, including some direct sun, but avoid direct summer sun through glass during the hottest part of the day.
Watering and feeding Water freely from spring to autumn, sparingly in winter. Feed regularly from spring to autumn.
Care Repot after flowering if saving an old plant, and shorten the shoots to keep growth compact. As they are easy to raise and cheap to buy, however, most people treat them as annuals and discard them when flowering is over. If raising your own plants they will only develop flower buds when day length is less than 12 hours. It is possible to adjust flowering time by artificially controlling daylight hours.
Propagation Cuttings; seed.

Kentia

See Howea.

Lilium

A genus of bulbous plants widely grown in gardens. Most species, especially those chosen as pot plants, are hybrids. They have become more popular as commercially grown houseplants with the introduction of compact varieties and new techniques with growth regulators to keep the plants dwarf. Apart from the hybrids, species such as *L. auratum, L. longiflorum, L. regale,* and *L. speciosum* are sometimes grown in pots.

Lilium hybrids

Most hybrids have trumpet-shaped or backward-curving petals, in shades of red, orange, yellow, and white, usually spotted, mottled, or flushed with another colour. There are hundreds of varieties, with new ones introduced annually. Consult a good bulb catalogue for the most appropriate varieties to grow in pots, and choose the most compact ones for the home. You may find it difficult to keep home-grown plants as compact as those produced by nurseries: special facilities and chemicals are used to produce small plants in full bloom.

HELPFUL HINTS
Temperature Aim for 3-10°C (37-50°F). Avoid high temperatures.
Humidity Mist occasionally.
Position Good light, but avoid exposing to direct summer sun.
Watering and feeding Keep the compost (potting soil) moist during the period of active growth, and feed regularly.
Care Bulbs are usually planted in autumn or mid to late winter, according to when they are available. Pot up large ones singly, smaller ones three to a pot. There should be at least 5cm (2in) of compost (potting soil) beneath the bulb and about 10cm (4in) above, but lilies vary in the way they form roots, so be guided by any instructions that come with the bulb or

LEFT: Lilium *hybrid*

in the catalogue. Keep the planted bulbs in a cool place, such as a garden frame, cellar or basement, with the soil just moist. Ensure there is good light once shoots appear, and keep at the recommended temperature once buds can be seen. When the buds show colour the pots can be moved to a warmer room, but avoid high temperatures that will shorten the life of the blooms. Plant in the garden after flowering.

Propagation Offsets or scales, but this is a slow job requiring an area where they can be grown on. Buy new bulbs each time for use indoors.

Lisianthus russellianus

See Eustoma grandiflora.

Lithops

Prostrate succulents with pairs of fused swollen leaves, which eventually grow into small clumps. They are interesting plants that mimic stones or pebbles, but are slow-growing. Many species are available but the one described below is typical of those you are likely to find.

BELOW: Lithops bella

Lithops bella
Pairs of pale brownish-yellow, fused leaves with slightly depressed darker patches. White daisy-like flowers in late summer or early autumn. About 2.5cm (1in) high.

HELPFUL HINTS
Temperature Winter minimum 7°C (45°F).
Humidity Tolerates dry air.
Position Good light with plenty of sun. Tolerates full summer sun.
Watering and feeding Water carefully at all times, only moderately in summer and not at all in winter. Start watering again when the old leaves split to reveal the new ones beneath. Feeding is seldom necessary, but if the plants have been in the same pot for many years, feed occasionally with a cactus fertilizer.
Care Repot only when the pot has become filled with leaves. Lithops look attractive if grown in a landscaped container with the surface decorated with gravel or pebbles to blend in with the plants.
Propagation Seed.

Lobivia

A genus of spherical to columnar cacti, forming clumps with age. Lobivias flower at an early age.

Lobivia densispina
Densely thorned, short-cylindrical body, sometimes branched. Wide, funnel-shaped, flowers. More correctly named *Echinopsis kuehnrichii*.

Lobivia famatimensis
Cylindrical body with about 20 ribs and yellowish thorns. The flowers appear in early summer, but are short-lived. More correctly named *Rebutia famatimensis*.

Lobivia hertrichiana
Spherical body with 11 notched ribs covered with yellow thorns. Red, short-lived flowers in early summer.

TOP: Lobivia densispina
ABOVE: Lobivia hertrichiana

HELPFUL HINTS
Temperature Aim for 5-7°C (41-45°F) in winter. Avoid high winter temperatures, but keep frost-free.
Humidity Tolerates dry air.
Position Best possible light, including some direct sun.
Watering and feeding Water moderately in summer, sparingly from autumn to spring. Keep practically dry in winter. Use soft water if possible. Feed with a weak fertilizer in summer.
Care Pay special attention to winter temperatures to encourage the plant to flower well. Repot young plants each spring.
Propagation Offsets (unrooted ones can be used as cuttings); seed.

Lytocaryum

See Cocos.

Mammillaria

A genus of about 150 hemispherical, spherical, or columnar cacti, most of which are compact in growth and free-flowering. Cacti specialists offer a wide range of species, and those described here are only a selection of those available.

Mammillaria bocasana
Spherical or cylindrical, maturing to form a clump, covered with hooked thorns and white hairs. Reddish flowers that are white inside.

Mammillaria elongata
Clump-forming with columnar stems, densely covered with yellow to brown spines. Cream flowers in summer.

Mammillaria wildii
Clump-forming, branching columnar stems with white thorns and long hairs. Rings of small white flowers appear in spring.

Mammillaria zeilmanniana
Clusters of short, cylindrical stems, with dense covering of hooked spines.

Bell-shaped flowers, deep purple to pink, sometimes white in spring.

HELPFUL HINTS
Temperature Winter minimum 7°C (45°F).
Humidity Tolerates dry air.
Position Best possible light, with some sun.
Watering and feeding Water moderately from spring to autumn, but keep almost dry in winter.
Care Repot young plants annually in spring; older ones will not require such frequent repotting.
Propagation Cuttings; seed.

ABOVE: Mammillaria zeilmanniana
BELOW: Mammillaria bocasana *(left)*
and M. wildii *(right)*

TOP: Maranta leuconeura erythroneura *(syn.* 'Erythrophylla' *and* M. tricolor)
ABOVE: Maranta leuconeura kerchoveana

Maranta

A small genus of tropical plants from regions of Central and South America, grown for their attractive foliage.

Maranta bicolor
Round to oval leaves up to 15cm (6in) long, with five to eight brown blotches on either side of the main vein and purple undersides. Small white flowers are sometimes produced.

Maranta leuconeura
A tuberous plant with slightly smaller leaves than the previous species. Varieties of this species most commonly grown include *M. l. erythroneura* (syn. 'Erythrophylla', sometimes sold

as *M. tricolor*), which has prominent red veins and yellow markings near main vein, and *M. l. kerchoveana*, with brown blotches turning green with age.

HELPFUL HINTS

Temperature Winter minimum 10°C (50°F).
Humidity Needs high humidity. Mist the leaves regularly.
Position Good light, but avoid exposing to direct summer sun. Best possible light in winter.
Watering and feeding Water freely from spring to autumn, sparingly in winter. Use soft water if possible. Feed regularly in summer.
Care Repot every second spring.
Propagation Division.

Microcoelum

See Cocos.

Mimosa

A large genus of shrubs, trees, climbers and annuals, including plants with very varied characteristics and requirements, but the one most likely to be grown as a houseplant is the species described here.

Mimosa pudica

Feathery-looking leaves with leaflets, which are highly responsive to being touched. First the leaflets fold, then the whole leaf droops (at night they fold naturally). After about a half to one hour the leaves resume their original position. Small flowers like pink balls are produced in summer. Although a short-lived shrub, it is usually treated as an annual, when it seldom exceeds 60cm (2ft).

HELPFUL HINTS

Temperature Winter minimum 16°C (60°F).
Humidity Mist the leaves regularly.
Position Good light with some direct sun, but avoid direct summer sun during the hottest part of the day.
Watering and feeding Water freely from spring to autumn, sparingly in summer. Use soft water if possible. Feed regularly in summer.
Care Repot in spring, but as plants are easily raised from seed, they are best treated as annuals.
Propagation Seed; cuttings.

BELOW: Mimosa pudica

ABOVE: Monstera deliciosa

Monstera

Woody climbers, most growing as epiphytes, from tropical regions of America.

Monstera deliciosa

Climber with thick stems and aerial roots by which it clings. The large leaves, up to 60cm (2ft) across, are entire and heart-shaped initially, but become incised and perforated with age. There is also a variegated variety. White lily-like flowers sometimes appear, but usually only on plants grown in a greenhouse or conservatory. Will easily grow to ceiling height. May be found under its old name of *Philodendron pertusum*.

HELPFUL HINTS

Temperature Winter minimum 10°C (50°F).
Humidity Mist the leaves regularly.
Position Good light or shade, out of direct sunlight.
Watering and feeding Water freely from spring to autumn, sparingly in winter.
Routine care Provide a suitable climbing support, such as a moss-covered pole. Lightly sponge the leaves occasionally.
Propagation Cuttings; air layering.

Nematanthus

See Hypocyrta.

Narcissus

A genus of well-known bulbous plants that includes the popular daffodil. Suitable varieties can be grown in pots for early flowering indoors.

Narcissus hybrids
There are hundreds of varieties, ranging from traditional trumpet daffodils to miniatures, mainly in the usual shades of yellow or white. Consult a bulb catalogue for varieties suitable for forcing in pots. 'Paperwhite' (white with yellow eye, fragrant) and 'Soleil d'Or' (yellow, with deep yellow centre) are sold primarily for indoor use.

HELPFUL HINTS
Temperature Aim for 15–21°C (59–70°F) for the varieties mentioned above. Garden varieties being used in the home should be kept cool until the flower buds have emerged from the bulb (*see* Care), then brought into warmth.
Humidity Undemanding.
Position The varieties mentioned above should be kept in good light all the time. Normal varieties should be in good light when the buds have emerged, but may be placed anywhere once in flower as they are short-term houseplants.
Watering and feeding Water moderately while the bulbs are growing. If keeping the bulbs to grow in the garden, continue watering until planted out. Feeding is unnecessary.
Care The two varieties mentioned specifically can be grown in pots, but are sometimes grown in bowls of water, supported by pebbles or marbles (keep base of bulb above the water). These are kept indoors, and will flower very early. Garden varieties forced in pots should be potted up then kept in a cool, dark place until rooted – aim for 7–10°C (45–50°F) at this

ABOVE: Narcissus *'Cheerfulness'*

stage. Bring indoors or into the warmth only when the flower buds have clearly emerged from the bulbs.
Propagation Offsets and scales (bulb-cuttings), but this is impractical in the home. Buy fresh bulbs each year.

Neanthe

See Chamaedorea.

Neoregelia

Rosette-forming epiphytic bromeliads, mainly from Brazil.

Neoregelia carolinae
Leaves about 40cm (16in) long and 5cm (2in) wide form a broad rosette, normally green but those that surround the top of the 'vase' created by the rosette are flushed red when the plant is in flower (usually in summer). *N. c. tricolor* has slightly narrower leaves streaked yellow along their length. The purple-blue flowers nestle in the water-filled 'vase'.

HELPFUL HINTS
Temperature Winter minimum 13°C (55°F).
Humidity Mist the leaves regularly.
Position Good light, but avoid exposing to direct sun.

BELOW: Neoregelia carolinae

Watering and feeding Water the compost (potting mixture) moderately at all times, but keep the 'vase' topped up with water. Use soft water if possible. Use a weak fertilizer (add it to the soil or 'vase') in summer.
Care The plant will die after flowering, so once in bloom it does not matter much where you place it. But if you want to propagate new plants from the offsets produced from around the parent, continue to feed and grow in good light. These are not easy plants to keep long-term in the home. It is best to grow them to flowering stage in a greenhouse or conservatory, bringing them indoors only when they begin to show colour.
Propagation Offsets.

Nephrolepis

Genus of about 30 terrestrial and epiphytic, evergreen or semi-evergreen ferns, distributed over tropical regions in all parts of the world. The species below is the only one widely grown as a pot plant.

Nephrolepis exaltata
Pinnate leaves about 45–60cm (1½-2ft) long, forming a dense clump. There are variations on the basic plant, including 'Bostoniensis', with more gracefully drooping leaves than the true species, 'Teddy Junior', with crimped and undulating leaflets, and 'Whitmanii', with deeply incised, lacy-looking leaflets.

HELPFUL HINTS
Temperature Winter minimum 18°C (64°F).
Humidity Mist the leaves regularly.
Position Good light, but not direct sun.
Watering and feeding Water freely in summer, cautiously in winter, but with care at all times. The plant is vulnerable to over- and under-watering, so try to keep the roots moist without being wet. Use soft water if possible.
Care Repot in spring if the plant becomes too large for its pot, but do not be surprised if the plant deteriorates before this stage is reached – it is difficult to keep in good condition in the home. Provide a position away from draughts.
Propagation Plantlets, which develop at intervals along the rhizomes. Spores can be used only for the species, and not the varieties.

Nerium

A genus of evergreen shrubs grown for their flowers. The species described here is widely grown as a pot plant, and is a very popular outdoor shrub in southern Europe and America.

ABOVE: Nerium oleander

Nerium oleander
Leathery, willow-like leaves 15–20cm (6–8in) long, arranged around the stem in groups of three. Clusters of white, red, pink, or lilac flowers. There are many varieties, including those with double blooms. Will make a large shrub of 1.8m (6ft) or more in suitable conditions, and, when fully grown, is more suitable for a conservatory than the home.

HELPFUL HINTS
Temperature Winter minimum 7°C (45°F).
Humidity Undemanding.
Position Good light, with some direct sun.
Watering and feeding Water freely spring to autumn, cautiously in winter; do not allow roots to become dry. Feed regularly in spring and summer.
Care The plant can be stood outdoors, perhaps on the patio, for the summer. Acclimatize it gradually, and bring in before the nights become cold. In autumn, shorten stems that have flowered by about half to keep the plant compact and encourage bushiness.
Propagation Cuttings.

LEFT: Nephrolepis exaltata *'Bostoniensis'*

Nertera

A small genus of creeping perennials grown for their bead-like berries. Only one species is cultivated.

Nertera depressa *see N. granadensis.*

Nertera granadensis
Mound-forming plant with creeping stems and small rounded leaves about 6mm (¼in) long. Tiny greenish-white flowers in spring followed by bright orange berries in autumn. You may find it sold under its other name of *N. depressa.*

HELPFUL HINTS
Temperature Winter minimum 7°C (45°F).
Humidity Mist the leaves occasionally.
Position Good light, with some direct sun.
Watering and feeding Water freely from spring to autumn, sparingly in winter. Never allow the roots to dry out completely.
Care The plant is unattactive until the berries appear, but you can stand it outdoors from early summer until the berries form. The plants are usually bought when in fruit and discarded afterwards, but they can be overwintered with care.
Propagation Division; seed.

BELOW: Nertera granadensis

Nidularium

Rosette-forming epiphytic bromeliads, similar to neoregelias.

Nidularium billbergioides citrinum
A rosette of arching strap-shaped leaves, to about 45–60cm (1½–2ft). The true flowers are white and inconspicuous, but the head of yellow bracts is bright and long-lasting.

Nidularium fulgens
Spreading rosettes of broad, strap-shaped, spiny-toothed leaves. Tubular white and purple flowers nestle in the 'vase' formed by the rosette of foliage, mainly in summer. When the plant is flowering the bright red bracts surrounding the 'vase' are the plant's main feature.

Nidularium innocentii
Similar to the previous species, but the undersides of the leaves are purple and the flowers white. The bracts also colour well at flowering.

LEFT BELOW: Nidularium innocentii striatum
LEFT ABOVE: Nidularium fulgens
ABOVE: Nidularium billbergiodes citrinum

HELPFUL HINTS
Temperature Winter minimum 10°C (50°F).
Humidity Mist occasionally.
Position Good light, but not direct sun.
Watering and feeding Water freely from spring to autumn, sparingly in winter. Keep the 'vase' topped up with water from spring to autumn. Feed with a weak fertilizer in summer.
Care The parent plant will die after flowering, and young plants propagated from offsets take a few years to make attractive specimens. If you do not have a greenhouse or conservatory where you can grow them on, it may be best to buy plants in flower and discard them afterwards.
Propagation Offsets.

Notocactus

A small genus of mainly spherical cacti, often ribbed and densely spiny, that flower young and prolifically.

Notocactus apricus
A small species forming a flattened and much-ribbed sphere. Very spiny. Yellow flowers about 7.5cm (3in) across in summer. Now also known as *Parodia concinna*.

Notocactus ottonis
A ribbed spherical body with stiff spines. Golden yellow flowers about 7.5cm (3in) across in summer. Now also known as *Parodia ottonis*.

HELPFUL HINTS
Temperature Winter minimum 10°C (50°F).
Humidity Tolerates dry air.
Position Good light but only limited direct sun. Provide shade from bright direct sun in spring; in summer a mixture of sun and some shade.

TOP: Notocactus apricus
ABOVE: Notocactus ottonis

Watering and feeding Water freely from spring to autumn, more sparingly in winter.
Care Generally trouble-free, but do not keep too warm in winter.
Propagation Seed; cuttings in species that produce offsets.

Odontoglossum

Epiphytic orchids from the mountain forests of tropical America. The species below is often particularly successful in a living-room, others can be more demanding in the home.

Odontoglossum grande

Large brown, yellow, and white flowers, up to 15cm (6in) across, produced in autumn. There are a number of varieties of this species. Now considered to be more correctly named *Rossioglossum grande*.

HELPFUL HINTS
Temperature Winter minimum 13°C (55°F).

Humidity Mist occasionally.
Position Good light, but not direct summer sun. Best possible light in winter.
Watering and feeding Water freely from spring to autumn, and very sparingly in winter (just enough to prevent the pseudobulbs from shrivelling). Use soft water if possible. Feed with a weak fertilizer from spring to autumn.
Care Use a special orchid compost (potting soil) when repotting. This becomes necessary when growth begins to wilt and die back.
Propagation Division.

BELOW: Odontoglossum grande
RIGHT BELOW: Opuntia microdasys

Opuntia

A large genus of more than 200 cacti, ranging from low ground-cover to tree-sized plants. Many of these are popular with collectors.

Opuntia cylindrica

Cylindrical stems which become branching with age. Older plants – usually those over 1.8m (6ft) tall – produce saucer-shaped, reddish-pink flowers in spring or early summer.

Opuntia microdasys

Flat, pale green pads, usually growing to about 30cm (1ft) as a houseplant, with tufts of tiny hooked barbs known as glochids. There are several varieties, and in *O. m. albinospina* the glochids are white. Flowers are usually yellow, about 5cm (2in) across, but only produced on larger plants than are usually found in the home.

Opuntia phaeacantha

Oval to round pads up to 15cm (6in) long, with brownish-yellow glochids. Yellow flowers. Cold tolerant.

Opuntia vestita

Cylindrical joints, the sections easily

ABOVE: Opuntia vestita *(left)*, O. cylindrica *(centre)*, O. phaeacantha *(right)*

broken off, with conspicuous wool and long hairs. Small, deep red flowers.

HELPFUL HINTS
Temperature Winter minimum 7°C (45°F).
Humidity Tolerates dry air.
Position Good light. Benefits from direct sun.
Watering and feeding Water moderately from spring to autumn, very sparingly in winter. Feed with a weak fertilizer, or one formulated for cacti, in summer.
Care Repot in spring if necessary — those with flat pads usually do well in an ordinary loam-based compost (potting soil), others prefer a cactus mixture. Avoid warm temperatures in winter. Some species can be grown outdoors if frosts are not severe.
Propagation Cuttings (detach pads from species that have them); seed.

Oxalis

A large genus of tuberous-, rhizomatous-, and fibrous-rooted perennials, most combining attractive foliage with pretty flowers. Some species are troublesome as garden weeds.

Oxalis deppei
A clover-like plant with four green leaflets blotched pinkish-brown at the base. Red or purplish-violet small, funnel-shaped flowers in late spring or summer. Frost-hardy. Is now considered by botanists to be more correctly named *O. tetraphylla*, but is still widely sold under the name given here.

Oxalis tetraphylla *see O. deppei.*

HELPFUL HINTS
Temperature Winter minimum 7°C (45°F). Some species are hardy, but indoors they are best kept at the minimum suggested.
Humidity Undemanding.
Position Good light or partial shade, out of direct summer sun.
Watering and feeding Water freely while in active growth. Feed regularly during the growing season.
Care Avoid high temperatures — otherwise the plant will be short-lived. Plants are sometimes sold for winter decoration indoors, but hardy species are best planted in the garden when flowering has finished.
Propagation Offsets.

BELOW: Oxalis deppei

Pachystachys

A genus of evergreen perennials and shrubs, with only one species being grown as a houseplant.

Pachystachys lutea
Cone-shaped yellow flower heads, about 10cm (4in) long, over a period from late spring to autumn. The true flowers are white and protrude from the longer-lasting yellow bracts. Pointed oval leaves.

HELPFUL HINTS
Temperature Winter minimum 13°C (55°F).
Humidity Mist the leaves regularly in summer.
Position Good light, but not direct summer sun during the hottest part of the day.
Watering and feeding Water freely from spring to autumn, sparingly in winter. Feed regularly in summer.
Care Cut off the flower heads when flowering is over, and shorten long shoots in spring to keep the plant compact. Repot annually in spring.
Propagation Cuttings.

BELOW: Pachystachys lutea

Paphiopedilum

A genus of about 60 orchids, but it is the hybrids that are usually grown.

Paphiopedilum hybrids
Striking flowers, about 5–10cm (2–4in) across, with a lower lip that forms a pouch, and wing-like petals. Colours vary according to variety but are usually in shades of brown, orange, amber, green, and purple, often heavily streaked or spotted. Most bloom in winter or spring. You may sometimes find paphiopedilums sold under their old name of cypripedium.

HELPFUL HINTS
Temperature Winter minimum 13°C (55°F).
Humidity Mist occasionally.
Position Good light, but avoid exposing to direct sun.
Watering and feeding Water freely from spring to autumn, sparingly in winter. Use soft water if possible. Feed with a weak fertilizer while growing actively.
Care Remove any old and yellowing leaves periodically and keep a watch for slugs, which may spoil the foliage.
Propagation Division.

RIGHT: Paphiopedilum 'Green Gable'

Parodia

Rounded cacti, some becoming cylindrical with age, with ribs and usually thorns. You may find that some plants have been grafted.

Parodia aureispina
A spherical body up to about 10cm (4in) across, with many conspicuous white and yellow thorns. Yellow flowers about 2.5cm (1in) across in spring.

Parodia chrysacanthion
A spherical body up to about 10cm (4in) across, sometimes flattened with age, with bristle-like spines. Yellow flowers in spring.

HELPFUL HINTS

Temperature Aim for 7–12°C (45–53°F) in winter.

Humidity Tolerates dry air.

Position Best possible light. Benefits from full sun.

Watering and feeding Water moderately from spring to autumn, keep practically dry in winter. Use soft water if possible. Feed in summer with a weak fertilizer or cactus food.

Care Plants are slow-growing, but if they need repotting use a special cactus mixture if possible.

Propagation Seed.

FAR RIGHT: Parodia chrysacanthion
RIGHT: Parodia aureispina

Pelargonium – Flowering

There are about 250 species of pelargonium, mainly from South Africa. However, those widely grown as flowering pot plants and for summer displays in our gardens, are hybrids that are the result of many years of intensive breeding.

Pelargonium grandiflorum (P. domesticum) hybrids

The result of crossing *P. grandiflorum*, *P. cordatum*, and other species. They are more popularly known as Regal or Martha Washington pelargoniums. The flowering season (early spring to mid summer) is shorter than in the zonal pelargoniums, but the blooms are larger, frillier, often more showy, and commonly bicoloured. The scalloped leaves with a serrated edge are about 7.5cm (3in) across and lack a distinctive zone. They make plants 30–60cm (1–2ft) tall in pots.

Pelargonium peltatum hybrids

Straggly, cascading stems, with shield-shaped, five-lobed leaves. Single or double, star-shaped flowers,

ABOVE LEFT: *A zonal pelargonium*
BELOW: *Regal pelargonium*

usually in shades of pink or red, sometimes white. Usually grown in a hanging basket or on a pedestal.

Pelargonium zonale hybrids

The traditional geraniums so widely grown as summer bedding. Rounded, slightly lobed leaves about 7.5–10cm (3–4in) across (smaller in miniatures), often attractively zoned and sometimes golden or variegated. Rounded heads of single or double flowers in shades of pink, orange, red, purple, and white. There are hundreds of varieties with variations in flower shape and size as well as colour and leaf patterning. Miniatures, growing only 15–23cm (6–9in) tall, are particularly useful for a windowsill.

HELPFUL HINTS

Temperature Winter minimum 7°C (45°F). Zonal pelargoniums will tolerate a few degrees lower, but are best maintained at the temperature recommended.
Humidity Tolerates dry air.
Position Good light with some sun.
Tolerates full sun.
Watering and feeding Water moderately from spring to autumn; pelargoniums they will tolerate dry soil more happily than most houseplants and are not demanding in this respect. Regal or Martha Washington pelargoniums need more water in summer than the other types. Feed regularly from spring to autumn.
Care Plants grown for the garden are often overwintered in a greenhouse, and kept in a semi-dormant state. Those grown as pot plants indoors can be kept in leaf and looking attractive if given sufficient – warmth at least 13°C (55°F) – and good light. Repot in spring if necessary. Deadhead regularly. Shorten long shoots in spring (autumn for Regal or Martha Washington types). Pinch out the growing tip of young plants to encourage bushy growth.
Propagation Cuttings; seed (some varieties).

ABOVE: Pelargonium peltatum *hybrid*
OPPOSITE: *Scented-leaved pelargoniums.*
Left to right: P. odoratissumum, P. graveolens, P. crispum *'Variegatum'*

Pelargonium — Foliage

Some of the zonal pelargoniums have attractive foliage as well as flowers, and are generally better looking than those grown specifically for their scented leaves. Pelargoniums with scented leaves sometimes have small flowers but these tend to be unexciting, and the foliage itself is often uninspiring although some varieties are variegated. They are grown for the strong aromas released when you brush against the leaves (and sometimes even when you don't).

Descriptions used to classify the scents sometimes appear to contradict one another, at other times to be fanciful, but this is largely because scent can be perceived differently from one person to another, and some of the plants give off a blend or mixture of smells. The best way to choose scented species and varieties is simply to follow your nose.

A selection of different species is listed here, but you will find many more scented species and hybrids at specialist nurseries.

Pelargonium capitatum
Deeply lobed leaves, smelling of roses. Mauve flowers. Will grow to about 90cm (3ft) if conditions suit.

Pelargonium crispum
Small, slightly lobed, green and cream leaves, with a lemon fragrance. Pink flowers. Grows to about 60cm (2ft).

Pelargonium graveolens
Deeply divided, lobed leaves, smelling of roses. Pink to rose-red flowers. Grows to about 90cm (3ft).

Pelargonium odoratissimum
Apple-scented foliage. White flowers. Grows to about 30cm (1ft).

Pelargonium tomentosum
Large, rounded, slightly lobed leaves, smelling of peppermint. Small white flowers. Grows to about 60cm (2ft).

Pellaea

Deciduous, semi-evergreen or evergreen ferns, generally found in dry areas of South America, South Africa and New Zealand. Being adapted to dry conditions, most species are better able to cope with conditions found in the home than most other types of fern.

Pellaea rotundifolia

Small, round, leathery leaflets on long arching fronds that grow from a creeping rootstock. The leaflets become more oval in shape with age. Low, spreading growth.

Pellaea viridis

More like a traditional fern than the previous species, with larger and more divided feathery fronds.

HELPFUL HINTS

Temperature Aim for 13–16°C (55–60°F) in winter.

Humidity Mist the leaves occasionally. Although better adapted to dry conditions than most ferns, growth will usually be improved if reasonable humidity is provided.

Position Good light, but avoid exposing to direct sun.

Watering and feeding Water moderately at all times. Never allow the roots to dry out entirely, but avoid very wet compost (potting soil). Feed with a weak fertilizer in summer.

Care If repotting use a shallow container or a hanging basket. In the wild often grow in rock crevices.

Propagation Division; spores.

RIGHT: Pellaea rotundifolia
BELOW: Pellaea viridis

Pellionia

A small genus of evergreen creeping perennials, a few of which may be used in large terrariums or bottle gardens, or as trailers for a hanging pot.

Pellionia daveauana

Creeping plant with oval leaves, olive green around the edge with a pale

central area. You may also find it more correctly called *P. repens*.

Pellionia pulchra
Creeping plant with almost oblong leaves about 4–8cm (1½–3in) long and 2.5cm (1in) wide. These have a mottled appearance with dark green veins over an olive-green background, and the reverse is brownish-purple.

Pellonia repens *see P. daveauana.*

HELPFUL HINTS
Temperature Winter minimum 13°C (55°F).
Humidity Mist the leaves regularly. Needs very high humidity.
Position Semi-shade or good light but no direct sun.
Watering and feeding Water freely from spring to autumn, sparingly in winter. Never allow the roots to become dry. Feed regularly in summer.
Care Misting alone is unlikely to provide sufficient humidity, so use other methods too, such as standing the pot over a dish of water, supporting the pot on marbles or pebbles to avoid direct contact.
Propagation Cuttings; division.

ABOVE: Pellionia daveauana

ABOVE: Pentas lanceolata

Pentas

A genus of about 30 mainly evergreen perennials and shrubs, generally found in areas such as the Middle East and tropical Africa.

Pentas carnea *see P. lanceolata.*

Pentas lanceolata
Small, star-shaped flowers in heads about 7.5–10cm (3–4in) across. Pink or red are the usual colours, but some varieties have white or mauve flowers. May be seen in flower in any month of the year, but winter is the most usual time. Hairy oval leaves about 5–7.5cm (2–3in) long. Also sold under its other name of *P. carnea.*

HELPFUL HINTS
Temperature Winter minimum 10°C (50°F).
Humidity Mist occasionally.
Position Good light with some sun, but not direct summer sun during the hottest part of the day.
Watering and feeding Water freely from spring to autumn, sparingly in winter. Never allow the roots to become dry. Feed regularly in summer.
Care Pinch out the growing tips of young plants to make them bushy. If you want the plant for winter flowering, pinch out early buds that form in autumn. Repot annually in spring.
Propagation Cuttings; seed.

Peperomia

Peperomias form a large genus of about 1,000 species, mainly from tropical and subtropical America. Some are epiphytes that grow on trees, others terrestrial plants from tropical rain forests. Some are annuals, but most are evergreen perennials. Some of the most popular ones used as houseplants are listed below, but you may sometimes find others that are equally pleasing in the home. Most of those that you are likely to find are undemanding to grow, and their variation in leaf shape, colouring and size makes them interesting to collect. Small poker-like, creamy-white flower spikes are sometimes produced, but on most species these are of marginal interest and they are grown mainly as foliage plants.

Peperomia argyreia
Shield-shaped leaves with dark green and silver blades and red stalks. Forms a neat, bushy clump. May also be found under its synonym *P. sandersii*.

Peperomia caperata
Heart-shaped leaves about 2.5cm (1in) long, deeply corrugated and grooved between the veins. Bushy, clump-forming growth. Varieties have variations in leaf shapes and colouring.

Peperomia clusiifolia
Leathery leaves about 7.5cm (3in) long, edged purple-red. *P. c.* 'Variegata' has cream and red margins. Upright growth to about 20cm (8in).

Peperomia fraseri
Circular to heart-shaped leaves, usually arranged in whorls on upright stems. The flower spikes are white and fragrant.

Peperomia glabella
Trailing stems with broadly oval, glossy, bright green leaves.

Peperomia griseoargentea
Heart-shaped to almost circular leaves on long pinkish stalks. Deep corrugations between the veins create a quilted look. The under surface is pale green. You are also likely to find this plant sold under its other name of *P. hederaefolia* (or *P. hederifolia*).

Peperomia hederaefolia (also P. hederifolia) *see P. griseoargentea.*

Peperomia magnoliaefolia (also P. magnoliifolia) *see P. obtusifolia.*

Peperomia nummulariifolia *see P. rotundifolia.*

Peperomia obtusifolia
Thick, fleshy leaves about 5–10cm (2–4in) long, on short stalks. The plain green form is not often grown as there are several variegated varieties

with yellow or cream markings. Upright but sprawling growth to about 25cm (10in). The nomenclature of these plants is confused – you will sometimes find them sold as *P. magnoliaefolia* (or *P. magnoliifolia*), and while some experts consider them synonymous others list them as distinct species, whatever the label.

OPPOSITE: *Peperomias:* P. *hybrid 'Columbiana' (far left)*, P. *hybrid 'Rauvema' (second from left), and three varieties of* P. caperata

BELOW: *Peperomias:* P. pereskiifolia *(top left)*, P. obtusifolia *'USA' (top right)*, P. clusiifolia *'Jeli' (bottom left)*, P. clusiifolia *variety (bottom right)*

Peperomia pereskiifolia
Whorls of dull green leaves tinged dull red. Spread to 30cm (12in).

Peperomia rotundifolia
A trailing species with round, bright green leaves, about 1cm (½in) across. Also known as *P. nummulariifolia*.

Peperomia verticillata
Distinctive upright growth to about 30cm (1ft) with the 2.5cm (1in) leaves in whorls of four to six along the stems. Foliage covered with fine hairs.

HELPFUL HINTS
Temperature Winter minimum 10°C (50°F).

Humidity Mist the leaves occasionally in warm weather, not in winter.
Position Semi-shade or good light, but not direct summer sun.
Watering and feeding Water moderately throughout the year, cautiously in winter. Use soft water if possible. Feed from spring to autumn.
Care Most peperomias have only a small root system and annual repotting is unnecessary. When necessary, move to a slightly larger pot in spring. A peat-based (peat moss) compost (potting mixture) is preferable to one based on loam.
Propagation Cuttings; leaf cuttings from species with rosettes of fleshy leaves.

Philodendron

A genus of about 350 evergreen shrubs and woody climbers from the rain forests of Central and South America. Although most of the species listed here are climbers and will reach ceiling height, many are fairly slow-growing and will put on less than 30cm (1ft) in a year, so they will give years of pleasure before they outgrow their space. Some of the non-climbing species can make large, spreading plants, and may be too large for a small home.

Philodendron angustisectum

Vigorous climber with large heart-shaped leaves, about 45–60cm (1½-2ft) long, incised almost to the main rib. Will readily grow to ceiling height. May also be found under its other name of *P. elegans*.

Philodendron bipennifolium *see P. panduriforme*.

Philodendron bipinnatifidum

Non-climbing species with a straight stem densely clothed with leathery, heart-shaped, deeply lobed leaves about 45–60cm (1½-2ft) long. Will make a large plant that can be 1.8m (6ft) or more across and about 1.2m (4ft) tall.

Philodendron domesticum

Climber with glossy, bright green leaves about 30–45cm (1–1½ft) long, arrow-shaped on young plants but with more prominent basal lobes when it matures. Will readily reach ceiling height. Also listed under its alternative name of *P. hastatum*.

Philodendron elegans *see P. angustisectum*.

Philodendron erubescens

Climber with young leaves surrounded by attractive rose-red sheaths that drop as the foliage expands. Arrow-shaped to heart-shaped, dark green leaves with a purple sheen and red edge. There are also named selections

with either greener or redder foliage than in the normal plants. Will easily reach ceiling height.

Philodendron hastatum *see P. domesticum*.

Philodendron hybrids

There are hybrids and selections usually sold just by their varietal name, such as 'Blue Mink', 'Burgundy', and 'Pink Prince'. These are generally climbers with large, attractive leaves, and can be treated in the same way as the other climbing species listed here.

Philodendron melanochrysum

Climber with heart-shaped leaves about 60cm (2ft) long, with a coppery surface and white veins. Fairly slow-growing but will easily reach ceiling height. The heart-shaped leaves become increasingly elongated as the plant matures.

Philodendron panduriforme

Climber with leaves about 23–30cm (9–12in) long, deeply lobed, with a distinct 'waist' on mature foliage. May also be named *P. bipennifolium*.

Philodendron pertusum *see Monstera deliciosa*.

Philodendron scandens

Climber or trailer with 7.5–13cm (3–5in) heart-shaped, glossy green leaves. Fairly rapid growth and will reach ceiling height if given a support, but is most often seen as a trailer.

Philodendron selloum

A non-climbing species, with leaves 60–90cm (2–3ft) long, deeply incised and with ruffled edges. Grows to about 1.5m (5ft).

HELPFUL HINTS

Temperature Winter minimum 13°C (55°F), but many, such as *P. melanochrysum*, prefer warmer temperatures and for these 18°C (64°F) or higher is preferable.

Humidity Mist the leaves regularly.

Position Good light, but not direct summer sun. *P. scandens* tolerates low light levels well.

Watering and feeding Water freely from spring to autumn, moderately in winter. Use soft water if possible. Feed from spring to autumn, but avoid high-nitrogen feeds if you want to limit the plant's growth.

Care Provide a suitable support for climbing species – moss poles are a popular method. Aerial roots that form low down on the plant can be trained to grow into the pot.

Propagation Cuttings; air layering.

ABOVE: Philodendron scandens
RIGHT TOP: Philodendron *hybrid 'Red Emerald'*
RIGHT MIDDLE: Philodendron *hybrid 'Blue Mink'*
RIGHT BOTTOM: Philodendron domesticum
FAR RIGHT: Philodendron *hybrid 'Purple Prince'*

Phlebodium aureum

See Polypodium aureum.

Phoenix

A genus of about 17 palms. Most become large trees where they grow outdoors, but some can make attractive pot plants while young.

Phoenix canariensis
Feathery fronds, stiff and erect at first, arching later, with narrow leaflets.

Phoenix dactylifera
The edible date. Similar to previous species, but not normally grown as a houseplant.

Phoenix roebelenii
Gracefully arching fronds, on a compact plant that seldom grows larger than 1.2m (4ft).

HELPFUL HINTS
Temperature Winter minimum 7°C (45°F); 16°C (60°F) for *P. roebelenii*.

BELOW: Phoenix canariensis

Humidity Tolerates dry air.
Position Good light. Benefits from direct sun.
Watering and feeding Water moderately from spring to autumn, sparingly in winter. Feed regularly from spring to autumn.
Care Repot only when the plant becomes pot-bound as the plant resents unnecessary root disturbance. Roots often penetrate through the bottom of the pot, and for this reason these plants are often planted in deeper containers than normal. Trim off any dead or yellowing leaves that are spoiling the plant's appearance.
Propagation Seed; division for *P. roebelenii*.

Pilea

A genus of about 600 bushy or trailing annuals and evergreen perennials from tropical regions, a small number of which are grown as foliage houseplants.

Pilea cadierei
Elliptical to oval leaves about 7.5–10cm (3–4in) long, with silver markings that look as though they have been painted on the green background.

Pilea hybrids
Some pileas are likely to be found with just their varietal name. The botanical status of these is sometimes confused or debatable, and more than one species may have been involved in their breeding. These vary in colouring and variegation, but the general cultural advice given below applies to them.

Pilea involucrata
Oval, slightly fleshy leaves, about 5–7.5cm (2–3in) long and deeply quilted. The species has dark green foliage with a coppery sheen and pale green margins, but varieties include 'Moon Valley' (bronze above, reddish-green below), and 'Norfolk' (bronze in good light, almost green in poor light, with several lengthwise white bands). You may find the latter listed as a variety of *P. spruceana*. They make bushy plants about 15–23cm (6–9in) tall.

Pilea microphylla
Small, pale green leaves only 2–6mm (⅛–¼in) long, on much-branched stems, forming a mass of fern-like foliage. Forms a dense, compact plant about 15cm (6in) tall. May also be found under its old name *P. muscosa*.

Pilea muscosa *see P. microphylla.*

Pilea nummulariifolia
Creeping reddish stems with round leaves about 1cm (½in) across, with a quilted surface, purplish on the underside. Grows to about 5cm (2in) tall.

ABOVE: Pilea microphylla
LEFT: Pilea spruceana *'Bronze' (left) and* Pilea repens *(right)*
LEFT BELOW: Pilea cadierei

Pilea spruceana

Oval, wrinkled leaves 5–7.5cm (2–3in) long. Most likely to be seen in one of its varieties, such as 'Bronze'. 'Norfolk' is often listed as a variety of this species, but other authorities consider it a variety of *P. involucrata*.

HELPFUL HINTS
Temperature Winter minimum 10°C (50°F).
Humidity Mist the leaves regularly.
Position Good light or partial shade, out of direct summer sun.
Watering and feeding Water freely while in active growth. Feed regularly from spring to autumn.
Care Pinch out the growing tips of young plants, and repeat the process a month or two later, to encourage bushy growth. Repot in spring.
Propagation Cuttings.

Pinguicula

A genus of more than 50 species of insectivorous plants that work on the fly-paper principle.

Pinguicula grandiflora

Broad, flat, ground-hugging, spatula-shaped leaves about 7.5–10cm (3–4in) long, slightly curled at the edges.

BELOW: Pinguicula moranensis

Long-spurred pink flowers on slender stems about 10cm (4in) long, carried well above the foliage.

Pinguicula moranensis

Rounded to oval leaves about 15cm (6in) long. Crimson, magenta or pink flowers with white throat.

HELPFUL HINTS
Temperature Winter minimum 7°C (45°F).
Humidity Needs moderate humidity. Occasional misting is useful, but standing the plant in a water-filled saucer will also help.
Position Good light, but avoid exposing to direct sun.
Watering and feeding Water freely at all times. These plants are used to damp or bog conditions and will react badly if the roots become dry. This is one of the few plants that benefits if the saucer in which the pot stands is kept topped up with water so that the soil in the pot is always moist.
Care Do not worry if some of the older leaves start to die, as these are recycled by the plant and new leaves are formed. Provided the young leaves look healthy, the whole plant is in good health.
Propagation Division; leaf cuttings (lay cuttings on chopped sphagnum moss); seed.

Platycerium

A small genus of epiphytic ferns whose natural habitat is high up in trees in tropical rain forests. Usually grown in cultivation in a hanging basket or wired to a piece of cork bark.

Platycerium alcicorne *see P. bifurcatum.*

Platycerium bifurcatum

The roots are hidden behind shield-shaped, sterile fronds that appear to clasp the plant's support. The broad, fertile fronds, which stand forwards, are divided and look like a stag's antlers. The plant may also be found under the name *P. alcicorne.*

HELPFUL HINTS
Temperature Winter minimum 10°C (50°F), although a few degrees lower should not harm plants.
Humidity Mist the leaves occasionally, more often in hot weather, but it is not as vulnerable as most ferns in dry air.
Position Good light, but avoid exposing to direct sun.
Watering and feeding Water freely from spring to autumn, sparingly in winter. Use soft water if possible. Feed with a weak fertilizer while growing actively. If you are growing

ABOVE: Platycerium bifurcatum

the fern on a piece of cork bark in the home, the easiest way to water it is to plunge the bark and fern in a bucket of water, and then allow it to drain before rehanging.
Care Although it can be grown in a pot, this fern looks much better displayed in a more natural way. In a greenhouse or conservatory, hanging baskets are satisfactory, but in the home a piece of cork bark is a better choice. Drill holes and insert wires for hanging the cork bark and to hold the plant securely in place. Pack plenty of sphagnum moss around the root-ball and wire in position on the piece of bark.
Propagation Offsets; spores.

Plectranthus

A genus of trailing or bushy evergreen perennials. Most of those grown as houseplants have variegated foliage.

Plectranthus coleoides

Low-growing creeper with green, scalloped leaves about 5cm (2in) long. It is the variegated varieties that are normally grown. The leaves of 'Marginatus' have white margins. Now more correctly named *P. forsteri.*

P. forsteri *see P. coleoides.*

Plectranthus fruticosus

Light green, oval to heart-shaped leaves, with a scalloped edge, up to 15cm (6in) long, on stems that grow to about 90cm (3ft). Spikes of lilac-blue flowers may grow in winter.

Plectranthus oertendahlii

A creeping plant with oval to round leaves about 2.5cm (1in) across, green with white veins above, purple-red on the reverse.

HELPFUL HINTS
Temperature Winter minimum 10°C (50°F).
Humidity Mist occasionally.
Position Good light or semi-shade, but not direct sunlight.
Watering and feeding Water freely from spring to autumn, sparingly in winter. Feed from spring to autumn.
Care Pinch stems back to keep trailing varieties compact and bushy.
Propagation Cuttings.

BELOW: Plectranthus coleoides 'Marginatus'

ABOVE: Polypodium aureum

Polypodium

A large and diverse group of deciduous, semi-evergreen and evergreen
ferns. The species described here is the
one you are most likely to find grown
as a houseplant.

Polypodium aureum

Blue-green, deeply-cut leaves sometimes 60cm (2ft) or more long. The
creeping rhizomes are densely covered
with orange-brown 'fur'. Although
normally beneath the soil, these are
sometimes visible. You may also find
this plant sold or listed under its other
name of *Phlebodium aureum*.

HELPFUL HINTS

Temperature Winter minimum
16°C (60°F).
Humidity Mist the leaves occasionally. Polypodium are more tolerant of
dry air than most ferns.
Position Good light, but avoid exposing to direct sun.
Watering and feeding Water mod-

erately from spring to autumn, sparingly in winter. Use soft water if
possible. Feed regularly from spring
to autumn.
Care Repot annually in spring.
Propagation Division of the rhizome;
spores.

Polyscias

A genus of more than 70 evergreen
trees and shrubs, a few of which are
grown as houseplants. Unfortunately
they can be difficult to grow successfully in the home.

Polyscias balfouriana

Leaves usually have three leaflets,
which are dark green and speckled grey
or paler green. Each leaflet, on a 15cm
(6in) stalk, is about 7.5cm (3in) across
and almost circular. 'Pennockii' has
white veins, 'Marginata' has a white
edge. Shrubby growth habit. Now
considered to be more accurately
named *P. scuttellaria* 'Balfourii'.

Polyscias fruticosa

Compound leaves usually with three
leaflets, each about 15cm (6in) long
and spiny-toothed, creating a feathery
appearance. Makes a large bushy, upright plant in time.

HELPFUL HINTS

Temperature Aim for 13–16°C (55–
60°F) in winter.
Humidity Mist the leaves regularly,
and provide as much additional
humidity as possible.
Position Good light, but avoid exposing to direct sun.
Watering and feeding Water freely
from spring to autumn, moderately in
winter. Use soft water if possible.
Feed regularly in summer.
Care Use an ericaceous (lime-free)
compost (potting soil) when you have
to repot the plant.
Propagation Cuttings.

BELOW: Polyscias balfouriana

Polystichum

A large group of evergreen, semi-evergreen and deciduous ferns, distributed over most parts of the world. Many species are used as hardy garden plants, and the two listed below cannot withstand severe frosts.

Polystichum falcatum
Tough, glossy fronds 30–60cm (1–2ft) long with large leathery leaflets. 'Rochfordianum' has more numerous holly-shaped leaflets. Although classed as a polystichum by some, you are likely to find it sold as *Cyrtomium falcatum*, which is considered by other botanists to be its correct name.

Polystichum tsus-simense
Broadly lance-shaped, semi-evergreen fronds with delicate-looking, spiny-edged leaflets. Grows to a height of about 30cm (1ft).

HELPFUL HINTS
Temperature Winter minimum 5°C (41°F), although short periods below this are unlikely to be detrimental.
Humidity Mist the leaves regularly, although these plants are not as demanding as many other ferns.

Position Semi-shade or good light, but not direct sun.
Watering and feeding Water freely from spring to autumn, sparingly in winter. Feed regularly in summer.
Care Remove faded or damaged

ABOVE: Polystichum falcatum (*syn.* Cyrtomium falcatum) *'Rochfordianum'*

fronds to keep the plants looking at their most attractive.
Propagation Division; spores.

Primula

A large genus with about 400 species of annuals, biennials and perennials, many of them hardy garden plants. Those listed below are popular commercial pot plants which you are most likely to come across.

Primula acaulis *see P. vulgaris.*

Primula malacoides
Dainty flowers about 1cm (½in) across, arranged in two to six tiers along the flower stalk, in shades of pink, purple, lilac, red, and white, with a yellow eye. Flowers are carried on stems about 30–45cm (1–1½ft) tall, above toothed oval leaves. Winter flowering.

Primula obconica
Large, rounded heads of 2.5–4cm (1–1½in) flowers mainly in shades of pink and blue, on stems about 23–30cm (9–12in) tall, appearing in winter and spring. The pale green hairy leaves may cause an allergic reaction in some people.

Primula vulgaris hybrids
The true species is the common primrose, with yellow flowers nestling in the rosette of leaves. These are unsuitable as houseplants. The modern hybrids, however, have large, colourful blooms in many shades, mainly yellows, reds, pinks, and blues, most with a bold contrasting eye, on stems

RIGHT: Primula obconica

carried higher above the leaves than in the species. These are widely sold as pot plants, and although they are not suitable for long-term use indoors they make a pretty short-term display in winter and spring.

HELPFUL HINTS
Temperature Winter minimum 13°C (55°F). To prolong the display, avoid high temperatures while plants are in flower.
Humidity Mist the leaves occasionally, especially if the air is dry.
Position Good light with some sun, but no direct summer sun during the hottest part of the day.
Watering and feeding Water freely from spring to autumn, but sparingly in winter. Feed quite regularly during the flowering season using a weak fertilizer.
Care The *P. vulgaris* hybrids should be bought in flower or raised in a greenhouse and taken indoors once the buds begin to open. After flowering they are best discarded or planted in the garden. The other primulas listed here are also often treated as short-term plants raised afresh each year and discarded after flowering. You can, however, successfully keep *P. obconica* from year to year. Keep it cool and out of strong sunlight, and water sparingly during the summer when it has its resting period. Resume normal watering in autumn.
Propagation Seed.

Pteris

A genus of about 280 deciduous, semi-evergreen and evergreen ferns from tropical and subtropical regions around the world.

Pteris cretica
Deeply divided green fronds with slender, slightly serrated leaflets on arching stems, growing to about 30cm (1ft). There are many varieties and these are more often grown than the species. Examples are 'Albolineata'

(pale stripe down the centre of each leaflet), and 'Alexandrae' (variegated but with the ends of the leaflets cut and fringed).

Pteris ensiformis
Similar to the previous species, but with darker leaves. There are variegated varieties, such as 'Evergemiensis' (broad white lengthwise bands on the leaflets) and 'Victoriae' (similar to the previous variety but with less pronounced markings).

HELPFUL HINTS
Temperature Winter minimum 13°C (55°F) for plain green forms, 16°C (60°F) for variegated varieties.
Humidity Mist the leaves regularly.
Position Good light, but not direct sun. Plain green forms will tolerate poorer light than the variegated varieties.
Watering and feeding Water freely from spring to autumn, sparingly in winter. Use soft water if possible. Feed regularly with a weak fertilizer from spring to autumn.
Care Be especially careful never to allow the roots to become dry.
Propagation Division; spores.

ABOVE: Pteris ensiformis *'Evergemiensis'*
BELOW: Pteris cretica *'Albolineata'*

Radermachera

A small genus of vigorous evergeeen trees and shrubs native to South-east Asia. The species below is the only one you are likely to find.

Radermachera sinica
Doubly pinnate foliage with individual leaflets about 2.5cm (1in) long, distinctly pointed at the ends. Makes a bushy plant about 60cm (2ft) tall in most home conditions. May sometimes be listed or sold as *Stereospermum suaveolens*.

HELPFUL HINTS
Temperature Winter minimum 13°C (55°F).
Humidity Undemanding.
Position Good light, but not direct summer sun during the hottest part of the day.
Watering and feeding Water freely from spring to autumn, moderately in winter.
Care Pinch out the growing tip of a young plant to encourage more compact, bushy growth.
Propagation Cuttings.

RIGHT: Radermachera sinica

Rebutia

Cacti originating from northern Argentina and parts of Bolivia, where they grow at high altitudes. There are about 40 species.

Rebutia minuscula
Spherical body, usually about 5cm (2in) across and somewhat flattened. Short white spines. Red to orange-red flowers about 2.5cm (1in) long, in spring and early summer.

Rebutia pygmaea
Oval to finger-shaped ribbed body,

RIGHT: Rebutia senilis *(left) and* Rebutia miniscula *(right)*
FAR RIGHT: Rebutia pygmaea

with tiny spines. It is often only about 2.5cm (1in) tall, but old specimens will reach 10cm (4in). Purple, pink, or red flowers, about 2.5cm (1in) long, in late spring and early summer.

Rebutia senilis

A flattened sphere, densely covered with white thorns. Bright-red, trumpet-shaped flowers, over 2.5cm (1in) long, in spring and summer. There are varieties with yellow, lilac, and orange flowers. Grows to about 7.5cm (3in).

HELPFUL HINTS
Temperature Winter minimum 5°C (41°F).
Humidity Tolerates dry air, but appreciates a humid atmosphere in spring and summer.
Position Good light. Benefits from direct sun.
Watering and feeding Water moderately from spring to autumn, keep practically dry in winter. Feed in summer with a weak fertilizer or a special cactus food.
Care Repot in spring when it becomes necessary, using a cactus mixture.
Propagation Cuttings (from offshoots); seed.

Rhaphidophora aurea

See Epipremnum aureum.

Rhipsalidopsis

A small genus of epiphytic cacti from the tropical forests of southern Brazil.

Rhipsalidopsis gaertneri

Flattened, segmented stems bearing clusters of bell-shaped scarlet flowers with multiple petals in mid and late spring. May sometimes be listed as *Schlumbergera gaertneri*, and now considered by botanists to be more correctly named *Hatiora gaertneri*.

ABOVE: Rhipsalidopsis gaertneri (*syn.* Schlumbergera gaertneri)

HELPFUL HINTS
Temperature Winter minimum 10°C (50°F).
Humidity Mist leaves occasionally.
Position Good light, but not direct summer sun.
Watering and feeding Water freely while in active growth. In winter give sufficient water only to prevent the stems from shrivelling. Feed with a weak fertilizer in spring and summer.
Care A cool resting period is essential for good flowering – so avoid keeping the plant in a hot room in winter. Do not move the plant once the buds have formed. Stand in a shady spot outdoors for the summer months.
Propagation Cuttings; seed.

Rhododendron

A very large genus of evergreen and deciduous shrubs, ranging from small alpine species to large plants of tree-like stature. Many of them are hardy and popular garden plants, especially the hybrids. Only a couple of species have been developed as houseplants, however, and these are popularly known as azaleas.

Rhododendron × obtusum

Semi-evergreen, with glossy leaves 2.5–4cm (1–1½in) long. Single or double, funnel-shaped flowers in clusters of two to five blooms, in late winter and spring. Varieties are available in a range of colours. They usually grow 30–45cm (1–1½ft) tall when kept as a pot plant.

Rhododendron simsii

Evergreen leathery leaves, about 4–5cm (1½-2in) long. Profusion of 4–5cm (1½-2in) single or double flowers in a range of colours, mainly pinks and reds, as well as white, in winter and spring. They grow to about 30–45cm (1–1½ft) tall as a pot plant.

HELPFUL HINTS

Temperature Aim for 10–16°C (50–60°F) in winter.

Humidity Mist the leaves regularly.

Position Good light, but avoid exposing to direct sun.

Watering and feeding Water freely at all times, using soft water if possible. Feed regularly in summer.

Care Pay special attention to watering – plants are often sold in a very peaty (peat moss) mixture that is difficult to moisten once it dries out. Always use an ericaceous (lime-free) compost (potting soil) for repotting, which is best done about a month after flowering has finished. Place the plants in a shady and sheltered spot in the garden once all danger of frost is past. *R.* × *obtusum* varieties can be planted permanently in the garden in sheltered areas where the winters are not very severe. *R. simsii* varieties must be brought indoors again in early autumn. If you stand the plants in the garden, plunge the pots into the ground to conserve moisture – don't forget to keep them watered and fed.

Propagation Cuttings.

BELOW: Rhododendron × obtusum
BOTTOM: Rhododendron simsii

Rosa

Roses are universally popular plants, and although there are only about 200 different species, there are thousands of hybrids and varieties. However, even dwarf and miniature varieties make only short-term houseplants.

Rosa, miniature hybrids

A scaled-down rose 15–30cm (6–12in) tall, with single, semi-double, or double flowers about 1–4cm (½-1½in) across. They are available as bushes or trained as miniature standards. Most are derived from *R. chinensis* 'Minima', but the breeding of those available today is complex and they will usually be sold simply with a variety name, or perhaps just labelled 'miniature rose'. Some are true miniatures, growing less than 15cm (6in) high, but the treatment is the same however they are labelled when you buy them.

HELPFUL HINTS

Temperature Frost-hardy. Aim for 10–21°C (50–70°F) when the plants are growing actively.
Humidity Undemanding, but it is beneficial to mist occasionally.
Position Best possible light. Will tolerate full sun.
Watering and feeding Water freely from spring to autumn, while they are in leaf. Feed regularly in summer.
Care The plants are best kept outdoors for as long as possible. After flowering stand them on the balcony or patio and keep watered, or plunge the pot in the garden soil. Pots kept on a balcony or patio for the winter may need some protection to prevent the root-ball from freezing solid. Repot in autumn if necessary. Prune in spring as you would an ordinary rose – although with very small plants it may be sufficient simply to remove dead or crossing shoots. Bring indoors again in late spring, or as soon as flowering starts.
Propagation Cuttings.

RIGHT: *Rose, miniature hybrids*

Saintpaulia

A small genus of rosette-forming perennials, just one species of which is well known. The large colour range and variation in flower form are the result of introducing genes from other species such as *S. confusa*, although they are usually all listed as varieties of *S. ionantha*. The original species is not grown as a houseplant.

Most of the saintpaulias sold in shops and garden centres will lack a specific name, but if you go to a specialist supplier you will have a choice of hundreds of varieties, all accurately named.

The huge range of varieties available, in many colours and variations in flower form and growth habit, make saintpaulias an ideal plant for collectors. They can be induced to flower throughout the year if you can provide suitable light intensities.

Sizes
Large varieties grow to 40cm (16in) or more across. Standard saintpaulias are the ones most often bought and generally grow between 20–40cm (8–16in) across. Miniatures are only 7.5–15cm (3–6in) across. There are also varieties intermediate in size, and microminiatures less than 7.5cm (3in) across when mature. Trailers have more widely spaced foliage than normal varieties, with drooping stems that tend to arch over the pot.

Flower shapes
Single flowers are the most common type. Semi-double flowers have more than five petals, but the centre is still clearly visible. Double flowers have at least ten petals, and the yellow centre is not visible. Frilled flowers have petals with a wavy edge. Star flowers have five equally sized and spaced petals, instead of the more usual two small and three large petals.

Leaf shapes
These are just a few of the leaf shapes identified by specialists. Boy leaves are plain green, and do not have a spot at the leaf base. Girl leaves are the same shape as boy leaves, but have a small white spot or blotch at the base. Lance leaves are longer and more pointed at the end. Spoon leaves have a rolled-up edge. Variegated leaves are mottled or speckled with white or cream.

Helpful hints

Temperature Winter minimum 16°C (60°F).

Humidity Saintpaulias appreciate high humidity, but regular misting is not appropriate as water may lodge on the hairy leaves and cause rotting. Provide the humidity in other ways, such as standing the pot over a saucer of water on pebbles or marbles so that the compost (potting soil) is not in direct contact with the water.

Position Good light, but not direct summer sun during the hottest part of the day. Strong light without direct sun is ideal. Saintpaulias grow very well under suitable artificial light (at least 5,000 lux).

Watering and feeding Water freely from spring to autumn, moderately in winter, but never allow the roots to remain wet – try to let the soil surface dry out a little before watering again. Use soft water if possible. Try to

ABOVE, OPPOSITE TOP LEFT AND ABOVE LEFT: Saintpaulia hybrids
OPPOSITE BELOW: Saintpaulias, showing the diversity of flower shapes and colouring, including a double. A miniature is shown bottom right.
OPPOSITE ABOVE RIGHT: Saintpaulias: 'Maggie May' (left), 'Fancy Pants' (centre), 'Colorado' (right)

water without wetting the leaves – use the immersion method or direct the spout of the watering-can below the rosette of leaves. Feed during active growth. However, if the plant produces lots of leaves and few flowers despite adequate light, you may be overfeeding – switch to a low-nitrogen fertilizer.

Care Most windowsill plants flower in spring and summer, when the light is good, but by supplementing the light they will continue blooming for most of the year. If you have the ability to maintain high light levels, however, it is best to rest the plant for about a month: lower the temperature close to the minimum, reduce watering and shorten the day length. After a month, place in good light to start into active growth again. Remove any old leaves that are marring the plant.

Propagation Leaf cuttings; seed.

Sansevieria

A small genus of evergreen rhizomatous perennials with stiff, fleshy leaves. These are desert plants that can tolerate poor conditions.

Sansevieria trifasciata

Tough, sword-like leaves, slightly crescent-shaped in cross-section, that can be 1.5m (5ft) long in good conditions, but usually only grow to half this height in the home. Dull green leaves with paler cross-banding that creates a mottled appearance. A more popular form is the variety 'Laurentii' which has yellow leaf margins. 'Hahnii' is a low-growing variety with a short, funnel-shaped rosette of leaves; 'Golden Hahnii' is similar but with broad yellow stripes along the edge of each leaf. Spikes of white flowers are sometimes produced.

BELOW: Sansevieria trifasciata *'Laurentii'*

HELPFUL HINTS

Temperature Winter minimum 10°C (50°F).
Humidity Tolerates dry air.
Position Best in bright, indirect light, but will tolerate direct sun and also a degree of shade.
Watering and feeding Water moderately from spring to autumn, very sparingly in winter. Always allow the soil to dry out slightly before watering. Feed regularly in summer.
Care Repotting is seldom required, as plants respond well to cramped conditions. However, always repot if the roots show signs of splitting the pot.
Propagation Division; leaf cuttings (but yellow-edged varieties will revert to the green form).

Sarracenia

Carnivorous plants with just eight species in the genus. Demanding as a houseplant, but grown as a curiosity.

Sarracenia flava

Leaves like long trumpets, hooded at the top, grow to about 30–60cm (1–2ft) long indoors. Insects are lured into the trap, attracted by nectar in special glands, and by the yellow colouring developed by the leaf traps. They are digested by enzymes and bacteria. Unusual yellow or cream flowers are sometimes produced in spring.

Sarracenia purpurea

Rosette-forming plants with erect to semi-prostrate growth to about 30cm (12in). Inflated green traps with red or purple veins and markings. Purple flowers in spring.

HELPFUL HINTS

Temperature Winter minimum 5°C (41°F).
Humidity Mist the leaves regularly, and try to maintain a humid atmosphere around the plant.
Position Good light with or without direct sun, but not direct summer sun

ABOVE: Sarracenia purpurea

during the hottest part of the day.
Watering and feeding Water freely from spring to autumn (when the plant likes to be kept constantly wet), sparingly in winter. Feeding is not normally necessary.
Care The plant is likely to do better in a greenhouse or conservatory than in a centrally-heated living-room.
Propagation Seed.

Saxifraga

A large genus with hundreds of species, mostly alpines, but only one is commonly grown as a houseplant.

Saxifraga sarmentosa *see S. stolonifera.*

Saxifraga stolonifera

Rounded leaves about 4–5cm (1½–2in) across, broadly toothed, olive green with white veins above, reddish beneath. 'Tricolor' has green and red or pink leaves with silver or white markings, reddish beneath. Height is up to about 23cm (9in), but plantlets will cascade if grown in a hanging pot. May also be found under its older name of *S. sarmentosa.*

ABOVE: Saxifraga stolonifera

HELPFUL HINTS
Temperature Winter minimum 7°C (45°F).
Humidity Mist occasionally.
Position Good light, but avoid exposing to direct sun.
Watering and feeding Water freely from spring to autumn, sparingly in winter. Feed regularly in summer.
Care The species listed above is frost-hardy and will grow in the garden where winters are mild. 'Tricolor' is more delicate, however, and is best kept indoors. Trim off long runners if they look untidy.
Propagation Plantlets (peg down into pots).

Schefflera

A large genus of evergreen shrubs and trees, a few of which are grown as focal-point houseplants.

Schefflera actinophylla

Although a large tree where it grows outdoors, in the home it makes a bushy plant up to ceiling height. Large, spreading leaves with 5–16 leaflets (the older the plant, the more it is likely to have), each of them about 10–20cm (4–8in) long.

Schefflera arboricola

Erect, well-branched growth with 7–16 oval leaflets which radiate from the top of the leaf stalk like an umbrella. There are several widely available varieties with variegated foliage. You may also find this plant sold or listed as *Heptapleurum arboricola*.

HELPFUL HINTS
Temperature Winter minimum 13°C (55°F).
Humidity Mist the leaves regularly.
Position Good light, but avoid exposing to direct sun.

Watering and feeding Water freely from spring to autumn, sparingly in winter. Feed regularly in summer.
Care Can be trained as an upright, unbranching plant if you stake the plant and do not remove the growing tip, or can be made to bush out by removing the growing tip. Repot annually in spring.
Propagation Cuttings.

BELOW: Schefflera arboricola *'Aurea'*

Schizanthus

A small group of annuals from Chile. Most of the plants grown in pots are hybrids, evolved through many years of breeding by seed companies.

Schizanthus hybrids

Feathery, light green leaves, divided and fern-like in appearance. Exotic-looking, open-mouthed flowers, often described as orchid-like. Flowers multicoloured and very freely produced. Height depends on variety – dwarf varieties are most appropriate for the home, and you should be able to restrict them to little more than 30cm (1ft). Some greenhouse varieties grow to 1.2m (4ft).

HELPFUL HINTS
Temperature Aim for 10–18°C (50–64°F).
Humidity Mist occasionally.

BELOW: Schizanthus *hybrid*

Position Best possible light. Will tolerate some direct sun.
Watering and feeding Water freely at all times. Remember to feed regularly.
Care If raising your own plant, pinch out the growing tips while the seedlings are still young in order to produce bushy growth. Repeat again later if the plants seem to be lanky. Move younger plants into larger pots to avoid checking their growth. Avoid very high temperatures. Discard plants when flowering has finished.
Propagation Seed.

Schlumbergera

See Rhipsalidopsis and Zygocactus.

Scindapsus aureus

See Epipremnum.

Sedum

A large genus of over 300 species, from temperate zones throughout the world. Many of them are fleshy or succulent, including the majority of those used as pot plants.

Sedum bellum

A small plant to about 7.5–15cm (3–6in), with leaves folded like buds that eventually spread apart and become spatula shaped. Small star-like white flowers in spring.

Sedum morganianum

Cascading growth with closely-packed grey-green, succulent cylindrical leaves that overlap like tiles, creating a tail-like appearance. Pink flowers may appear in summer.

ABOVE: Sedum sieboldii
'Mediovariegatum'
LEFT ABOVE: Sedum pachyphyllum
LEFT BELOW: Sedum × rubrotinctum

Sedum pachyphyllum

Erect with pale blue-green cylindrical leaves about 2.5cm (1in) long, slightly upturned and flushed red at the tips. Yellow flowers may appear in spring.

Sedum × rubrotinctum

Similar to the previous species, but more of the leaf tends to be flushed red, especially in strong sunlight.

Sedum sieboldii

Thin, flattish leaves, in groups of three, blue-green with a white edge. In the variety 'Mediovariegatum' the leaves have a central creamy-white blotch. Pink flowers may appear in late summer or autumn. Botanists have now moved this to another genus and called it *Hylotelephium sieboldii*, but it is still sold as a sedum.

HELPFUL HINTS
Temperature Winter minimum 5°C (41°F).
Humidity Tolerates dry air.
Position Best possible light.

Watering and feeding Water sparingly from spring to autumn, and keep practically dry in winter (water only to prevent the leaves from shrivelling up). Feeding is not normally necessary.
Care Repot in spring, using a potting soil that drains freely. A cactus mixture suits well.
Propagation Leaf cuttings (for varieties with large, fleshy leaves such as *S. pachyphyllum* and *S. morganianum*); stem cuttings.

Selaginella

A genus of about 700 species of moss-like perennials, most of them coming from tropical rain forests.

Selaginella kraussiana

Creeping stems with filigreed green foliage, yellowish-green in 'Aurea'. Individual stems may be 30cm (1ft) long, and they root readily as they spread over the surface.

Selaginella lepidophylla

Looks like a ball of rolled-up, dead foliage in its dry state (the form in which it is often sold as a curiosity plant). Within hours of being given water it opens to a rosette shape, and the green colouring gradually returns.

Selaginella martensii

Upright-growing stems to about 30cm (1ft), which later become decumbent and produce aerial roots. Frond-like sprays of feathery green foliage. There are variegated varieties, such as 'Watsoniana', which has silvery-white tips.

HELPFUL HINTS
Temperature Winter minimum 13°C (55°F).
Humidity Mist the leaves regularly. Additional humidity from other sources must be provided.
Position Partial shade – avoid direct sun all year round. Plants do well in bottle gardens and terrariums, where the atmosphere is humid and protected.
Watering and feeding Keep moist at all times, but reduce watering in winter to suit the lower temperatures. Feed occasionally in summer using a foliar feed.
Care Provide as much humidity as possible and avoid cold draughts and very hot, sunny windows. Do not be surprised if plants are short-lived in living-room conditions.
Propagation Division (pot up rooted pieces).

BELOW: Selaginella lepidophylla
BELOW LEFT: Selaginella martensii

Senecio

A very large group of plants, with over 1,000 species, distributed throughout the world. It includes plants as diverse as annuals and perennials, succulents and non-succulent perennials, evergreen shrubs, sub-shrubs and climbers. Relatively few are used as houseplants.

Senecio cruentus hybrids

Dense head of colourful daisy-like flowers in winter and spring. Colours include shades of red, pink, purple, white, and blue. Large, irregularly lobed, hairy leaves, which can almost be hidden when a compact plant is in full flower. Height ranges from about 23–75cm (9–30in), and flower size from 2.5–7.5cm (1–3in) depending on the variety. Choose compact varieties for the home. You will usually find this plant called cineraria. Although botanists have now reclassified it as *Pericallis cruenta*, it is not sold under this name.

Senecio macroglossus

Trailer or climber with small succulent, roughly triangular leaves resembling common ivy (*Hedera helix*). 'Variegatus' has white margins.

Senecio mikanioides

Trailer or climber similar to the previous species, but the leaves have five

ABOVE: Senecio rowleyanus
BELOW: Senecio macroglossus *'Variegatus'*

to seven sharply pointed lobes. Now reclassified as *Delairea odorata*.

Senecio rowleyanus

Trailer with pendent, thread-like stems clustered with pea-like leaves that resemble beads.

HELPFUL HINTS

Temperature Winter minimum 7°C (45°F). Try to keep *S. cruentus* varieties below 13°C (55°F).
Humidity Succulent types are tolerant of dry air, but mist *S. cruentus, S. macroglossus,* and *S. mikanioides* occasionally.
Position Best possible light, but not direct sun for *S. cruentus. S. rowleyanus* should receive some direct sun. The other species listed here need good light but not direct summer sun, and

will tolerate semi-shade, but in winter provide as much light as possible.
Watering and feeding Water the non-succulent types freely from spring to autumn, sparingly in winter. Water *S. rowleyanus* sparingly at all times, and keep practically dry in winter. Feed all types when they are growing actively.
Care *S. cruentus* will die after flowering, so discard once blooming is over.
Propagation Although you can raise senecios from seed in the greenhouse, they are difficult to grow on from seed in the home. Most people buy them in flower if they cannot keep them in a greenhouse until flowering starts.

Sinningia

A small genus of tuberous perennials and deciduous sub-shrubs. Those commonly grown are widely known and sold as gloxinias, and have been bred from *S. speciosa*.

Sinningia speciosa

Large, oval to oblong leaves arising directly from the tuber, about 20–25cm (8–10in) long and hairy. The underside is sometimes reddish. Large, showy, bell-shaped flowers about 5cm (2in) long, in pink, red, blue, purple, or white, some with contrasting rim, others attractively speckled.

HELPFUL HINTS

Temperature Minimum 16°C (60°F) during growing season.
Humidity Mist around plants regularly, but avoid wetting the leaves or blooms. Provide as much humidity as possible by other methods.
Position Good light, but avoid exposing to direct sun.
Watering and feeding Water freely once the tubers have rooted well. Decrease watering at the end of the growing season (*see* Care). Feed regularly in summer.
Care When flowering has finished, gradually reduce the amount of water given and stop feeding. Remove the

ABOVE: Sinningia speciosa

sometimes mottled. Height in flower is usually about 30–38cm (12–15in).

HELPFUL HINTS

Temperature Winter minimum 13°C (55°F).

Humidity Mist regularly, but try not to over-wet the leaves. Use soft water if possible.

Position Good light, but avoid exposing to direct sun.

Watering and feeding Water freely from spring to autumn, while plants are growing. Keep almost dry in winter if the top growth has died down. Feed regularly in summer.

Care After flowering, gradually reduce the amount of water given and stop feeding. Leave the rhizome in its old pot for most of the winter, but repot and start into active growth again in late winter.

Propagation Division of rhizomes; leaf cuttings.

leaves when they have turned yellow. If you have space, store the tubers in the pot in a frost-free, place ideally at about 10°C (50°F).

Repot afresh in the spring, making sure you plant them the right way up and at about the same depth as before.

Propagation Leaf cuttings; seed.

Smithiantha

Only a few species are known, and these come from humid mountain forests in Mexico and Guatemala. These have been used to provide some attractive hybrids, however, that are especially worth growing if you have a conservatory. They are not easy to grow in a living-room.

Smithiantha hybrids
Loose heads of pendent, tubular flowers about 5cm (2in) long, with a slightly flared mouth, in autumn. Hairy, round to heart-shaped leaves, usually about 10cm (4in) long and

RIGHT: Smithiantha × hybrida

Solanum

A genus of about 1,400 species, from all parts of the world, and including annuals, perennials, shrubs, sub-shrubs and climbers. The only ones used in the home are the two species described below. These are grown for their decorative fruits, which are poisonous.

Solanum capsicastrum

A sub-shrub usually grown as an annual, generally reaching 30–60cm (1–2ft) as a pot plant, but this depends on variety. Lance-shaped leaves about 5cm (2in) long, and small white star-shaped flowers in summer. These are followed by egg-shaped or round green fruits that turn orange-red or scarlet by winter.

Solanum pseudocapsicum

Very similar to the previous species, but the stems are smoother and the fruits usually larger.

HELPFUL HINTS

Temperature Aim for 10–16°C (50–60°F) in winter.
Humidity Mist the leaves regularly.
Position Best possible light. Tolerates some direct sun.
Watering and feeding Water freely

BELOW: Solanum capsicastrum

throughout the growing period. Feed regularly in summer.
Care Most people buy the plants already in fruit, but they are easy to raise from seed. As they are uninteresting until the fruits colour, and conditions indoors are not really suitable, it is best to raise them in a greenhouse to take indoors later. If you want to try to keep an old plant, cut the stems back to half their length after flowering and water sparingly until spring, when you can repot the plant. Stand the plant in a garden frame or outside in the garden for the summer, but spray the flowers with water to try to assist pollination. Bring indoors in autumn, before the evenings turn cold.
Propagation Seed; cuttings.

Soleirolia

There is only one species in this genus, a native of Corsica. It is frost-hardy, but easily damaged or killed by hard winter frosts so is only suitable for growing outdoors in mild areas.

Soleirolia soleirolii

Creeping, ground-hugging plant with very small round leaves that give a mossy appearance from a distance. The species itself is green, but there are silver and gold varieties that masquerade under several names. The silver form 'Variegata' is also sold as 'Argentea' and 'Silver Queen'. The golden form 'Aurea' is also sold as 'Golden Queen'. They all grow to form compact mounds not more than 5cm (2in) tall. You are also likely to find the plant under its older name of *Helxine soleirolii*.

HELPFUL HINTS

Temperature Frost-hardy, but aim for 7°C (45°F) when growing it as a pot plant.
Humidity Mist the leaves regularly.
Position Good light, but avoid exposing to direct sun.
Watering and feeding Water freely

TOP AND ABOVE: Soleirolia soleirolii

at all times. Feeding is normally un-necessary.
Care Repot in spring. A low, wide container is better than a normal pot, as the growth quickly spreads and hangs over the edge.
Propagation Division.

Solenostemon

See Coleus.

Sparmannia

A small group of evergreen trees and shrubs. The only species normally grown as a pot plant is the one pictured and described on this page, *Sparmannia africana*.

Sparmannia africana
Large, pale green downy leaves up to 25cm (10in) across. Long-stalked clusters of white flowers with yellow and purplish-red stamens in spring. Makes a large plant that will reach ceiling height.

HELPFUL HINTS
Temperature Winter minimum 7°C (45°F).
Humidity Mist occasionally.
Position Good light, but not direct summer sun during the hottest part of the day.
Watering and feeding Water freely from spring to autumn, sparingly in winter. Feed regularly in spring and summer.
Care Cut back the stems when flowering is over — this helps to keep the plants compact and may encourage a later flush of flowers. When you re-pot, you can cut it back severely to a height of about 30cm (1ft) if necessary. Young plants may need repotting several times in a year. The plant can be stood outdoors for the summer, but choose a sheltered position out of direct sun, and bring indoors again before the evenings turn cold. Pinch out the growing tip of a young plant if you want to encourage a bushy shape.
Propagation Cuttings.

RIGHT: Sparmannia africana

ABOVE: Spathiphyllum wallisii

Spathiphyllum

Rhizomatous evergreen perennials, grown for their arum lily-like flowers. Other species and hybrids are available, but the one below is compact and one of the most popular.

Spathiphyllum wallisii
Tuft-forming clusters of thin, lance-shaped leaves arising from soil level. Arum lily-type flowers with a sail-like white spathe and fragrant florets on a white spadix, in spring and sometimes autumn. Height 30–45cm (1–1½ft).

HELPFUL HINTS
Temperature Winter minimum 16°C (60°F).
Humidity Mist the leaves regularly. Provide additional humidity by other means too.
Position Best possible light in winter, semi-shade in summer, out of direct summer sun.
Watering and feeding Water freely from spring to autumn, sparingly in winter. Feed regularly in summer.
Care Pay special attention to providing high humidity, and avoid cold draughts. Repot annually, in spring.
Propagation Division.

Stapelia

A genus of about 100 clump-forming succulents, most of them from South and South West Africa.

Stapelia variegata
Angular, fleshy green stems arising from the base of the plant and forming a small clump, usually about 10–15cm (4–6in) long. Star-shaped flowers about 5–7.5cm (2–3in) across, variable in colour but usually blotched or mottled yellow, purple, and brown, appearing in summer or autumn. Now reclassified as *Orbea variegata*, but likely to be sold as a stapelia.

HELPFUL HINTS
Temperature Winter minimum 10°C (50°F).
Humidity Tolerates dry air.
Position Best possible light.
Watering and feeding Water freely from spring to autumn, sparingly in winter. Feeding not necessary if plant is repotted periodically.
Care Repot in spring, annually if growth is good.
Propagation Cuttings; seed.

BELOW: Stapelia variegata

ABOVE: Stephanotis floribunda

Stephanotis

A small genus of climbers. The species described below is the one most commonly grown. This is a popular plant for bridal bouquets in some countries.

Stephanotis floribunda
Glossy, oval leaves 7.5–10cm (3–4in) long. Clusters of very fragrant star-shaped tubular white flowers in spring and summer. Will reach 3m (10ft) in good conditions. Often trained around wire hoops as a small plant, but is a vigorous climber requiring a proper support in a conservatory.

HELPFUL HINTS
Temperature Aim for 13–16°C (55–60°F) in winter. Avoid high winter temperatures.
Humidity Mist occasionally.
Position Best possible light, but not direct summer sun during the hottest part of the day.

Watering and feeding Water freely from spring to autumn, sparingly in winter. Feed regularly in summer, only in moderation if the plant is already large and seems too vigorous.
Care Train plant to a support. Shorten over-long shoots in spring, and cut out overcrowded stems at the same time. Repot every second spring.
Propagation Cuttings.

Stereospermum suaveolens

See Radermachera sinica.

Strelitzia

A small genus of large and exotic-looking plants from South Africa. Only the species described here is grown as a houseplant.

Strelitzia reginae

Clump-forming with large paddle-shaped leaves about 90cm (3ft) tall, including the stalk. Spectacular and long-lasting orange and blue flowers sitting in a boat-like bract. Spring is the main flowering period, but they may bloom at other times.

HELPFUL HINTS
Temperature Aim for a winter temperature of 13–16°C (55–60°F).
Humidity Mist occasionally.
Position Best possible light, but not direct summer sun during the hottest part of the day.
Watering and feeding Water freely from spring to autumn, sparingly in winter. Feed regularly from spring to autumn.
Care Repot as infrequently as possible as the roots are easily damaged. Be patient if you buy a small plant or raise your own from seed, as they can take four or five years to flower.
Propagation Division; seed.

BELOW: Strelitzia reginae

Streptocarpus

A genus of woodland plants from South Africa and Madagascar, but the ones grown in the home are almost always hybrids.

Streptocarpus hybrids

Long, stemless, strap-shaped leaves, 20–30cm (8–12in) long, growing more or less horizontally and often arching over the edge of the pot. Trumpet-shaped flowers about 5cm (2in) across in shades of pink, red, and blue, on stems about 23cm (9in) tall. Late spring to late summer is the normal flowering time. The leaf sap sometimes causes an irritating rash.

Streptocarpus saxorum

Woody-based perennial with whorls of small, oval, hairy leaves. Lilac flowers, like a smaller version of the hybrids, in summer and autumn.

HELPFUL HINTS
Temperature Winter minimum 13°C (55°F).
Humidity Mist the leaves occasional-ly, lightly so as not to soak them.
Position Good light, but not direct summer sun.
Watering and feeding Water freely from spring to autumn, sparingly in winter. Feed regularly in summer.
Care Benefits from a dormant winter season, with the compost (potting soil) only slightly moist and the temperature close to the minimum suggested. Repot in mid spring.
Propagation Leaf cuttings; seed.

Stromanthe

A small genus, from the maranta family, native to tropical regions of South America. They are easily confused with some species of ctenanthe and calathea.

Stromanthe amabilis

Pale green oval leaves, attractively cross-banded either side of the midrib with grey streaks. The reverse of the leaf is grey-green. This has now been reclassified as *Ctenanthe amabilis*.

Stromanthe sanguinea

Stiff, erect growth, with glossy, lance-shaped leaves about 38cm (15in) long, olive green above with a pale central vein. The reverse is purplish-red. Many-stemmed flower heads may be produced in spring. The true flowers are small and white, but the conspi-cuous bracts are vivid scarlet.

HELPFUL HINTS
Temperature Winter minimum 18°C (64°F).
Humidity Mist the leaves regularly,

ABOVE: Stromanthe amabilis
OPPOSITE ABOVE: Streptocarpus saxorum
OPPOSITE BELOW: Streptocarpus *hybrid*

and supplement with other methods of raising the humidity level.

Position Good light, but not direct summer sun during the hottest part of the day.

Watering and feeding Water freely from spring to autumn, sparingly in winter. Use soft water if possible. Feed regularly in summer.

Care These are difficult plants to care for indoors. If you have a heated greenhouse or conservatory, keep them there for most of the year, only bringing them into the home for short periods. When repotting, use a soil mixture that drains freely.

Propagation Division.

Syagrus weddeliana

See Cocos weddeliana.

Syngonium

A genus of about 30 species, from tropical rain forests in Central and South America. These woody climbers have leaves that change shape according to the plant's stage of growth, and adult leaf forms are often much more lobed than the juvenile forms usually seen on small pot plants.

Syngonium podophyllum

Foot-shaped compound leaves, arrow-shaped on young plants. There are several variegated varieties, the main differences being in the position and extent of the cream or white markings. Some leaves are almost entirely white or yellow. Grows to about 1.8m (6ft) with a suitable support.

HELPFUL HINTS

Temperature Winter minimum 16°C (60°F).

Humidity Mist the leaves regularly.
Position Good light, but not direct sun. Tolerant of low light levels.
Watering and feeding Water freely from spring to autumn, sparingly in winter. Feed regularly in spring and summer.
Care If you prefer the juvenile foliage, cut off the climbing stems that develop – the plant will remain bushy rather than climb, and the leaves will be more arrow-shaped. Repot every second spring.
Propagation Cuttings; air layering.

BELOW: Syngonium *hybrid* 'White Butterfly'

Tillandsia

About 400 species of mainly epiphytic plants. Many of those that derive nutrients from air alone are now popular as novelty plants, and are often used as decorations even by non-gardeners. These are usually displayed for sale glued or wired to accessories such as shells, mirrors or pieces of wood. A few of the species planted in pots are grown for their interesting or unusual flowers.

Air plant tillandsias

These interesting plants have special scaly leaves, capable of trapping moisture from the air, and they can even absorb nutrients from dust and any nutrient-rich moisture that may be about. *T. usneoides* grows best in a humid greenhouse, but the other species listed here are compact and tough enough to grow in the home.

The scales that give the air plants their unique quality reflect light in such a way that the plants all tend to look grey in colour. For that reason they are sometimes referred to as the grey tillandsias. The species listed here provide a cross-section of some of the most popular, but specialist suppliers will offer many more.

Tillandsia argentea
Rosettes of very narrow, thread-like leaves, with a bulb-like base. Loose sprays of small red flowers may appear in summer.

Tillandsia caput-medusae
Thick, twisted, reflexed leaves, broadening at the base to form a bulb-like structure. Quite showy red flowers in blue bracts in summer.

Tillandsia ionantha
Compact rosettes of silvery arching leaves. The inner leaves turn red when the small spikes of violet-blue flowers emerge in summer.

Tillandsia juncea
Tufts of rush-like foliage reflexing outwards, forming a thick, bushy rosette.

Tillandsia magnusiana
Thread-like leaves covered in grey scales, bulbous at base.

Tillandsia oaxacana
Dense rosette of rolled grey-green foliage. Flowers not a feature.

Tillandsia usneoides
Cylindrical leaves about 5cm (2in) long on slender drooping stems. Forms a long cascading chain of grey leaves suspended from the plant's support. There are inconspicuous yellowish-green flowers in summer, which tend to be lost among the foliage.

Opposite far left: Tillandsia usneoides
Opposite above: Tillandsia magnusiana
Opposite middle: *Tillandsias. From left to right:* T. oaxacana, T. caput-medusae, T. juncea, *and* T. ionantha
Opposite below: Tillandsia argentea

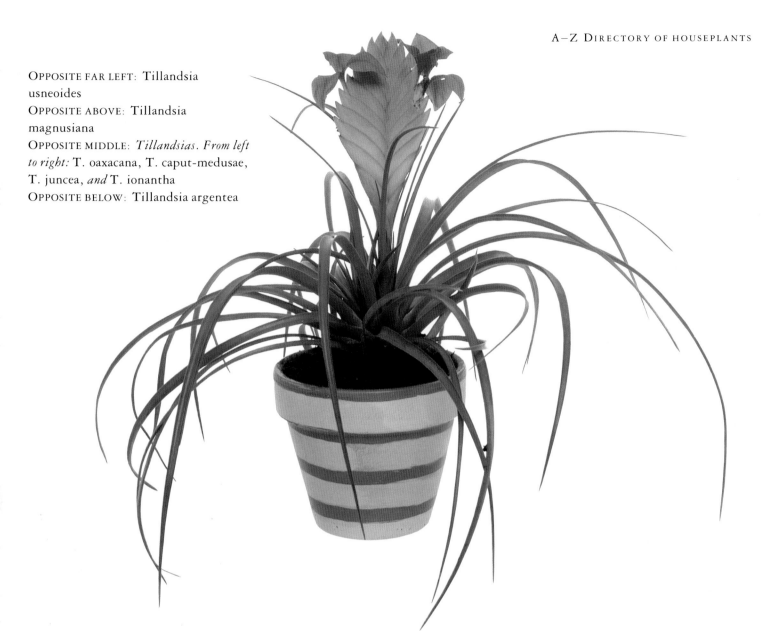

Above: Tillandsia cyanea

Flowering pot tillandsias

Tillandsias grown for their flowers are very different in appearance to air plant species. Although their root systems are not extensive, they are grown in pots like a conventional houseplant.

Tillandsia cyanea

Rosette of narrow, grass-like leaves, reddish-brown at the base and striped brown along the length. Blade-like flower spike in summer, from which purple-blue, pansy-shaped flowers appear along the edge of the spike from the pink or red bracts. The plant grows to about 25cm (10in).

Tillandsia lindenii

Similar to the previous species, but the blue flowers have a white eye.

Helpful hints

Temperature Winter minimum 13°C (55°F) for air plant tillandsias, 18°F (64°F) for the flowering species.
Humidity Mist regularly. This is especially important for the air plants, as these depend on atmospheric moisture. If possible, provide additional humidity by other methods as well.
Position Good light, but not direct sun in summer. The air plants can tolerate quite low light levels.
Watering and feeding Air plants receive their moisture by regular – preferably daily – misting. Water the other species freely from spring to autumn, sparingly in winter. Use soft water if possible. Air plants are fed via the leaves using a mister, but use a very weak solution of the fertilizer, and only apply when the plants are growing actively. Feed pot-grown species in the same way, or by adding the fertilizer to the soil.
Care Air plants are often wired into position on a bromeliad 'tree' or suitable support. If you want to fix them to a mirror or ornament, use adhesives sold for the purpose by many garden centres. Other species can be potted in spring. Although the flowered part will die, other shoots will appear.
Propagation Offsets.

Tolmiea

The single species below is the only one in the genus, a native of the west coast of North America. It is hardy enough to be grown in the garden.

Tolmiea menziesii

Bright green foliage arranged in a rosette and forming a mound of heart-shaped lobed leaves about 5cm (2in) across. The leaf stalks are long and when the plant is grown in a hanging pot this sometimes gives the plant a cascading appearance. Young plantlets form at the base of the leaf blade. 'Taff's Gold' is a variegated variety that you may also find under the names 'Goldsplash', 'Maculata', and 'Variegata'. It is sometimes semi-evergreen.

HELPFUL HINTS

Temperature Hardy, but usually requires a winter minimum of 5°C (41°F) when grown as a houseplant. Avoid high winter temperatures.
Humidity Mist occasionally.
Position Good light or semi-shade, but not direct sun.

ABOVE: Tolmiea menziesii

Watering and feeding Water freely from spring to autumn, sparingly in winter. Feed regularly in summer.
Care If the plant becomes too large and its stems are congested, try cutting it back in spring to allow new leaves to grow from the base. Repot annually in spring. The plant can be stood outside for the summer, but choose a position out of direct sun.
Propagation Division, or pot up plantlets.

Tradescantia

A genus of about 70 species, including hardy border plants as well as tender trailers. It now includes *Zebrina pendula*, another popular trailing houseplant.

Tradescantia albiflora *see T. fluminensis.*

Tradescantia blossfeldiana
Narrowly oval, slightly fleshy leaves 5–10cm (2–4in) long in two distinct rows on hairy, trailing stems. In the species the leaves are glossy green above and sometimes tinged purple beneath. It is the variegated varieties that are usually grown, however, and 'Variegata' has longitudinal cream stripes. The flowers are pink with a white base. This species is now more correctly *T. cerinthoides*.

Tradescantia cerinthoides *see T. blossfeldiana.*

Tradescantia fluminensis
Trailing, rooting, hairless stems, with short-stalked green leaves about 5–7.5cm (2–3in) long, sometimes tinged purple beneath. It is the variegated varieties that are grown, however, and these include 'Albovittata' (creamy-white lengthwise stripes), 'Quicksilver' (clear white markings), and 'Tricolor' (white and pale purple stripes). The white flowers are unspectacular. This species was once considered distinct from *T. albiflora* (colourless sap in *albiflora*, violet in *fluminensis*), but they are now classed by botanists as one species. You may find them under either name.

Tradescantia zebrina

Pointed oval leaves about 5cm (2in) long on creeping or trailing stems. The upper surface is pale green with a silvery sheen and lengthwise purple stripe, and the underside is purple. Small white or rose-red flowers. This plant is still widely known and sold as *Zebrina pendula.* The variety 'Purpusii' is a little larger and more robust, with purple-tinged, bluish-green leaves and pink flowers. This is likely to be found also as *Zebrina purpusii* or *Tradescantia purpusii.*

HELPFUL HINTS
Temperature Keep temperature in

LEFT: Tradescantia blossfeldiana
'*Variegata*'
BELOW: Tradescantia fluminensis
'*Albovittata*'
BOTTOM: Tradescantia zebrina

winter to a minimum of 7°C (45°F).
Humidity Mist occasionally.
Position Good light, including some direct sun. Variegation will be inferior in poor light.
Watering and feeding Water freely from spring to autumn, sparingly in winter. Feed regularly from spring to autumn.
Care The plants soon look untidy with tangled growth, and if conditions are not good the leaves may turn brown or shrivel. Trim them back by pinching out unattractive shoots – this will encourage bushy new growth from near the base.
Propagation Cuttings.

Tulipa

Although there are only about 100 species of tulip, breeding has produced a huge range of hybrids and varieties that are planted in their millions every year. None of them can be considered true houseplants, but some are forced for early flowering in winter and may be used as a short-term houseplant.

Tulipa hybrids

The tulip needs no description, but there are many kinds. Consult a good bulb catalogue for those varieties suitable for growing in pots for early flowering – these will usually be compact types such as early singles and early doubles, and specialists will also offer bulbs that have been specially treated or 'prepared' so that they come into flower early. Florists and garden centres also offer pots of tulips that are just coming into flower, and these are a useful option.

HELPFUL HINTS
Temperature Hardy, and once in flower the cooler the room, the longer the flowers should last. See below for advice on earlier treatment.
Humidity Undemanding.
Position If brought indoors just as the flowers open, they can be placed anywhere you choose.

ABOVE: *Tulip, early double*

Watering and feeding Water moderately while in the home.
Care In early or mid autumn, plant the bulbs with their necks just below the compost (deep planting is impractical in a pot). Place in a sheltered position outdoors, and cover with fine gravel, pulverized bark, or some other suitable mulch, to a depth of at least 5cm (2in). Keep the soil in the pots just moist but be careful not to overwater. When the shoots are about 4–5cm (1½–2in) tall, or as soon as you can detect signs of a bud, bring into the light. Keep the pots in a light place at about 15°C (59°F) – ideally in a greenhouse or conservatory – until the buds show colour. Then bring them into the home. Discard or plant in the garden once flowering is over.
Propagation Bulb offsets, but this is not a practical option in the home. Buy fresh bulbs each year.

Veltheilmia

There are only a handful of species in this genus of bulbous plants, which originate from South Africa.

Veltheilmia capensis
Strap-shaped, wavy-edged leaves about 30cm (1ft) long. The flower spike, consisting of about 60 small, bell-like, pink or red blooms, arises from the centre of the plant in winter.

Helpful hints
Temperature Winter minimum 10°C (50°F), but at higher than 13°C (55°F) the flowers tend to drop.
Humidity Undemanding.
Position Good light, including sun in winter.
Watering and feeding Water cautiously until growth appears, moderately throughout the growing period, then gradually reduce the amount of water given in late spring or early summer. The leaves will then die down as the bulb enters its dormant period.

Once growth is well established,

feed regularly until flowering is over.
Care Plant the bulbs in autumn, and keep at about 21°C (70°F) until growth starts. After the bulbs have flowered and entered their resting period, keep the pots practically dry until early autumn. During the dor-

Above: Veltheilmia capensis

mant stage you can stand the pots in a sheltered position outdoors.
Propagation Bulb offsets; seed (slow).

Vriesea

Bromeliads with about 250 species in the genus, occurring naturally in Central and South America.

Vriesea hieroglyphica
A species grown for foliage effect. Large rosette of wide, strap-shaped leaves with very dark green, sometimes almost black, markings. Seldom flowers in cultivation.

Vriesea hybrids
Hybrids are sometimes available ('Elan' is illustrated). Others include 'Perfecta' (a cross between V. *carinata* and V. 'Poelmannii') and 'Poelmannii' (a cross between V. *gloriosa* and V. *vangertii*).

Opposite above: Vriesea splendens
Left: Vriesea *hybrid 'Elan'*

Vriesea splendens
Rosette of arching, strap-shaped leaves, 30–45cm (1–1½ft) long on a mature plant, with brown cross-bands. The bright red flower head, 60cm (2ft) long, rises above the rosette of leaves. The true flowers are yellow but the plant is grown for the colour-ful red bracts, which appear mainly in summer and autumn.

HELPFUL HINTS
Temperature Winter minimum 15°C (59°F).
Humidity Mist the leaves regularly.
Position Light shade or good light out of direct sun.
Watering and feeding Water freely from spring to autumn, sparingly in winter. Keep the 'vase' formed by the leaves topped up with water from mid spring to mid autumn. Use soft water if possible. Feed with a weak fertilizer in summer.
Care The species grown for their col-ourful flower spikes are often dis-carded after flowering, but offsets will form around the old plant and these can be grown on to flower in due course. They are difficult to grow successfully in the home throughout their lives, however. If repotting, use an ericaceous (lime-free) mixture. You can also grow them attached to a bromeliad 'tree' made from an old branch, if you have space.
Propagation Offsets.

Washingtonia

A very small genus of just two species of tall palms. Both are occasionally used as a houseplants, but the species described below is the one you are most likely to find.

Washingtonia filifera
Fan-shaped, long-stalked, grey-green leaves with fibrous threads at the ends. Will make a large specimen if condi-tions suit, but is often short-lived in the home.

BELOW: Washingtonia filifera

HELPFUL HINTS
Temperature Winter minimum 10°C (50°F).
Humidity Undemanding.
Position Best possible light, with some direct sun, but avoid sunlight through glass during the hottest part of the day in summer.
Watering and feeding Water freely from spring to autumn, sparingly in winter. Feed regularly in summer.
Care The plant will appreciate being stood outside, perhaps on the patio, for the warmest months. In winter, the plant is better in a cool conserva-tory than in a living-room.
Propagation Seed (difficult).

Yucca

A genus of about 40 species of evergreen trees and shrubs, some of which are hardy. The two species listed below are the ones most commonly seen as houseplants.

Yucca aloifolia

The leaves, up to 50cm (20in) long, grow in a dense rosette, and have very sharp points. A pronounced trunk gives it a tree-like shape.

Yucca elephantipes

Similar to the previous species, but the leaf tips are not sharp. This is the species commonly sold, and in Europe large quantities of the sawn stems are imported from countries such as Honduras. These 'trunks' are then started into growth like giant cuttings, to produce attractive plants with a thick trunk. Commercial growers sometimes refer to this species as *Y. elegantissima* but you are unlikely to see this name used.

HELPFUL HINTS
Temperature Winter minimum 7°C (45°F).
Humidity Tolerates dry air.
Position Good light with some sun.
Watering and feeding Water freely from spring to autumn, sparingly in winter. Feed regularly in summer.
Care Repot small plants if necessary, large ones can remain in the same container for many years, but in this case it is worth removing and replacing the top 2in (5cm) of the compost (potting mixture). The plant will be happy standing on the patio for the summer, but keep in shade for the first few weeks to acclimatize.
Propagation Sideshoots can be used as cuttings. The large-trunked plants seen in shops are raised from imported stems.

BELOW: Yucca elephantipes

Zebrina

See Tradescantia.

Zephyranthes

A genus of bulbous plants from Central and South America. Growing plants are not often sold, but you can obtain the bulbs easily from specialist bulb companies.

Zephyranthes candida

Fine, grass-like leaves, and crocus-like white flowers, sometimes with a hint of purple, in autumn. Grows to about 15cm (6in).

BELOW: Zephyranthes grandiflora

ABOVE: Zephyranthes candida

Zephyranthes grandiflora

Similar to the previous species but with larger, rosy-pink flowers with a yellow throat on 30cm (1ft) stems, in early summer.

HELPFUL HINTS
Temperature Winter minimum 5°C (41°F).
Humidity Undemanding.
Position Best possible light, with some direct sun.
Watering and feeding Water freely when the bulbs are growing actively, sparingly when they are resting. Never let the soil become completely dry even during the resting period.
Care If necessary, repot when the bulbs are dormant, but do not repot unnecessarily. The display is usually better when the pot is densely planted with bulbs.
Propagation Division; seed.

Zygocactus

Forest cacti with flattened stems. The plants widely grown for the home are hybrids of *Z. truncatus*, but you may also find them allocated to the genus schlumbergera. Some may be hybrids between more than one genus.

Zygocactus truncatus hybrids

Flattened, winged segments forming arching branches. Exotic-looking flowers with two tiers of reflexed petals and forward-thrusting stems and stigma. The flowers, up to 7.5cm (3in) long, are borne on the tips of the shoots. Bright violet flowers are most common, but they vary from orange to lilac, as well as white. Late autumn and winter are the main flowering times. Also labelled under what some consider to be their more correct name of *Schlumbergera truncata*.

HELPFUL HINTS
Temperature Winter minimum 13°C (55°F).
Humidity Mist the leaves regularly.
Position Good light, but not direct summer sun.
Watering and feeding Water freely from late autumn, sparingly from late winter onwards. Increase the amount of water given again when buds start to form in the autumn. Use soft water if possible. Feed with a weak fertilizer during the period of active growth.
Care Stand the plant outdoors in a shady spot for the summer, but bring in before the evenings turn too cold. Avoid turning or moving the plant once the buds are well developed as they may drop. Repot young plants each spring, mature ones only every second or third year.
Propagation Cuttings.

BELOW: Zygocactus truncatus (*syn.* Schlumbergera truncata)

Glossary

Aerial root A root that grows from the stem above ground level. Plants such as philodendrons use them to assist climbing, as well as to absorb moisture and nutrients.

Air layering Method of propagating a plant by encouraging a stem to root while still on the plant. After careful wounding the stem is protected with sphagnum moss or other moisture-holding material and covered with plastic or foil until roots form.

Alkaline compost A growing medium containing lime, and having a high pH.

Annual A plant that lives for only one year.

Areole A small depression or raised, cushion-like area on a cactus that bears spines or wool.

Aroid A member of the *Araceae* family, which includes anthuriums, philodendrons and monsteras among the houseplants.

Bloom When used to describe the appearance of a leaf or fruit, a whitish or bluish powdery or waxy coating, which is easily removed by rubbing or handling.

Bract A modified leaf, often brightly coloured and petal-like, associated with flowers that themselves lack size or colour. Some bracts are small and scale-like, however, and serve mainly to protect buds.

Bromeliad A member of the *Brome-liaceae* family. Most are ephiphytic, and the leaves usually form a rosette.

Bulb Although the term is often used to include corms and tubers, strictly speaking, a bulb is a structure consist-

ing of modified leaves that protects the next season's embryo shoots and flowers.

Bulbil A small bulb that forms above ground on a few plants. Bulbils can be removed and potted up to grow into normal bulbs.

Callus A growth of corky tissue that forms over a wound, sealing and healing it.

Cane cuttings Method of propagation using a piece of stem cut into small lengths placed horizontally in the rooting medium.

Capillary mat An absorbent mat that holds a lot of water. Plants placed on it can draw up moisture by capillary action.

Chlorophyll The green pigment in plants which enables them to manufacture food from sunlight (photosynthesize).

Chlorosis An unhealthy yellowing of the foliage, usually caused by a deficiency of iron or other trace elements. Often appears in lime-hating plants which have been grown in an alkaline medium.

Cladode *See Cladophyll*

Cladophyll Also called a cladode. A modified stem that simulates a leaf in appearance and function. They can be found in the garden plant *Ruscus aculeatus*. One of the best-known houseplants with cladophylls is *Asparagus densiflorus*.

Compost (potting soil) The medium in which pot plants are grown.

Corm A swollen stem base that usually remains underground and stores food during the dormant season. If cut across, no distinct layers of leaves can be seen, unlike a bulb.

Corolla A term applied to the petals of a flower, or the inner ring of them, the petals being either separate or fused.

Crocks Pieces of broken clay pot (also known as shards), placed over the drainage hole of a clay pot to prevent the compost (potting soil) from being washed through the hole.

Crown The point at which stem and roots meet.

Dormant period The time when growth slows down and the plant needs less warmth and water. Some plants have no discernible dormant period, but with others – such as cyclamen – it is pronounced.

Epiphyte A plant that grows above ground level, usually in trees. Epiphytes are not parasites and only use their host for physical support.

Epiphytic A plant that grows on other plants without being parasitic.

Ericaceous When used specifically the term applies to members of the *Ericaceae* family, but is sometimes applied broadly to include similar plants. If applied to potting soils (potting composts) it means one specially formulated with a low pH to suit acid-loving plants.

Eye A term with several meanings. If used with reference to a flower it indicates that the centre of the bloom is a different colour. In propagation it refers to a stem cutting with a single lateral bud. If applied to a tuber, it is used to describe a dormant (undeveloped) bud on its surface.

Eye cuttings Method of propagation using a short section of ripened stem with a growth bud, the cutting being placed horizontally in the rooting medium.

Foliar feed A quick-acting liquid fertilizer that can be absorbed through the leaves as well as the roots.

Genus A group of species with enough common characteristics to group them together like a 'family'.

Glochid A tiny barbed spine or bristle, usually occurring in tufts on the areoles of some cacti. These penetrate the skin easily and can often set up irritation, making some cacti hazardous to handle. A good way to remove them from the skin is to lay a surgical plaster or tape over the area then peel it off.

Hardy Frost-tolerant.

Hormone, rooting hormone An organic compound that stimulates a cutting into forming roots.

Humidifier A device for raising the humidity in a room. Sometimes a tray of evaporating water is used, but more

sophisticated humidifiers are electrically powered.

Hydroponics A method of growing plants in nutrient solutions, without compost (potting soil).

Loam-based compost (potting soil) A soil mix in which the main ingredient is sterilized loam, to which peat (peat moss), sand and fertilizer are added.

Lux The scientific unit by which light levels are measured.

Mulch A protective covering for soil. In this book it refers to a loose covering of chipped bark, peat (peat moss), or similar material used to cover bulbs planted in pots, giving them a period of darkness in preparation for early flowering.

Offset A small plant that is produced alongside its parent.

Peat-based compost (peat-moss-based potting soil) A soil mix in which peat is the main ingredient. Sometimes sand and other substances are added, and the mixture always includes fertilizers and something to neutralize the acidity of the peat. Peat substitutes, such as coir, are increasingly used to avoid depletion of natural peat reserves.

Perennial A plant that lives for more than two years.

Perlite An inert growing medium, sometimes used as a compost (potting soil) additive or for rooting cuttings.

Petiole A leaf stalk.

pH A scale expressing the degree of acidity or alkalinity of a substance. It runs from 0 to 14, 7 being technically neutral, though most plants prefer a pH of about 6.5. Above 7 is alkaline, below 7 is acid.

Photosynthesis The mechanism by which plants convert sunlight into energy.

Phyllode A leaf stalk that takes on the function and appearance of a leaf. They are commonly found in acacias.

Pinnate A compound leaf with the leaflets arranged in parallel rows.

Pot-bound A term used to describe a plant whose growth is being inhibited by roots that have filled the pot.

Prop roots Special roots that arise above ground level and help to give the mature plant stability.

Pseudobulb A thickened, bulb-like stem found on some orchids, used by the plant for water storage. They vary considerably in shape and size and can be long and narrow or short and rounded. They are always produced above the ground.

Relative humidity The amount of water contained in the air at a particular temperature. It is calculated against the maximum amount of water that could be held in the air at that temperature.

Resting period *see* **Dormant period**

Rhizome A special, modified stem, sometimes thick and fleshy but not always, that lies close to the surface of the soil (except in epiphytes) and produces both roots and aerial parts such as leaves and flowers. You can tell that a rhizome is not a root by the presence of nodes (joints) and often scale-like leaves or buds.

Root-ball A mass of roots and compost (potting soil) together.

Spadix A special type of fleshy flower spike, found in aroids and palms, in which small flowers are more or less embedded. In aroids it is surrounded by a spathe, and in this case forms a single erect organ. In palms it is often branched.

Spathe The term usually refers to the conspicuous bract that protects a spadix (see above). In aroids (members of the *Araceae* family, such as philodendrons and monsteras) it is leafy, more or less fleshy, and often brightly coloured. The term is sometimes used for palms (in which it could be fleshy or woody) and other plants — for example, the membranous sheath that surrounds a daffodil bud is technically

a spathe. In this book it is always used in the sense described for aroids.

Sphagnum moss A moss belonging to the genus *Sphagnum*, found in boggy places and capable of holding a large amount of water.

Spores Minute reproductive structure found on non-flowering plants such as ferns and mosses. Can be sown like seeds but need special treatment.

Stem cutting Method of propagation using a length of stem. There are many kinds, including soft, unripened wood, hardwood, and semi-ripe cuttings, the length varying according to the type of plant.

Stipule A leafy or bract-like appendage at the base of a leaf stalk. It is usually small and inconspicuous.

Sucker A shoot growing from a plant's roots or underground stem, producing leaves of its own. Suckers can be a problem on grafted plants in the garden, but for pot plants they usually provide a useful method of propagation. The term also applies to a group of insects, but is not used in that sense in this book.

Terrestrial Growing in soil — a land plant.

Tip cutting Method of propagation using only the soft tips of actively growing plants.

Tuber A swollen underground stem or root used by plants to store food during the dormant period.

Vermiculite An inert growing medium, sometimes used as a compost (potting soil) additive or for rooting cuttings.

Viviparous Producing live young. When applied to plants it refers to buds or bulbs that become plantlets while still attached to the parent plant. It also refers to seeds that germinate while on the parent plant.

Whorl Three or more organs, such as leaves, arranged in a circle around the same axis.

Index of common plant names

Jerusalem cherry – *Solanum capsicastrum, S. pseudocapsicum*
Joseph's coat – Codiaeum
Kaffir lily – *Clivia miniata*
Kangaroo vine – *Cissus antarctica*
Kentia palm – Howea
Kentia palm – *Howeia forsteriana* (syn. *Kentia forsteriana*)
Lace cactus – *Mammillaria elongata*
Lace fern – *Nephrolepis exaltata* 'Whitmanii'
Lacy tree philodendron – *Philodendron selloum*
Ladder fern – Nephrolepis
Lady's slipper – Cypripedium (syn. Paphiopedilum)
Leopard lily – Dieffenbachia
Lily – Lilium
Lily, regal – *Lilium regale*
Lily, golden-rayed – *Lilium auratum*
Lily, Easter – *Lilium longifolium*
Lily, Japanese – *Lilium speciosum*
Lollipop plant – *Pachystachys lutea*
Lucky clover – *Oxalis deppei*
Madagascar dragon tree – *Cordyline terminalis* (syn. *Dracaena terminalis*)
Madagascar jasmine – *Stephanotis floribunda*
Madagascar periwinkle – *Catharanthus roseus*
Maidenhair fern – Adiantum
Meadow saffron – Colchicum
Mexican breadfruit – *Monstera deliciosa*
Mexican sunball – *Rebutia minuscula*
Mind your own business – *Soleirolia soleirolii* (syn. *Helxine soleirolii*)
Mistletoe fig – *Ficus deltoidea*
Monarch-of-the-East – *Sauromatum venosum*
Money tree – *Crassula argentea*
Mother fern – *Asplenium bulbiferum*
Mother of thousands – *Saxifraga stolonifera* (syn. *S. sarmentosa*)
Mother-in-law's tongue – *Sansevieria trifasciata* 'Laurentii'
Naked ladies – Colchicum
Natal ivy – *Cissus rhombifolia*
Never-never plant – *Ctenanthe oppenheimiana*
New Zealand cabbage plant – *Cordyline australis*
New Zealand cliffbrake – *Pellaea rotundifolia*
Nipple cactus – Mammillaria
Norfolk Island pine – *Araucaria heterophylla* (syn. *A. excelsa*)
Old man cactus – *Cephalocereus senilis*

Oleander – *Nerium oleander*
Orchid cactus – Epiphyllum
Painted net leaf – *Fittonia verschaffeltii*
Pansy orchid – Miltonia
Paper flower – Bougainvillea
Paradise palm – *Howea forsteriana*
Parasol plant – *Schefflera arboricola* (syn. *Heptapleurum arboricola*)
Parlour palm – *Chamaedorea elegans* (syn. *Neanthe bella*)
Peace lily – Spathiphyllum
Peacock plant – *Calathea makoyana*
Peanut cacus – *Chamaecereus silvestrii*
Pepper, annual – *Capsicum annuum*
Persian violet – *Exacum affine*
Peruvian daffodil – *Hymenocallis narcissiflora*
Pick-a-back plant – *Tolmeia menziesii*
Piggyback plant – *Tolmiea menziesii*
Pincushion cactus – Mammillaria
Pineapple, red – *Ananas bracteatus striatus*
Pineapple, ivory – *Ananas comosus* 'Variegatus'
Plantain lily – Hosta
Plume flower – *Celosia plumosa*
Poinsettia – *Euphorbia pulcherrima*
Polka dot plant – *Hypoestes sanguinolenta* (syn. *H. phyllostachya*)
Poor man's orchid – Schizanthus

Powder puff cactus – *Mammillaria bocasana*
Prairie gentian – *Eustoma grandiflorum*
Prayer plant – Maranta
Prickly pear – Opuntia
Primrose – *Primula vulgaris*
Pygmy date palm – *Phoenix roebelenii*
Queen's tears – *Billbergia nutans*
Rabbit's ears – *Opuntia microdasys*
Rainbow star – *Cryptanthus bromelioides*
Rat tail plant – *Crassula lycopodioides*
Rattlesnake plant – *Calathea lancifolia*
Regal pelargonium – *Pelargonium* x *domesticum*
Resurrection plant – *Selaginella lepidophylla*
Ribbon fern – Pteris
Ribbon plant – *Dracaena sanderiana*
Rosary vine – *Ceropegia woodii*
Rose of China – *Hibiscus rosa-sinensis*
Rose pincushion – *Mammillaria zeilmanniana*
Rubber plant – *Ficus elastica*
Scarlet star – *Guzmania lingulata* (and hybrids)
Sensitive plant – *Mimosa pudica*
Sentry palm – *Howeia belmoreana* (syn. *Kentia belmoreana*)
Shrimp plant – *Beloperone guttata*
Silk bark oak – *Grevillea robusta*
Silver jade plant – *Crassula arborescens*
Silver net leaf – *Fittonia verschaffeltii argyroncura*
Slipper flower – *Calceolaria* hybrids
Slipper orchid – Cypripedium (syn. Paphiopedilum)
Snakeskin plant – Fittonia

Spade leaf – *Philodendron domesticum*
Spanish bayonet – *Yucca aloifolia*
Spanish moss – *Tillandsia usneoides*
Spathe flower – Spathiphyllum
Spider lily – *Hymenocallis* x *festalis*
Spider plant – *Chlorophytum comosum*
Spineless yucca – *Yucca elephantipes*
Spiraea, perennial – Astilbe
Spotted laurel – *Aucuba japonica*
Spreading clubmoss – *Selaginella kraussiana*
Stag's horn fern – *Platycerium bifurcatum*
Star of Bethelehem – *Campanula isophylla*
Starfish flower – *Stapelia variegata*
Stonecrop – Sedum
Stove fern – *Pteris cretica*
Strawberry geranium – *Saxifraga stolonifera* (syn. *S. sarmentosa*)
String of hearts – *Ceropegia woodii*
Sundew – *Drosera capensis*
Sunset cactus – *Lobivia famatimensis*
Swedish ivy – *Plectanthus oertendahlii*
Sweetheart plant – *Philodendron scandens*
Swiss cheese plant – *Monstera deliciosa*
Sword fern – *Nephrolepis exaltata*
Table fern – *Pteris cretica*
Temple bells – Smithiantha
Ti tree – *Cordyline fruticosa*
Tiger jaws – *Faucaria tigrina*
Tiger orchid – *Odontoglossum grande*
Torch thistle – Cereus
Transvaal daisy – *Gerbera jamesonii*
Tree ivy – × *Fatshedera lizei*
Tree philodendron – *Philodendron bipinnatifidum*
Tsus-simense holly fern – *Polystichum tsus-simense*
Tulip – Tulipa
Umbrella plant – Cyperus
Umbrella plant – *Schefflera actinophylla*
Urn plant – *Aechmea fasciata*
Velvet plant – Gynura
Venus fly trap – *Dionaea muscipula*
Voodoo lily – *Sauromatum venosum* (syn. *S. guttatum*)
Wandering Jew – Tradescantia, Zebrina
Washington palm – Washingtonia
Watermelon plant – *Peperomia argyreia*
Wax begonia – *Begonia semperflorens*
Wax flower – Hoya, *Stephanotis floribunda*
Wax privet – *Peperomia glabella*
Wax vine – *Senecio macroglossus*
Weeping fig – *Ficus benjamina*
Whorled peperomia – *Peperomia verticillata*
Winter cherry – *Solanum capsicastrum, S. pseudocapsicum*
Zebra plant – *Aphelandra squarrosa, Calathea zebrina*
Zonal pelargonium – *Pelargonium zonale*

Index

Acknowledgements and credits

The publishers would like to thank the following for their generous help in the production of this book: Andrew J Smith, Manor Nurseries, Stockbridge Road, Timsbury, Hants, for providing plants, a location and their time for much of the photography; Sean Flynn, The Garden Studio, 146 Columbia Road, London E2, for kindly lending a range of plant containers and equipment featured in the chapter on Creative Displays; Peter Watkins, Lease-a-Plant Ltd, M.K.M. Nurseries, Bulls Lane, Bell Bar, Herts, for providing plants for photography; The Dutch Nursery, Bell Bar, Brookmans Park, Herts, for providing plants for photography; The Camden Garden Centre, 2 Barker Drive, St Pancras Way, London NW1, for lending plants for photography; Chessington Nurseries, Ltd, Leatherhead Road, Chessington, Surrey; for providing plants for photography; The Hollygate Cactus Nursery, Billingshurst Lane, Ashington, West Sussex for providing plants for photography; and The Chelsea Gardener, 125 Sydney Street, Kings Road, London SW3 for providing plants and containers for photography.

Special thanks are due to Stephanie Donaldson, who created and styled the plant displays featured in the chapter on Creative Displays; thanks also to Ann Venn, Nicky Walton and Diane Redfern for kindly opening up their homes to provide the settings for these plant displays.

All photography by John Freeman, with additional photographs, as follows:

Key: t = top; b = b ottom; l = left; c = centre; r = right.

Peter McHoy, pages 20 b, 23 t, 24 t, 26 b, 27 tl br, 28 b, 29 tl tc tr b, 30 t, 31 b, 32 t b, 33 t c bl br, 39 t, 46, 47 cr br, 58, 59, 63 b, 64, 70 br, 71, 73 cl cr bl br, 80 tr bc, 81 tl tc bl, 82 b, 83 tr, 84 bl br, 85 tl tr bl, 99 bl, 100, 101 tr, 103 tl bl br, 104, 112 b, 113 b, 128 c b, 129 cr, 141, 142 bl, 145 t, 149, 154 b, 160 t, 2 br, 175 bl cl, 184, 185 b, 188 tc, 193 tr br, 205 b, 207 t, 208 b, 224 t b, 230 bl, 237 and 247 t b; The Garden Picture Library/Erika Craddock 126; The Garden Picture Library/John Sira 202t; The Garden Picture Library/Mayer Lescanff 234 and The Garden Picture Library/John Sira 246 br; A-Z Botanical 204 l; and Photos Horticultural 129 tl, 190 t, 215 bl and 233 b.

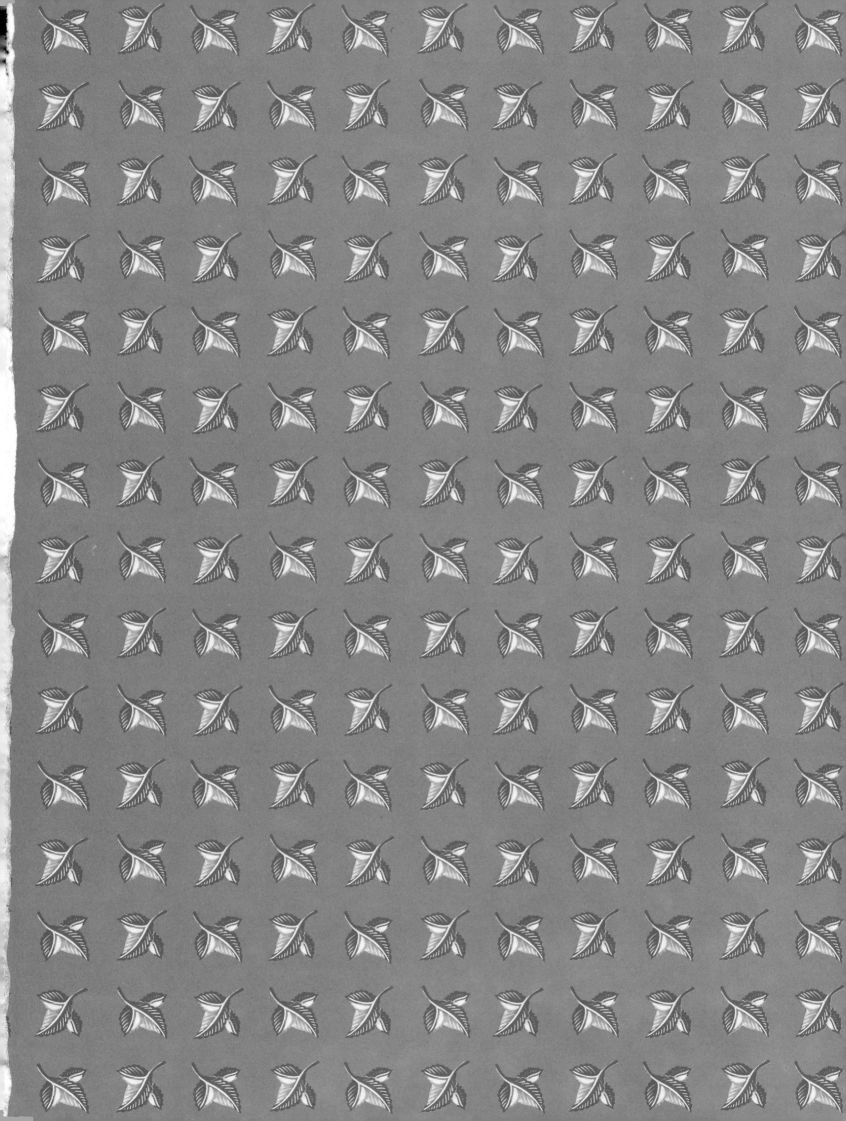

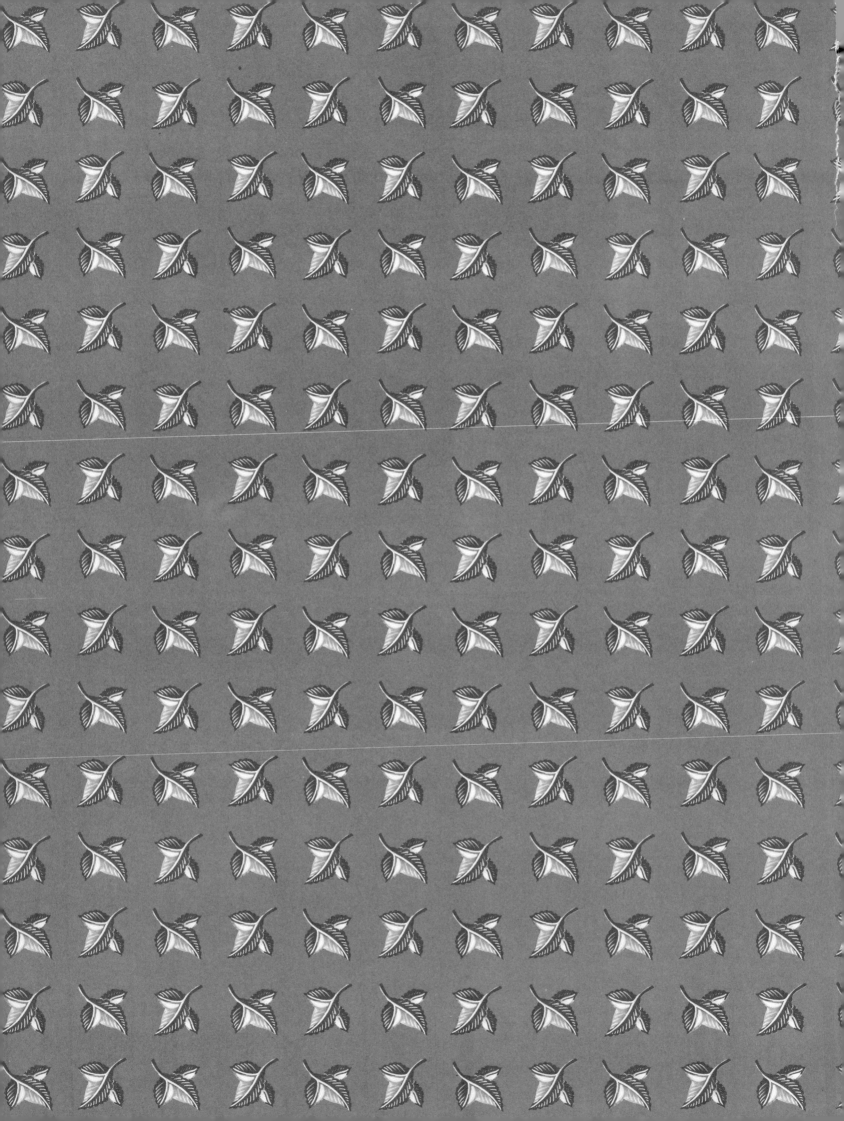